Exploring Resources, Life-Balance and Well-Being of Women Who Work in a Global Context

Roxane L. Gervais • Prudence M. Millear
Editors

Exploring Resources, Life-Balance and Well-Being of Women Who Work in a Global Context

Springer

Editors
Roxane L. Gervais
Independent Practitioner
Goole, UK

Prudence M. Millear
School of Social Sciences
University of the Sunshine Coast
Maroochydore DC, QLD, Australia

ISBN 978-3-319-31734-2 ISBN 978-3-319-31736-6 (eBook)
DOI 10.1007/978-3-319-31736-6

Library of Congress Control Number: 2016943129

Printed on acid-free paper

This Springer imprint is published by Springer Nature
The registered company is Springer International Publishing AG Switzerland

Acknowledgements

The editors recognise gratefully the efforts of the chapter authors in preparing their various contributions, especially their diligence and quick response to our many queries. We thank our families for their support during the many days we spent in front of computer screens. We appreciate the opportunity from Springer Publishing in having confidence in our work and allowing us to translate our intense focus on women who work into this book and especially to Mireille van Kan and Stefan Einarson, for their support throughout this process. The authors appreciate the comments and suggestions from the anonymous reviewers in moving the manuscript forward and thank them for these.

Independent Practitioner
Goole, UK
Roxane L. Gervais

University of the Sunshine Coast
Maroochydore DC, QLD, Australia
Prudence M. Millear

Contents

Editors and Contributors

Editors

Roxane L. Gervais Independent Practitioner, Goole, UK

Prudence M. Millear School of Social Sciences, University of the Sunshine Coast, Maroochydore DC, QLD, Australia

Contributors

Haya Al-Dajani Futures Entrepreneurship Centre, Plymouth Business School, Plymouth University, Plymouth, Devon, UK

Angelika Bader Women's Health Centre, Medical University of Innsbruck, Innsbruck, Austria

Beate Baldauf Warwick Institute for Employment Research, University of Warwick, Coventry, UK

Heike Behle Warwick Institute for Employment Research, University of Warwick, Coventry, UK

Wendy Boyd School of Education, Southern Cross University, Lismore, NSW, Australia

Sara Carter Hunter Centre for Entrepreneurship, Strathclyde Business School, University of Strathclyde, Glasgow, UK

Kate Crawford Eviva Pty Ltd, Kuranda, QLD, Australia

Roxane L. Gervais Independent Practitioner, Goole, UK

Margarethe Hochleitner Women's Health Centre, Medical University of Innsbruck, Innsbruck, Austria

Syed S.M. Sadrul Huda Department of Business Administration, East West University, Dhaka, Bangladesh

Christian Jones Discipline of Psychology and the Engage Laboratory, University of the Sunshine Coast, Maroochydore, QLD, Australia

Mary Katsikitis Discipline of Psychology and the Engage Laboratory, University of the Sunshine Coast, Maroochydore, QLD, Australia

Gail Kinman Department of Psychology, University of Bedfordshire, Luton, UK

Clare Lyonette Warwick Institute for Employment Research, University of Warwick, Coventry, UK

Prudence M. Millear School of Social Sciences, University of the Sunshine Coast, Maroochydore DC, QLD, Australia

Melody Muscat Discipline of Psychology and the Engage Laboratory, University of the Sunshine Coast, Maroochydore, QLD, Australia

Floor Rink The Faculty of Economics and Business, The University of Groningen, Groningen, The Netherlands

Michelle K. Ryan The Faculty of Economics and Business, The University of Groningen, Groningen, The Netherlands

Social and Organizational Psychology, University of Exeter, Exeter, UK

Heidi Siller Women's Health Centre, Medical University of Innsbruck, Innsbruck, Austria

Janka I. Stoker The Faculty of Economics and Business, The University of Groningen, Groningen, The Netherlands

Karen L. Thorpe School of Psychology and Counselling, Queensland University of Technology, Kelvin Grove, QLD, Australia

Sue Walker School of Early Childhood, Queensland University of Technology, Kelvin Grove, QLD, Australia

Jennifer Webster Independent Practitioner, Stoke-on-Trent, UK

Colin Williams Inter-disciplinary Centre of the Social Sciences, University of Sheffield, Sheffield, UK

About the Editors and Contributors

Editors

Roxane L. Gervais has worked in diverse organisations, and at present, she is a Senior Psychologist at the Health and Safety Laboratory in the United Kingdom. In her role, she researches and promotes solutions to work-related issues. This research covers stress and well-being at work, and this aspect of her research has led to her facilitating training on work-related stress and well-being as well as undertaking stress audits within organisations. Her research interests include also assessing women over the life-course, especially with respect to their work patterns and practices, along with those other organisational practices, such as work-life balance, engagement, resilience and organisational change processes that allow a more holistic view of today's workforce. Due to the changing work environment that includes globalisation and a stronger focus on diversity, her research includes generational differences as well as other diversity issues. She has presented these aspects of her research at international conferences and contributes to her profession by editing papers for three journals and two international conference committees. As well, Roxane volunteers with one of her professional bodies, the British Psychological Society, as she to wants to assist in ensuring that both the science and practice of occupational psychology is maintained and reinforced. She gained her PhD at the University of Hull.

Prudence M. Millear completed her PhD from the Queensland University of Technology (QUT) in 2010. Her doctoral research programme focused on the benefits and effects of individual and workplace resources on well-being, mental health and work engagement in the Australian workforce. She joined the University of the Sunshine Coast as a Lecturer in Psychology in early 2011, as an ongoing position. Prudence's research focuses on how individuals are actively involved in constructing their own lives, in particular, the importance of personal resources, such as optimism and self-efficacy, acting with workplace resources to promote well-being and work engagement. Her research has a particular focus on the intersection of work and family roles across the lifespan. She is interested in women's engagement in the paid workforce, from the important role of childcare provision, to the consequences of menopause on women's work lives. In addition, her research is framed through the lens of successful ageing and how the characteristics of persons drive their experiences and behaviours to experience a full and happy life. Bringing together the resources of individuals with the resources of their work and family roles will enable better understanding of resilient well-being, better mental health and continued engagement in life's tasks.

Contributors

Haya Al-Dajani is Associate Professor (Reader) in Entrepreneurship at the Plymouth Graduate School of Management and the Plymouth Business School (Faculty of Business) in the United Kingdom. Her research is predominantly focused on the intersection between entrepreneurship, empowerment and gender in developing economy contexts.

Angelika Bader, Dr.^{in} med., MSc, works at the Women's Health Centre at the Innsbruck University Hospital, Austria. Angelika Bader is a physician at the Women's Health Centre at the University Hospital. She is involved in several projects on migrant's health, gender and career (in physicians) and gender and health (sexuality and violence in medical history taking). Her research foci are cardiology, gender studies, preventive medicine, women's health and migrants.

Beate Baldauf is a Senior Research Fellow at the Institute for Employment Research at the University of Warwick. She is a social scientist and has conducted research on a range of subject areas, including quality part-time work. Her research primarily focuses on health and social care labour markets, (higher) education and training and paid/voluntary work by older people. This has involved both quantitative and qualitative research methods, as well as collaborative work at national and European level. She joined the Institute in 2000, having previously worked in other research centres in the UK and Germany.

Dr. Heike Behle a Research Fellow at the Institute for Employment Research at the University of Warwick since 2004, is an experienced quantitative sociologist. Her research mainly focuses on the acquirement and maintenance of employability skills, especially in an international context. Up until March 2014, she lead a project funded by the Society for the Research into Higher Education entitled *The transferability of (under-)graduate knowledge gained in United Kingdom higher education institutions (HEIs) within the European Higher Education Area* in which the experiences of UK-educated graduates in other European countries were observed. Her work is mainly based around the analysis of quantitative data such as the Labour Force Survey (LFS).

Wendy Boyd is a Lecturer and Researcher in Early Childhood Education and Care at Southern Cross University. Her research focuses on the provision of quality early childhood education. Of particular interest are the qualities of early childhood teachers and their work with a focus on teachers developing professional identity regarding their knowledge and pedagogical approaches to early childhood including environmental education, mathematics, art making, and children's health and well-being. Wendy's PhD was a longitudinal prospective study titled: *Parents' decisions regarding paid work and care of the child*. Prior to academia, she had 25 years early childhood education experience working with children, aged from birth to 5 years, their families and other key stakeholders.

Sara Carter is a Professor of Entrepreneurship and Associate Deputy Principal at the University of Strathclyde in Glasgow, Scotland, and Visiting Professor at Nordland Research Institute in Norway. She is also an Associate Director of the Enterprise Research Centre, a co-funded multi-partner centre which aims to improve the evidence base for enterprise policy.

Kate Crawford has had successful careers as an academic and software developer, and is now the director of a consultancy company Eviva Pty Ltd, an Honorary Principle Research Fellow at the University of Wollongong and a founding member of Peel St Campus Inc., a think tank with a focus on emerging digital cultures. She works to support research, innovation and development projects in communities, business, government and universities. She has a commitment to creating conditions for confidence, commitment, adaptability and operational success in volatile, innovative or changing conditions. She applies her knowledge from research and business to catalyse higher levels of participation in learning leadership, co-operation, strategic planning, adaptive behaviours, team work, developmental research and effective innovation.

Margarethe Hochleitner, Univ.-Prof.^{in} Dr.^{in} med, is a Professor for Gender Medicine and Director of the Women's Health Centre at the Innsbruck University Hospital. From 2005 to 2009, she was the Vice-Rector for Human Resources, Human Resources Development and Gender Equality; from 1991 to date, the chairperson of the Committee for Equal Rights at the Innsbruck University; 1988–2005 head of the Ludwig Boltzmann Institute for Cardiological Gender Studies; from 1999 to date, the scientific head of the Women's Health Office of the State of Tyrol; since 2008, the Director of the Women's Health Centre at the Innsbruck University Hospital; in the summer term 2001, she was the Aigner-Rollett-Gastprofessur for Women's and Gender Studies at the Karl Franzens University Graz, Austria; and in 2005, she received the Gabriele Possanner State Award of the Federal Ministry of Education, Science and Culture. Her research focus is on cardiology, preventive medicine, gender studies, women's health and migrants.

Syed S.M. Sadrul Huda joined East West University as a lecturer in 1999 and is now an Assistant Professor in the department of Business Administration. Apart from teaching, he has been actively engaged in academic research and with extra-curricular activities. He has published many research articles in national and international journals and participated in various workshops and conferences. His research agenda includes employee empowerment, work-family conflict, customer satisfaction and gender. He was awarded a fellowship by the Japanese Government in 2013 to conduct work-life research on Japanese executives and won a research grant from EWU Center of Research and Training (CRT). He participated in the International Conference on Bangladesh, organised by the Ash Institute of Kennedy School of Governance, BDI and BBDF, held at Harvard University, gaining a travel grant by the American Centre. He was nominated for a sustainable tourism workshop organised by WICE, The Netherlands, held in Vietnam in 2009 and funded by a Dutch Government Fellowship programme. He received his MSc from Wageningen University, the Netherlands, in 1999.

Christian Jones is the Director of the Engage Research Lab (www.engageresearch.org) and Associate Dean of Research at the University of the Sunshine Coast. Christian researches and develops innovative solutions for social change, empowering people to flourish in their worlds, have positive and playful experiences, make social connections, find meaning, experience accomplishments and achieve well-being. He designs digital technologies that are familiar to users (such as videogames, smartphone/tablet applications, social networks, interactive media and artwork) to provide free-to-use environments for users to become informed, inspired and motivated to make changes for the social good. He is also a commercial entrepreneur and has a successful track record of managing large-scale research projects and spinning out Intellectual Property for industrial commercialisation.

Mary Katsikitis is the Foundation Professor of Psychology and Discipline Leader at the University of the Sunshine Coast. She has spent many years in a clinical/health environment (major teaching hospital) and also managing accreditation and professional development processes for the members of the largest professional association for psychologists in Australia. Mary is a member of the Board of the Australian Psychology Accreditation Council and also currently holds the position of National Course Approvals Chair for the APS College of Clinical Psychologists. Her recent grants have funded research focused on using web-based media to deliver positive interventions and to measure their effect on adolescent and adult mental health.

Gail Kinman is a Professor of Occupational Health Psychology at the University of Bedfordshire, United Kingdom. She is a Chartered Psychologist with a long-standing research interest in the well-being and work-life balance of academic employees and has published widely in this area. Gail has also conducted research on the work-related well-being of several professional groups whose work could be considered emotionally demanding, such as social workers, nurses, police officers and prison officers. Gail co-chairs the British Psychological Society's Work-life Balance Working Group, which seeks to promote a psychological perspective to the management of the work-home interface. She is currently involved in research projects at a national level to enhance emotional resilience in social workers and a book on this topic was published in 2014. A further book that examines work-related well-being in the university sector is scheduled for publication in 2016.

Clare Lyonette is a Principal Research Fellow at the Institute for Employment Research at the University of Warwick. Her research focuses primarily on work-family balance and conflict, career choices, career barriers and career outcomes, gender roles, fatherhood, atypical working and flexible working/part-time work. In 2009–2010, she ran an evaluation of the Quality Part-Time Work Fund, commissioned by the Government Equalities Office, and has recently been awarded funding by the Nuffield Foundation to conduct a mixed-methods project examining the experiences of student mothers accessing and continuing into higher education and upon entry into the labour market. She has extensive knowledge of conducting both quantitative and qualitative research and data analysis and regularly undertakes in-depth interviewing and case study work. Clare has published widely in her fields of expertise and is a member of the British Psychological Society Work-Life Balance working group.

Melody Muscat is a Senior Lecturer of Indigenous Health and Health Promotion in the College of Public Health, Medical and Veterinary Sciences at James Cook University, Australia. Her research focuses on co-designing alternate reality games as a participatory health promotion approach, to mobilise her knowledge in communities to capture Indigenous youth's interest in becoming social engineers of their own identity, health and future. Her interest in this area was stimulated while working as a research assistant investigating the feasibility, acceptability and effectiveness of using new media and technology for health promotion. The research specifically focused on exploring the best ways to harness technology to promote positive communication between mothers and daughters to promote safer behaviours relating to alcohol use during adolescence.

Floor Rink is an Associate Professor at the University of Groningen (The Netherlands). She is interested in the psychological mechanisms underlying organisational behaviour and examines the conditions that facilitate the upward mobility of minority members within organisations.

Michelle K. Ryan is a Professor of Social and Organisational Psychology at the University of Exeter (United Kingdom) and a Professor of Diversity at the University of Groningen (The Netherlands). Together with Alex Haslam, she uncovered the 'glass cliff' phenomenon. Her work has been featured in many scientific articles and popular journals and was named as one of the ideas that shaped 2008 by the *New York Times*.

Heidi Siller, Mag.a Dr.in, is a Clinical and Health Psychologist and works as a researcher at the Women's Health Centre at the Innsbruck University Hospital, Medical University Innsbruck, Austria. She worked as a project assistant on European Union projects on psychosocial support after crisis, and lay counselling (University of Innsbruck). She has been involved in several projects on gender and health (e.g. sexuality and violence in medical history taking), gender and psychotraumatology (e.g. post-traumatic stress disorder and intersectionality, humanitarian aid workers) and gender and career (gender and career of physicians). Her research foci are psychotraumatology, health psychology with special focus on gender, gender studies and women's health.

Janka I. Stoker is a full Professor in Leadership and Organisational Change at the University of Groningen (The Netherlands) and examines a broad range of issues related to leadership, power and diversity.

Karen L. Thorpe is a Developmental Scientist and Professor at the School of Psychology and Counselling at Queensland University of Technology. Her research examines the effects of early life experiences on social, learning and health trajectories across the lifespan. A particular interest is the effect of early childcare and education experiences on children and families. She collaborates with a range of government and non-government organisations to effect positive change for children and families. In 2013, she was named one of Australia's *100 Women of Influence* for her research impacts on educational and family policy.

Sue Walker is a Professor within the School of Early Childhood at Queensland University of Technology. Her research foci include the effect of early experiences on children's outcomes particularly across the transition to school. A particular concern is child outcomes in relation to inclusive early childhood education programmes and early intervention. A range of research projects explore these issues along with the development of children's epistemic beliefs and moral values and personal epistemologies in teacher education.

Jennifer Webster is an Associate Fellow of the British Psychological Society and registered Occupational Psychologist and is part of a team of psychologists and human factors specialists at the Health and Safety Laboratory in the United Kingdom. Previously, she was employed with Jobcentreplus, working with individuals who acquired a disability or health condition during the course of their working lives to help them find or retain employment, and to encourage employers to identify reasonable workplace adjustments and accommodations. Her research interests include extended working lives, managing multi-generational workforces and burnout.

Colin Williams is a Professor of Public Policy in the Management School at the University of Sheffield in the United Kingdom. His research interests include the informal economy, work organisation and the future of work, subjects on which he has published some 20 monographs and 300 journal articles over the past 25 years. His recent books include *Informal Work in Developed Nations* (2010, Routledge), *Rethinking the Future of Work: Directions and Visions* (2007, Palgrave Macmillan), *The Hidden Enterprise Culture* (2006, Edward Elgar), *A Commodified World? Mapping the Limits of Capitalism* (2005, Zed) and *Cash-in-Hand Work* (2004, Palgrave Macmillan).

Part I
Introduction: Women and Work

Chapter 1
Introduction: Key Issues on Women Who Work

Roxane L. Gervais and Prudence M. Millear

Introduction

The world of work is ever changing and while women have contributed, do contribute and will continue to contribute to the labour market, this contribution is vested still within policy; culture; the economies of their respective countries; and the concept of gender. These overarching factors, when combined with various other micro factors for example, their level of education, their caring responsibilities and the resources that are available to them, influence how, where and for how long women enter and remain in the workforce. The aim of this present volume is to provide an overview of women at work in different environments, countries, and contexts; focusing on how they utilise available resources to assist in managing life and work. The chapter starts with an overview of gender theory, then discusses the various attributes under which the chapters fall.

This chapter is based on data collected independently by the authors and represents solely their opinions and/or conclusions.

R.L. Gervais (✉)
Independent Practitioner, Goole DN14 6XN, UK
e-mail: roxane_gervais@alumni.fdu.edu

P.M. Millear
School of Social Sciences, University of the Sunshine Coast,
Locked Bag 4, Maroochydore DC, QLD 4558, Australia

R.L. Gervais, P.M. Millear (eds.), *Exploring Resources, Life-Balance and Well-Being of Women Who Work in a Global Context*,
DOI 10.1007/978-3-319-31736-6_1

The Gender Perspective

Gender theory has advanced over the past decades, moving from the sole differences between the sexes to focusing on the development of self that is rooted within social structures around the individual, their interactions with others, and the institutions within which they function (Risman & Davis, 2013). Despite these advances, it is important to realise that gender remains a concept deeply entrenched within society (Risman, 2004). There is constant interaction between these two domains; a fluidity that allows changes to occur and fosters a dynamic environment. Gender is not static. As such, proposals in how gender should be studied has included using a trans-disciplinary model that employs multi-methods and multi-perspectives (Cohen & Jeffrey, 2009).

This more inclusive approach has been outlined in intersectionality. Intersectionality was meant to take into account the many facets against which a woman could be identified, such as race, culture and sexual orientation (McCall, 2005), allowing for an identity that is seen as complex and multidimensional. This tactic could add to the discourse in this present volume on the many agencies under women who work function. However, the usefulness of this type of definition has been challenged as in reality, any woman could choose to 'use' or focus on only one of her 'identities' at any point in time (Nash, 2008); or that the defined concept would have to be adapted dependent on the context in which it is being used (see e.g., Smooth, 2011). Moreover, there are questions around its methodology and the challenges it has in its inclusivity across dimensions (Nash, 2008). And as seen in the present volume migrant women in Jordan (Chap. 3, Al-Dajani, Carter and Williams) were discriminated against regardless of their level of education and skill set. Their discrimination was on one facet and did not take into account their other identities. The importance of that particular chapter highlights that women and their experiences with work cannot be confined to one 'catch-all' concept.

What is evident over the past few decades, as stated, is that gender can be fluid and cannot be contained within one dimension that separates the sexes. Moreover, one interpretation of 'gender' and how the various issues associated with that concept interacts, cannot be realised through one definitive understanding. This is seen as experiences differ among and within the same groups of individuals (Appelrouth & Desfor, 2011). Gender remains a dynamic process (Risman, 2009). The present volume adds to the debate that feminist research and gender theory cannot be considered within one paradigm (Annandale & Clark, 1996). Indeed, the concept of women and women who work cannot be confided to a set paradigm, as experiences, opportunities, and support systems would differ across countries, cultures and workplaces. This volume therefore adds to the importance of considering experience (Brah & Phoenix, 2004) and not confining 'women' to one unit or identity (Appelrouth & Desfor, 2011), when exploring, in this instance, women within the workplace. Moreover, gender equality cannot be separated from economic development as higher incomes facilitate more equality between the genders (World Bank, 2011).

Another aspect of gender has been to focus on the reproductive differences between the sexes (Risman, 2004). However, the different experiences of the women in the chapters by Boyd and colleagues (Chap. 9; first time mothers returning to work), Siller and colleagues (Chap. 7; Austrian women doctors and their children), and Millear (Chap. 11; comparing women across the lifespan) demonstrate that the presence or absence of children alone cannot define a woman's trajectory in life. It is a misperception that reproductive abilities can lock women into only one particular role (Annandale & Clark, 1996). As such, women should not be defined on their ability to reproduce or the choices they make about childbearing.

Concepts and Their Interpretations

Resources

Amongst researchers (e.g., Bakker & Demerouti, 2006; Hakanen, Perhoniemi, & Toppinen-Tanner, 2008; Hobfoll, 2002; Schaufeli & Bakker, 2004; Voydanoff, 2005), there is general agreement on what constitutes the demands and resources of the work-life interface. Work demands within this domain include work hours (paid and overtime), workload and job insecurity, whilst the demands between domains include travelling away from home for work and working at home. Family domain demands can include care for young children or elderly relatives, household chores and responsibilities, in addition to the commute to work and family responsibilities that intrude on the work day.

Resources on the other hand are those aspects within work/non-work that make life function more easily; such as autonomy at work, the support of supervisors and co-workers, as well as support from family and relatives, along with the activities that give rewards for the efforts that are made, such as pride in one's work or parental rewards. It is proposed that individuals will be distressed by the loss, the threatened loss or the failure to gain resources after appropriate effort (Hobfoll, 2002). Resources, therefore, are those facets that individuals value in their own right, and find ways to accrue more of these over time which Hobfoll proposed that individuals will strive to do, to act as buffers in future challenging times. Examples of these resources include sense of optimism, time for work, time with loved ones, positive challenging routine, personal health, feelings of control over life, and the ability to organise tasks (Hobfoll, 2002). In line with Bronfenbrenner and Morris's (1998) ecological systems theory, such actions to accumulate resources would lead the active individual to interact with their environment in ways that promote their competent development in the longer term.

While a lack of resources could and has hindered how some women are able to function effectively in the workforce, those women who have been resourceful in using their abilities and skills have managed to achieve work success regardless of the lack of resources (see Al-Dajani, Chap. 3)

Well-Being

Well-being is being used increasingly to capture various aspects of feeling good and being healthy. Within the literature, there are various interpretations of well-being, e.g., affective well-being (Warr, 1987), which cuts across dimensions ranging from anxiety-contentment and depression-enthusiasm (Warr, 1990). It can encompass also achieving happiness or self-actualisation (Ryan & Deci, 2001). In addition, within the work setting, well-being has been shown to be linked to job characteristics (see de Jonge & Schaufeli, 1998; Warr, 1987), including demands, control and overall resources. Further, as work adds to well-being (Vaughan-Jones & Barham, 2009), it has been shown conversely that unemployment can affect mental health and thereby affect adversely well-being (Warr, 1987).

In the present volume, due to the nature of the various aspects of the research, well-being is considered from the affective perspective. In this respect, the fullness of any person's life combines both work and non-work/family outcomes and encompasses satisfaction with individual roles (e.g., Judge, Bono, Erez, & Locke, 2005), purposeful and meaningful activities (e.g., Ryan & Deci, 2001; Ryff & Keyes, 1995) and ongoing energy and motivation for all of these (e.g., Bakker & Demerouti, 2006). Throughout this volume, women's well-being is examined separately and in combination across these facets, reflecting that well-being can be defined in diverse and extensive ways. Moreover, well-being is defined through women's active participation in constructing the conditions of their lives, thereby contributing to more positive outcomes for them, in their work and for their families.

Work-Life Balance

The relationship between work and non-work activities has generated extensive research over time; which in turn has resulted in various terms to address this work-non-work/life/family balance (conflict, imbalance) interface. There is general agreement within the literature that there is no singular terminology to describe the concept (see e.g., Kalliath & Brough, 2008). It can be considered to be a noun (as what is achieved), a verb (as the daily balancing of roles), or as an adjective (in that it is positive or negative) (Greenhaus, Collins, & Shaw, 2003). As such, in the concept of the present volume, the preferred term of work-life balance refers to achieving a positive relationship between those activities that occur within the work and non-work domains. In the present volume, Huda (Chap. 4) and Kinman (Chap. 8) provide more specific interpretations of their use of the concept within their respective research.

The various terms have been gaining more prominence due to the dynamic work environment, the 24/7 society, dual-earners within families and globalisation that exist at present. Due to the varying increasing demands on individuals' time, it has highlighted that there is a need for a more positive integration of work/non-work activities to allow individuals to fulfil those personal, work, family, and community duties (Grzywacz & Carlson, 2007; Morris & Madsen, 2007) that arise over the course of any 1 day or period. As research has shown, the concept can contribute to a higher quality of life for those who are able to devote considerable time to both work and family, or have a greater focus on family responsibilities (e.g., Greenhaus et al., 2003). While work-life balance is a key concern for both genders, women still do the majority of household work (Risman, 2011) and are considered still as the person 'responsible' for this task, even when engaged in paid work and despite social class (Risman, 2011). In this respect, work-life balance becomes even more significant in women's overall well-being.

That work-family conflict has been the focus of much research also highlights that the belief that parents, and mothers in particular, would be more likely to have conflicts between their roles than non-parents. Research, however, shows that both parents and non-parents are appreciative on family-friendly benefits, showing increased attachment to their workplaces (Grover & Crooker, 1995). Understanding the work-life interface acknowledges that people are involved in many activities beyond childcare, and that eldercare, volunteer activities and leisure pursuits can occupy time and energy in the same manner as raising children can. Work-family, work-nonwork, and work-life are all terms that can be used interchangeably, acknowledging that many of the factors that affect parents also affect non-parents (Geurts & Demerouti, 2003), such as working hours (Moen & Sweet, 2003) and burnout (Maslach & Leiter, 2008).

Entrepreneurship

Entrepreneurship is an established part of business. However, since the start of the 2008 global recession, it has gained in prominence due to the various levels of job cuts that have occurred (Pines, Lerner, & Schwartz, 2010). It has allowed persons to start their own businesses. While, it has been noted that the concept lacks a conceptual framework, which makes it difficult to define (Shane & Venkataraman, 2000); in the present volume, an "entrepreneur" refers to 'individuals who are self-employed with no employees own account workers and with employees employers' (World Bank, 2011, p. 39).

It has been noted that while entrepreneurship is a good business opportunity for women, women are less likely to become entrepreneurs (Pines et al., 2010). Within developing countries, this could be due to social exclusion and the difficulty in gaining the appropriate funding to start a business (Pines et al., 2010). Al-Dajani and colleagues in Chap. 3 explore entrepreneurship within a developing country and in the informal economy. The informal economy stands outside the regulatory framework (ILO, 2010), thereby consisting of work and jobs that are not regulated; it is thereby easier to enter and exit, and provide a good option for those wishing to start a business, however small and unique.

Method

The challenges in conducting research and collecting data within some developing countries have been noted (de Baessa, 2008; World Bank, 2011). Further, due to the differences within western and non-western cultures and countries, findings collected from one arena should be extrapolated to the other. Despite these difficulties, it is important to continue to collect data across countries and cultures to facilitate a greater understanding of work conditions and the resources that women use and can obtain.

The current volume includes diverse research methods and samples, and spans the divide between Western and non-western research. This volume presents research on women's experiences, attitudes and perceptions, particularly in their work roles. The research is varied and the methods used within the chapters include cross-sectional and longitudinal research, reviews of literature, as well as experiences and practical suggestions from clinical, organisational, health and occupational health psychologists, in addition to occupational safety and health practitioners. The chapters present theoretical underpinnings of how, what, when and where women approach work options, approach life and approach living. The research represents women in all walks of life, from part-time employees and those in vulnerable positions in the informal economy to women in mainstream, full-time employment, and explores their options across all life stages, from first-time mothers returning to work, to those pursuing entrepreneurial work options in developing countries, to those transitioning through the menopause. In addition, working women are considered in their family roles, as they seek to balance their work and family roles and as they learn to effectively communicate with their adolescent daughters. Exploring women in the many and varied roles and responsibilities across the lifespan allows this volume to progress the knowledge of women's work-life experiences, based on appropriate theoretical frameworks, to ensure that women are acknowledged and supported as essential to the workforce. Moreover, the overarching factor that links these chapters is the focus on women as a vital resource in the world economy, with an exploration of the options that are available to them and how these could be maximised to retain a productive and healthy female workforce.

Moreover, there are various methodological considerations in respect of gender that should be considered, some of which have been undertaken in this volume. For example, research should focus on analysing any research independently for men and women, but research should look also at any issue across both genders (European Agency for Safety and Health at Work, 2013). This approach to understating women's issues as distinct from men's have been done in for example, Chap. 4 (Huda) and Chap. 7 (Siller and colleagues).

Plan of the Book

The conceptual framework that is used in this volume reflects the integration of biological, psychological, social and cultural perspectives, which interact with each other to determine how, where and why women work. The chapters are framed by ecological systems theory (e.g., Bronfenbrenner & Morris, 1998; Grzywacz & Marks, 2000), where the outcomes of a person's life are the results of the ongoing interactions between the person and her/his environment. The primary focus of the

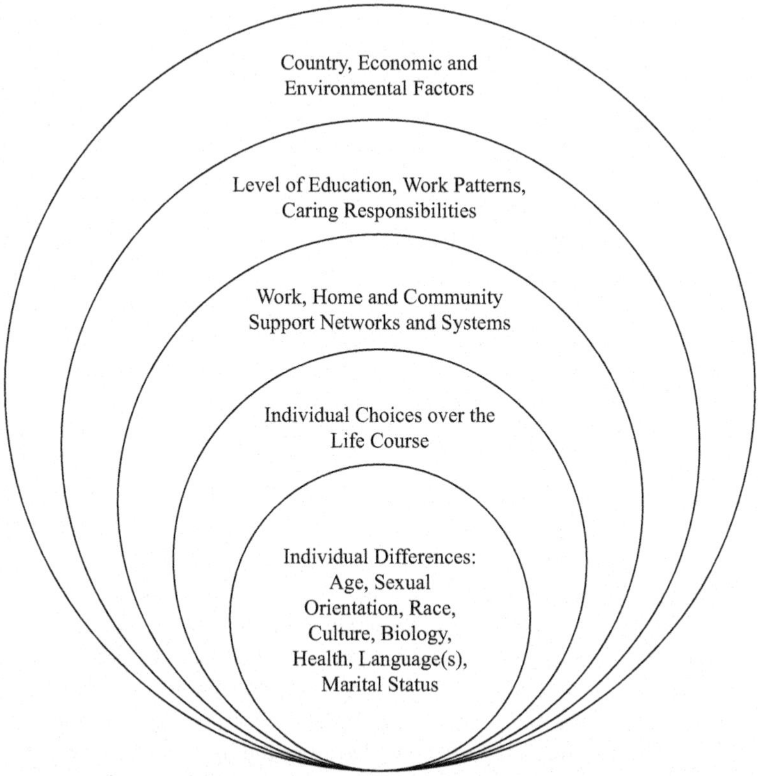

Fig. 1.1 Factors that contribute to women's work choices across the lifespan

book is women in the environment of their working roles. However, women also have their family roles, which can both complement and contradict their engagement in work, and their good health, where menstruation and menopause can interrupt both roles. Figure 1.1 uses a modification of Bronfenbrenner's classic arrangement of widening circles of influence. Immediate influences are shown as choices over the life course; the support networks (resources); influencing factors on how she works; and country, economic and environmental factors.

Women throughout this book demonstrate that they were active agents in shaping their lives, whether they were in part-time work, working within the informal economy, or as executives and highly qualified professionals; and especially in responding to the challenges that they face. The book represents a great diversity in circumstances, yet throughout, women used the resources that are available to them in making the most of their particular situation. From women in the refugee camps in Jordan, cities in Bangladesh, to prosperous western countries, where they are highly qualified women working as executives and in universities and hospitals, women are pursuing work opportunities that provide for personal accomplishments as well as security for their families. The chapters that follow explore the various choices available to women, from women in countries considered still as 'developing' and as such, women tend to have fewer choices available to them. In Australia, women can choose to a certain extent if to have children, and when to return to work; while in Jordan, a country where women are the main carers of their child and responsible for the entire family, they could choose to enter the informal economy as entrepreneurs to have the 'choice' of earning an income as well as having the flexibility to address work and life issues.

The book consists of six parts. The first part introduces the volume, and includes an overview of the book (Gervais and Millear), followed by Gervais (Chap. 2) outlining those issues that impact on women at work. The second part explores the work choices and resources available to women in developing countries. Beginning with women in developing countries, Al-Dajani and colleagues (Chap. 3) have conducted valuable research in the difficulties that refugee women face in Jordan. Al-Hajani et al. outline the entrepreneurial activities of refugee and displaced women in Jordan and their reasons for staying in the informal economy. The women found creative solutions to generate income and security for themselves and their families, when opportunities were not obvious or not permitted for refugees. In contrast, the women involved in Huda's research (Chap. 4) were employed as mid-level executives in Bangladesh. There were strong correlations between the women's efficient work performance, reduced conflict between work, and greater work to family enrichment. This section allows two different, distinct and essential dimensions of developing countries to be highlighted: the informal economy and senior management. Further, despite the cultural barriers for women's employment; the women and their families benefited from the opportunities they obtained from work.

The third part focuses on those challenges, choices and constraints that women face in choosing to work or wishing to advance their career. The part starts with Lyonette and colleagues discussing women's reasons for working part-time. Part-time work is a solution for women with younger children, but Lyonette, Baldauf, and Behle's research (Chap. 5) shows the practical constraints for women and businesses to make this option a successful alternative for both parties. It is interesting that the arrangements were most successful where the women involved were more proactive about ensuring the strategies were enacted on an ongoing basis and where organisations showed that they valued the contribution that women made to their organisations.

Rink, Ryan and Stoker's research on the glass cliff in Chap. 6 provides an interesting comment on how gender stereotypes of women's strengths can be seen as a double-edged compliment. On the one hand, women are seen as best suited to help an organisation through difficult financial times, but are considered less suitable to lead those organisations in good times. The irony that the ability to 'nurture' was only valued during difficult times should not be lost on policy makers and organisations. The strengths that women can bring to leadership should be consistently valued, rather than to place them in unduly precarious leadership positions.

In traditional and to a great extent, still male-dominated professions, such as medicine, Siller and colleagues (Chap. 7) examined the support experienced by male and female physicians in a university hospital. They found that women physicians showed many similarities to their male colleagues, except that the women with children devoted less time to research than all others. It was this research time that was foregone for family time, rather than patient care, that was the trade-off that professional women made when combining medicine and parenting.

The fourth part considers how women could balance the work-life-family interface and those resources that are available to them to assist with this. The experience of the physicians in Chap. 7 (Siller and colleagues) is expanded in the chapters in this section that are concerned with working mothers and their family roles.

Kinman's research (Chap. 8) examined how women academics managed the interface between work and life, and found that they face similar challenges to the Austrian physicians. In common with women in part-time positions, work-life balance relied on the academics' own strategies as well as supportive organisations to be achieved. Combining work and family requires women to make choices, such as when to return to work (Boyd et al., Chap. 9) after the birth of a first child; what type of work they will pursue, and how to maintain relationships when children reach the challenging time of adolescence (Katsikitis et al., Chap. 10). However, there are benefits for women later in life where they show the consequences of managing work and family roles across the life span (Millear, in Chap. 11).

All choices have consequences so whilst Lyonette and colleagues considered the work issues of mothers of young children in part-time work, Boyd and her colleagues (Chap. 9) examined the decisions about when to return to work and how this affected women's beliefs about costs and benefits of working in the first 18 months of their new child's life. Boyd et al. describes the transition back to work when children are young and the gradual accommodation to the work role. Once women returned to work, they became accustomed to the challenges of combining work and family roles, compared to mothers not yet in the workforce, who were more negative about the work role.

Moreover, while work-family tensions often focus on mothers of young children, Katsikitis and colleagues (Chap. 10) showed that mothers can also struggle to maintain good relationships with their adolescent children. Whilst mothers and their adolescent daughters may desire better communication, a technology-specific intervention posed additional, unexpected challenges for mothers. Technology is a ubiquitous part of modern life, and adolescents are often more at ease than their parents with such devices. The usefulness of such an intervention to assist with positive engagement is explored. Good intentions for additional time to be spent with children may have been impacted by the existing time constraints from other roles. However, Millear's research (Chap. 11) suggests that older women with multiple roles may show an accumulated advantage from their experiences. Young mothers are undoubtedly at the busiest times of their lives, but children grow up and eventually require less parental involvement. Older mothers showed greater well-being and work engagement compared to all other ages in that study. Working through the challenges of earlier ages was associated with greater resources for older working women.

The fifth part looks at two of the physiological changes that women experience over their work life, menstruation and menopause. It starts with Gervais assessing the impact of menstruation on work performance. Gervais (Chap. 12) examined nurses' experiences of menstruation through a diary study, with psychosomatic symptoms increasing the nurses' job strain and impacting work performance. Job resources assisted the nurses in managing their symptoms and contributed to positive work outcomes. Job resources also contributed to managing the experience of menopause, as shown in the study of middle-aged women by Millear and Gervais (Chap. 13). Women with more workplace resources, such as support from colleagues, and more personal resources (and therefore personal agency) could moderate the poor experience of menopause and associated poor mental health, to maintain well-being, job satisfaction and work performance. Webster (Chap. 14) details more of the personal concerns that menopause brings and outlines workplace strategies that can assist women. Menopause is a natural part of a woman's life, and like their earlier experiences of combining work and family roles, women can be proactive in managing their symptoms and gaining assistance from their organisations.

The sixth and final part summaries the present research and investigates the future for women at work and how the resources that they need could be obtained. As noted in Chap. 2, women are a much needed resource for the workplace and have to be supported as valued workers.

References

Annandale, E., & Clark, J. (1996). What is gender? Feminist theory and the sociology of human reproduction. *Sociology of Health & Illness, 18*(1), 17–44. doi:10.1111/1467-9566.ep10934409.

Appelrouth, S., & Desfor, E. L. (2011). *Sociological theory in the contemporary era: Text and readings* (2nd ed.). Thousand Oaks, CA: Sage.

Bakker, A. B., & Demerouti, E. (2006). The jobs demands-resources model: State of the art. *Journal of Managerial Psychology, 22*(3), 309–328. doi:10.1108/02683940710733115.

Brah, A., & Phoenix, A. (2004). Ain't I a woman? Revisiting intersectionality. *Journal of International Women's Studies, 5*(3), 75–86.

Bronfenbrenner, U., & Morris, P. A. (1998). The ecology of developmental processes. In W. Damon & R. M. Lerner (Eds.), *Handbook of child psychology* (5th ed., Vol. 1, pp. 993–1028). New York: Wiley.

Cohen, J. W. (2009). *What's sex gotta do with it?: The study of gender in criminology and the social sciences*. Indiana University of Pennsylvania. Retrieved from http://dspace.iup.edu/bitstream/handle/2069/154/Jeffrey%20Cohen.pdf?sequence=1

de Baessa, Y. (2008). *Research in a developing country*. Psychology International, December. Retrieved from http://www.apa.org/international/pi/2008/12/de-baessa.aspx

de Jonge, J., & Schaufeli, W. B. (1998). Job characteristics and employee well-being: A test of Warr's vitamin model in health care workers using structural equation modelling. *Journal of Organizational Behavior, 19*(4), 387–407.

European Agency for Safety and Health at Work. (2013). *New risks and trends in the safety and health of women at work*. Luxembourg: Publications Office of the European Union. Retrieved from https://osha.europa.eu/en/publications/reports/new-risks-trends-osh-women. Accessed 27 May 2013.

Geurts, S., & Demerouti, E. (2003). Work/non-work interface: A review of theories and findings. In M. J. Schabracq, J. A. M. Winnubst, & C. L. Cooper (Eds.), *Handbook of work and health psychology* (2nd ed., pp. 279–312). Chichester, UK: Wiley.

Greenhaus, J. H., Collins, K. M., & Shaw, J. D. (2003). The relation between work-family balance and quality of life. *Journal of Vocational Behavior, 63*(3), 510–531. doi:10.1016/S0001-8791(02)00042-8.

Grover, S. L., & Crooker, K. J. (1995). Who appreciates family-responsive human resource policies: The impact of family-friendly policies on the organizational attachment of parents and non-parents. *Personnel Psychology, 48*(2), 271–288. doi:10.1111/j.1744-6570.1995.tb01757.x:.

Grzywacz, J. G., & Carlson, D. S. (2007). Conceptualizing work-family balance: Implications for practice and research. *Advances in Developing Human Resources, 9*, 455–471. doi:10.1177/1523422307305487.

Grzywacz, J. G., & Marks, N. F. (2000). Reconceptualizing the work-family interface: An ecological perspective on the correlates of positive and negative spillover between work and family. *Journal of Occupational Health Psychology, 5*(1), 111–126. doi:10.1037/1076-8998.5.1.111.

Hakanen, J. J., Perhoniemi, R., & Toppinen-Tanner, S. (2008). Positive gain spirals at work: From job resources to work engagement, personal initiative and work-unit effectiveness. *Journal of Vocational Behavior, 73*(1), 78–91. doi:10.1016/j.jvb.2008.01.003.

Hobfoll, S. E. (2002). Social and psychological resources and adaptation. *Review of General Psychology, 6*(4), 307–324. doi:10.137//1089-2680.6.4.307.

International Labour Organization. (2010). Women in labour markets: Measuring progress and identifying challenges. Geneva: International Labour Office. http://www.ilo.org/wcmsp5/groups/public/---ed_emp/---emp_elm/---trends/documents/publication/wcms_123835.pdf. Accessed 15 Aug 2014.

Judge, T. A., Bono, J. E., Erez, A., & Locke, E. (2005). Core self-evaluations and job and life satisfaction: The role of self-concordance and goal attainment. *Journal of Applied Psychology, 90*(2), 257–268. doi:10.1037/0021-9010.90.2.257.

Kalliath, T., & Brough, P. (2008). Work-life balance: A review of the meaning of the balance construct. *Journal of Management & Organization, 14*, 323–327. doi:10.1017/S1833367200003308.

Maslach, C., & Leiter, M. P. (2008). Early predictors of job burnout and engagement. *Journal of Applied Psychology, 93*(3), 498–512. doi:10.1037/0021-9010.93.3.498.

McCall, L. (2005). The complexity of intersectionality. *Signs: Journal of Women in Culture and Society, 30*(3), 1771–1800. doi:10.1086/426800.

Moen, P., & Sweet, S. (2003). Time clocks: Work-hour strategies. In P. Moen (Ed.), *It's about time: Couples and careers* (pp. 18–34). Ithaca, NY: Cornell University Press.

Morris, M. L., & Madsen, S. R. (2007). Advancing work-life integration in individuals, organizations, and communities. *Advances in Developing Human Resources, 9*, 439–454. doi:10.1177/1523422307305486.

Nash, J. C. (2008). Re-thinking intersectionality. *Feminist Review, 89*, 1–15. doi:10.1057/fr.2008.4.

Pines, A. M., Lerner, M., & Schwartz, D. (2010). Gender differences in entrepreneurship: Equality, diversity and inclusion in times of global crisis. *Equality, Diversity and Inclusion: An International Journal, 29*(2), 186–198. doi: http://dx.doi.org/10.1108/02610151011024493.

Risman, B. J. (2004). Gender as a social structure: Theory wrestling with activism. *Gender & Society, 18*(4), 429–450. doi:10.1177/0891243204265349.

Risman, B. J. (2009). From doing to undoing: Gender as we know it. *Gender & Society, 23*(1), 81–84. doi:10.1177/0891243208326874.

Risman, B. J. (2011). Gender as structure or trump card? *Journal of Family Theory & Review, 3*(1), 18–22. doi:10.1111/j.1756-2589.2010.00076.x.

Risman, B. J., & Davis, G. (2013). From sex roles to gender structure. *Current Sociology, 61*(5–6), 733–755. doi:10.1177/0011392113479315.

Ryan, R. M., & Deci, E. L. (2001). On happiness and human potentials: A review of research on hedonic and eudaimonic well-being. *Annual Review of Psychology, 52*(1), 141–166. doi:10.1146/annurev.psych.52.1.141.

Ryff, C. D., & Keyes, C. L. M. (1995). The structure of psychological well-being revisited. *Journal of Personality and Social Psychology, 69*(4), 719–727. doi:10.1037/0022-3514.69.4.719.

Schaufeli, W. B., & Bakker, A. B. (2004). Job demands, job resources, and their relationship with burnout and engagement: A multi-sample study. *Journal of Organizational Behavior, 25*, 293–315. doi:10.1002/job.248.

Shane, S., & Venkataraman, S. (2000). The promise of entrepreneurship as a field of research. *The Academy of Management Review, 25*(1), 217–226.

Smooth, W. (2011). Standing for women? Which women? The substantive representation of women's interests and the research imperative of intersectionality. *Politics and Gender, 7*(3), 436–441.

Vaughan-Jones, H., & Barham, L. (2009). *Healthy work challenges and opportunities to 2030.* London: BUPA. http://www.theworkfoundation.com/assets/docs/publications/216_Bupa_report.pdf. Accessed 16 Aug 2014.

Voydanoff, P. (2005). Toward a conceptualization of perceived work-family fit and balance: A demands and resources approach. *Journal of Marriage & the Family, 67*, 822–836. doi:10.1111/j.1741-3737.2005.00178.x.

Warr, P. (1990). The measurement of well-being and other aspects of mental health. *The Journal of Occupational Psychology, 63*, 193–210.

Warr, P. B. W. (1987). *Work, unemployment, and mental health*. Oxford: Clarendon.

World Bank. (2011). *World development report 2012. Gender equality and development.* Washington DC: The International Bank for Reconstruction and Development/The World Bank. http://siteresources.worldbank.org/INTWDR2012/Resources/7778105-1299699968583/7786210-1315936222006/Complete-Report.pdf. Accessed 26 Mar 2013.

Chapter 2
Women's Contribution to the Workplace

Roxane L. Gervais

Introduction

The contributions that women have made and continue to make to the workplace cannot be understated. They constitute half of the population, and in 2014, 50 % of global working age women were actively employed (International Labour Organization (ILO, 2014a). This rate reflects a fairly large disparity when compared with men whose employment rate stood at 77 % (ILO, 2014a). As would be expected, this employment rate differs by region, with for example, more women employed in East Asia (63 %), Sub-Saharan Africa (65 %) and South East Asia and the Pacific (60 %); while fewer women work in the Middle East (20 %) and in North Africa (26 %); and within the developed economies and the European Union just over half of the women of working age were employed (54 %; ILO, 2014a). These figures support the entry of more women in the workforce. Within the European Union (EU), the European Commission in 2010 set an employment rate of 75 % by 2020 for those aged 20–64, with a focus on increasing the rates for women, older workers and ensuring that migrant workers are integrated to a better extent in the workforce (European Commission, 2010). This encouragement of a healthier employment rate is required as a review of employment patterns showed that if the constant employment rate for women was held at its present level in the EU, this would result in an expected shortfall of 24 million people in the active workforce by 2040; conversely, if women's employment rate could increase to equal that of men,

---

This chapter is based on data collected independently by the author and represents solely her opinions and/or conclusions.

R.L. Gervais (✉)
Independent Practitioner, Goole DN14 6XN, UK
e-mail: roxane_gervais@alumni.fdu.edu

R.L. Gervais, P.M. Millear (eds.), *Exploring Resources, Life-Balance and Well-Being of Women Who Work in a Global Context*,
DOI 10.1007/978-3-319-31736-6_2

then the projected shortfall reduces to 3 million (Desvaux, Devillard-Hoellinger & Baumgarten, 2007). A greater entry of women in the workforce is not limited to Europe, but would benefit economies worldwide (World Bank, 2011). For, as noted, unless the employment rates rise for both men and women, economies will not be able to sustain their growing and elderly populations (Korczyc, Matia, Vincelette, Cuaresma & Loichinger, 2013). These figures are compounded further by estimations outlining that since the start of the global recession in 2008, 29 million net jobs have been lost worldwide and these have not been replaced (ILO, 2012). These data support the EU's strategy in wishing to increase participation rates, including women's; moreover, in supporting women, as a resource in the workforce, women as workers are entrenched more in the work environment.

While women are an available resource in helping to realise an active and sustainable source of labour, there is still much more to be done, especially for older and younger women, to encourage their entry into the labour market. One essential component of the work environment therefore is to ensure that all workers work in decent jobs. An increase in the workforce requires more than just placing people into jobs. There is an understanding that the workplace has to improve to ensure that it allows for better work practices and facilities, i.e., the modern organisation of work, having in place a knowledge economy, encouraging competitiveness, the creation of more and very importantly better jobs, as the availability of better quality jobs are one of the requirements in supporting a country's development (ILO, 2014a).

'Decent work' resonates for women as they tend generally to be employed in a few specific industries such as education and healthcare (European Agency for Safety and Health at Work (EU-OSHA), 2013), and are over-represented among unpaid and wage workers and in the informal economy. Figures from research published in 2010 showed that women accounted for 58 % of all unpaid work, 44 % of wage employment, and 50 % of informal employment (ILO, 2010). While none of these characteristics of women's work counteract their contribution to economies, they have to be considered when assessing women's reasons for working and in promoting decent work for all.

In this respect, encouraging women to enter and then remain in the workforce should encompass more than just acknowledging their contribution to the economy; and that work would assist with their well-being. It is known that individuals in work are more likely to have better health than those out of work (Vaughan Jones & Barham, 2009); with paid employment influencing positively women's mental and physical health (Repetti, Matthews, & Waldron, 1989). Therefore, while not discounting the benefits of work, such as improved well-being; the financial security of work to women has to remain a strong focus across all economies. It is essential to ensure that women have an income and a way to support themselves as they get older. It is established that women more than men are likely to face poverty over the course of their lives, and this is a higher risk for single mothers and those women who are over 65 (EC, 2009). This increased risk of poverty continues as women get older and, by the age of 65, it has been predicted that women are 1.5 times more likely than men of the same age to live in poverty (OECD, 2012); which in turn contributes to the feminisation of poverty. Some of the causes to women's lower earnings over their life course are due to their (historical) earlier retirement ages and in some countries from not being encouraged to work, due to social and 'protective' motives (World Bank, 2011).

Even though there has been a concerted effort to raise the occupational safety and health (OSH) aspects of the work in which women are engaged (see Messing, 1997; Messing, Dumais, Courville, Seifert, & Boucher, 1994; Messing & Mager Stellman, 2006), assumptions exist still on what constitutes women's work. The work in which women engage generally is seen for the most part as safe, allowing for the real risks in the types of work in which women are involved to be ignored (Hazards, 2008). Due to the greater focus on improving work conditions, especially in Western societies, work is becoming safer and accidents at the workplace have been decreasing steadily (EU-OSHA, 2013). There has been an acceptance that men's work-related injury rates remain higher than women's due to their greater involvement in high risk jobs (EU-OSHA, 2013; Eurostat, 2002); but it needs to be acknowledged also that as more women are entering male-dominated professions to a greater extent, their potential for harm is likely to increase (EU-OSHA, 2013). It has been shown that there are methodological concerns in how these rates are assessed. When various characteristics are controlled, such as age, occupation, type of employment (full-time, part-time), then the stark differences between the two genders tend to decrease (see Alamgir, Yu, Drebit, Fast, & Kidd, 2009; Eurostat, 2002; Kelsh & Sahl, 1996), with Davies and Jones (2005) calling for a 'like with like' comparison of injury rates. There is research that reflects also that for some industries such as manufacturing, women's injury rates are higher (Taiwo et al., 2009; Tessier-Sherman et al., 2014).

The increasing research on women in more high-risk industries should work at dispelling the pre-existing assumption that women do not do the high risks jobs as men, classified as 3D – *dirty, difficult and dangerous* – jobs, and subsequently leading to the presumption that women are safe at work, rather than in reality:

- Women are more exposed to repetitive and monotonous work and to stressful conditions;
- Young women are more likely than men to be physically assaulted at work; and
- Women are more likely than men to experience back strain, skin diseases, headaches and eyestrain (Hazards, 1999).

The three listed areas above are ones that are problematic for women still based on recent research (see Eng et al., 2011; EU-OSHA, 2013). Research on *women* and their *work* has increased and these studies are beneficial, but a lower focus on women as participants in research remains (Messing, 1998), with limited research being conducted into the health and safety hazards of female dominated industries (Stellman, 2000). Increased research could facilitate much quicker the development of decent jobs, for both genders.

Women and Part-Time Work

Women tend to work part-time to a greater extent than men. In the EU, part-time work shows a great disparity between the genders with a part-time rate for women (32 %) that is four times the part-time rate for men (8 %, Eurofound, 2011). Part-time work allows more women to enter the workforce, thereby boosting women's participation rates (European Working Conditions Observatory (EWCO), 2010); but it must be acknowledged that part-time work for women is more common in countries with poorer child care facilities (EU-OSHA, 2013; The World Bank, 2011). Despite this, the reasons for women's working time are varied, but for women with child care responsibilities, it is one viable option to remain employed, whilst fulfilling care responsibilities. (See Lyonette et al., Chap. 5 this volume). Moreover, there are no differences in terms of the job characteristics or income of women with children who work part-time for care reasons from those women who work part-time out of personal choice (Horemans, 2012). In 2007, a study of seven European countries found that for three of these countries, Finland, Poland and Spain, most of the respondents cited their reasons for working part-time was their inability to find full-time work or they were working part-time to complete their education (Michoñ, 2007). Interestingly, the proportion of part-time workers from Finland and Poland was higher among childless women. Child care therefore cannot be seen as the main reason that women opt for this form of employment.

Regardless of the motives for women choosing to work in a part-time capacity, other issues around part-time work are relevant to discuss; research has found that part-time workers were less likely than full-time workers to be promoted or to receive a pay rise (Grant, Yeandle, & Buckner, 2005; Michoñ, 2007), and part-time women workers have described themselves as being peripheral in their organisations and were more likely to be laid off (Barker, 1993). Another aspect associated with this form of employment is that while women with more qualifications are less likely to work part-time (EWCO, 2010), for some of those women, they may be working below their potential, i.e., not using all their skills, neither their labour market experience, nor their qualifications in the jobs in which they were employed (Grant et al., 2005). Women who work part-time receive lower wages than those who work full-time (EWCO, 2010) and as mentioned previously in this chapter, women are more likely to live in poverty as they get older; making this form of work even more relevant to the debate.

Women's work pattern tends to change as their children get older (Horemans, 2012), and some may choose to work full-time as their children become independent, or they may choose to continue to work part-time to maintain their work-life balance (Gash, Mertens, & Romeu Gordo, 2009). The option of a choice for women in how to work is discussed in Boyd et al. and Millear, Chaps. 9 and 11 respectfully, this volume. There are positive aspects to part-time working as it has been associated with achieving work-life balance (Eurofound, 2012; Hill, Martinson, Ferris, & Baker, 2004). Further, there is some evidence that women who choose to reduce their working hours, moving from full-time employment to part-time, were able to achieve higher levels of well-being, i.e., life satisfaction (Gash et al., 2009) and higher job satisfaction, with lower role conflict and role overload (Barker, 1993). Another positive aspect of reduced hours of work is that it might help with well-being, due to the increase in psychological distress that could occur when long hours negatively impacts on the work-family interface (Major, Klein, & Ehrhart, 2002).

Women and Psychosocial Risks

Psychosocial risks continue to facilitate discussion within the work environment, perhaps driven by a few of the major theories of the past few decades: the demand-control model (Karasek, 1979), the person-environment fit model (French, Caplan, & Harrison, 1982), and the effort-reward imbalance model (Siegrist, 1996). These models continued the importance of considering work-related characteristics in understanding those factors that contribute to ill health within the work environment. Despite the intensity of research that has been dedicated to understanding and promoting ways to address psychosocial risks, there are challenges still in how the term is best interpreted (Egan, Tannahill, Petticrew, & Thomas, 2008; Martikainen, Bartley, & Lahelma, 2002). However, some of the most used terms within the work environment have included high demands, low control, effort-reward imbalance, decision authority, decision latitude, social support, emotional labour, harassment, and violence (see Dollard, Skinner, Tuckey, & Bailey, 2007; Siegrist & Marmot, 2004; Stansfeld & Candy, 2006). These risks are influenced heavily by the design, organisation and management of the workplace.

One potential outcome of experiencing psychosocial risks is ill health, such as stress. Studies on occupational stress that were assessed by gender, found that women are subjected to the same stressors as men (see Barnett & Brennan, 1997; Martocchio & O'Leary, 1989; Piltch, Walsh, Mangione, & Jennings, 1994). Haynes (1991) found also that women in high strain jobs have the same stress related diseases in common with men, such as heart disease and alcohol-related illnesses. They also have higher morbidity rates (Piltch et al., 1994; Verbrugge, 1985), use the health services more and have more illnesses and disabilities (Verbrugge).

Psychosocial risks are of concern for women workers therefore as they are more likely to experience these risks at the workplace than are men (Campos-Serna, Ronda-Perez, Artazcoz, Moen, & Benavides, 2013; Campos-Serna, Ronda-Perez, Moen, Artazcoz, & Benavides, 2013), and are more likely to be affected adversely by psychosocial risks than men (Lund, Labriola, Christensen, Bültmann, & Villadsen, 2006). This is especially when a combination of poor physical work conditions with poor psychosocial work conditions exist (Lund et al., 2006).

For women, there are certain psychosocial risks that can affect adversely their OSH over the course of their working lives. These include musculoskeletal disorders (MSDs; Strazdins & Bammer, 2004), and stress due to greater unpaid workload (Lundberg & Frankenhaeuser, 1999). Moreover, men and women differ in their responses to work stressors, and as one study has shown, men are more likely to experience job stress due to workload, and conversely, women were found to be adversely affected by emotional and intellectual demands (Rivera-Torres, Araque-Padilla, & Montero-Simó, 2013). However, when workload is considered as part of the family domain, the stressors to which women in high level positions are subjected revolve still around family issues, such as the extra workload from unpaid work (Lundberg & Frankenhaeuser, 1999) and this aspect is discussed further in Siller et al., Chap. 7 this volume.

Low control at work remains problematic for women, perhaps driven by the sectors in which they work. Low control could contribute to poor health and psychological distress, as reported by women employees who were then more likely to take more sick leave than those with more control; a similar effect was not found in men (Ala-Mursula, Vahtera, Kivimäki, Kevin, & Pentti, 2002). The gender difference in roles at home might lend to an explanation of those results (see Benavides, Benach, & Muntaner, 2002).

Maintaining Balance

Women still do most of the housework, regardless of working part-time or full-time, even when married (EU-OSHA, 2013) and regardless of income (World Bank, 2011). They continue to be the main caregivers, looking after children and due to the ageing population, the Generation X and Baby Boomers tending to have increasing dual care roles, i.e., looking after both children and elder relatives (parents, in-laws, extended family members); it is another role to which they have to adjust. While the literature is mixed on the adverse effects of a dual care role (see Dautzenberg et al., 2000; Künemund, 2006; Loomis & Booth, 1995; Williams, 2004), this does not negate that women continue to engage in these various roles, which may restrict options in moving forward in their chosen occupation. Siller et al., Chap. 7 this volume, explores some of the work-home factors that could limit career advancement for female physicians.

One of the ways that women who work cope with multiple responsibilities is to use their sick leave allowances for child or elderly care, which then results in them needing to work when they are ill themselves (Quinn & Woskie, 1988). This element of presenteeism contributes to higher sick leave rates, and could lower productivity within organisations (Hillier, Fewell, Cann, & Shephard, 2005).

Recent research has shown that women more so than men were more likely to be affected adversely when contacted outside of work hours. Their feelings of guilt and distress when this was done increased, whilst these emotional and mental health feelings were not associated with men (Glavin, Schieman, & Reid, 2011). Similarly, there is the factor of psychological distress that could occur when long hours negatively impacts on the work-family interface (Major et al., 2002). Kinman, Chap. 8 this volume, explores the work-family interface among academics, with Huda, Chap. 4, this volume, focusing on the concept among executives. A meta-analysis to evaluate the linkage between long work hours and coronary heart disease (CHD) was published in 2012 (Virtanen et al., 2012). The findings confirmed the hypothesised relationship, in that long hours at work would lead to increased risk for CHD, but noted also that there was an elevated risk of CHD for part-time workers. Interestingly, although women work part-time more than men (EU-OSHA, 2013), the research that has explored this relationship has tended to include mainly samples of men (e.g., Sokejima & Kagamimori, 1998). While it is important to assess these risks that result in ill health for all workers, if part-time work, when combined with long hours, is indeed a predictor of CHD, then it is essential that research studies include more samples of women when assessing this condition. When women's work hours are considered solely from the workplace, it is recognised that they work fewer hours than men; but when combined with the hours they work outside of the workplace, their active time is significantly increased (EU-OSHA, 2013). This is even more relevant for women when they are employed full-time (Eurostat, 2006; Forastieri, 2000).

Overall, women engage in more roles than men (Barnett & Marshall, 1991; Gutek, Repetti, & Silver, 1988). This could have some benefits, as studies have shown that multiple roles when combined with paid work can result in positive health effects on women (e.g., Barnett, Marshall, & Sayer, 1992) and as noted by Lundberg and Frankenhaeuser (1999) challenging work could function therefore as a stress buffer. In addition to challenging work, the quality of the roles in which women function contributes to their well-being (Baruch & Barnett, 1986), as does a good challenging paid job, and high quality of life (Ryff & Singer, 1998). The longer term consequences of multiple roles are explored in Millear, Chap. 11 this volume, and women's roles as mothers, in their communications with their daughters are considered in Katsikitis et al., Chap. 10 this volume.

Women and Their Bodies

Women during their working lives could experience physiological changes due to menstruation, pregnancy and the menopause. Despite these constant and expected changes in women's lives, there remains a lack of research in these areas (EU-OSHA, 2003, 2013), and especially better focused research on reproductive issues in respect of overall working conditions (EU-OSHA, 2003). Research has increased on pregnant women and new mothers, but the same comment cannot be made about the other life experiences that women go through while at work, such as menstruation and menopause. Boyd et al., Chap. 9 this volume, outlines the options available to new mothers in respect of returning to work.

As discussed earlier, older women are required to enter the workforce, due to the overall ageing population across, for example Europe and to assist with sustaining economies; but the research that is available to assist women at work during this period of their lives, has to improve. The scarcity of research on the menopause from both developed and developing countries to support health promotion in this area was noted in 1996 (World Health Organization (WHO), 1996) and seems to be relevant still today. Millear and Gervais, Chap. 13 this volume, and Webster, Chap. 14 this volume, provide some insight into this aspect of women's working lives. These chapters are especially relevant to challenge some of the anecdotal evidence that women find it difficult to deal with 'the change' and are less productive during this phase. In reality, most women are not depressed when experiencing menopause (Brown, Gallicchio, Flaws, & Tracy, 2009), neither are they liable to be less productive at work (DiBonaventura, Wagner, Alvir & Whiteley, 2012).

Similarly, there have been extensive negative perceptions about women's work ability during their 'time of the month', the menstrual cycle. The research that is in the public domain about the impact of menstruation on women while at work is not extensive. Gervais, Chap. 12 this volume, adds to the literature in this area by exploring its impact on performance.

The physical features of the work environment such as open plan offices; the ambient conditions, such as light, sound, and ventilation; as well as thermal comfort, are rarely considered as being significant contributors to workers' well-being and productivity. It would be expected that due to women's physiological changes that progress throughout their life course that is even while they work; that these features are very relevant for women when menstruating, pregnant or menopausal. As such, more research in this area should be encouraged. See Webster, Chap. 14 and Millear and Gervais, Chap. 13, this volume. Briner (2000) noted that the work environment contributes to both positive and negative impacts on the psychological well-being of employees. To add to this discussion, Klitzman and Stellman (1989) found that the physical environment could increase workers' stress levels, while Vischer (2007) found that it affected both job performance and job satisfaction. Mccoy and Evans (2005) in examining the impact of the features of the physical environment on work objectives found that stressors therein could affect adversely employee performance, motivation, and social interaction, resulting in a loss of productivity and performance. Moreover, any time and attention that workers spend coping with their particular physical environment represents a loss of time and attention from the performance of their work (Vischer, 2007). Ergo, different aspects of the physical work environment can affect psychological well-being, productivity and performance, and as every employee may have different interpretations of these, it is not possible to state which aspect of the physical working environment has the biggest negative impact. However an investment into creating an ambient working environment will result in an increase in productivity and performance (see Vischer, 2007).

Discrimination at Work

Discrimination remains relevant to women's increased presence in the workplace. An EU-OSHA report in 2013 highlighted the various factors that could be used to discriminate against women at work, much more than men. These could focus on many facets, so in addition to their gender, age, ethnicity, disability and sexual orientation, migrant women could face discrimination due to their origin or class, or this could occur when they work in the informal economy. Further, women could experience multiple forms of discrimination via a combination of any of these factors. Other vulnerable groups include young women; women with care obligations in countries where resources for these are limited; women in multiple jobs, very young mothers and older women, depending on the country in which they live (EU-OSHA, 2013). Banks and Milestone (2011) have proposed that women despite being discriminated against in the workplace, have managed to carve a niche for themselves in this arena.

Another issue that is very relevant to women within the workforce is that pay is still an issue for them (Grant et al., 2005). Due to the segmentation of the genders in specific sectors, women tend to work still in sectors with low pay (ILO, 2010). This links again to the concern of women living in poverty as they get older and has to remain on the agenda as a resource that must improve for women. Interestingly, women who choose an entrepreneurial approach to work, due to lack of choice, could increase their income from women who work in set workplaces. Al-Dajani et al., Chap. 3 this volume, explore this situation for women working in the informal economy.

As women's discrimination in the workplace cuts across a variety of issues, sexual harassment is still a significant risk for women workers, more than for men workers (EU-OSHA, 2013; Gervais, 2013). One of these is the gender-based discrimination, usually combined with sexual harassment, when they move into traditionally male dominated occupations, such as those within the construction industry (see Goldenhar, Swanson, Hurrell, Ruder & Deddens, 1998). The construction industry is one with an acknowledged ageing workforce (Schwatka, Butler & Rosecrance, 2012). It requires therefore the recruitment of workers, such as women, minority groups and younger workers, who have not been explored previously nor to any great extent, on the opportunities that it provides. It is established that more work needs to be done to improve the OSH in the construction industry, especially in respect of women workers, in order to improve the work environment and thereby allow more entrants (Occupational Safety & Health Administration (OSHA), 1999). Overall, the negative consequences of sexual harassment at work, such as lower psychological well-being, have been well documented (e.g., Glomb, Munson, Hulin, Bergman, Drasgow, 1999; Schneider, Swan & Fitzgerald, 1997).

Race and ethnicity are other factors that could encourage discrimination (Wadsworth et al., 2007), and is relevant especially for migrant women, leaving them no option but to enter the informal economy. See Al-Dajani et al., Chap. 3 this volume, for a greater discussion of this issue.

Informal Work as a Viable Option for Women

Informal work tends to attract particular groups who may have limited access to more decent and quality jobs. These groups include those with less education, the young, the elderly, those individuals who have chronic health problems and migrant workers (ILO, 2014b). Informal work may provide therefore an option for those individuals who would need to move to a worse job to cope with e.g., illness or fewer demands, and thereby *drift* to a situation that may not in the long term improve their well-being (de Jonge et al., 2001; Frese, 1982). Informal work tends to offer poorer working conditions and lower earnings than individuals would gain from obtaining jobs within the formal economy (ILO, 2014b).

Figures from the ILO show that informal work remains a substantial form of global employment. For example, within Eastern Europe, the Commonwealth of Independent States (CIS) countries and in a few advanced economies, informal employment tends to account for over 20 % of total employment. While in Latin America, informal employment rates could range from below 50 to 70 % or higher. For some countries in South and South-East Asia, the informality rates could approach up to 90 % of total employment, and are mainly due to the lack of formal employment opportunities (ILO, 2014b).

Informal work is increasing among women, and has to be focused in terms of OSH concerns, as these types of jobs are more likely to be unstable, unprotected and precarious (EU-OSHA, 2013). These could include those 'invisible' areas of informal work, such as domestic labour, piece-rate home work and assistance in small family enterprises (Ascoly, 2004). Another factor that serves to have women seeking work within the informal economy is the perception that they are 'less flexible' workers if they are married, pregnant or have children and therefore are not able to cope with these responsibilities as well as working in a full-time paid job (Ascoly). Some of the reasons for engaging in work in the informal economy are discussed in Al-Dajani et al., Chap. 3 this volume. Due to the nature of how work is contracted in the informal economy, it is difficult to get precise data on employment levels, especially when those involved in the work try their best not to be identified. Researchers propose that a qualitative approach as the most appropriate method to use to get information on those in these areas due to the sensitivities around informal paid work (Katungi, Neale, & Barbour, 2006).

Organisational Leadership and Women

Women still have difficulties in attaining senior positions within organisations because of the 'glass ceiling effect'; i.e. the idea that senior management, usually men, promote those similar to themselves, and thereby restricting women from 'fitting' into the established model of senior positions (Kumra & Vinnicombe, 2008). Moreover, although the number of women in managerial roles is increasing than in the past, they continue to be subjected to traditional stereotypes and tend to be discriminated against based on institutionalised systems that maintain subjective assessments of leadership capability (Melero, 2004). The glass ceiling effect remains relevant still in hampering women's position in organisations (Banks & Milestone, 2011).

In addition to the glass ceiling effect, women who are black and from other minority groups (BME) and aspire to leadership positions have to conquer as well the concrete ceiling (Davidson, 1997). A more recent phenomenon, described as the glass cliff effect, in which women are appointed to leadership positions during time of crisis, while men are appointed during periods of prosperous times (Bruckmuller & Branscombe, 2010), has been generating quite a lot of research. See Rink et al., Chap. 6 this volume, which discusses women's recruitment into situations that limit the relationships that they can develop within the organisation, thereby directly limiting their social capital, and allowing them to fall victim to glass cliffs.

For those women who do break through the glass ceiling, regardless of the restrictions that they encounter, their leadership abilities are accepted as no different to those of men (Rosette & Tost, 2010). One suggestion for women is that they should improve on how they access social capital (i.e., those relevant elements of knowledge, resources and networks), as these tend to assist men in their career development (Timberlake, 2005). Timberlake, in her review, emphasises that, although women and men enter the workplace with the same amount of human capital (intelligence, education, skills and experience), men are more successful at accessing social capital, that is membership in networks that provides an understanding and adopting of organisational norms, values and aims, which in turn strengthens their ability to gain organisational power.

Despite the constraints women managers might face in advancing in their careers, once they do, they have been able to achieve positive outcomes in respect of human resources policies. Organisations that have chosen to include more women at the management level have seen improved interpersonal communication, greater involvement of managers in employees' career administration and more democracy in decision-making at the workplace (Melero, 2004).

Summary

The issues raised in this chapter provide some insight into the many contributions that women make to the workplace. It outlines also some of the challenges that women continue to face within the work environment. These aspects of women's work will remain relevant over time, but they are being addressed. The chapters that follow will provide more insight into how, where and why women work; the resources that are available to them and overcoming constraints as well as recommending various options to address these.

References

Alamgir, H., Yu, S., Drebit, S., Fast, C., & Kidd, C. (2009). Are female healthcare workers at higher risk of occupational injury? *Occupational Medicine, 59*(3), 149–152. doi:10.1093/occmed/kqp011.

Ala-Mursula, L., Vahtera, J., Kivimäki, M., Kevin, M. V., & Pentti, J. (2002). Employee control over working times: Associations with subjective health and sickness absences. *Journal of Epidemiological Community Health, 56*(4), 272–278. doi:10.1136/jech.56.4.272.

Ascoly, N. (2004). *The global garment industry and the informal economy: Critical issues for labour rights advocates* (IRENE/CCC discussion paper). http://www.cleanclothes.org/documents/04-09-informal_labour_seminar_discussion_paper_CCC.pdf. Accessed 16 August 2014.

Banks, M., & Milestone, K. (2011). Individualization, gender and cultural work. *Gender, Work & Organization*. Special Issue: The Knowledge Society, *18*(1), 3–89. doi: 10.1111/j.1468-0432.2010.00535.xGender

Barker, K. (1993). Changing assumptions and contingent solutions: The costs and benefits of women working full- and part-time. *Sex Roles, 28*(1–2), 47–71.

Barnett, R. C., & Brennan, R. T. (1997). Change in job conditions, change in psychological distress, and gender: A longitudinal study of dual-earner couples. *Journal of Organizational Behavior, 18*(3), 253–274. doi:10.1002/(SICI)1099-1379(199705)18:3.

Barnett, R. C., & Marshall, N. L. (1991). The relationship between women's work and family roles and their subjective well-being and psychological distress. In M. Frankenhaeuser, U. Lundberg, & M. A. Chesney (Eds.), *Women, work, and health: Stress and opportunities* (pp. 111–136). New York: Plenum Press.

Barnett, R. C., Marshall, N. L., & Sayer, A. (1992). Positive-spillover effects from job to home: A closer look. *Women Health, 19*(2–3), 13–41. doi:10.1300/J013v19n02_02.

Baruch, G. K., & Barnett, R. C. (1986). Role quality, multiple role involvement, and psychological well-being in midlife women. *Journal of Personality and Social Psychology, 51*(3), 578–585. doi:10.1037/0022-3514.51.3.578.

Benavides, F. G., Benach, J., & Muntaner, C. (2002). Psychosocial risk factors at the workplace: Is there enough evidence to establish reference values? *Journal of Epidemiological Community Health, 56*(4), 244–245. doi:10.1136/jech.56.4.244.

Briner, R. B. (2000). Relationship between work environments, psychological environments and psychological well-being. *Occupational Medicine, 50*(5), 299–303. doi:10.1093/occmed/50.5.299.

Brown, J. P., Gallicchio, L., Flaws, J. A., & Tracy, J. K. (2009). Relations among menopausal symptoms, sleep disturbance and depressive symptoms in midlife. *Maturitas, 62*(2), 184–189. doi:10.1016/j.maturitas.2008.11.019.

Bruckmuller, S., & Branscombe, N. R. (2010). The glass cliff: When and why women are selected as leaders in crisis contexts. *British Journal of Social Psychology, 49*(3), 433–451. doi:10.1348/014466609X466594.

Campos-Serna, J., Ronda-Perez, E., Artazcoz, L., Moen, B. E., & Benavides, F. G. (2013). Gender inequalities in occupational health related to the unequal distribution of working and employment conditions: A systematic review. *International Journal for Equity in Health, 12*, 57. doi:10.1186/1475-9276-12-57.

Campos-Serna, J., Ronda-Perez, E., Moen, B. E., Artazcoz, L., & Benavides, F. G. (2013). Welfare state regimes and gender inequalities in the exposure to work-related psychosocial hazards. *International Journal of Occupational and Environmental Health, 19*(3), 179–195. doi:10.1179/2049396713Y.0000000030.

Dautzenberg, M. G. H., Diederiks, J. P. M., Philipsen, H., Stevens, F. C. J., Tan, F. E. S., & Vernooij-Dassen, M. J. F. J. (2000). The competing demands of paid work and parent care: middle-aged daughters providing assistance to elderly parents. *Research on Aging, 22*, 165–187. doi:10.1177/0164027500222004.

Davidson, M. J. (1997). *The black and ethnic minority woman manager: Cracking the concrete ceiling*. London: Sage Publications.

Davies, R., & Jones, P. (2005). *Trends and context to rates of workplace injury*. Health and Safety Executive. London: Her Majesty's Stationery Office. http://www.hse.gov.uk/research/rrpdf/rr386.pdf. Accessed 16 August 2014.

de Jonge, J., Dormann, C., Janssen, P. P. M., Dollard, M. F., Landeweerd, J. A., & Nijhuis, F. J. N. (2001). Testing reciprocal relationships between job characteristics and psychological well-being: A cross-lagged structural equation model. *Journal of Occupational and Organizational Psychology, 74*(1), 29–46. doi:10.1348/096317901167217.

Desvaux, G., Devillard-Hoellinger, S., & Baumgarten, P. (2007). *Women matter. Gender diversity, a corporate performance driver*. McKinsey & Company, Inc. http://www.mckinsey.com/locations/paris/home/womenmatter/pdfs/Women_matter_oct2007_english.pdf.Accessed 26 March 2012.

DiBonaventura, M. da C., Wagner, J-S., Alvir, J., & Whiteley, J. (2012). Depression, quality of life, work productivity, resource use, and costs among women experiencing menopause and hot flashes: A cross-sectional study. *The Primary Care Companion for CNS Disorders, 14*(6): PCC.12 m01410. doi: 10.4088/PCC.12m01410

Dollard, M., Skinner, N., Tuckey, M. R., & Bailey, T. (2007). National surveillance of psychosocial risk factors in the workplace: An international overview. *Work & Stress: An International Journal of Work, Health & Organisations, 21*(1), 1–29. doi:10.1080/02678370701254082.

Egan, M., Tannahill, M., Petticrew, M., & Thomas, S. (2008). Psychosocial risk factors in home and community settings and their associations with population health and health inequalities: A systematic meta-review. *BMC Public Health, 8*, 239. doi:10.1186/1471-2458-8-239.

Eng, A., 't Mannetje, A., McLean, D., Ellison-Loschmann, L., Cheng, S., & Pearce, N. (2011). Gender differences in occupational exposure patterns. *Occupational and Environmental Medicine, 68*(12), 888–894. doi:10.1136/oem.2010.064097.

European Agency for Safety and Health at Work. (2003). *Gender issues in safety and health at work: A review*. Luxembourg: Publications Office of the European Union. http://osha.europa.eu/en/publications/reports/209. Accessed 27 May 2013.

European Agency for Safety and Health at Work. (2013). *New risks and trends in the safety and health of women at Work*. Luxembourg: Publications Office of the European Union. Retrieved from https://osha.europa.eu/en/publications/reports/new-risks-trends-osh-women. Accessed 27 May 2013.

European Commission. (2009). Report on equality between women and men: 2009. http://europa.eu/legislation_summaries/employment_and_social_policy/equality_between_men_and_women/em0015_en.htm. Accessed 26 August 2010.

European Commission. (2010). Communication from the Commission of 3 March 2010 – Europe 2020. A strategy for smart, sustainable and inclusive growth [COM(2010) 2020]. http://eur-lex.europa.eu/legal-content/EN/TXT/PDF/?uri=CELEX:52010DC2020&from=EN. Accessed 17 August 2014.

European Foundation for the Improvement of Living and Working Conditions. (2012). *Fifth European working conditions survey*. Luxembourg: Publications Office of the European Union. http://www.eurofound.europa.eu/pubdocs/2011/82/en/1/EF1182EN.pdf. Accessed 16 August 2014.

European Foundation for the Improvement of Living and Working Conditions. (2011). *European company survey 2009. Part-time work in Europe*. Luxembourg: Publications Office of the European Union. http://www.eurofound.europa.eu/pubdocs/2010/86/en/3/EF1086EN.pdf. Accessed 23 August 2014.

European Working Conditions Observatory (2010). *Women and part-time work*. http://www.eurofound.europa.eu/ewco/2010/02/AT1002019I.htm. Accessed 17 August 2014.

Eurostat. (2002). The health and safety of men and women at work. *Statistics in Focus, 3-4/2002*. http://epp.eurostat.ec.europa.eu/cache/ITY_OFFPUB/KS-NK-02-004/EN/KS-NK-02-004-EN.PDF. Accessed 16 August 2014.

Eurostat. (2006). Aliaga, C., 'How is the time of women and men distributed in Europe?' *Statistics in Focus, 4/2006*. Available at: http://epp.eurostat.ec.europa.eu/cache/ITY_OFFPUB/KS-NK-06-004/EN/KS-NK-06-004-EN.PDF

Forastieri, V. (2000). Women workers and gender issues on occupational safety and health. Information note. *Safe Work*. Geneva, Switzerland: International Labour Office. http://www.ilo.org/public/english/protection/safework/gender/womenwk.htm. Accessed 17 August 2014.

French, J. R., Caplan, R. D., & Harrison, R. V. (1982). *The mechanisms of job stress and strain*. Chichester, UK: Wiley.

Frese, M. (1982). Occupational socialization and psychological development: An underemphasized research perspective in industrial psychology. *Journal of Occupational Psychology, 55*(3), 209–224. doi:10.1111/j.2044-8325.1982.tb00095.x.

Gash, V., Mertens, A., & Romeu Gordo, L. (2009). *Women between part-time and full-time work: The influence of changing hours of work on happiness and life-satisfaction* (CCSR working paper 2009–06). Cathie Marsh Centre for Census and Survey Research (CCSR). Manchester: University of Manchester. http://www.ccsr.ac.uk/publications/working/2009-06.pdf. Accessed 27 May 2014.

Gervais, R. (2013). *Sexual harassment and victimisation: what happens in the workplace*. European Agency for Safety and Health at Work. Available from http://oshwiki.eu/wiki/Sexual_harassment_and_victimisation:_what_happens_in_the_workplace. Accessed 10 August 2014.

Glavin, P., Schieman, S., & Reid, S. (2011). Boundary-spanning work demands and their consequences for guilt and psychological distress. *Journal of Health and Social Behavior, 52*(1), 43–57. http://dx.doi.org/10.1177/0022146510395023.

Glomb, T. M., Munson, L. J., Hulin, C. L., Bergman, M. E., & Drasgow, F. (1999). Structural equation models of sexual harassment: Longitudinal explorations and cross-sectional generalizations. *Journal of Applied Psychology, 84*(1), 14–28. doi:10.1037/0021-9010.84.1.14.

Goldenhar, L. M., Swanson, N. G., Hurrell, J. J., Jr., Ruder, A., & Deddens, J. (1998). Stressors and adverse outcomes for female construction workers. *Journal of Occupational Health Psychology, 3*(1), 19–32. doi:10.1037/1076-8998.3.1.19.

Grant, L., Yeandle, S., & Buckner, L. (2005). *Working below potential: women and part-time work* (Working paper series no. 40). Equal Opportunities Commission. http://www.shu.ac.uk/_assets/pdf/ceir-workingbelowpotential.pdf. Accessed 27 May 2014.

Gutek, B. A., Repetti, R. L., & Silver, D. L. (1988). Nonwork roles and stress at work. In C. L. Cooper & R. Payne (Eds.), *Causes, coping and consequences of stress at work* (pp. 141–174). Chichester, UK: Wiley.

Haynes, S. G. (1991). The effect of job demands, job control, and new technologies on the health of employed women: A review. In M. Frankenhaeuser, U. Lundberg, & M. A. Chesney (Eds.), *Women, work, and health. stress and opportunities* (pp. 157–169). New York: Plenum Press.

Hazards. (1999). *Women hurt at work.* Factsheet 67. Hazards 67, July-September 1999. http://www.hazards.org/women/womenhurtatwork.pdf. Accessed 10 August 2014.

Hazards (2008). Women's work. *Hazards 101*, January–March 2008. http://www.hazards.org/haz101/h101centre.pdf. Accessed 10 August 2014.

Hill, E. J., Martinson, V. K., Ferris, M., & Baker, R. Z. (2004). Beyond the mommy track: The influence of new-concept part-time work for professional women on work and family. *Journal of Family and Economic Issues, 25*(1), 121–136. doi:10.1023/B:JEEI.0000016726.06264.91.

Hillier, D., Fewell, F., Cann, W., & Shephard, V. (2005). Wellness at work: Enhancing the quality of our working lives. *International Review of Psychiatry, 17*(5), 419–431. doi:10.1080/09540260500238363.

Horemans, J. (2012). Understanding women's reasons for working part-time: A multi-country study. In *ESPAnet (the European Social Policy Analysis network) conference, Edinburgh. 6–8 September 2012.* http://www.espanet2012.info/__data/assets/word_doc/0008/88991/Horemans_-_Stream_6.docx. Accessed 27 May 2014.

International Labour Organization. (2010). *Women in labour markets: Measuring progress and identifying challenges*. Geneva, Switzerland: International Labour Office. http://www.ilo.org/wcmsp5/groups/public/---ed_emp/---emp_elm/---trends/documents/publication/wcms_123835.pdf. Accessed 15 August 2014.

International Labour Organization. (2012). *Global employment trends for women 2012*. Geneva, Switzerland: International Labour Office. http://www.ilo.org/wcmsp5/groups/public/---dgreports/---dcomm/documents/publication/wcms_195447.pdf. Accessed 19 May 2013.

International Labour Organization. (2014a). *World of work report 2014: Developing with jobs*. Geneva, Switzerland: International Labour Office. http://www.ilo.org/wcmsp5/groups/public/---dgreports/---dcomm/documents/publication/wcms_243961.pdf. Accessed 16 August 2014.

International Labour Organization. (2014b). *Global employment trends 2014: Risk of a jobless recovery?* Geneva, Switzerland: International Labour Office. http://www.ilo.org/wcmsp5/groups/public/---dgreports/---dcomm/---publ/documents/publication/wcms_233953.pdf. Accessed 16 August 2014.

Karasek, R. A., Jr. (1979). Job demands, job decision latitude, and mental strain: Implications for job redesign. *Administrative Science Quarterly, 24*(2), 285–308.

Katungi, D., Neale, E., & Barbour, A. (2006). *People in low-paid informal work: Need not greed. Joseph Rowntree Foundation*. Bristol, UK: The Policy Press. http://www.jrf.org.uk/sites/files/jrf/9781861348937.pdf. Accessed 16 August 2014.

Kelsh, M. A., & Sahl, J. D. (1996). Sex differences in work-related injury rates among electric utility workers. *American Journal of Epidemiology, 143*(10), 1050–1058.

Klitzman, S., & Stellman, J. M. (1989). The impact of the physical environment on the psychological well-being of office workers. *Social Science & Medicine, 29*(6), 733–742. doi:10.1016/0277-9536(89)90153-6.

Korczyc, E., Matia, L., Vincelette, G. A., Cuaresma, J. C., & Loichinger, E. (2013). *EU11 regular economic report – Macroeconomic report: faltering recovery – special topic: the economic growth implications of an aging European Union*. Washington, DC: The World Bank. http://documents.worldbank.org/curated/en/2013/01/17183435/eu11-regular-economic-report-macroeconomic-report-faltering-recovery-special-topic-economic-growth-implications-aging-european-union. Accessed 25 May 2013.

Kumra, S., & Vinnicombe, S. (2008). A study of the promotion to partner process in a professional services firm: How women are disadvantaged. *British Journal of Management, 19*(1), S65–S74. doi:10.1111/j.1467-8551.2008.00572.x.

Künemund, H. (2006). Changing welfare states and the "Sandwich Generation": Increasing burden for the Next Generation? *International Journal of Ageing and Later Life, 1*(2), 11–29.

Loomis, L., & Booth, A. (1995). Multigenerational caregiving and well-being: The myth of the beleaguered Sandwich Generation. *Journal of Family Issues, 16*(2), 131–148. doi:10.1177/019251395016002001.

Lund, T., Labriola, M., Christensen, K. B., Bültmann, U., & Villadsen, E. (2006). Physical work environment risk factors for long term sickness absence: Prospective findings among a cohort of 5357 employees in Denmark. *BMJ, 332*(7539), 449–452. doi:10.1136/bmj.38731.622975.3A.

Lundberg, U., & Frankenhaeuser, M. (1999). Stress and workload of men and women in high-ranking positions. *Journal of Occupational Health Psychology, 4*(2), 142–151. doi:10.1037/1076-8998.4.2.142.

Major, V. S., Klein, K. J., & Ehrhart, M. G. (2002). Work time, work interference with family, and psychological distress. *Journal of Applied Psychology, 87*(3), 427–436. doi:10.1037//0021-9010.87.3.427.

Martikainen, P., Bartley, M., & Lahelma, E. (2002). Psychosocial determinants of health in social epidemiology. *The International Journal of Epidemiology, 31*(6), 1091–1093. doi:10.1093/ije/31.6.1091.

Martocchio, J. J., & O'Leary, A. M. (1989). Sex differences in occupational stress: A meta-analytic review. *Journal of Applied Psychology, 74*(3), 495–501. doi:10.1037/0021-9010.74.3.495.

McCoy, J. M., & Evans, G. W. (2005). Physical work environment. In J. Barling, E. K. Kelloway, & M. Frone (Eds.), *Handbook of work stress* (pp. 219–245). Thousand Oaks, CA: Sage.

Melero, E. (2004). *Sex differences in managerial style: From individual leadership to organizational labour relationships* (Discussion paper no. 1387). Bonn: Institute for the Study of Labor. http://ftp.iza.org/dp1387.pdf. Accessed 16 August 2014.

Messing, K. (1997). Women's occupational health: A critical review and discussion of current issues. *Women & Health, 25*(4), 39–68. doi:10.1300/J013v25n04_03.

Messing, K. (1998). *One-eyed science: Occupational health and women workers*. Philadelphia: Temple University Press.

Messing, K., Dumais, L., Courville, J., Seifert, A. M., & Boucher, M. (1994). Evaluation of exposure data from men and women with the same job title. *Journal of Occupational Medicine, 36*(8), 913–917.

Messing, K., & Mager Stellman, J. (2006). Sex, gender and women's occupational health: The importance of considering mechanism. *Environmental Research, 101*(2), 149–162. doi:10.1016/j.envres.2005.03.015.

Michoñ, P. (2007). *Quality, preferences, reasons, satisfaction: Part-time employment in seven European Union countries* (WOLIWEB D10a Working papers on working time). http://www.wageindicator.org/documents/publicationslist/WOLIWEBparttime07. Accessed 23 August 2014.

Occupational Safety and Health Administration. (1999). *Women in the construction workplace: Providing equitable safety and health protection*. Occupational Safety & Health Administration. Washington, DC: U.S. Department of Labor. Available from https://www.osha.gov/doc/accsh/haswicformal.html

Organisation for Economic Co-operation and Development. (2012). *Closing the gender gap. Act now*. doi:10.1787/9789264179370-en. Retrieved from http://www.oecd-ilibrary.org/social-issues-migration-health/close-the-gender-gap-now_9789264179370-en. Accessed 27 Sept 2014.

Piltch, C. A., Walsh, D. C., Mangione, T. W., & Jennings, S. E. (1994). Gender, work, and mental distress in an industrial labour force: An expansion of Karasek's job strain model. In G. P. Keita & J. J. Hurrell Jr. (Eds.), *Job stress in a changing workforce. Investigating gender, diversity, and family issues* (pp. 39–54). Washington, DC: APA.

Quinn, M. M., & Woskie, S. R. (1988). Women and work. In B. S. Levy & D. H. Wegman (Eds.), *Occupational health: Recognizing and preventing work-related disease* (2nd ed., pp. 479–499). Boston, MA: Little, Brown & Co.

Repetti, R. L., Matthews, K. A., & Waldron, I. (1989). Employment and women's health: Effects of paid employment on women's mental and physical health. *American Psychologist, 44*(11), 1394–1401.

Rivera-Torres, P., Araque-Padilla, R. A., & Montero-Simó, M. J. (2013). Job stress across gender: The importance of emotional and intellectual demands and social support in women. *International Journal of Environmental Research and Public Health, 10*(1), 375–389. doi:10.3390/ijerph10010375.

Rosette, A. S., & Tost, L. P. (2010). Agnetic women and communal leadership: how role prescriptions confer advantage to top women leaders. *Journal of Applied Psychology, 95*(2), 221–235. doi:10.1037/a0018204.

Ryff, C. D., & Singer, B. (1998). The contours of positive human health. *Psychological Inquiry, 9*(1), 1–28. doi:10.1207/s15327965pli0901_1.

Schneider, K. T., Swan, S., & Fitzgerald, L. F. (1997). Job-related and psychological effects of sexual harassment in the workplace: Empirical evidence from two organizations. *Journal of Applied Psychology, 82*(3), 401–415. doi:10.1037/0021-9010.82.3.401.

Schwatka, N. V., Butler, L. M., & Rosecrance, J. R. (2012). An aging workforce and injury in the construction industry. *Epidemiologic Reviews, 34*(1), 156–167. doi:10.1093/epirev/mxr020.

Siegrist, J. (1996). Adverse health effects of high-effort/low-reward conditions. *Journal of Occupational Health Psychology, 1*(1), 27–41. doi:10.1037/1076-8998.1.1.27.

Siegrist, J., & Marmot, M. (2004). Health inequalities and the psychosocial environment – two scientific challenges. *Social Science & Medicine, 58*(8), 1463–1473. doi:10.1016/S0277-9536(03)00349-6.

Sokejima, S., & Kagamimori, S. (1998). Working hours as a risk factor for acute myocardial infarction in Japan: case-control study. *BMJ, 317*(7161), 775–780. doi: http://dx.doi.org/10.1136/bmj.317.7161.775

Stansfeld, S., & Candy, B. (2006). Psychosocial work environment and mental health – A meta-analytic review. *Scandinavian Journal of Work, Environment & Health, 32*(6), 443–462. doi:10.5271/sjweh.1050.

Stellman, J. M. (2000). Perspectives on women's occupational health. *Journal of the American Medical Women's Association, 55*(2), 69–72.

Strazdins, L., & Bammer, G. (2004). Women, work and musculoskeletal health. *Social Science & Medicine, 58*(6), 997–1005. doi:10.1016/S0277-9536(03)00260-0.

Taiwo, O. A., Cantley, L. F., Slade, M. D., Pollack, K. M., Vegso, S., Fiellin, M. G., et al. (2009). Sex differences in injury patterns among workers in heavy manufacturing. *American Journal of Epidemiology, 169*(2), 161–166. doi:10.1093/aje/kwn304.

Tessier-Sherman, B., Cantley, L. F., Galusha, D., Slade, M. D., Taiwo, O. A., & Cullen, M. R. (2014). Occupational injury risk by sex in a manufacturing cohort. *Occupational & Environmental Medicine, 71*(9), 605–610. doi:10.1136/oemed-2014-102083.

Timberlake, S. (2005). Social capital and gender in the workplace. *Journal of Management Development, 24*(1), 34–44. doi:10.1108/02621710510572335.

Vaughan-Jones, H., & Barham, L. (2009). *Healthy work challenges and opportunities to 2030.* London: BUPA. http://www.theworkfoundation.com/assets/docs/publications/216_Bupa_report.pdf. Accessed 16 August 2014.

Verbrugge, L. M. (1985). Gender and health: An update on hypothesis and evidence. *Journal of Health and Social Behavior, 26*(3), 156–182.

Virtanen, M., Heikkilä, K., Jokela, M., Ferrie, J. E., Batty, G. D., Vahtera, J., et al. (2012). Long working hours and coronary heart disease: A systematic review and meta-analysis. *American Journal of Epidemiology, 176*(7), 586–596. doi:10.1093/aje/kws139.

Vischer, J. C. (2007). The effects of the physical environment on job performance: Towards a theoretical model of workplace stress. *Stress and Health, 23*(3), 175–184. doi:10.1002/smi.1134.

Wadsworth, E., Dhillon, K., Shaw, C., Bhui, K., Stansfeld, S., & Smith, A. (2007). Racial discrimination, ethnicity and work stress. *Occupational Medicine (London), 57*(1), 18–24. doi:10.1093/occmed/kql088.

Williams, C. (2004, September). The sandwich generation. *Perspectives on Labour and Income*, 7–14.

World Bank. (2011). *World development report 2012. Gender equality and development.* Washington, DC: The International Bank for Reconstruction and Development/The World Bank. http://siteresources.worldbank.org/INTWDR2012/Resources/7778105-1299699968583/7786210-1315936222006/Complete-Report.pdf. Accessed 26 March 2013.

World Health Organization. (1996). *Research on the menopause in the 1990s.* WHO technical report series 866. Geneva, Switzerland: World Health Organization. http://whqlibdoc.who.int/trs/WHO_TRS_866.pdf. Accessed 28 June 2014.

Part II
Women in Developing Economies: Exploring Work Choices and Resourcefulness

Chapter 3
Women's Resourcefulness in the Informal Economy: Evidence from Jordan

Haya Al-Dajani, Sara Carter, and Colin Williams

Introduction: Entrepreneurship Within the Informal Economy

Entrepreneurial activities within the informal economy are profoundly different from those that have informed much of the entrepreneurship discourse (Baker & Nelson, 2005; Williams & Nadin, 2010). These consist of legitimate economic actions (Webb, Tihanyi, Ireland, & Sirmon, 2009) that are excluded from both the protection and the costs of legal and administrative regulations covering "property relationships, commercial licensing, labour contracts, torts, financial credit, and social security systems" (Feige, 1990, p. 992). They are typified by unregulated and unrecorded work, unrecognised by local governments, often taking place within independent, very small scale units of self-employed men and women (Castells & Portes, 1989).

In exploring the economic activities of refugee and displaced women operating in Jordan's informal economy, we respond to calls for enriching our understanding of how entrepreneurship can break the chains of poverty and improve the lives of

H. Al-Dajani (✉)
Futures Entrepreneurship Centre, Plymouth Business School, Plymouth University, Plymouth PL4 8AA, Devon, UK
e-mail: haya.al-dajani@plymouth.ac.uk

S. Carter
Hunter Centre for Entrepreneurship, Strathclyde Business School, University of Strathclyde, Cathedral Street, Glasgow G40QU, UK
e-mail: sara.carter@strath.ac.uk

C. Williams
Inter-disciplinary Centre of the Social Sciences, University of Sheffield, Sheffield, UK
e-mail: c.c.williams@sheffield.ac.uk

R.L. Gervais, P.M. Millear (eds.), *Exploring Resources, Life-Balance and Well-Being of Women Who Work in a Global Context*,
DOI 10.1007/978-3-319-31736-6_3

the desperately poor (Bruton, 2011), and contribute to enhancing contemporary understandings of women's 'emancipatory entrepreneuring', as well as making a contribution to the development and enhancement of contemporary theorising in entrepreneurship studies. Here, emancipatory entrepreneuring is defined as informally organised, everyday micro-enterprise activity through which individuals attempt to resist their economic and social oppression. This definition builds on those offered by others including Rancière (2009), Rindova, Barry, and Ketchen (2009) and Huault, Perret, and Spicer (2014). It recognises individual as well as collectively shared entrepreneurial activity, which aims to 'emancipate' those involved and therefore supports their potential to overcome overwhelmingly restrictive conditions. This is often challenging for women who are nationals of countries where patriarchal cultures and systems dominate and remain largely unopposed. However, for refugee and displaced women in host nations where they are denied full citizenship, this challenge is intensified and requires substantial resourcefulness. Alvarez and Barney (2007) and Baker and Nelson (2005) argued that motivations for entrepreneurship are often associated with discovery and creation through freedom and independence from regulating environments, rather than wealth creation. Rindova et al. (2009, p. 478) advised that "viewing entrepreneurial projects and emancipatory efforts focuses on understanding the factors that cause individuals to seek to disrupt the status quo and change their position in the social order in which they are embedded – and, on occasion, the social order itself."

Although resourceful entrepreneurship among the 'bottom of the pyramid' population is not a new phenomenon, indeed it has been considered as a poverty alleviation priority by international aid agencies and neo-liberal political agendas for decades (Al-Dajani & Carter, 2010), it has only relatively recently become recognised as being within the parameters of normative mainstream entrepreneurship studies that reflect a male United States of America (US) and Eurocentric bias (Abu-Lughod, 2009; Al-Dajani & Marlow, 2010), and an assumption that the "essence of entrepreneurship research rests upon analyses of associations between opportunity recognition and resulting wealth creation" (Al-Dajani & Marlow, 2013a, p. 503). Feminist critiques of entrepreneurship have frequently exposed the gender blindness of mainstream theses of entrepreneurship (Ahl, 2006; Marlow & McAdam, 2013; Neergaard, Frederiksen, & Marlow, 2011) and argue that the powerful roles of institutional influences embedded in culture and context on the gendering of entrepreneurial activity must be recognised in entrepreneurship research (Welter, 2011; Welter, Brush, & De Bruin, 2014).

This chapter starts by reviewing the existing literature on the role of the informal economy, where most of the entrepreneurial activities of displaced and refugee women occurs, and then focuses on Jordan's informal economy. This is followed by a discussion of the qualitative research methodology adopted in this exploratory study. The results of our data draw attention to three areas of resourceful action exhibited by the six women participants in this study. Following a discussion of the research findings, conclusions are presented.

Development and the Informal Economy

During the twentieth century, the widespread assumption which prevailed was that economic endeavour was gradually moving into the formal economy. Those engaged in work in the informal economy were therefore commonly depicted as a leftover or historical legacy from an earlier mode of production. Viewed through this lens, the continuing existence of entrepreneurship in the informal economy signified the 'under-development', 'traditionalism' and 'backwardness' of societies whilst the emergence of the formal economy signalled the advent of 'development', 'advancement' and 'progress' (Geertz, 1963; Lewis, 1959). Entrepreneurship in the informal economy was consequently portrayed as part of a pre-modern traditional mode of production that survived only at the fringes of modern society in a few minor enclaves.

Since the turn of the millennium, however, a burgeoning literature has revealed not only that the informal economy (Charmes, 2009; ILO, 2013; Jütting & Laiglesia, 2009; Schneider, 2008; Williams & Lansky, 2013), but also informal sector entrepreneurship (De Soto, 2001; Minard, 2009; Small Business Council, 2004; Venkatesh, 2006; Webb et al., 2009; Williams, 2006, 2013), is an extensive, enduring and expanding phenomenon in the contemporary global economy. The outcome has been the advent of new explanations for its persistence and growth. Until now, commentators have largely adopted one of two broad perspectives.

On the one hand, an 'exclusion' perspective has portrayed informal sector entrepreneurs as unwilling and unfortunate pawns of an exploitative global economic system (Castells & Portes, 1989; Davis, 2006; Gallin, 2001; Portes & Roberts, 2005; Sassen, 1997; Slavnic, 2010; Taiwo, 2013). They are the surplus labour 'excluded' from the circuits of the modern economy participating in this endeavour out of necessity as a survival tactic in the absence of alternative livelihoods. Viewed in this manner, informal sector entrepreneurship is an absorber of surplus labour and provider of income earning opportunities for the poor (Bhatt, 2006; Nelson & Bruijn, 2005; Tokman, 2001). Those no longer of use to capitalism are no longer maintained as a reserve army of labour. Instead, they are off-loaded onto the informal economy resulting in their increasing reliance on informal entrepreneurship as a survival tactic. As such, informal entrepreneurship is extensive in excluded populations acting as a substitute for the formal economy due to the inability of populations to gain access to formal work. It is thus conducted by those who involuntarily engage in this form of work that has few benefits, low wages and poor working conditions (Castells & Portes, 1989; Gallin, 2001; ILO, 2002; Sassen, 1997).

On the other hand, an 'exit' perspective has depicted engagement in entrepreneurship in the informal economy as a matter of choice rather than due to a lack of choice. This has been argued by two separate groups of commentators. Firstly, a neo-liberal perspective has argued that entrepreneurship in the informal economy is a rational economic decision resulting from a desire to avoid the costs, time and effort of formal registration (Cross & Morales, 2007; De Soto, 1989, 2001; Perry & Maloney, 2007; Small Business Council, 2004). Informal sector entrepreneurship therefore marks an opposition to over-regulation and is 'the people's spontaneous and creative response to the state's incapacity to satisfy the basic needs of the impoverished masses' (De Soto, 1989, pp. xiv–xv). As such, pursuing entrepreneurial endeavour in the informal economy is asserted to be conducted due to the many benefits it offers, including flexible hours, ease of doing business, the opportunity for economic independence, better wages and the avoidance of taxes, labour laws and inefficient government regulation (Gurtoo & Williams, 2011; Maloney, 2004; Packard, 2007). Secondly, a post-structuralist perspective has emerged which again views entrepreneurship in the informal economy as voluntarily chosen but views it more as a lifestyle choice pursued by social actors because of the greater personal freedom and flexibility it affords and because it allows them to gain control over their lives (Cross, 2000; Hart, 1973). An outcome is that not only do business and friendship relations blur between informal entrepreneurs because there is greater solidarity and reciprocity (Stillerman & Sundt, 2007), but so too do relations between informal entrepreneurs and their customers because without recourse to a legal contract, interpersonal relations and trust become more important (Cross & Morales, 2007).

Until now, these exit and exclusion perspectives have been largely treated as mutually exclusive and informal entrepreneurship as taking place according to a single unique 'logic' (De Soto, 2001; Snyder, 2004). It is seen to be conducted either for purely exclusion rationales or for purely exit rationales. In recent years, however, this has begun to be questioned. Some have started to call for the crude depiction of informal entrepreneurship as universally caused by exit or universally caused by exclusion to be transcended. As Perry and Maloney (2007, p. 2) point out, 'these two lenses, focusing, respectively, on informality driven by exclusion from state benefits and on voluntary exit decisions resulting from private cost-benefit calculations, are complementary rather than competing analytical frameworks'. Analyses have revealed for instance that deprived populations tend to be driven more by exclusion rationales and affluent populations more by exit rationales in English localities (Williams, 2006, 2009a; Williams & Nadin, 2011), Ukraine (Williams, Nadin, & Rodgers, 2012; Williams, Round, & Rodgers, 2010) and Moscow (Williams & Round, 2009, 2010).

Women's Entrepreneurship in the Informal Economy

Until now, the vast majority of the literature on the gendering of entrepreneurship has focused upon the gendering of formal sector entrepreneurship (for reviews, see Hughes, Jennings, Brush, Carter, & Welter, 2012; Pines, Lerner, & Schwartz, 2010; Rouse, Treanor, & Fleck, 2013). So far, few studies have considered the gendering of entrepreneurship in the informal economy. When this issue has been studied, the finding has been that women are lower paid than men (e.g., Fortin, Garneau, Lacroix, Lemieux, & Montmarquette, 1996; Lemieux, Fortin, & Frechette, 1994; McInnis-Dittrich, 1995) and that such endeavour is confined to similar sectors and occupations to those which women and men occupy in the formal labour market (McInnis-Dittrich, 1995). Women engage in service activities such as commercial cleaning, domestic help, childcare and cooking. Men, on the other hand, are argued to largely conduct what are conventionally seen as 'masculine tasks' such as building and repair work (Fortin et al., 1996; Jensen, Cornwell, & Findeis, 1995). So, not only is the informal economy characterised by the same sector divisions as the formal economy, but the gender disparities in wage rates prevalent in the formal economy appear to be replicated in the informal economy.

Turning to the motives of women engaged in entrepreneurship in the informal economy, most scholars start from the *a priori* assumption that women entrepreneurs in the informal economy are necessity-driven by exclusion rationales (Franck, 2012; Grant, 2013; Williams, 2009a, 2009b; Williams & Gurtoo, 2011a, 2011b; Williams & Martinez-Perez, 2014; Williams & Round, 2009; Williams & Youssef, 2013). Based on this assumption, they have then focused on measuring the amount and nature of their access to credit, welfare funds, insurance and so forth. These studies consequently first argue that reliance on day-to-day profits for survival is high because they have little or no access to institutional credit (Schneider & Bajada, 2005), second, that they have to protect themselves from harassment by local authorities (Bhatt, 2006; Carr & Chen, 2002, 2004; Charmes, 1998; ILO, 2002, 2006; Nelson, 1997), third, that often their entrepreneurial endeavour is not constituted as a separate legal entity independent from the household (Chen, Carr, & Vanek, 2004; Chen, Sebstad, & Connell, 1999; Fawzi, 2003) and finally, that their activities tend to get locked into traditional roles such as selling flowers at the temple and keeping a basket of fruits (Bhatt, 2006; Charmes, 1998). Until now, therefore, there has been little attempt to consider whether women informal sector entrepreneurs are engaged in anything but purely necessity-based entrepreneurship.

Refugee and Displaced Women in Jordan's Informal Economy

Since the outbreak of the civil war in neighbouring Syria in 2011, Jordan continues to be a refuge for Syrian citizens escaping their war ravaged nation in search of peace and stability either within the three specially designated Syrian refugee camps in Jordan, or within the neighbourhoods of Jordan's capital Amman and other Jordanian cities in the north of the country. The United Nations High Commission for Refugees registered 613,104 Syrian refugees in Jordan by April 2014. A large proportion of this population (122,723) reside in the Zaatri refugee camp located close to the Syrian border; a place now known as Jordan's fourth largest city, and the world's second largest refugee camp (Migration Policy, 2014; Wall Street & (Sept, 2013).

However, the Syrian refugee population is not Jordan's only refugee population. Between 15–20 % of the Jordanian national population is made up of displaced Iraqi nationals who have also made Jordan their home since the first Gulf War in 1990 (Tobin, 2011; UNHCR, 2010). Furthermore, Jordan's national 6.18 million population

(Hausmann, Tyson, & Zahidi, 2012) also comprises two million displaced Palestinians (Minority Rights Group International, 2008) of whom 17 % still reside within the ten official and three unofficial refugee camps (Alnsour & Meaton, 2014). With such a high refugee population presence within the country, Jordan has become "the first country in the world in terms of the refugee to total population ratio" (Olwan & Shiyab, 2012, p. 2). As Jordan rejects policies of total integration (UNHCR, 2010), the protection of displaced persons and refugees is regarded as temporary, irrespective of how prolonged the length of stay within the country. Thus, 'right of return' to their national homelands or resettlement in other countries are Jordan's only long-term policy solutions for refugees and displaced persons. Until this happens however, Jordan remains as a long-term transit destination for refuge.

While residing in Jordan, refugees are entitled to protection through several international conventions on refugees' human rights and protection to which Jordan is party. However, Jordan is yet to ratify the most important 1951 Convention on the Status of Refugees and its 1967 protocol update on the status of refugees (UNHCR, 2014). Because of this, displaced persons and refugees in Jordan are considered 'foreign nationals', subject to Jordan's entry and residency national laws which do not acknowledge or separate 'refugee status' directly or specifically from a 'foreign national' status. Thus, while displaced persons and refugees are permitted to reside in Jordan and access some benefits and services provided either by international agencies, national governmental agencies and non-governmental organisations, they are prohibited from employment unless they obtain a work permit. Obtaining such permits is exceptionally difficult for all forms of employment, due to the high national unemployment rate (especially among those aged under 30) and policies that give preference to the employment of nationals. As yet, Jordan has not adopted a quota system for work permits for displaced and refugee persons. Hence, many displaced persons and refugees create their opportunities within the thriving informal economy (UNDP, 2012) operating at the boundaries of the formal economy and often, within it. A study conducted by the Jordanian Ministry of Planning in collaboration with the UNDP, found that Jordan's informal economy constituted 39.6 % of the overall Jordanian economy, compared to the IMF's (2013) reported figure of 26 %. However, this study also noted the invisibility of Jordan's non-nationals operating within the informal economy as a limitation of the research.

Whilst data accounting for Jordanian women operating within the formal economy are now widely available and show an official 24 % female unemployment rate, 16 % rate of women in wage employment (non-agricultural employment), and 13 % of firms with female participation in ownership (Hausmann et al., 2012), information relating to Jordanian women's participation with the informal economy is starting to emerge. Indeed, the study conducted by the Jordanian Ministry of Planning in collaboration with the UNDP (2012), found that 27 % of Jordanian women were operating within the informal economy either as employees or entrepreneurs. This figure is almost equal to the percentage of Jordanian women operating within the formal economy either as employees or entrepreneurs. With regard to the business ownership and labour participation of women who are displaced or refugees in

Jordan, there is wide recognition of this trend among policy makers, third sector organisations and international agencies (Charmes, 2007; Destremau, 2007; ILO, 2007), yet official and reliable data focusing specifically on this population is negligible (Chant & Pedwell, 2008; ILO, 2014). While this presents a significant research gap, "officially accounting for such female economic activity could unleash damaging social and political consequences for the implicated women" (Al-Dajani & Marlow, 2013b, p. 8). Their resourcefulness therefore, influences their survival as well as the creation of their entrepreneurial activity and its operationalisation.

Method

The qualitative research approach is best suited for undertaking exploratory research in under-researched contexts and when researching issues that are seldom documented in the existing literature (Miles & Huberman, 1994). Such research is driven by "a conceptual question, not by a concern for representativeness" (Miles & Huberman, p. 29) and therefore, constructing generalisations from the data is not a priority. It is grounded in "the interpretive approach to social reality and in the description of the lived experience of human beings" (Holloway & Wheeler, 2013, p. 3). The qualitative research approach is also apposite for conducting research with vulnerable peoples where trust, confidentiality and security are essential (Al-Dajani & Carter, 2010; Creswell, 2012; Rubin & Rubin, 2012). To this extent, the adoption of this methodological approach was ideal for our research with refugee and displaced women operating within Jordan's informal economy, as they remain vulnerable, powerless and largely invisible (Olwan & Shiyab, 2012).

Data Collection Methods

While it is easy to locate and identify refugee and displaced women street vendors on the pavements of downtown Amman selling cigarettes, lighters, chewing gum and tissue packs among other similar small items attractively organised on large trays that can be easily transported, they are very cautious and refuse to engage in any extended discussion within this public space. Keen to engage entrepreneurial refugee and displaced women who are not so visible and given the difficulty in locating and accessing them, we resorted to utilising non-governmental, grassroots women-led organisations that were locally active within the refugee and displaced communities. One such organisation, at risk of closure due to the diminishing national and international aid funds, was eager to provide assistance in recruiting participants for our research. However, to avoid bias from the organisation's potential selection bias, the Arabic speaking research team member spent 1 week in January 2013 at the organisation's premises and randomly invited for an interview, refugee and displaced women entrepreneurs arriving at the organisation.

Clarifying that the study was for academic purposes only, and guaranteeing that all identities would be anonymous, the women became agreeable and embraced the chance to tell their story to an active listener rather than interviewer (Rubin & Rubin, 2012). Active listening is ideal for conducting semi-structured, exploratory in-depth interviews as it facilitates data reliability through gaining participants' immediate confirmation of the interviewer's interpretations of their responses, through the use of paraphrasing and reflection techniques (Weger, Castle, & Emmett, 2010). The conversations addressed the transition from their native home country to Jordan, prior experience of employment and entrepreneurship before arrival in Jordan, current family dynamics and those previous to displacement, current entrepreneurial activities, challenges and opportunities, and visions for the future. All semi-structured interviews were conducted in Arabic, recorded, and lasted approximately 1.5–2 h. All participants were given the option of having the interview either at their home or at the premises of the women-led organisation. Four participants opted to be interviewed in their homes rather than at the premises of the women-led organisation as they were more comfortable and at ease within their own familiar surroundings. Two participants opted to have the interview at the premises of the women-led organisation to avoid their husbands' questions and the crowdedness and distractions within their own homes.

Sampling Refugee and Displaced Women

To capture the diversity amongst Jordan's refugee and displaced population, our sample includes Iraqi, Palestinian and Syrian women displaced to Jordan and currently residing in the poor, overcrowded and deprived neighbourhoods of the capital, Amman. Since the focus of the study is on women's resourcefulness and entrepreneurial activities within the host country of Jordan, three criteria were set for participation in the study. These were that they had resided in Jordan for a minimum period of 12 months; they engaged in informal entrepreneurship in Jordan for a minimum period of 6 months; and that they operated home-based micro enterprises.

Table 3.1 highlights some characteristics of the six women in our sample, and shows that they are all married and operating home-based micro enterprises within the craft sector. The monthly earnings of all participants were above the Jordanian poverty line equivalent to £550 per year (UNDP, 2012). The average age was 40 years – the youngest participant (Hania) was aged 32, and the oldest participant (Rajha) was aged 53. The two displaced Palestinian women in the sample (Hania and Najat) were born in Jordan and have always resided there, and one Iraqi participant (Sudad) arrived with her family 22 years ago. All three women met their husbands who were of the same displaced nationality, and married in Jordan. In contrast, the two Syrian women in the sample (Amira and Raida) and the other Iraqi participant (Rajha) were married in their native countries prior to arriving in Jordan. With the exception of Rajha, all participants' children were within school age and

Table 3.1 Characteristics of the participants

	Pseudonym	Age	Education level	Marital status	Children	Years in Jordan	Current business	Monthly income equivalent to GB£
Iraqi	Rajha	53	Primary School	Married	5	7	Beaded Jewellery	£140
	Sudad	34	College	Married	4	22	Beaded Jewellery	£90
Palestinian	Hania	32	College	Married	4	32	Traditional embroidery	£190
	Najat	37	College	Married	3	37	Tailoring	£240
Syrian	Amira	48	Secondary School	Married	4	2	Crochet	£80
	Raida	36	College	Married	4	1	Tailoring	£150

Note: To protect the identities of the participants, pseudonyms are used throughout

attended state schools within their neighbourhoods. In Rajha's case, three of her five children are deaf and mute, and are now aged in their late teens – early twenties. However, her five children remain illiterate as they were not entitled to schooling in Jordan, as they do not hold any national identity – neither Iraqi nor Jordanian.

With the exception of Rajha and Amira, all women were educated to tertiary level. Hania and Najat's college education in Jordan was funded by UNRWA (the United Nations Relief Work Agency), which is dedicated to the affairs of displaced Palestinians in the Middle East region. Raida's college education was completed in Syria while she was residing there, and prior to the civil war, which erupted in 2011. Sudad's college education was completed in Jordan and was funded by an Iraqi charitable organisation.

Consistent with the political turbulence in the region, the parents of Hania and Najat were displaced to Jordan following the 1967 war with Israel, Sudad arrived in Jordan with her parents and siblings during the first Gulf war in 1991, and Rajha and her family arrived in Jordan following the execution of Iraq's Saddam Hussein in 2006. Amira and Raida, and their children are the latest arrivals in Jordan as they left their native Syria following the start of the uprising and ensuing civil war. Both their husbands remained in Syria, and Sudad's husband returned to Iraq in May 2013 to seek employment there. The husbands of Rajha, Hania and Najat reside with them in Jordan. Rajha's husband is unemployed, but the husbands of Hania and Najat are employed within the informal economy as car mechanics.

Results and Discussion

To ensure that the data analysis remained focused upon the research themes, we adopted the template analysis technique (King, 2004) as this "allows for textual data to be thematically organised and analysed according to a set of codes developed a priori" (Sang, Al-Dajani, & Özbilgin, 2013, p. 162). The exploratory themes for which the data were organised and analysed were congruent with the interview guide's themes of transition from their native home country to Jordan, employment and entrepreneurship prior to arrival in Jordan, current family dynamics and those previous to displacement, current entrepreneurial activities, and visions for the future. Similarities and differences among the participants for each of these identified themes were recorded thus allowing for within and between cases analysis (King, 2004). The researchers decided that the template met the research needs when the obtained data reached saturation and no further changes or differences were being identified in the interviews. That is, when new interview data became repetitive which occurred by interview four.

The Arabic speaking research team member and an external bilingual Arabic / English researcher were involved in the data analysis. Both researchers conducted the analysis in Arabic (the language in which the interviews were conducted) and subjected each broad theme to a detailed manual analysis independently, and later compared their results, which led to the formation of the finalised themes. Relevant quotes presented in this chapter were then translated into English by one bilingual researcher and back translated into Arabic by another bilingual research to guarantee accuracy of the translated quotes. For the purposes of this chapter, the data analysis presented below focuses on the theme of current entrepreneurial actions within Jordan's informal economy, and its relevant sub-themes of learning the trade, challenges and opportunities. This informs our overall analysis of the refugee and displaced women's resourcefulness.

Learning the Trade

Given the sampling criteria for this study, all participants operated home-based micro-enterprises. A notable result however, is the participants' concentration within the feminised handicraft sector. This is consistent with other studies, which found that women are more likely to engage in traditional crafts enterprises (Wilkinson-Weber, 2001). Much of this research raises concern about the reproduction of gender inequalities through such feminised sectors (León, 2009), which arc often saturated and therefore, characterised by heightened competition amongst the producers operating within them (Al-Dajani & Marlow, 2013b). As shown in Table 3.1, Hania is engaged in Palestinian traditional embroidery, Amira crochets, and Rajha and Sudad make beaded jewellery. Hania and Amira are the only participants in this sample who learnt their craft from family members during childhood rather than through women-led organisations. Hania learnt to embroider from her grandmother. In her words, "*My mother used to be away all day long cleaning houses and my grandmother looked after me and my sisters. She embroidered all day for her clients and to keep us occupied, she would give me and my sisters a needle and thread and ask us to copy her. When we finished the embroidery, she always rewarded us with delicious date cakes, and Pepsi. I got hooked*!"

Similarly, Amira learnt to crochet from her female relatives and commented that, "*When I was much younger, as a teenager, we often spent the three month summer holiday at the village where my father originally came from and there, all the women - young and old spent all day and night drinking tea and coffee, chatting, laughing and crocheting, so I joined in. It might seem strange to you, but those were the best days of my life. We were carefree, all together, happy and warm ... I'm so thankful that I did join in then or what would I do now*".

Whilst the craft activities in which Hania and Amira engage sparks endearing memories of their families and childhoods, Rajha and Sudad learnt to make beaded jewellery under very different and harsh circumstances, after they became refugees in Jordan. Rajha explained that, "*A few days after we arrived here from Baghdad, a neighbour knocked on my door and invited me to go with her to the Centre (women-led non-profit organisation) where they were running a free beaded jewellery making course for Iraqi refugee women. I hesitated but she pulled me and said this is the only way to adjust to your life here - we are all the same and there is nothing to be ashamed of or scared of*".

Sudad also attended a beaded jewellery making course for Iraqi refugee women at the same women-led organisation as Rajha, albeit at a different time. Sudad described this experience as, "*One of the worst things in my life. I had graduated from college and was looking forward to my dream job and salary. But after hundreds of rejections I had to face the reality of this never happening because I will always be an Iraqi refugee here. One day I ran to the Centre as I didn't want my parents to see how upset and angry I was and Um Jasem* [pseudonym] *spent hours calming me down then took me along to the course to distract me from my misery*".

Najat and Raida both had college diplomas in dressmaking, Najat studied in Amman (Jordan) and Raida in Aleppo (Syria). Najat stated that, "*This professional qualification enhanced my credibility when I started my business*", but Raida said, "*It seems that the Syrian qualification doesn't count here. Because I'm a Syrian refugee, customers expect my prices to be much cheaper than local tailors. Whether I'm better than those tailors or not does not seem to matter. They say that if I charge the same as the others, why should they come to me?*" Such challenges will be expanded upon in the ensuing section.

These results show three dominant approaches to the participants' methods of learning their craft trades either in their home countries or following displacement to another country. The approaches are firstly during childhood through female family members, secondly through training offered and funded by aid agencies and lastly, through formal education channels. All three approaches have been previously documented, but not with specific reference to refugee and displaced women in Jordan. The impact that these learning methods have on refugee and displaced women's resourcefulness presents a worthwhile future research direction.

Entrepreneurial Challenges

By coincidence rather than design, the sample was equally split between participants who had been residing in Jordan for less than or more than ten years. When analysing the reported entrepreneurial challenges, this variation had a substantial effect. As Table 3.2 shows, most entrepreneurial challenges were reported by participants who had resided in Jordan for less than ten years. That is, Rajha (Iraqi refugee arriving in Jordan in 2006), Amira (Syrian refugee arriving in Jordan in 2011) and Raida (Syrian refugee arriving in Jordan in 2012). The main challenges stated by Amira, Raida and Rajha only; were learning about understanding and navigating the Jordanian market. The difficulty in overcoming this challenge for Amira and Rajha was exacerbated by the fact that neither had previously engaged in paid or self-employment in their home countries.

Sudad was the only participant to consider seeking and securing employment as an entrepreneurial challenge. None of the remaining participants had any interest in seeking or securing employment because they agreed that, "*We don't have the legal right to get employment in this country*" (Raida). Indeed, all participants with the exception of Hania and Najat reported the inability to secure a work permit as an entrepreneurial challenge.

Only Najat associated paid employment with the inability to manage family responsibilities by stating that, "*If I worked away from my home, and had to comply with specific attendance regulations, I would not be able to fulfil my duty towards my family and home*". Paradoxically however, all other participants claimed that managing the combination of enterprise and family responsibilities as an entrepreneurial challenge. This was most pertinent for Rajha as three of her five children were disabled, and none of her children had received basic literacy education.

Table 3.2 Participants' entrepreneurial challenges

	Less than 10 years in Jordan			More than 10 years in Jordan		
	Rajha	Amira	Raida	Sudad	Hania	Najat
Seeking and securing employment				X		
Learning & understanding Jordanian market	X	X	X			
Finding clients	X	X	X	X		
Navigating Jordanian market	X	X	X			
Managing enterprise and family responsibilities	X	X	X	X	X	
Business recognition and growth					X	X
Threatened business closure	X	X	X	X	X	X
Competition from local nationals	X	X	X	X		X
Inability to secure work permit	X	X	X	X		
Obtaining official identity documents such as a passport	X			X		

Indeed, she reported one of her main successes as, "*convincing the Centre to offer my children and other Iraqi children like them literacy classes*".

Threatened business closure was an entrepreneurial challenge reported by all six participants and highlights their recognition of the precariousness of their economic existence. Perhaps unsurprisingly, Hania and Najat who have spent all their lives in Jordan as 'displaced Palestinians' and never travelled beyond its borders, reported the fewest entrepreneurial challenges as they succumbed to their circumstances as "*this is the only reality we know. We have not lived a different life somewhere else to compare this life with, like the Syrians and Iraqis do*" (Najat). Indeed, Najat seemed to be in control of her situation and unlike the remaining participants, her entrepreneurial challenges were predominantly enterprise focused; business recognition and growth, competition from local nationals and threatened business closure. Her tailoring micro-enterprise was sustainable, her clients were reliable and loyal, and she understood the local market well enough to identify her competition as well as associates. With the exception of the themes of 'inability to secure work permit' and 'obtaining official identity document', the often stifling challenges presented here are not unique to refugee and displaced women. Indeed, understanding and navigating the market, managing enterprise and family responsibilities, competition and business recognition and growth, are well documented entrepreneurial challenges faced by women entrepreneurs operating in very different developed economy contexts.

Entrepreneurial Opportunities

Unlike the participants' entrepreneurial challenges, their opportunities were not time-bound. That is, entrepreneurial opportunities for gaining credibility and recognition, and increasing trade, customers and sales were sought and created irrespective of how long the participants' had resided in Jordan. Knowing that their informal entrepreneurship had to remain hidden from the prying eyes of landlords, aid agencies and government officials, all of the women in the sample proactively sought local men and women as their sales representatives, and paid them sales commissions. These sales representatives were recruited through channels including the local women-led organisation, husbands' networks, neighbours and the local shops.

Subcontracts from local businesses and partnerships were also pursued and secured. The participants' resourcefulness in achieving this was exceptional, given that "*No one teaches you how to negotiate a deal or contract, or how to avoid exploitation or how to convince others that they should work with you. I had to teach myself and I'm sure that all the women you speak to will tell you the same thing*" (Najat). Similarly, Sudad added, "*At centres like this one they teach you skills like jewellery making or embroidery or cooking or hairdressing, but they don't teach you how to sell your products or how to set up a business or how to secure contracts.*" After some contemplation she then added, "*Maybe they don't teach these skills because we are not supposed to do these things in this country*".

Instead of relying on women-led organisations or aid agencies to guide them in their business venturing, all the study participants reported examples of grassroots informal relationships and friendships as the accelerator for entrepreneurial opportunities. Najat for example, explained that, "*There are a few professionally trained Iraqi women in my neighbourhood who are excellent at beading and applying sequins, silk painting and so on, so I subcontract them when my clients want that kind of thing on their tailoring*". Similarly, Hania shared her willingness to "*exhibit the items made by my Iraqi neighbours alongside my items at the embroidery bazaar for a small fee. And, for their items that sold, they gave me a commission too*".

Such contracts were conducted internationally as well as locally. Rajha described how this was facilitated; "*when my Iraqi friend and soul mate secured immigration to the USA with her family two years ago, she took a suitcase full of beaded jewellery that I, my daughters and other women made so she could sell them there. She didn't have the money to pay upfront for the stock, so every month, she transferred a payment through Western Union. Her business there is doing very well and since she left, we have sent her beaded jewellery stocks several times … if I think about it, we probably sell more of our products there than we do here*".

Similarly, Hania added, "*you probably will not believe me when I tell you that most of my products are sold in Iraq and not in Jordan*!" She then explained that after being told by Iraqi neighbours that the traditional Palestinian embroidery is highly sought after in Iraq but seldom available, she devised a plan to enter that market. She convinced her husband to persuade his customer, Abu Iyad [pseudonym], to take a selection of her products to see if they sell in Iraq. She stated that "*Abu Iyad drives a big truck regularly to Baghdad to deliver fruit and vegetables grown in Jordan. When he returned from Baghdad the first time, he told me that my embroidery items disappeared immediately and that he would be happy to take a regular supply with him, for a fee and commission of course*."

Evidently, the refugee and displaced women's resourcefulness enhanced their entrepreneurial opportunities and expanded their reach beyond the confines of Jordan's informal economy. Further research into the pursuit of entrepreneurial opportunities among refugee and displaced women will expand our understanding of resourcefulness and international entrepreneurship within the informal economy.

Conclusions

Our study of six displaced and refugee women uncovered expansive resourcefulness in their entrepreneurial activities. This was seen in their ability to acquire skills that had the potential to develop into income-generating production, recognise new opportunities for successful exchange, and also in the ways they were able to expand into new markets, even internationally, through local contacts and networks. Their resourcefulness helped these refugee and displaced women adapt to the restrictive conditions imposed on them as a consequence of past or present conflicts within their homelands.

While there has been a great deal of research interest in the informal economy across a variety of country contexts (Castells & Portes, 1989; Feige, 1990; Williams, 2009b), few studies have focused on the development of informal entrepreneurship within refugee camps and among displaced communities. Many observers may assume that refugee camps are temporary communities whose inhabitants will move on, either returning to their homelands when conflict subsides or to settle in a new permanent location either within their country of sanctuary or further abroad. As this study highlights, far from being transient communities, many refugee camps within the Middle East have become long-term, even permanent, settlements for displaced populations. Unable to secure employment within their new host country of sanctuary, informal entrepreneurship is often their only means of earning a living or the best of a limited range of income generation options given the situation in which they find themselves. As such, these communities may provide important insights into the nature of informal entrepreneurship and how individuals may pursue economic opportunities and demonstrate individual resourcefulness even within the most unpromising and restrictive conditions.

For the women in this study, their status as refugees or displaced persons was exacerbated by the social, cultural and organisational barriers that shape and define women's roles and activity within this society (Mosedale, 2005). While it may be tempting to view their resourcefulness and entrepreneurial actions as evidence of what Rindova et al. (2009) describe as 'emancipatory entrepreneuring', or as contributing to a wider process of collective social change as identified by Calás, Smircich, and Bourne (2009), their experiences suggest otherwise. For the six women interviewed in this study, displacement and destitution was sustained over decades and is potentially life-long. Informal entrepreneurship provided the means of earning an income above the national poverty level. Their remarkable resourcefulness in acquiring new skills, spotting economic opportunities and selling their craft skills and products provided some alleviation of their immediate poverty, but their vulnerability and their political, economic and social exclusion persist. They were proud of being recognised by their Arabic accents as nationals of their home countries, and integrating into Jordanian society was not an ambition. Rather, it was considered as a necessity for improving entrepreneuring practice and profit, mobility within and beyond Jordan, and enhancing their overall quality of life.

References

Abu-Lughod, L. (2009). Dialects of women's empowerment: the international circuitry of the Arab human development report 2005. *International Journal of Middle East Studies, 41*(1), 83–103.

Ahl, H. (2006). Why research on women entrepreneurs needs new directions. *Entrepreneurship Theory and Practice, 30*(5), 595–621.

Al-Dajani, H., & Carter, S. (2010). Women empowering women: How female entrepreneurs support home-based producers in Jordan. In C. Brush, A. De Bruin, E. Gatewood, & C. Henry (Eds.), *Women entrepreneurs and the global environment for growth: A research perspective* (pp. 118–137). Northampton, UK: Edward Elgar.

Al-Dajani, H., & Marlow, S. (2010). The impact of women's home-based enterprise on marriage dynamics: evidence from Jordan. *International Small Business Journal, 28*(5), 470–487.

Al-Dajani, H., & Marlow, S. (2013a). Empowerment and entrepreneurship: a theoretical framework. *International Journal of Entrepreneurial Behaviour & Research, 19*(5), 503–524.

Al-Dajani, H., & Marlow, S. (2013b). *"It's a civic and moral responsibility": Analysing Arab women's entrepreneurship as an articulation of political activism.* Paper presented at the 8th international conference in critical management studies, Manchester, UK, July

Alnsour, J., & Meaton, J. (2014). Housing conditions in Palestinian refugee camps, Jordan. *Cities, 36*, 65–73.

Alvarez, S. A., & Barney, J. (2007). Discovery and creation: Alternative theories of entrepreneurial action. *Strategic Entrepreneurship Journal, 1*, 11–26.

Baker, T., & Nelson, R. (2005). Creating something from nothing: Resource construction through entrepreneurial bricolage. *Administrative Science Quarterly, 50*, 329–366.

Bhatt, E. (2006). *We are poor but so many: The story of self-employed women in India.* Oxford, UK: Oxford University Press.

Bruton, G. (2011). *Garry Bruton discusses his research on entrepreneurship & emerging economies.* Scientist Interview: Science Watch, http://www.sciencewatch.com/inter/aut/2011/11-feb/11febBrut/ Accessed 28 October 2011.

Calás, M. B., Smircich, L., & Bourne, K. A. (2009). Extending the boundaries: Reframing "entrepreneurship as social change" through feminist perspectives. *Academy of Management Review, 34*, 552–569.

Carr, M., & Chen, M. (2002). *Globalization and the informal economy: How global trade and investment impact on the working poor.* Geneva, Switzerland: The Informal Economy Working Paper No. 1, Policy Integration Department, International Labor Office.

Carr, M., & Chen, M. (2004). *Globalization, social exclusion and work with special reference to informal employment and gender.* Geneva, Switzerland: Working Paper No. 20, Policy Integration Department, International Labor Office.

Castells, M., & Portes, A. (1989). World underneath: the origins, dynamics and effects of the informal economy. In A. Portes, M. Castells, & L. A. Benton (Eds.), *The informal economy: Studies in advanced and less developing countries* (pp. 19–42). Baltimore, MD: John Hopkins University Press.

Chant, S., & Pedwell, C. (2008). *Women, gender and the informal economy: An assessment of ILO research and suggested ways forward.* Geneva, Switzerland: International Labour Office.

Charmes, J. (1998). *Street vendors in Africa: Data and methods.* New York: United Nations Statistical Division.

Charmes, J. (2007). *Statistics on informal employment in the Arab region.* Geneva, Switzerland: International Labour Office.

Charmes, J. (2009). Concepts, measurement and trends'. In J. P. Jütting & J. R. Laiglesia (Eds.), *Is informal normal? Towards more and better jobs in developing countries* (pp. 19–35). Paris: OECD.

Chen, M., Carr, M., & Vanek, J. (2004). *Mainstreaming informal employment and gender in poverty reduction: A handbook for policymakers and other stakeholders.* London: Commonwealth Secretariat.

Chen, M., Sebstad, J., & Connell, L. (1999). Counting the invisible workforce: The case of home-based workers. *World Development, 27*(3), 603–610.

Creswell, J. W. (2012). *Qualitative inquiry and research design: Choosing among five approaches.* Thousand Oaks, CA: Sage.

Cross, J. C. (2000). Street vendors, modernity and postmodernity: Conflict and compromise in the global economy. *International Journal of Sociology and Social Policy, 20*(1), 29–51.

Cross, J., & Morales, A. (2007). Introduction: Locating street markets in the modern/postmodern world. In J. Cross & A. Morales (Eds.), *Street entrepreneurs: People, place and politics in local and global perspective* (pp. 1–13). London: Routledge.

Davis, M. (2006). *Planet of slums.* London: Verso.

De Soto, H. (1989). *The other path: The economic answer to terrorism*. London: Harper and Row.
De Soto, H. (2001). *The mystery of capital: Why capitalism triumphs in the West and fails everywhere else*. London: Black Swan.
Destremau, B. (2007). *Gender and rights in the informal economies of Arab States*. Presentation for workshop on the informal economy held in Tunis, April 2007, organised by the Regional Office for Arab States, ILO.
Fawzi, C. (2003). *Gender, poverty and employment in the Arab region*. Geneva, Switzerland: Capacity-Building Program on Gender, Poverty and Employment, Discussion Paper, International Labor Office.
Feige, E. L. (1990). Defining and estimating underground and informal economies: The new institutional economics approach. *World Development, 18*, 989–1002.
Fortin, B., Garneau, G., Lacroix, G., Lemieux, T., & Montmarquette, C. (1996). *L'Economie Souterraine au Quebec: mythes et realites*. Laval, QC, Canada: Presses de l'Universite Laval.
Franck, A. K. (2012). Factors motivating women's informal micro-entrepreneurship: Experiences from Penang, Malaysia. *International Journal of Gender and Entrepreneurship, 4*(1), 65–78.
Gallin, D. (2001). Propositions on trade unions and informal employment in time of globalization. *Antipode, 19*(4), 531–549.
Geertz, C. (1963). *Peddlers and princes: Social change and economic modernization in two Indonesian towns*. Chicago: University of Chicago.
Grant, R. (2013). Gendered spaces of informal entrepreneurship in Soweto, South Africa. *Urban Geography, 34*(1), 86–108.
Gurtoo, A., & Williams, C. C. (2011). Women entrepreneurs in the Indian informal sector: Marginalisation dynamics or institutional rational choice? *International Journal of Gender and Entrepreneurship, 3*(1), 6–22.
Hart, K. (1973). Informal income opportunities and urban employment in Ghana. *Journal of Modern African Studies, 11*(1), 61–89.
Hausmann, R., Tyson, L., & Zahidi, S. (2012). *The global gender gap report 2012*. Geneva, Switzerland: World Economic Forum.
Holloway, I., & Wheeler, S. (2013). *Qualitative research in nursing and healthcare*. Chichester, UK: Wiley.
Huault, I., Perret, V., & Spicer, A. (2014). Beyond macro- and micro- emancipation: Rethinking emancipation in organisation studies. *Organisation, 21*(1), 22–49.
Hughes, K. D., Jennings, J. E., Brush, C., Carter, S., & Welter, F. (2012). Extending women's entrepreneurship research in new directions. *Entrepreneurship Theory and Practice, 36*(3), 429–442.
International Labour Office (ILO). (2002). *Women and men in the informal economy*. Geneva, Switzerland: International Labor Office.
International Labour Office (ILO). (2006). *Decent work for women and men in the informal economy: Profile and good practices in Cambodia*. Geneva: International Labor Office.
International Labour Office (ILO). (2007). *Gender equality and workers' rights in the informal economies of Arab states: Training component outline*. Geneva, Switzerland: International Labour Office.
International Labour Office (ILO). (2013). *Statistical update on employment in the informal economy*. Geneva, Switzerland: ILO Department of Statistics.
International Labour Office (ILO). (2014). *ILO Response to the Syrian Refugee Crisis in Jordan and Lebanon*. Geneva, Switzerland: International Labour Office.
International Monetary Fund (IMF). (2013). *Regional economic outlook: Middle East and Central Asia*. Washington, DC: International Monetary Fund.
Jensen, L., Cornwell, G. T., & Findeis, J. L. (1995). Informal work in nonmetropolitan Pennsylvania. *Rural Sociology, 60*(1), 91–107.
Jütting, J. P., & Laiglesia, J. R. (2009). Employment, poverty reduction and development: What's new? In J. P. Jütting & J. R. Laiglesia (Eds.), *Is informal normal? Towards more and better jobs in developing countries*. Paris: OECD.

King, N. (2004). Using templates in the thematic analysis of text. In N. King, C. Cassell, & G. Symon (Eds.), *Essential guide to qualitative methods in organisational research* (pp. 256–270). London: Sage.

Lemieux, T., Fortin, B., & Frechette, P. (1994). The effect of taxes on labor supply in the underground economy. *American Economic Review, 84*(1), 231–254.

León, J. (2009). *Handicraft trade and women entrepreneurs: A case study in Lima, Perú*. Ottowa: North–South Institute.

Lewis, A. (1959). *The theory of economic growth*. London: Allen and Unwin.

Maloney, W. F. (2004). Informality revisited. *World Development, 32*(7), 1159–1178.

Marlow, S., & McAdam, M. (2013). Advancing debate and challenging myths – Exploring the alleged case of the under-performing female entrepreneur. *International Journal of Entrepreneurial Behaviour and Research, 19*(1), 114–124.

McInnis-Dittrich, K. (1995). Women of the shadows: Appalachian women's participation in the informal economy. *Affilia: Journal of Women and Social Work, 10*(4), 398–412.

Migration Policy Centre. (2014). *Syrian refugees: A snapshot of the crisis in the Middle East and Europe – Jordan report*. http://syrianrefugees.eu/?page_id=87 Accessed 4 March 2014.

Miles, M. B., & Huberman, A. M. (1994). *Qualitative data analysis*. London: Sage.

Minard, S. C. L. (2009). Valuing entrepreneurship in the informal economy in Senegal. *Social Enterprise Journal, 5*(3), 186–209.

Minority Rights Group International. (2008). World *directory of minorities and indigenous peoples – Jordan: Palestinians*. http://www.refworld.org/docid/49749cfcc.html. Accessed 16 May 2013.

Mosedale, S. (2005). Assessing women's empowerment: Towards a conceptual framework. *Journal of International Development, 17*, 243–257.

Neergaard, H., Frederiksen, S., & Marlow, S. (2011, June). *The emperor's new clothes: Rendering a feminist theory of entrepreneurship visible*. Paper presented at the 56th ICSB conference, Stockholm.

Nelson, E., & Bruijn, E. (2005). The voluntary formation of enterprises in a developing economy: The case of Tanzania. *Journal of International Development, 17*, 575–593.

Nelson, N. (1997). How women and men get by and still get by, only not so well: The sexual division of labor in the informal sector of a Nairobi squatter settlement. In J. Gugler (Ed.), *Cities in the developing world: Issues, theory, policy* (pp. 141–165). Oxford: Oxford University Press.

Olwan, M., & Shiyab, A. (2012). *Forced migration of Syrians to Jordan: An exploratory study*. San Domenico di Fiesole (FI), Italy: Robert Schuman Centre for Advanced Studies, European University Institute.

Packard, T. (2007). *Do workers in Chile choose informal employment? A dynamic analysis of sector choice*. Washington, DC: World Bank Latin American and the Caribbean Region Social Projection Unit.

Perry, G. E., & Maloney, W. F. (2007). Overview: Informality – Exit and exclusion. In G. E. Perry, W. F. Maloney, O. S. Arias, P. Fajnzylber, A. D. Mason, & J. Saavedra-Chanduvi (Eds.), *Informality: Exit and exclusion* (pp. 1–20). Washington, DC: World Bank.

Pines, A. M., Lerner, M., & Schwartz, D. (2010). Gender differences in entrepreneurship: equality, diversity and inclusion in times of global crisis. *Equality, Diversity and Inclusion: an International Journal, 29*(2), 186–198.

Portes, A., & Roberts, B. (2005). The free-market city: Latin American urbanization in the years of the neoliberal experiment. *Studies in Comparative International Development, 40*(1), 43–82.

Rancière, J. (2009). *The emancipated spectator*. London: Verso.

Rindova, V., Barry, D., & Ketchen, D. J. (2009). Entrepreneuring as emancipation. *Academy of Management Review, 34*(3), 477–491.

Rouse, J., Treanor, L., & Fleck, E. (2013). The gendering of entrepreneurship: Theoretical and empirical insights. *International Journal of Entrepreneurial Behaviour and Research, 19*(6), 452–459.

Rubin, H. J., & Rubin, I. S. (2012). *Qualitative interviewing: The art of hearing data*. Thousand Oaks, CA: Sage Publications.

Sang, K., Al-Dajani, H., & Özbilgin, M. (2013). Frayed careers of migrant female professors in British Academia: An intersectional perspective. *Gender, Work & Organisation, 20*(2), 158–171.

Sassen, S. (1997). *Informalisation in advanced market economies* (Issues in development discussion paper 20). Geneva, Switzerland: International Labour Organisation.

Schneider, F. (Ed.). (2008). *The hidden economy*. Cheltenham, UK: Edward Elgar.

Schneider, F., & Bajada, C. (2005). An international comparison of underground economic activity. In C. Bajada & F. Schneider (Eds.), *Size, causes and consequences of the underground economy: An international perspective*. Aldershot, UK: Ashgate.

Slavnic, Z. (2010). Political economy of informalization. *European Societies, 12*(1), 3–23.

Small Business Council. (2004). *Small business in the informal economy: Making the transition to the formal economy*. London: Small Business Council.

Snyder, K. A. (2004). Routes to the informal economy in New York's East village: Crisis, economics and identity. *Sociological Perspectives, 47*(2), 215–240.

Stillerman, J., & Sundt, C. (2007). Embeddedness and business strategies amongst Santiago Chel's street and flea market vendors. In J. Cross & A. Morales (Eds.), *Street entrepreneurs: People, place and politics in local and global perspective* (pp. 180–198). London: Routledge.

Taiwo, O. (2013). Employment choice and mobility in multi-sector labour markets: Theoretical model and evidence from Ghana. *International Labour Review, 152*(3–4), 469–492.

Tobin, S. (2011). *Jordan's Arab Spring: The middle class and anti-revolution*. Washington, DC: Middle East Policy Council.

Tokman, V. (2001). Integrating the informal sector on the modernization process. *SAIS Review, 21*(1), 45–60.

United Nations Development Program (UNDP). (2012). *Thinking differently about the poor findings from poverty pockets survey in Jordan, United Nations United Nations Development Programme*. Jordan: Department of Statistics, and Ministry of Planning and International Cooperation.

United Nations High Commissioner for Refugees (UNHCR). (2010). *UNHCR global report 2009, Iraq*. http://www.refworld.org/docid/4c57cc550.html. Accessed 02 November 2013.

United Nations High Commissioner for Refugees (UNHCR). (2014). *2014 UNHCR country operations profile – Jordan*. http://www.unhcr.org/cgi-bin/texis/vtx/page?page=49e486566. Accessed 13 April 2014.

Venkatesh, S. A. (2006). *Off the books: The underground economy of the urban poor*. Cambridge, MA: Harvard University Press.

Wall Street Journal. (2013, September). *Ten largest refugee camps*. http://online.wsj.com/news/articles/SB10001424127887323932604579052742703621858. Accessed 22 December 2013.

Webb, J. W., Tihanyi, L., Ireland, R. D., & Sirmon, D. G. (2009). You say illegal, I say legitimate: Entrepreneurship in the informal economy. *Academy of Management Review, 34*(3), 492–510.

Weger, H., Jr., Castle, G. R., & Emmett, M. C. (2010). Active listening in peer interviews: The influence of message paraphrasing on perceptions of listening skill. *The International Journal of Listening, 24*(1), 34–49.

Welter, F. (2011). Contextualising entrepreneurship – Conceptual challenges and ways forward. *Entrepreneurship Theory and Practice, 35*(1), 165–184.

Welter, F., Brush, C., & De Bruin, A. (2014). *The gendering of entrepreneurship context* (No. 01/14). Working Paper, Institut für Mittelstandsforschung (IfM) Bonn. http://hdl.handle.net/10419/95879

Wilkinson-Weber, C. M. (2001). Gender, handicrafts, and development in Pakistan: A critical review. *Pakistan Journal of Women's Studies, 8*(2), 91–104.

Williams, C. C. (2013). Beyond the formal economy: Evaluating the level of employment in informal sector enterprises in global perspective. *Journal of Developmental Entrepreneurship, 18*(4). doi: 10.1142/S1084946713500271

Williams, C. C. (2006). *The hidden enterprise culture: Entrepreneurship in the underground economy*. Cheltenham, UK: Edward Elgar.
Williams, C. C. (2009a). Explaining participation in off-the-books entrepreneurship in Ukraine: A gendered evaluation. *International Entrepreneurship and Management Journal, 5*(4), 497–513.
Williams, C. C. (2009b). Informal entrepreneurs and their motives: A gender perspective. *International Journal of Gender and Entrepreneurship, 1*(3), 219–225.
Williams, C. C., & Gurtoo, A. (2011a). Women entrepreneurs in the Indian informal sector: Marginalisation dynamics or institutional rational choice? *International Journal of Gender and Entrepreneurship, 3*(1), 6–22.
Williams, C. C., & Gurtoo, A. (2011b). Evaluating women entrepreneurs in the informal sector: Some evidence from India. *Journal of Developmental Entrepreneurship, 16*(3), 351–369.
Williams, C. C., & Lansky, M. (2013). Informal employment in developed and emerging economies: Perspectives and policy responses. *International Labour Review, 152*(3–4), 355–380.
Williams, C. C., & Martinez-Perez, A. (2014). Is the informal economy an incubator for new enterprise creation? A gender perspective. *International Journal of Entrepreneurial Behaviour and Research, 20*(1), 4–19.
Williams, C. C., & Nadin, S. (2010). Entrepreneurship and the informal economy: An overview. *Journal of Developmental Entrepreneurship, 15*(4), 361–378.
Williams, C. C., & Nadin, S. (2011). Theorising the hidden enterprise culture: The nature of entrepreneurship in the shadow economy. *International Journal of Entrepreneurship and Small Business, 14*(3), 334–338.
Williams, C. C., Nadin, S., & Rodgers, P. (2012). Evaluating competing theories of informal entrepreneurship: Some lessons from Ukraine. *International Journal of Entrepreneurial Behaviour & Research, 18*(5), 528–543.
Williams, C. C., & Round, J. (2009). Evaluating informal entrepreneurs' motives: Some lessons from Moscow. *International Journal of Entrepreneurial Behaviour and Research, 15*(1), 94–107.
Williams, C. C., & Round, J. (2010). Spatial variations in the character of off-the-books entrepreneurship: Lessons from a study of contrasting districts in Moscow. *International Journal of Entrepreneurship and Small Business, 10*(2), 287–301.
Williams, C. C., Round, J., & Rodgers, P. (2010). Explaining the off-the-books enterprise culture of Ukraine: Reluctant or willing entrepreneurship? *International Journal of Entrepreneurship and Small Business, 10*(2), 165–180.
Williams, C. C., & Youssef, Y. (2013). Evaluating the gender variations in informal sector entrepreneurship: Some lessons from Brazil. *Journal of Developmental Entrepreneurship, 18*(1), 1–16.

Chapter 4
Work-Family Interface: Studying Dhaka City Executives

Syed S.M. Sadrul Huda

Introduction

Two separate areas of life, Work and Family, have joined together to form a new field, "Work and Family". This field is denoted by various terminologies such as 'Work/Family' or 'Work and Family' or Work-Family. The hyphen connecting the two originally separated fields, in the latter term, confirms the "relationships," "interactions," and/or "interfaces" between these two domains (Pitt-Catsouphes, Kossek, & Sweet, 2006). It is generally believed that a significant increase in women's participation in the workforce has raised concerns around the work and family issue (McElwain, Korabik, & Rosin, 2005); as women's outward engagement breaks down the traditional set-up of households and the interactions between work and family life becomes unpleasant not only for women, but also for men. Barnett (1998) observed that this unpleasant interaction between these two domains did not necessarily exist, when women lived at home and men worked to earn an income. Therefore, research with respect to work-family issues needs to focus both on the male and female members of the households and this paper deals with the work and family interfaces of Dhaka City executives, considering both genders.

Work and family roles may interact with each other through a variety of ways (Edwards & Rothbard, 2000). These relationships are believed to be culture specific. Individualist cultures have a tendency to consider the work and family domains as detached entities, while collectivist cultures see these domains as integrated (Yang, 2005). The cultural differences have a profound impact on gravity, antecedents and outcomes of work-family interfaces (Aycan, 2008). For example, Yang, Chen, Choi, and Zou (2000) found that due to work demands, work interference with family (WIF) in China was higher than in the United States of America (USA),

S.S.M.S. Huda (✉)
Department of Business Administration, East West University, Dhaka, Bangladesh
e-mail: sadrul@ewubd.edu

R.L. Gervais, P.M. Millear (eds.), *Exploring Resources, Life-Balance and Well-Being of Women Who Work in a Global Context*,
DOI 10.1007/978-3-319-31736-6_4

whereas, in respect of family demand, work interference with family (WIF) was higher in the USA compared to China, because of the differences in individualism-collectivism cultural dimensions. Spector et al. (2004) in a 15 country study found working hours to have a stronger relationship with work family conflict (WFC) in individualist Anglo countries (western) but not in collectivist countries (eastern). The work-family relationships in Bangladesh are expected to coincide with collectivist culture because it is located in the east. This chapter explores the work-family interfaces of male and female executives primarily in respect of an eastern culture.

Theoretical Framework

A wide range of connections are assumed to describe the pattern of the relationship between work and family lives (Edwards & Rothbard, 2000). The most discussed relationships are conflict, accommodation, enrichment, compensation, and segmentation. Alternatively, the whole notion of work-family interface can be categorised in three dimensions: work-family conflict (negative linkage), work-life balance (neutral phase) and work-family enrichment (positive linkage). These three different perspectives of work-family study are discussed briefly in the following paragraphs.

Work-Family Conflict

Among the three concepts, the notion of work-family conflict gets the highest level of research attention. Role theory has long been accepted as the basis for work-family research (Kahn, Wolfe, Quinn, Snoek, & Rosenthal, 1964). It also relates generally to Goode's (1960) argument that several life roles produce stress, which leads to conceptualisations of the work-family conflict construct. The role theory identifies four categories of employee behaviours, e.g., role-taking, role-consensus, role-compliance and role-conflict (Wickham & Parker, 2007) and all of these situations might affect the emotional and physical state of employees either positively or negatively. The notion of work-family conflict is based on the concept of role conflict. Work-family conflict arises when multiple life roles (i.e., work or family) have incompatible demands (Greenhaus & Beutell, 1985). The issue of work-family conflict was originally considered as unidimensional (e.g., Kopelman, Greenhaus, & Connolly, 1983), however the later development of the construct considered its bidirectional nature, e.g., work interference with family and family interference with work (Frone, Russell, & Cooper, 1992; Gutek & Searle, 1991).

One of the consequences of someone's high involvement with both work and family is the loss at the individual level (e.g., energy, health, mental stress), and at the organisational level (e.g., productivity, employee retention, employee morale, strength; Warner & Hausdorf, 2009). Thus, organisational psychologists took an active interest in researching work-family issues (Thompson & Prottas, 2006). They found substantive negative consequences for those employees who face incompatible demands from their work and family domains, which included: disturbed personal lives (Balmforth & Gardner, 2006); job dissatisfaction (Ford, Heinen, & Langkamer, 2007; Frone, Russell, & Cooper, 1997); poor health (Frone et al., 1992); decreased overall life satisfaction (Carlson, Kacmar, & Williams, 2000; Ford et al., 2007); and absenteeism (Barling, MacEwen, Kelloway, & Higginbottom, 1994; Cooper & Williams, 1994; Hepburn & Barling, 1996; Kossek & Nichol, 1992; Thomas & Ganster, 1995).

Work-Family Enrichment

Work-family enrichment is a new dimension of work-family research, which shows how the work role and the family role help each other (Greenhaus & Powell, 2006). This construct is based on the idea that each of the life domains equips individuals with resources, e.g., self-esteem, earnings, and other support mechanisms that eventually enable the individual to perform better in both life domains (Barnett & Hyde, 2001; Greenhaus & Powell, 2006). However, as opposed to conflict, the notion of enrichment receives a lower level of research attention (Frone, 2003). Yet, initial research confirms the synergies between work and family domains (Barnett & Hyde, 2001).

Work-family enrichment may be described as the degree to which experiences in one domain increase performance in the other domain (Greenhaus & Powell, 2006). Greenhaus and Powell posited that enrichment can take place in two ways: direct and/or indirect. The direct effect is known as the instrumental path, while the indirect effect is known as the affective path. Previous research has provided evidence of the instrumental path. For example, Crouter (1984) and Kirchmeyer (1992) highlighted the many skills employees learnt from their families, which helped them to deal effectively with their co-workers at work. Rothbard's (2001) research outlined evidence of the affective pathway. For example, higher involvement with one domain is connected indirectly with increased participation in another domain through positive affect. This could involve, e.g., an employee leaving the office in a bad mood and might interact therefore more negatively with family members, which eventually reduces his or her affect and performance as a parent and/or spouse.

Work-family enrichment, like work-family conflict, is bidirectional in nature, which means, resource transfer can occur both ways, from work to family (work to-family enrichment and family to work (family-to-work enrichment). Those resources gained from work may enhance employee performance in family situations (work to-family enrichment; Barnett, Marshall, & Sayer, 1992) and resource gained from the family may produce better performance in work (family-to-work enrichment; Crouter, 1984).

Work-Family Balance

The neutral work and family interface phase is a situation when individuals combine both spheres of life comfortably, leading to work-family balance. Work-family balance may refer to a situation when individuals wish to establish a balance between work and family, to the act of balancing work and family demands or to an already balanced life. It also means reducing work time and spending it with family (Greenhaus, Collins, & Shaw, 2003). Several scholars have attempted to define work-family balance distinguishing it from other work-family concepts (Greenhaus et al., 2003; Hill, Hawkins, Ferris, & Weitzman, 2001; Kofodimos, 1993; Marks, Huston, Johnson, & MacDermid, 2001; Marks & MacDermid, 1996).

The traditional view concerning multiple life roles is that individuals generally categorise life roles in order of importance. Conversely, Marks and MacDermid (1996), referring to Mead (1964), posited that individuals are able to give the same level of importance to all life roles. Marks and MacDermid observed that role balance can be achieved by ensuring full participation in every aspect of life and by handling each role and all role partners seriously.

Work-family balance is considered as a tool for promoting well-being, with Marks and MacDermid (1996) finding that reduced role overload enhanced role ease, and lowered levels of depression, which are some of the individual outcomes of work-life balance. Kofodimos (1993) observed that imbalance in general, and work imbalance in work life in particular, increased levels of stress, diminished quality of life, and eventually decreased productivity. Therefore, organisations have been urged to promote work-life balance (Cummings, 2001; Fisher, 2001).

Sources of Tensions Between Work and Family Roles

Beutell and Greenhaus (1982) found that women whose career orientations are dissimilar from those of their husbands experienced relatively intense conflict between work and non-work roles. Husband and wife disagreements about family roles (Chadwick, Albrecht, & Kunz, 1976) and husband and wife dissimilarities in their attitudes toward a wife's employment status (Eiswirth-Neems & Handal, 1978) also can contribute to family tension. Presumably, spouse dissimilarity in fundamental beliefs can weaken the mutual support system and produce stress. It has also been documented that employees with significant dependant care responsibilities (e.g., employees who have responsibilities of caring for young children, employees with large families, employees who care for dependant elders) tend to report higher levels of work-family conflict (Frone et al., 1992; Greenhaus & Beutell, 1985). Individuals with families or those with family responsibilities tend to experience both higher time-based and strain-based conflicts (e.g., Lyness & Kropf, 2005).

Numerous studies have identified also workplace factors as sources of work-family conflict. Much of this research found that workplace culture has a profound impact on employees' perception of work-family conflict (Galinsky, Bond, & Friedman, 1996; Greenhaus & Beutell, 1985; Thompson, Beauvais, & Lyness, 1999). For example, Jones and Butler (1980) and Kopelman et al. (1983) observed that ambiguity about work role and/or conflict of interest within the work role heightened the level of work-family conflict.

A lack of leader support may cause also work-family conflict (Jones & Butler, 1980), as would a higher level of physical and mental involvement with work (Pleck, Staines, & Lang, 1980). Other factors could involve a rapid change in the workplace; pursuing a boundary-spanning role; stressful communications; and a high level of mental involvement with work (Burke, Weir, & Duwors, 1980). An indirect consequence would entail a negative effect on an employee's mental health and overall life satisfaction due to job burnout (Hakanen & Schaufel, 2012).

Empirical Context: The Case of Bangladesh

The scenario of Bangladesh - a developing country where women represent roughly half of the total population is no different from the developed world's situation. Interestingly, there is a similar trend of employment comparable to western affluent countries, namely the increasing number of dual-earner families, the increasing rate of weekly hours worked and the numbers of women in paid work, which have a direct impact on work-family interface. The Ministry of Planning of the Bangladeshi Government, in a report looking at gender issues, highlighted that 26 % of employed women worked 40–49 h in 1 week, 15 % worked 30–39 h and 17 % worked less than 15 h. At the same time 80 % of women are engaged in household work (Ministry of Planning, 2009).

Relatively very little research has been done in Bangladesh on the issues of work-family interface. Past research has concluded that mothers who work outside the home are affected adversely, e.g., in the preparation of food and care for children (Chowdhury, 1976). None of the research mentioned took a comprehensive approach to detect the work-family interface of urban educated women in Bangladesh. Majumder's (1982) research, a pioneer in this field, had very interesting findings that reflected that women's participation in economic activity outside the home, did not necessarily make them a worse mother, wife or housewife than that of their non-working counterparts. Rather the evidence showed that working women were even better and / or equally as good a mother as non-working women. The reason for this conclusion lay in the time management plans of the working women. They had to sacrifice their own leisure times to organise child and home care (Huda, 2010).

The Majumder and Huda studies highlighted that working women have to sacrifice their own leisure time in order to manage the time demands placed on them by their dual role, i.e., as *executives* and *home managers*. Yet another study by Huda, Zubayer, and Akhtar (2005) on the work-family conflict situation of Dhaka City's women managers confirmed the findings of previous studies in that women managers' are under heavy pressure both from their work and homes in fulfilling their obligations as expected. In doing so, the women managers were curtailing their personal time and felt stressed, suffered from anxiety and often became ill (Akter & Rashid, 2006) and they also sacrificed their career progression (Alam, Biswas, & Hassan, 2009; Chowdhury, 2008). Alam, Satter and Chowdhury (2011) concluded that though this area of WFC research is new for the Dhaka City's context, it is a situation that is becoming gradually more severe.

Interestingly, all of the studies recommended interventions by concerned circles, i.e., employers, governments, civil society group, etc., to neutralise the situation. But no research was found that systematically explored the views of all the relevant people, i.e., executives, employers, government policy makers, civil society people to develop a policy map for intervention and neutralise the gradually increasing problem. It is very clearly established from the results of the discussion above that Dhaka City's women managers are facing serious problems arising from their poor management of the time between work and family responsibilities; with them having to sacrifice their own leisure in favour of either their family or their work. There is therefore a need to understand the opportunities for intervention between these domains especially in the Bangladeshi context, as most of the studies on this topic have been done in respect of the western viewpoint. Accordingly, the objectives of this paper is established, which is presented in the next section.

Objectives

Based on the above discussions on different theories, practices and evidence concerning the work and family interface, the present chapter aims to measure the three major perspectives of work-family interfaces, i.e., work-family conflict, work-family balance and work-family enrichment in the lives of mid-level executives working in Dhaka City, Bangladesh considering the gender perspectives. Moreover, it tries to find out whether the three interfaces correlate with work performance.

Method

This chapter is based on survey research on a small sample of mid-level executives of Dhaka City. A purposive sampling method was employed to cover both male and female executives. The response rate was 77 % as 144 respondents out of 186 responded, representing 21 organisations from various sectors: consumer goods, service and trade. The respondents were from diverse backgrounds as shown in the analysis of their demographic profile. This showed, 45 % belonged to the 22–33 age group, 42 % belonged to the 34–49 age group and the rest were in the 50+ age group. With respect to their educational levels, 32 % had completed honours degree, 58 % completed Masters and 10 % had pre-university degrees. Two thirds were female (67 %), with one-third male (33 %), and a similar proportion in terms of marital status, unmarried (36 %), married (65 %). Among the respondents, 23 % had less than 2 years of job experience, 27 % had 2–4 years of experience, 34 % had 4–6 years of experience, while 16 % had 8+ years of job experience.

A structured questionnaire was used as the survey instrument. The questionnaire consisted of multiple choice questions (MCQ); adapted work-family interfaces scales, with items constructed along a Likert scale; and one open-ended question.

Multiple Choice Questions The MCQ items (e.g., in which of the following income levels do you belong?) provided the respondents with options to choose from multiple alternatives.

Work-Family Interfaces Scales The items for the work-family balance, work-family conflict and work-family enrichment scales (e.g., *I always get support from my spouse*) were rated on a five-point Likert scale. Adopted versions of standard measurement instrument were used to measure the research constructs (e.g., work-family balance, work-family conflict and work-family enrichment). Carlson et al. (2000) and Carlson, Kacmar, Wayne and Grzywacz (2006) scales of work-family enrichment and work-family conflict were primarily used to measure the work-family conflict and work-family enrichment construct. The sample items for the adopted scale are '*I have difficulties combining work and family life* (conflict, 3 items)', '*I comfortably combine work and family life* (balance, 4 items)', and '*My experiences in one role improve the quality of life in the other role* (enrichment, 3 items)'. The reliabilities exceeded the conventional level of acceptance of .70 (Nunnally, 1978). The Cronbach's alpha values for these constructs were .89 (work-family conflict), .80 (work-life balance) and .70 (work-family enrichment). Carlson et al. (2000) examined the reported reliability of various work-family conflict scales used by different researchers and found that .87 was the highest and .63 was the lowest alpha score. The reliability score of this study fits well with this range. The work performance was measured with a self-developed scale, based on Diener's, Emmons, Larsen, and Griffin (1985) satisfaction with life scale, with 3 items and Cronbach's alpha of .71.

Open Ended Question There was only one open ended question i.e., *Do you want to share your experience about work-family balance initiatives of your company*? The typical answer to that question was, "No Comment".

The data were analysed to provide simple frequency analysis, mean independent samples *t*-test and correlation analyses (Table 4.1).

Table 4.1 Descriptive statistics and alpha values of the work-family interface scales

Scale	Items	Item statistics		Summary item statistics		
		M	*SD*	*M*	*SD*	α
Work-family conflict	I have difficulties in combining work and family life	3.58	.81	3.50	.78	.89
	I often experience a conflict between work and family	3.70	.98			
	My work and family life interfere with each other	3.20	1.08			
Work-life balance	I comfortably combine work and family life	2.70	93	2.87	.78	.80
	I never experience conflict between work and family life	2.10	1.10			
	My work and family life never interfere with each other	2.41	.91			
	I can easily manage time between work and family life	3.08	.86			
Work family enrichment	My work and family life each provides me with resource that increases my performance in both life domains	3.60	.64	4.26	.87	.70
	My experience in one role improves the quality of life in the other role	3.78	.88			
	I have mutually beneficial interaction between work and family life	3.34	.81			
Work performance	Most days I am happy with my work performance	3.29	1.02	3.11	.85	.71
	I can perform my work efficiently most of the times	3.12	.93			
	I can see the output of my work	2.90	1.11			

Results

Measurement of Work-Family Interfaces

The mean distribution of the sample shows that work-family enrichment was the dominant form of work-family interface for both men and women executives, though the women's mean score was slightly higher than the men's (Men = 4.25; Women = 4.29). Work-family conflict was the second most frequently experienced dimension of work-family interface for both male and female executives. The mean score for men was higher than women (Male = 3.79; Female = 3.06). Interestingly, work-life balance secured the lowest mean again with the men's score slightly higher than the women's (Male = 2.89; Female = 2.84). The standard deviations in all cases were less than 1, which indicates conformity of the responses among the respondents (See Table 4.2).

Table 4.2 Mean values of the work-family interface by gender

	Male $n=96$		Female $n=48$	
Scale	*M*	*SD*	*M*	*SD*
Work-family conflict	3.79	.72	3.06	.66
Work-life balance	2.89	.77	2.84	.97
Work family enrichment	4.20	.85	4.29	.82

Table 4.3 Correlations between work performance, and work-family conflict, balance and enrichment for men ($n=96$) and women ($n=48$) in the sample

Gender		1	2	3	4
Male	1. Work performance	1	−.44***	.32**	.01
	2. Work family conflict		1	−.011	−.26*
	3. Work family balance			1	.20*
	4. Work family enrichment				1
Female	1. Work performance	1	−.71***	.28†	.62***
	2. Work family conflict		1	.24†	.20
	3. Work family balance			1	−.09
	4. Work family enrichment				1

† $p<.10$, * $p<.05$, ** $p<.01$, *** $p<.001$

The observed differences in mean score between the men and women sample was compared with the *t*-tests. The results showed that only the mean difference of work-family conflict between the genders was statistically significant, $t(118)=5.57$, $p<.001$. The mean differences of work-family balance, $t(118)=0.31$, $p=.75$, and work-family enrichment, $t(118)=0.25$, $p=.80$, for gender were insignificant. These results suggest that work-family conflict does differ in respect of gender, with men more likely than women to experience it, while the effect of work-family balance and work-family enrichment did not vary gender wise.

Moreover, the relationship between the three dimensions of work-family interfaces and work performance of the executives was explored by Pearson correlation. In this case, the gendered view was also considered, with the relationships considered separately for men and for women.

The results showed that for the men, work-family balance showed a positive and significantly correlation with work performance ($r=.31$, $p<.01$, $n=96$), with work-family conflict ($r=-.43$, $p<.001$, $n=72$), having a significant negative correlation with the construct. However, work-family conflict was negatively, ($r=-.71$, $p<.001$, $n=48$), and work-family enrichment, ($r=.62$, $p<.001$, $n=36$), was positively correlated with work performance among women. Moreover, in the male sample, work-family enrichment showed a negative and significant correlation with work-family conflict, but a positive and significant correlation with work-family balance (See Table 4.3).

The relationships found in the female sample were quite strong, whereas in the male sample they were low to moderate. These provide indications of the nature of impact of work-family interfaces on work performance. For example, work-family conflict with a negative relationship ($r = -.71, p < .01, n = 48$) indicated that as work family conflict increased among female executives, their work performance declined. Besides, in the female sample work-family balance approached significance. It was positively related with work performance but with a weak relationship.

In considering all of the results, it can be said that work-family conflict and work-family enrichment have profound impact on work performance. The gender comparison showed that the work-family interfaces have a stronger impact on the work performance of the female executives than the male executives.

Discussion

The present chapter with a small sample size tried to uncover the basic nature of work-family interfaces in the lives of Dhaka City executives considering the male and female views. The results of this chapter showed that the executives have positive experiences about work-family interfaces as work-family enrichment scored the highest mean values though no significant gender difference was found. The descriptive analysis for this variable favoured women over men. The overall findings conform exactly to an earlier finding on an Indian sample, which also found that executives experience more work-family enrichment than work-family conflict and this study also found no significant gender difference in employee perceptions of work-family enrichment (Baral, 2014).

Besides, other research (e.g., Greenhaus & Powell, 2006) found that involvement with more than one role (e.g., within work and family) is favourable for employees. Barnett and Hyde (2001) explained that the tension and stress inherent in the management of both the work and family domains expected to be counterbalanced by the socio-psychological benefits that arise from the dual involvement in work and family roles. Consequently, positive aspects of the work-family interconnectedness are recognised by the present day executives. This growing interest in the positive interface between work and family coincides with the rising interest in positive psychology (Seligman & Csikszentmihalyi, 2000) and also positive organisational behaviour (Luthans, 2002), both of which highlight the strengths and optimal operations of individual as well as social systems while ignoring the weaknesses and malfunctioning.

The conflicting mode of work-family interaction is also prevalent in the present sample. Both the male and female sample experienced work-family conflict and reflected a significant gender difference. The incidence of work-life conflict is increasing and the magnitude of it perhaps is higher now than it was 20 years ago (Siegel, Post, Brockner, Fishman, & Garden, 2005). A literature review (Kelly et al., 2008) found 163 articles that addressed the impact of work-family conflict on different aspects of human life. Earlier research on Dhaka executives also found evidence of work-family conflict (Alam, Biswas, et al., 2009; Alam, Satter, et al., 2011; Chowdhury, 2008).

However, research is inconclusive on whether women experience a higher level of work-family conflict than men. Some studies found that women reported higher work-family conflict than men (Duxbury, Higgins, Lee, & Mills, 1991; Voydanoff, 2004), but other studies found no gender difference (Milkie & Peltola, 1999; Voydanoff, 1988). This varying output may be the results of the research method which may not have taken total time allocations into consideration. For example, Bianchi, Robinson, and Milkie (2006) found limited gender differences in total work and family hours, perhaps due to fathers spending less time at home and compensate this by extending their work hours. As has been reported by Wood and Eagly (2002) women put the family role as central to their value system and attach significantly higher importance to their family than to their work roles than do men; so when they see that family interferes with their work they consider it as natural, rather than as a conflict. Consequently, women may face lower degrees of conflict than men, and researchers are urged to examine the meanings individuals attach to women's life roles, while studying work-family interfaces.

The findings of the study related to work-life balance is interesting in that it scored the lowest mean compared to other two constructs and no gender difference was found. However, it correlated positively with work performance in the male sample and was marginally insignificant in the female sample in the correlation analysis. Although several studies (Clark, 2000; Greenhaus et al., 2003; Kofodimos, 1993) found a connection between balance and satisfaction, this satisfaction is expected to prevail in all life roles equally (Marks & MacDermid, 1996), in order to maintain balance. The equal level of satisfaction with work and family roles is called positive balance and the equal level of satisfaction comes from satisfactory performance in each of the roles. Thus, a relationship can be drawn between work performance and work-life balance. Besides, Malik, Saif, Gomez, Khan and Hussain (2010) reported a positive and significant relationship between job performance and work-family balance in a sample of working women of Pakistan. Thus, the findings of the present research command support from the existing literature. Kossek and Ozeki (1998) found that job satisfaction for men and women was affected equally by work-family conflict, in general, and family to work conflict, in particular.

Kofodimos (1993) suggests that imbalance or work-family conflict creates stress, hampers quality of life, and eventually reduces individuals' productivity or work performance. The present research also found significant negative correlation relationships between work-family conflict and work performance for both men and women. The relationship was much stronger for women than men, which means women facing much hardship in managing both the work and home life, which affects their work performance significantly. Earlier research (Yavas & Karatepe, 2008) found that women are more relationship oriented, with men more task- or goal-oriented. As a result, it becomes difficult for women to ignore family demands and concentrate on work, causing ineffectiveness at work.

Interestingly, this chapter found significant positive correlations between work-family enrichment and work performance in women but not in men. The relationship is quite strong among women, which means if female employees can positively transfer resources between the domains, their work performance increases. Baral (2014) found that work-family enrichment is related positively with job satisfaction, psychological well-being, organisational commitment and organisational citizenship behaviour in a female sample, which supports the findings of the present research. One of the outcomes of work-family enrichment is the development of psychosocial resources (e.g. security, confidence, accomplishment, or self-fulfilment), that helps the employees to become more effective (Witt & Carlson, 2006), which increases their work performance as well.

It also found that women with multiple life roles (e.g., mother, wife, employee) are more cheerful (less depressed), have higher level of confidence and are happier with family and work life compared to other employees (e.g., unmarried/unemployed/childless women and men (Baruch & Barnett, 1987; Crosby, 1991). The findings of the present research re-affirmed the fact that women with multiple roles become more effective both at home and work.

Finally, it can be said that through understanding the type, direction, and nature of the work-family interfaces, organisations and managers can design appropriate workplace interventions to develop and support an ideal form of work-family interface. Therefore, it is important to examine the varying types of relationships between work-family initiatives and work-life balance. This chapter contributes significantly to the study of effectiveness of work-life initiatives. It finds positive relationship among selected work-family variables and work-life balance for the female executives of Dhaka City. Further research is required to explore the other dimensions of the phenomena.

References

Akter, N., & Rashid, N. (2006). Stress of married women executives of private business concern in Bangladesh. *Journal of Business, South East University, 1*(2), 39–56.

Alam, M. S., Biswas, K., & Hassan, K. (2009). A test of association between working hour and work-family conflict: A glimpse on Dhaka's female white collar professionals. *International Journal of Business and Management, 4*(5), 27–35.

Alam, M. S., Satter, A., Chaudhury, S. I., & Nusrat, A. (2011). Work family conflict of women managers in Dhaka. *Asian Social Science, 7*(7), 108–114. doi:10.5539/ass.v7n7p108.

Aycan, Z. (2008). Cross-cultural approaches to work-family conflict. In K. Korabik, D. S. Lero, & D. L. Whitehead (Eds.), *Handbook of work-family integration: Research, theory and best practices*. Boston: Academic Press/Elsevier.

Balmforth, K., & Gardner, D. (2006). Conflict and facilitation between work and family: Realizing the outcomes for organizations. *New Zealand Journal of Psychology, 35*(2), 69–76.

Baral, R. (2014). *Work-family enrichment: Benefits of combining work and family*. Paycheck.in. Retrieved from http://www.paycheck.in/main/career-tips/women-paycheck/articles/work-family-enrichment-benefits-of-combining-work-and-family. Accessed 20 Aug 2014.

Barling, J., MacEwen, K. E., Kelloway, E. K., & Higginbottom, S. F. (1994). Predictors and outcomes of elder-care-based interrole conflict. *Psychology and Aging, 9*(3), 391–397. doi:10.1037/0882-7974.9.3.391.

Barnett, R. C. (1998). Toward a review and reconceptualisation of the work/family literature. *Genetic, Social, and General Psychology Monographs, 124*(2), 125–184.

Barnett, R. C., & Hyde, J. S. (2001). Women, men, work, and family: An expansionist theory. American Psychologist, 56, 781–796.

Barnett, R. C., Marshall, N. L., & Sayer, A. (1992). Positive spillover effects from job to home: A closer look. *Women & Health, 19*(2/3), 13–41.

Baruch, G. K., & Barnett, R. C. (1987). Role quality, multiple role involvement, and psychological well-being in midlife women. *Journal of Personality and Social Psychology, 51*, 578–585.

Beutell, N. J., & Greenhaus, J. H. (1982). Inter role conflict among married women: The influence of husband and wife characteristics on conflict and coping behavior. *Journal of Vocational Behavior, 21*, 99–110.

Bianchi, S. M., Robinson, J. P., & Milkie, M. A. (2006). *Changing rhythms of American family life*. New York: Russell Sage.

Burke, R. J., Weir, T., & Duwors, R. E. (1980). Work demands on administrators and spouses well being. *Human Relations, 33*, 253–278.

Carlson, D. S., Kacmar, K. M., Wayne, J. H., & Grzywacz, J. G. (2006). Measuring the positive side of the work-family interface: Development and validation of a work-family enrichment scale. *Journal of Vocational Behavior, 68*(1), 131–164. doi:10.1016/j.jvb.2005.02.002.

Carlson, D. S., Kacmar, M. K., & Williams, L. J. (2000). Construction and validation of a multidimensional measure of work-family conflict. *Journal of Vocational Behavior, 56*(2), 249–276. doi:10.1006/jvbe.1999.1713.

Chadwick, B. S., Albrecht, S. L., & Kunz, P. R. (1976). Marital and family role satisfaction. *Journal of Marriage and the Family, 38*, 431–440.

Chowdhury, R. H. (1976). *Married women in urban occupations of Bangladesh: Some problems and issues* (Research report series, no.22). Dacca, Bangladesh: Bangladesh Institute of Development Studies.

Chowdhury, S. F. (2008). Balancing career & family: Challenge for working women. In R. S. Datta & R. S. Mukherjee (Eds.), *Women in changing world: Experiences and challenges* (pp. 125–150). Kolkata, India: Levent Books.

Clark, S. C. (2000). Work/family border theory: A new theory of work/family balance. *Human Relations, 53*, 747–770.

Cooper, C. L., & Williams, S. (1994). *Creating healthy work organizations*. Chichester, UK: Wiley.

Crosby, F. J. (1991). *Juggling: The unexpected advantages of balancing career and home for women and their families*. New York: Free Press.

Crouter, A. C. (1984). Spillover from family to work: The neglected side of the work-family interface. *Human Relations, 37*(6), 425–441. doi:10.1177/001872678403700601.

Cummings, B. (2001). Sales ruined my personal life. *Sales & Marketing Management, 153*(11), 44–51.

Diener, E., Emmons, R., Larsen, J., & Griffin, S. (1985). The satisfaction with life scale. *Journal of Personality Assessment, 49*(1), 71–75.

Duxbury, L., Higgins, C., Lee, C., & Mills, S. (1991). Balancing work and family: A study of the Canadian public sector, Prepared for The Department of Health and Welfare Canada (NHRDP), Ottawa, Ontario.

Edwards, J. R., & Rothbard, N. P. (2000). Mechanisms linking work and family: Clarifying the relationship between work and family constructs. *The Academy of Management Review, 25*, 178–199.

Eiswirth-Neems, N. A., & Handal, P. J. (1978). Spouse's attitudes to- ward maternal occupational status and effects on family climate. *Journal of Community Psychology, 6*, 168–172.

Eiswirth-Neems, N. A., & Handal, P. J. (1978). Spouse's attitudes to- ward maternal occupational status and effects on family climate. *Journal of Community Psychology, 6*, 168–172.

Ford, M. T., Heinen, B. A., & Langkamer, K. L. (2007). Work and family satisfaction and conflict: A meta-analysis of cross-domain relations. *Journal of Applied Psychology, 92*(1), 57–80.

Frone, M. R. (2003). Work-family balance. In J. C. Quick & L. E. Tetrick (Eds.), *Handbook of occupational health psychology* (pp. 142–163). Washington, DC: American Psychological Association.

Frone, M. R., Russell, M., & Cooper, M. L. (1992). Antecedents and outcomes of work–family conflict: Testing a model of the work-family interface. *Journal of Applied Psychology, 77*(1), 65–78.

Frone, M. R., Russell, M., & Cooper, M. L. (1997). Relation of work and family conflict to health outcomes: A four-year longitudinal study of employed parents. *Journal of Occupational & Organizational Psychology, 70*, 325–335.

Galinsky, E., Bond, J. T., & Friedman, D. E. (1996). The role of employers in addressing the needs of employed parents. *Journal of Social Issues, 52*, 111–136.

Goode, W. J. (1960). A theory of role strain. *American Sociological Review, 25*, 483–496.

Greenhaus, J. H., & Beutell, N. J. (1985). Sources of conflict between work and family roles. *Academy of Management Review, 10*, 76–88.

Greenhaus, J. H., Collins, K. M., & Shaw, J. D. (2003). The relation between work-family balance and quality of life. *Journal of Vocational Behavior, 63*(3), 510–531.

Greenhaus, J. H., & Powell, G. N. (2006). When work and family are allies: A theory of work-family enrichment. *Academy of Management Review, 31*(1), 72–92. doi:10.2307/20159186.

Gutek, B. A., & Searle, S. (1991). Rational versus gender role explanations for work-family conflict. *Journal of Applied Psychology, 76*, 560–568.

Hakanen, J. J., & Schaufeli, B. W. (2012). Do burnout and work engagement predict depressive symptoms and life satisfaction? A three-wave seven-year prospective study. *Journal of Affective Disorders, 141*(2–3), 415–424. doi:10.1016/j.jad.2012.02.043.

Hepburn, C. G., & Barling, J. (1996). Eldercare responsibilities, inter role conflict, and employee absence: A daily study. *Journal of Occupational Health Psychology, 1*, 311–318.

Hill, E. J., Hawkins, A. J., Ferris, M., & Weitzman, M. (2001). Finding an extra day a week: The positive influence of perceived job flexibility on work and family life balance. *Family Relations, 50*(1), 49. doi:10.1111/j.1741-3729.2001.00049.x.

Huda, S. S. M. (2010). *Free time management and working women*. Berlin: LAP Lambert Academic Publishing AG & Co KG.

Huda, S. S. M., Zubayer, M., & Akhtar, A. (2005). Work-family conflict: A study of employees in Dhaka city. *Journal of Business, South East University, 1*(2), 155–163.

Jones, A. P., & Butler, M. C. (1980). A role transition approach to the stresses of organizationally-induced family disruption. *Journal of Marriage and the Family, 43*, 367–376.

Kahn, R. L., Wolfe, D. M., Quinn, R. P., Snoek, J. D., & Rosenthal, R. A. (1964). *Organizational stress: Studies in role conflict and ambiguity*. New York: Wiley.

Kelly, E. L., Kossek, E. E., Hammer, L. B., Durham, M., Bray, J., Chermack, K., et al. (2008). Getting there from here: Research on the effects of work-family initiatives on work-family conflict and business outcomes. *Academy of Management Annals, 2*, 305–349. doi:10.1080/19416520802211610.

Kirchmeyer, C. (1992). Perceptions of non-work-to-work spillover: Challenging the common view of conflict-ridden domain relationship. *Basic and Applied Social Psychology, 13*(2), 231–249.

Kofodimos, J. (1993). *Balancing act*. San Francisco: Jossey-Bass.

Kopelman, R. E., Greenhaus, J. H., & Connolly, T. F. (1983). A model of work, family, and inter-role conflict: A construct validation study. *Organizational Behavior and Human Performance, 32*, 198–215.

Kossek, E. E., & Ozekie, C. (1998). Work-family conflict policies and the job-life satisfaction relationship, a review and direction for organization behavior human resources research. *Journal of Applied Psychology, 83*, 139–149.

Kossek, E. Y., & Nichol, V. (1992). The effects of on-site child care on employee attitudes and performance. *Personnel Psychology, 45*, 485–509. doi:10.1111/j.1744-6570.1992.tb00857.x.

Luthans, F. (2002). The need for and meaning of positive organizational behavior. *Journal of Organizational Behavior, 23*(6), 695–706. doi:10.1002/job.165.

Lyness, K. S., & Kropf, M. B. (2005). Work-family balance: A study of European managers. *Human Relations, 58*(1), 33–60.

Majumder, P. P. (1982). *Women, work and home* (Research report 49). Dhaka: Bangladesh Institute of Development Studies: Human Resource Division.

Malik, M. I., Saif, M. I., Gomez, S. F., Khan, N., & Hussain, S. (2010). Balancing work and family through social support among working women in Pakistan. *African Journal of Business Management, 4*(13), 2864–2870.

Marks, S. R., Huston, T. L., Johnson, E. M., & MacDermid, S. M. (2001). Role balance among White married couples. *Journal of Marriage and the Family, 63*, 1083–1098. doi:10.1111/j.1741-3737.2001.01083.x.

Marks, S. R., & MacDermid, S. M. (1996). Multiple roles and the self: A theory of role balance. *Journal of Marriage and the Family, 58*, 417–432.

McElwain, A. K., Korabik, K., & Rosin, H. M. (2005). An examination of gender differences in work-family conflict. *Canadian Journal of Behavioural Science, 37*(4), 283–298.

Mead, G. H. (1964). *Selected writings*. Indianapolis, IN: Bobbs-Merrill.

Milkie, M. A., & Peltola, P. (1999). Playing all the roles: Gender and the work-family balancing act. *Journal of Marriage and the Family, 61*, 476–490.

Ministry of Planning. Gender Statistics Bangladesh. (2009). *Bangladesh Bureau of statistics*. Retrieved from www.bbs.gov.bd/WebTestApplication/userfiles/.../statisticsbook.pdf

Nunnally, J. C. (1978). *Psychometric theory* (2nd ed.). New York: McGraw-Hill.

Pitt-Catsouphes, M., Kossek, E., & Sweet, S. (2006). Multi-disciplinary perspectives, methods, and approaches in the study of work and family. In M. Pitt-Catsouphes, E. E. Kossek, & S. Sweet (Eds.), *The handbook of work-family: Multi-disciplinary perspectives, methods, and approaches* (pp. 1–17). Mahwah, NJ: Lawrence Erlbaum.

Pleck, J. H., Staines, G. L., & Lang, L. (1980). Conflicts between work and family life. *Monthly Labour Review, 103*(3), 29–32.

Rothbard, N. P. (2001). Enriching or deleting? The dynamics of engagement in work and family roles. *Administrative Science Quarterly, 40*, 655–684.

Seligman, M. E. P., & Csikszentmihalyi, M. (2000). Positive psychology: An introduction. *American Psychologist, 55*(1), 5–14. doi:10.1037//0003-066X.55.1.5.

Siegel, P. A., Post, C., Brockner, J., Fishman, A., & Garden, C. (2005). The moderating influence of procedural fairness on the relationship between work-life conflict and organizational commitment. *Journal of Applied Psychology, 90*(1), 13–24. doi:10.1037/0021-9010.90.1.13.

Spector, P. E., Cooper, C. L., Poelmans, S., Allen, T. D., O'Driscoll, M., Sanchez, J. I., et al. (2004). A cross-national comparative study of work-family stressors, working hours, and well-being: china and Latin America versus the Anglo world. *Personnel Psychology, 57*(1), 119–142. doi:10.1111/j.1744-6570.2004.tb02486.x.

Thomas, L. T., & Ganster, D. C. (1995). Impact of family-supportive work variables on work-family conflict and strain: A control perspective. *Journal of Applied Psychology, 80*, 6–15. doi:10.1037/0021-9010.80.1.6.

Thompson, C. A., Beauvais, L., & Lyness, K. S. (1999). When work-family benefits are not enough: The influence of work-family culture on benefit utilization, organizational attachment, and work-family conflict. *Journal of Vocational Behavior, 54*, 392–415. doi:10.1006/jvbe.1998.1681.

Thompson, C. A., & Prottas, D. J. (2006). Relationships among organizational family support, job autonomy, perceived control, and employee well-being. *Journal of Occupational Health Psychology, 10*, 100–118. doi:10.1037/1076-8998.10.4.100.

Voydanoff, P. (1988). Work role characteristics, family structure demands, and work/family conflict. *Journal of Marriage and the Family, 50*, 749–761.

Voydanoff, P. (2004). The effects of work demands and resources on work-to-family conflict and facilitation. *Journal of Marriage and Family, 66*(2), 398–412. doi:10.1111/j.1741-3737.2004.00028.x.

Warner, M., & Hausdorf, A. P. (2009). The positive interaction of work and family roles: Using need theory to further understand the work-family interface. *Journal of Managerial Psychology, 24*(4), 372–385.

Wickham, M. D., & Parker, M. (2007). Reconceptualising organisational role theory for contemporary organizational contexts. *Journal of Managerial Psychology, 22*(5), 440–464.

Witt, L. A., & Carlson, D. S. (2006). The work-family interface and job performance: Moderating effects of conscientiousness and perceived organizational support. *Journal of Occupational Health Psychology, 11*(4), 343–357. doi:10.1037/1076-8998.11.4.343.

Wood, W., & Eagly, A. H. (2002). A cross-cultural analysis of the behavior of women and men: Implications for the origins of sex differences. *Psychological Bulletin, 128*(5), 699–727. doi:10.1037//0033-2909.128.5.699.

Yang, N. (2005). Individualism-collectivism and work-family interfaces: A Sino-U.S. comparison. In S. A. Y. Poelmans (Ed.), *Work and family: An international research perspective*. Mahwah, NJ: Lawrence Erlbaum.

Yang, N., Chen, C. C., Choi, J., & Zou, Y. (2000). Sources of work-family conflict: A Sino-U.S. comparison of the effects of work and family demands. *Academy of Management Journal, 43*, 113–123.

Yavas, U. E., & Karatepe, O. M. (2008). Attitudinal and behavioral consequences of work-family conflict and family-work conflict: Does gender matter? *International Journal of Service Industry Management, 19*(1), 7–31.

Part III
Challenges, Choices and Constraints

Chapter 5
Making the Best of a Bad Job? Women and Part-Time Work in the United Kingdom

Clare Lyonette, Beate Baldauf, and Heike Behle

Introduction

Forty-two per cent of the female workforce, many of whom have young children, now work part-time, and the more children a woman has, the more likely she is to work either part-time or not at all (Labour Force Survey (LFS), Oct–Dec 2013). Researchers have argued that part-time work is "recognisably *the* way of reconciling work and family" (Lewis, Campbell, & Huerta, 2008, p. 25). Over two million men (13 % of all employed men) also work part-time in their main job (LFS, Oct-Dec 2013), but are much less likely than women to do so after having children. In fact, there is evidence that fathers work longer hours than non-fathers (e.g., Biggart & O'Brien, 2009). However, extensive research has shown that most part-time work is offered in lower-level jobs, with lower training and promotion prospects than full-time jobs (e.g., Hoque & Kirkpatrick, 2003). Part-time work has also been consistently shown to pay less than similar full-time work (Connolly & Gregory, 2009; Warren, 2003).

This chapter begins by outlining the choices and constraints which women face in relation to paid employment and the complex - and sometimes competing - explanations for women's reliance on part-time work. We also describe the efforts made by individual women and by various organisations to improve the situation for women wishing to work part-time in better quality jobs. In so doing, we draw on evidence from the Quality Part-time Work Fund initiative, funded by the Government Equalities Office under the previous New Labour government in the United Kingdom (UK).

C. Lyonette (✉) • B. Baldauf • H. Behle
Warwick Institute for Employment Research, University of Warwick, Coventry, UK
e-mail: C.Lyonette@warwick.ac.uk; B.Baldauf@warwick.ac.uk; Heike.Behle@warwick.ac.uk

R.L. Gervais, P.M. Millear (eds.), *Exploring Resources, Life-Balance and Well-Being of Women Who Work in a Global Context*,
DOI 10.1007/978-3-319-31736-6_5

The Current Status of Part-Time Work in the United Kingdom (UK)

Not only are there clear gender differences, but also occupational class differences, in part-time working in the UK (e.g., Lyonette, Baldauf, & Behle, 2010; Warren, 2003). Only 23 % of higher professional and managerial women work part-time, compared with 58 % of women in semi-routine occupations and 64 % in routine occupations[1] (LFS, Oct–Dec 2013). Research using LFS data demonstrated that 60 % of mothers working part-time were employed in four occupational areas: 'elementary administration and service', 'sales and customer service', 'caring personal service' and 'administrative' jobs (Durbin & Tomlinson, 2010). At the same time, only 3 % of mothers working part-time were corporate managers (Tomlinson, Olsen, & Purdam, 2009). Anxo and colleagues (2007) also found that 'long' part-time working (defined as 80 % of full-time hours) is more prevalent in professional occupations than in lower-level jobs.

Full-time working hours are relatively high in the UK: fathers working full-time work on average 46 h per week, and over a third of fathers also work over 48 h per week (Biggart & O'Brien, 2009), meaning that women often bear the major responsibility for childcare and domestic work. There is an assumption by many that women's orientations to work are somewhat different to those of men and that most women give less priority to paid work than to family (e.g., Hakim, 1991). It has been argued that countries such as the UK, with its flexible, deregulated labour market, allow women to freely exercise their choices with regard to work and family responsibilities and particularly with regard to part-time working (Hakim, 2004). Others have challenged this view (e.g. Ginn et al., 1996; McRae, 2003; Procter & Padfield, 1998) and still others have argued that constraints, as well as individual preferences, have some part to play in the 'choices' that women make. For example, previous UK research (Crompton & Lyonette, 2008) has shown that mothers in professional/managerial occupations are much more likely to work or stay at home in accordance with their own attitudes to women's employment and childcare, than women from lower occupational groups who are forced to work out of necessity. Moreover, those with fewer resources are even more constrained in their work decisions. Although childcare costs have been subsidised for those working parents on lower or medium incomes over recent years, and there were new plans by the 2010–2015 Coalition government to supplement the high costs of childcare for working parents, UK families still spend more on childcare than any other country included in OECD analyses (2010). Not surprisingly, therefore, less affluent women are more likely to solve their childcare responsibilities by working part-time

[1] e.g., Routine sales and service occupations; Routine production occupations; Routine technical occupations; Routine operative occupations; Routine agricultural occupations. These positions have the least need for employee discretion and employees are regulated by a basic labour contract (ONS).

(Rubery & Fagan, 1994), while simultaneously drawing on informal childcare such as grandparents and other relatives (e.g., Finch, 2006; Warren, Pascall, & Fox, 2010; Wheelock & Jones, 2002).

The Need for More "Quality" Part-Time Jobs

In spite of their greater ability to pay for full-time childcare, many women in higher-level jobs would prefer to work part-time, at least for a short period while their children are young (Fagan, 2001). However, a recognised lack of part-time opportunities available to women in senior occupations means that many women 'downgrade' when reducing their hours (Connolly & Gregory, 2009), working below their capabilities (Darton & Hurrell, 2005; Women and Work Commission (WWC), 2006) and crowding into lower-level jobs (Grant, Yeandle, & Buckner, 2005). This lack of quality part-time jobs has obvious implications, not only for the women who often become stuck in lower-level jobs, thereby reducing their career opportunities, lifetime earnings and pensions (Connolly & Gregory, 2009; Warren, 2008), but also for the women with lower qualifications and skills who will potentially be displaced by better-qualified women.

Not only has part-time work been conclusively demonstrated to be associated with lower levels of occupational success, but the UK also has the lowest rates of pay and the poorest working conditions for part-timers across much of Europe (Aston et al., 2004). Figures from the UK Office for National Statistics demonstrate the consistent pay gap between full-time and part-time employees. For full-time employees in April 2012, women's hourly earnings were £12.00 and men's hourly earnings were £13.27 (median, excluding overtime, full-time employees only). For part-time employees working 30 h or less per week (for those in teaching professions, less than 25 h per week), women earned a median hourly rate (excluding overtime) of £8.12 in April 2012, compared with men working in part-time jobs who earned an average of £7.72 (Bovil, 2013). There has been a substantial rise in part-time working since the recession of 2008, and most especially for men (Grimshaw & Rafferty, 2011; ONS, 2012). However, this growth in part-time working was more heavily skewed towards lower-level jobs and many new part-timers were 'involuntary' part-time workers who took a part-time job because they were unable to find suitable full-time work (Bell & Blanchflower, 2011, 2013), which may explain the lower salary levels of part-time male workers, in comparison with similar women.

Although the UK has one of the largest shares of female part-time workers across Europe, the Netherlands has by far the highest proportion at over 60 %. Here, however, part-time work is more integrated into the national employment structure and specific policies have been developed to protect part-time workers (Anxo, Fagan, Smith, Letablier, & Perraudin, 2007). Legislation prohibits employers from differentiating between full-time and part-time employees, without any objective justification, so recognising part-time work as equivalent to full-time work. Part-time workers are entitled to the same (pro-rata) pay and pension rights, bonuses and holidays, and employees have the right to reduce or increase their working hours. Although such jobs could therefore be justifiably described as quality part-time work in the Netherlands, chances for promotion are still limited and the part-time pay penalty is equally prevalent (see for example, Román, 2006).

Pressures from the European Commission have led over more recent years to significant changes to regulations protecting part-time workers' rights in the workplace in the UK, whilst rights to request flexible working (the Employment Act of 2002) have opened up part-time work to more and diverse workers (Lyonette et al., 2010). The Part-time Work Directive in the UK came into effect in July 2000. This stipulated that part-time workers:

- Must not be treated less favourably than comparable full-time workers;
- Should receive equal hourly rates of pay;
- Should receive equal overtime pay, as well as equal enhanced rates of pay for working outside normal contractual hours;
- Should get equal access to any company pension scheme, training and career development, rights to career breaks, rights to receive enhanced sick, maternity, paternity and adoption leave and pay, parental leave rights and consideration for promotion; and
- Should receive contractual benefits pro-rata.

Although national legislation has aimed to eradicate any remaining sex discrimination or unfavourable treatment within the workplace for many years, women working part-time continue to be disadvantaged, even in highly feminised sectors such as catering, cleaning, caring and teaching assistance (e.g., Thornley, 2007). In a study of part-time work in the service industries, Tomlinson (2006) refers to Connell's use of "hegemonic masculinity" to describe the process whereby male views become recognised as 'normal'. As a consequence, Tomlinson argues, the traditional 'male full-time work' trajectory becomes the normal way to measure work commitment (2006, p. 69) and thus, part-time work will always be devalued and marginalised. Tomlinson's analysis further demonstrates the negative effects on part-time workers of informal workplace practices, often implemented by line managers, even when strict equality policies are in place. Although rarely perceived as discriminatory by managers or full-time workers, these practices effectively close off the career prospects of part-time employees. Similarly, the EHRC (2009) report on the financial services sector found that negative management attitudes towards women can have serious repercussions on women's career progression, in spite of strong employment policies.

In spite of the overwhelming evidence that part-time work has negative effects on women's careers, it cannot be ignored that women like part-time work and flexibility in their working hours (Scott & Dex, 2009) and women working part-time report lower levels of work-to-family conflict than full-time workers (Crompton & Lyonette, 2007). Part-time working women also express more happiness and greater job satisfaction than full-time women (Booth & van Ours, 2008). However, although research has shown that women in the UK reported higher life satisfaction when switching from full-time to part-time work after having children, those with higher levels of education appeared to be less likely to do so (Gash, Mertens, & Gordo, 2012).

The research presented here focuses on a recent government initiative to increase quality part-time jobs. Twelve organisations (see Table 5.1) received government funding to support new initiatives aimed at achieving a culture change, so that more

Table 5.1 Organisations involved in the quality part-time work project

Organisation	Size of organisation	Individual pilot project's objectives	Amount of funding awarded[a]
Flexworks (initially named Equals One Recruitment)	Small	Develop an online Jobs Board for quality part-time or job-share posts	Large
Working families	Small	Develop case studies and a toolkit for employers and employees	Medium/large
Youth action	Small	Develop case studies on black and minority ethnic part-time role models and a toolkit for employers and employees	Medium/large
East riding of Yorkshire council	Large	Increase the number of part-time posts overall and help to fill 'service-critical' posts within the local authority	Medium/large
Medical women's federation	Small	Conduct research and publish a report on part-time work and training in the medical profession	Medium/large
Kellogg's	Large	Develop a coaching programme and women's network for senior part-time women	Medium/large
Royal mail	Large	Increase recruitment and employment of part-time management posts	Medium
Workers' educational association – West Midlands	Small	Conduct research on flexible working within the Workers' Educational Association, feeding into revised management practices throughout the organisation	Medium
Swindon Borough council	Large	Increase communication between part-time workers and managers and produce case studies of part-time workers for managers and employees	Small
Wisework	Small	Develop a toolkit for managers and employees on part-time work	Small
Tesco	Large	Develop a women's network and organise events	Small
Durham constabulary	Large	Conduct research on the barriers to senior part-time working for women in the police force	Small

[a]Funding: Small: £15,000 or less, Medium: £15,001 to 30,000, Medium/large: £30,001 to 60,000, Large: more than £60,000

senior jobs – particularly in the skilled occupations and the professions - are more open to part-time and flexible working. Projects were funded for 1–2 years, varying in size and scope. One pilot organisation declined further involvement and is therefore not included in the research reported here. The following section outlines the methods employed in the research programme.

Method

Defining Quality Part-Time Work

Drawing first upon a literature review undertaken as part of the research, we identified seven key themes relating to the quality of part-time jobs. All the literature included in the review specifically focused upon the "quality" of part-time or reduced-hours jobs, and included international evidence, where relevant (e.g., Chalmers, Campbell, & Charlesworth, 2005; Charlesworth, Campbell, Probert, Allan, & Morgan, 2002; Tilly, 1996). In spite of the minimal evidence available, we have categorised these themes as follows:

- **Reversibility between full- and part-time work**: many women working part time end up in lower-level jobs with little opportunity for progression; enabling women to move back into full-time work or allowing them to increase their part-time hours, if desired, would help to avoid this.
- **Retaining skill levels and experience**: evidence shows that women who return to work part-time after childbirth tend to move into female-dominated lower-level occupations which are less well paid. If more jobs were opened up on a part-time basis at senior levels, women working part-time would stand a greater chance of retaining their skills and experience and moving up the career ladder, and employers would be less likely to lose vital talent.
- **Access to training and development**: although women overall appear to receive more training than men, women working part-time do not receive as much training as similar women working full-time.
- **Access to promotion**: women working part-time are less likely than full-time workers to receive training and development opportunities, and will also have less relevant work experience if working part-time for longer periods, which will impact on opportunities for promotion. Negative perceptions of part-time workers, by colleagues and by line managers, also present a barrier to women's progression.
- **Internal communication and consultation**: evidence suggests that all part-time workers (where the data allow for comparisons, this appears to affect women in particular) are less likely to be consulted about work-related matters than full-time workers, even at higher levels, for example, if meetings occur on days when part-time workers are not present. Communication problems can also be reported between part-time workers and managers; for part-time workers who

may already be absent for some meetings and training courses, good communication with colleagues and managers may be doubly important.

- **Job content - assigned tasks**: some research, in specific occupational sectors, suggests that women working part-time are given different, less challenging tasks and roles to similar full-time workers, and that this practice is not only common in male-dominated occupations, but also in highly feminised occupations.
- **Workload and perceived commitment**: research into female part-time workers suggests that some managers view part-time workers as less committed or motivated than full-time workers (e.g., Tomlinson, 2006), especially where being present in the office is desirable and positively evaluated, e.g., in Accountancy (Lyonette & Crompton, 2008; Smithson, Lewis, Cooper, & Dyer, 2004) and Finance (EHRC, 2009).

This is not an exhaustive list, as other occupation-specific issues are likely to be important. However, our aim was to provide a comprehensive list of issues that represent female part-time workers across different sectors, and so the most important themes were drawn out from the literature. Each theme has been identified as a potential problem for women who move into part-time work, and all clearly need to be addressed in order to improve the experiences of part-time employees.

As a result of this review, we developed a framework (see Annex 5.A1) to develop a definition of "quality" part-time work, which is defined here as jobs: (a) which provide the same terms and conditions, development and progression opportunities as comparable full-time work; (b) which enable the job-holder to maintain or enhance his or her skills; (c) which enable the achievement of an acceptable work-life 'balance', meeting the needs of both employer and employee; and, (d) where a business case can be made, provide the opportunity to increase the number of hours to full-time work, if desired, at the same or a higher job level.

The Pilot Study Organisations

Eleven case studies were conducted,[2] combining interview and focus group data, company records, and research and policy documents. Twenty-six interviews were conducted which included: 10 project managers, usually working in Human Resources (HR) departments (5 male, 5 female); 3 other HR representatives (1 male, 2 female); 8 part-time employees (all female); 3 line managers of part-time employees (all male); and 2 others, e.g. clients of pilot organisations (both female).

While all the named organisations are in the public domain, the actual research findings have been anonymised in order to protect individual respondents. Interviews

[2] One organisation declined further involvement with the project, in spite of numerous attempts to contact the relevant project manager.

Table 5.2 Evidence base of the quality part-time work fund pilot programme

Organisation	PM	LM	PT	HR	Others	Focus groups	Add'n material	Total interviews
Flexworks (FWK)	1						R	1
Working Families (WF)	1						R	1
Youth Action (YA)	1							1
East Riding of Yorkshire Council (ERYC)	1	1	1	1		1 (LMs of PTs)	■	4
Medical Women's Federation (MWF)	1						R	1
Kellogg's (Kell)	1		1				■	2
Royal Mail (RM)	1	2	1	1		1 (PT managers)	■	5
Workers' Educational Association (WEA)	1				1		R	2
Swindon Borough Council (SBC)	1		1	1			■	3
Wisework (WWK)	1				1			2
Tesco								0
Durham Constabulary (DC)			4			1 (PTs)	■	4
No. of interviews	10	3	8	3	2	3		26

PM project manager, *LM* line manager, *PT* part-time employee, *HR*: human resources representative
■: e.g. PM's evaluation report, statistical data etc
R: (research) reports produced as part of the pilot

were organised in various ways. The research team attempted to interview up to four employees within each organisation but due to the limited number of respondents available within the time allocated to the project, the findings from four organisations were based on information provided by the project manager only, potentially limiting their reliability (see Table 5.2).

Interviews lasted for around an hour, following a semi-structured topic guide designed to gauge the positive and negative aspects of the pilot programme and what respondents perceived to be the costs and benefits of increasing quality part-time work within their organisations. Key examples of good or best practice were also identified.

In addition, three focus groups were held, two with part-time employees and one with line managers, representing a mix of male and female participants from various ethnic backgrounds. For the focus groups with part-time workers, participants ranged widely in age but all were parents.

Focus groups lasted for around an hour to an hour and a half, following a topic guide designed to gauge the positive and negative aspects of the pilot programme, participants' current roles and any drawbacks or difficulties with part-time working, as well as any perceived differences between full- and part-time work. Where possible, interviews and focus groups took place in a private room in the pilot organisation and confidentiality was assured. Two researchers attended all the focus groups. After gaining permission, the interviews and focus groups were audiotaped and extensive notes were taken. The qualitative data were analysed using thematic analysis (Boyatzis, 1998), codes were constructed inductively from the raw information using data-driven coding methods and the data were initially analysed to identify common or similar themes.

Results

Assessing the New Definition of 'Quality' Part-Time Work

Pilot organisations usually reported that their current part-time jobs satisfied a maximum of three of the four criteria outlined earlier (the ability to increase hours at a later time was often the most difficult to satisfy, as this depended on work available and the current economic climate). Although fulfilling all criteria is recognised as an ideal, and many organisations were struggling to do so, many were striving to open up or create better jobs on a part-time basis.

The Costs and Benefits of Increasing Quality Part-Time Work

All interview respondents were asked to identify any costs and benefits of increasing quality part-time work. Most project managers and line managers recognised the potential requirement for additional recruitment and training costs, management time, review processes and appraisals, particularly for job share posts, as well as continuity and communication difficulties between managers and part-time workers. Some project managers referred to the extra costs of training line managers effectively in dealing with part-time workers.

However, representatives from all organisations (whether project managers, line managers or part-time employees) were almost universally convinced that the benefits of increasing quality part-time work outweighed the costs. Many referred to increased employee satisfaction and happiness, greater focus, motivation, flexibility and loyalty of part-time workers. Others outlined improved creativity and productivity, as well as greater retention, leading to reduced recruitment costs. Some pointed to improved job coverage by two people in a job-share post (Table 5.3).

Table 5.3 The main costs and benefits of quality part-time work, as identified by pilot respondents

Actual or potential costs	Actual or potential benefits
Extra training (if job-share)	Increased commitment and loyalty
Extra appraisals (if job share)	Improved retention
Communication problems	Improved work satisfaction
Extra advertising and recruitment costs (if job-share)	Reduced sickness and absenteeism
Management of more people	Better productivity
Extra training needed for managers	Better coverage of a role (if job share)

How and Why Are New Quality Part-Time Jobs Being Developed by Employers?

Due to long-term recruitment and retention problems in certain sectors and occupations, and the need for greater diversity within workforces, there has been a degree of optimism from researchers over more recent years that employers will increasingly recognise the 'business case' for increasing quality part-time jobs (e.g., Edwards & Robinson, 2004). As a result of this increased flexibility, employers may expect greater loyalty and positive working attitudes from their employees. Several pilot organisations were making efforts to increase the provision of, or raise awareness of, existing part-time opportunities. The following section highlights some examples.

(a) Managers within a local authority which had responsibility for a wide range of services, including education in schools, were aware of the need for part-time workers, especially in 'service-critical' areas. For example, two line managers commented: "*without part-time workers, there would be no social care*", and "*schools would not be able to run without part-time staff*". While there are national shortages of school head teachers, traditionally full-time workers with long hours, the local authority's predominantly rural location deterred many potential applicants. As a result, active efforts were being made to find new models of working, such as allowing one head teacher to move to part-time working, while another (more junior) co-head "stepped up", working part-time in both roles. This was seen as a 'win-win' strategy, with the co-head being potentially ready to take over from the more senior employee upon retirement (*Source*: focus group with line managers).

(b) A large private sector organisation recognised the need for senior women to progress and identified four future female leaders with young children, all of whom were working part-time or who had expressed an interest in doing so. The company organised one-to-one coaching sessions with an external facilitator which helped the women to manage their workload and to delegate appropriately, so leading to a better balance between work and family responsibilities. The women then coached their managers in turn to show how it could work effectively, and also acted as positive role models within their own departments.

Results were reported to be very successful, with one woman commenting that, as a consequence of having more senior women such as herself working part-time, more women at junior levels were returning from maternity leave and asking for reduced hours. As a result of the workshop, therefore, the women acted as successful role models: *"I as the individual have got to make this work because that then shows the management that when it is managed effectively and when you have the right person with the right support doing it, it is absolutely no different to someone working full-time"*. (*Source*: interviews with the project manager and one woman on the coaching course).

How Do Women Working Part-Time Help to Make Changes Within Their Organisations?

Women within the various organisations included in the project reported on a variety of strategies designed to improve and increase the acceptance of part-time working. Some were individual-level strategies, whereas other women were more vocal in their efforts to change the organisational culture as a whole. In one case, a woman described her experience of working in the first senior job share post within a large organisation. The sometimes extreme efforts of the two women involved in the job-sharing arrangement were deliberately kept hidden in order to ensure the success of the shared post: *"…we used to say is 'this is going to work', and we had an agreement that I would just pick up her work without any problems…and we would call each other. And I don't think people knew we were doing that but we were so determined it wasn't going to fail, we weren't going to be criticised for it"* (Female HR Manager). Since that time, more senior job share posts were opened up within the organisation and, in spite of some cross-over difficulties, these were working successfully.

Working "above and beyond" the requirements of the part-time role was a common strategy used by the more senior women working part-time in an effort to succeed. However, many saw this as a pay-off for being allowed to work reduced hours and did not resent these extra duties. For example, a woman described how, if working longer on one project in a particular working week, she would reduce her working hours the next week. She was also willing to attend meetings on her day off: *"Because of how flexible they have been with me, I will come in and offer time for a meeting…no-one forces me, no-one pushes me, and they try their best to arrange meetings in the hours that I'm there". "I feel that it's two-way."* (Female Manager)

Other women were less positive about their experiences and insisted on their rights as part-time workers, actively resisting attempts to reduce their duties or responsibilities. For example, when a female manager was not invited on a business trip, her manager told her: *"'because you've got children and you're part-time, I didn't think you could'* [attend]*…so I put him right on that and after that, he always did ask in advance…As a professional he should have treated me the same as the* *others.*" (Female Manager). This woman's experience of working part-time had improved significantly since her intervention, suggesting slow but positive organisational progress.

Another woman working in a traditional, male-dominated workplace described herself as a "*saviour*" in being the first to move to part-time work. She had been made redundant from a part-time managerial role, and after applying for her current role she initially had to work full-time, but eventually persuaded her manager to let her work reduced hours. This was working successfully and she was now acting as a positive role model, with other women planning to reduce their hours in the future.

Persisting Barriers to Quality Part-Time Work

The organisational context acted either as a facilitator or as a barrier in achieving reconciliation for the women (and the limited number of men) included in the pilot study. Table 5.4 describes the different 'types' of organisations within the pilot study.

In spite of some real progress demonstrated within several of the more progressive pilot organisations, other organisations remained steadfastly opposed to reduced-hours working in more senior roles. This sometimes took the form of negative reactions from other co-workers or line managers, of reduced responsibilities, rewards and benefits such as enhanced pay for working on Bank holidays, or of inadequate provision of support for those attempting to balance such roles on a part-time basis.

One woman in a 'Traditional' workplace worked 36 h per week but had effectively decided that she could not progress within the male-dominated workforce where both she and her husband worked. When pregnant, she was put on restricted schedule: "*Both roles that I carried out…were soul-destroying, not very*

Table 5.4 Typology of workplaces included in the pilot programme

Progressive	Progressive but also some resistance (at unit level)	Traditional
High % of female workers, many part-time	Average % of female workers, some part-time but rarely at higher levels	Low % of female workers, some part-time but rarely at higher levels
Recognised need for part-time workers by HR and senior management	Recognition of diversity issues and retention problems by HR	Recognition that female part-timers are not progressing but some jobs difficult to accommodate on part-time basis
Supportive HR policies, strictly adhered to	Generally supportive HR policies, mostly adhered to	Generally supportive HR policies, rarely adhered to
Line manager training widespread	Some line managers still resistant	Most line managers male and resistant

career-developmental, tortuous...when I was pregnant with my second child, I didn't declare it until I was over 20 weeks pregnant". She went on to argue that part-time work within her workplace environment was still perceived - and rewarded - negatively: *"You've got to work twice as hard to prove yourself. You do less hours but twice the work*". Even to progress to the next level within the organisation, she argued, the hours "*would be just too unforgiving...so I think career-wise, my career pretty much stops at this level*". The experience of working part-time during pregnancy had demonstrated that the organisation did not easily accommodate and support part-time workers at senior levels, forcing her to abandon any hopes for career progression.

Another woman within the same organisation accepted that it can be more difficult to accommodate people with childcare issues, especially in a "*demand-driven*" organisation: the demand cannot be met with fewer hours, and some full-timers complain. Although she described the organisation as "*reasonably pro-flexible working*," supervisors nevertheless have the ability to discourage such types of work. The resistance to part-time working within the organisation was deeply entrenched, even though working part-time hours did not provide the same benefits as full-time jobs. Legislation, at least in this case, did not appear to have made effective changes to organisational practice.

One project manager within a 'Progressive' pilot organisation argued: *"The biggest hurdle was convincing operational managers that this was worthwhile, that potentially there was a barrier for people progressing into part-time managerial roles and once we'd made that case and got managers on side, then they can make it or break it"*. When line managers and senior managers were supportive of part-time workers, and when HR policies regarding part-time working were adhered strictly to (in those organisations with a recognised need for part-time workers, and which had trained line managers in dealing with part-time employees), organisations were generally successful in increasing quality part-time work.

Discussion

Previous researchers have argued that 'moves towards opening up management jobs on a part-time basis' were 'slow' and 'embryonic' (Burchell, Dale, & Joshi, 1997, p. 215), and that this 'remains the case more than a decade later' (Durbin & Tomlinson, 2010, p. 624). These findings are generally supported in the research reported here. However, there were several examples of positive moves towards more quality part-time working and representatives from all organisations were almost universally convinced that the benefits of increasing quality part-time work outweighed the costs. Part-time employees in higher-quality jobs can serve as effective role models which in turn leads to wider acceptance overall, although there is some recognition that not all jobs can be done on a part-time basis.

The HR representatives who were interviewed were generally supportive and recognised that they had an important role to play in promoting quality part-time work, including the ability to draw on employment policies if necessary. Selling the business case for increasing quality part-time work is crucial in increasing managerial commitment, and those with a recognised need for part-time workers were more likely to embrace the increased provision (and resultant take-up) of such jobs. In an earlier examination of work-family culture in the United States of America (US), Thompson and colleagues (1999) found that '*the cultural dimension of managerial support was significantly related to utilisation, suggesting that managerial support on a daily basis may be the most critical cultural variable in employees' decisions to use family-friendly benefits and programs*' (p. 408).

Training line managers in how to deal with part-time employees was a key strategy involved in creating a more supportive workplace culture. In those workplaces where employers *had* accommodated the needs of part-time workers, these workers in turn demonstrated a high degree of loyalty and flexibility. Other women had developed strategies of their own to challenge the organisational culture in increasing part-time work at more senior levels.

Even in those workplaces where part-time work has become accepted, sometimes at more senior levels, these jobs often require the employee to be available on days off, with no alternative cover in place. Furthermore, there was some evidence that part-time managers in operational roles did not have sufficient time to fulfil extra duties and worked significantly longer hours than contracted. In order to encourage more women and men to work part-time in senior roles, quality part-time jobs need to be recognised as such, and not as full-time jobs worked in fewer days. While many employees (full-time or part-time) work longer hours than contracted, this is especially difficult for working parents with young children, who are often limited in their working hours by inflexible and expensive childcare arrangements and additional domestic responsibilities. One senior woman in the study described the number of well-qualified women who are not working because "*the whole concept is exhausting*".

The research data demonstrate that there is still a long way to go before women working part-time are treated the same as other women and men working on a full-time basis. In order for this to happen, there seems to be a recognised need for more men to work on a part-time basis, and especially those in senior positions, which may have the effect of 'mainstreaming' part-time work. Smithson and colleagues (2004) found that flexible working policies in accountancy appeared to have the most effect when senior staff, especially men, acted as role models. This in turn led to a greater acceptance of part-time work within organisations. In reality, however, men's requests for part-time work tend to be viewed less sympathetically than women's (e.g., Fagan, Hegewisch, & Pillinger, 2006). Merely increasing the number of quality part-time jobs specifically targeted at women has the potential to polarise men's and women's work even further: senior part-time women may be in a more advantageous position in comparison with lower-level part-time women, but will still be disadvantaged in comparison with full-time men.

This research was undertaken shortly after the start in 2008/2009 of the economic recession, providing new information on the extent of quality part-time working at the onset of a critical time period. It will be interesting to note how the impact of the government spending cuts in the public sector will affect the provision of quality part-time work and other forms of flexible working in the future. There is evidence that more men are working in (lower-level) part-time jobs as a result of the recession. However, it seems likely that this is a short-term outcome of fewer jobs available on a full-time basis. This, in turn, is unlikely to improve the prospects for part-time workers, with potential male role models moving back into better-paid jobs with longer hours as the current situation improves.

Persisting expectations for women to be the main carer mean that government initiatives to increase quality part-time work are unlikely to affect women's ability to progress within the workplace, with women themselves choosing not to pursue more demanding roles. Reducing childcare costs and full-time working hours, while simultaneously encouraging more men to work part-time and take on greater child-care and routine domestic responsibilities, will go some way towards addressing these ongoing inequalities.

Annex A1: Framework Used for the Development of the Definition of Quality Part-Time Work

No.	Dimensions	Operationalisation	Comments
1.	Pro-rata wages	PT workers receive the same pro-rata wages as a comparable full-time worker. Pro-rata wages include basic pay and performance-related pay	1st bullet point of the working definition
2.	Pro-rata access to benefits	PT workers receive the same pro-rata access to benefits as a comparable full-time worker, such as sick leave, annual leave and pension	1st bullet point of the working definition
3.	Same protection as full-timers with regard to job, contracted hours and discrimination	PT workers receive the same protection as full-timers with regard to job protection, contracted hours and discrimination as a comparable full-time worker	1st bullet point of the working definition
4.	Equal opportunities to participate in training	PT workers have the same equal opportunities to participate in training as a comparable full-time worker (ideally including access to career-enhancing training, at a time when PT workers can access the training during their contracted hours or make alternative arrangements to do so)	1st bullet point of the working definition

(continued)

No.	Dimensions	Operationalisation	Comments
5.	Equal access to career progression	PT workers have the same opportunities as FT workers to apply for promotion, with applications being considered on their merit	1st bullet point of the working definition
			Some qualitative studies suggest that there is an informal closure of promotion opportunities at the workplace even where official policies support equal opportunities
6.	Employment reflects the qualification level and the skills of the employee	PT work is commensurate with the qualification and skill level of the job-holder, e.g. staff reducing their hours on return from a short break, where their skills are still current, can continue working in the same job or a job at the same grade	2nd bullet point of the working definition
			There may be sector specific differences in what constitutes a short leave where skills have remained current. (e.g. science/engineering versus other areas)
7.	Predictability and control over the working hours	The hours of PT workers have either been set to meet their own needs or theirs and the employer's needs	3rd bullet point of the working definition
8.	Reversibility of mode of work (from FT to PT and from PT to FT)	It is relatively easy for workers to reduce or increase their working hours, given a certain lead time. The change in hours does not have a detrimental effect on the job-holder's utilisation of skills or the grade attained	4th bullet point of the working definition
			Statistical data (Anxo et al., 2007) show that a change of mode of work in either direction or both ways is not commonplace in organisations and varies according to a number of factors (e.g. size of the company, scope of part-time work)

NB. *PT* part-time, *FT* full-time

References

Aston, J., Clegg, M., Diplock, E., Ritchie, H., & Willison, R. (2004). *Interim update of key indicators of women's position in Britain* (Institute for employment studies). London: Women and Equality Unit/Department of Trade and Industry.

Anxo, D., Fagan, C., Smith, M., Letablier, M. T., & Perraudin, C. (2007). *Part-time work in European companies: Establishment survey on working time 2004–2005*. Dublin, OH: European Foundation for the Improvement of Living and Working Conditions.

Bell, D., & Blanchflower, D. (2011). Young people and the Great recession. *Oxford Review of Economic Policy, 27*(2), 241–267. doi:10.1093/oxrep/grr011.

Bell, D., & Blanchflower, D. (2013). Underemployment in the UK revisited. *National Institute Economic Review, 224*(1), F8–F22. doi:10.1177/002795011322400110.

Biggart, L., & O'Brien, M. (2009, November). *Fathers' working hours: Parental analysis from the third work-life balance employee survey and maternity and paternity rights and benefits survey of parents*. Department for Business, Innovation and Skills, Employment Relations Occasional Paper.

Booth, A. L., & van Ours, J. C. (2008). Job satisfaction and family happiness: The part-time work puzzle. *The Economic Journal, 118*(526), F77–F99. doi:10.1111/j.1468-0297.2007.02117.x.

Bovil, D. (2013). Patterns of pay: Results from the annual survey of hours and earnings, 1997 to 2012. *Office for National Statistics (ONS)* http://www.ons.gov.uk/ons/dcp171766_300035.pdf. Accessed 17 June 2014.

Boyatzis, R. E. (1998). *Transforming qualitative information: Thematic analysis and code development*. London: Sage.

Burchell, B., Dale, A., & Joshi, H. (1997). Part-time work among British women. In H. P. Blossfeld & C. Hakim (Eds.), *Between equalization and marginalization: Women working part-time in Europe and the United States of America* (pp. 210–246). Oxford: Oxford University Press.

Chalmers, J., Campbell, I., & Charlesworth, S. (2005). Part-time work and caring responsibilities in Australia: Towards an assessment of job quality. *Labour and Industry, 15*(3), 41–66. doi:10.1080/10301763.2005.10669317.

Charlesworth, S., Campbell, I., Probert, B., Allan, J., & Morgan, L. (2002). *Balancing work and family responsibilities: Policy implementation options*. Project summary: A report for the Department of Premier and Cabinet (Victoria) and Department of Innovation, Industry and Regional Development (Victoria). Centre for Applied Social Research, RMIT University, Melbourne.

Connolly, M., & Gregory, M. (2009). The part-time pay penalty: Earnings trajectories of British women. *Oxford Economic Papers, 61*(1), i76–i97. doi:10.1093/oep/gpn043.

Crompton, R., & Lyonette, C. (2007). Are we all working too hard? Women, men, and changing attitudes to paid employment. In A. Park, J. Curtice, K. Thomson, M. Phillips, & M. Johnson (Eds.), *British social attitudes: The 23rd report – Perspectives on a changing society* (pp. 55–70). London: Sage.

Crompton, R., & Lyonette, C. (2008). Mothers' employment, work-life conflict, careers and class. In J. Scott, S. Dex, & H. Joshi (Eds.), *Women and employment: Changing lives and new challenges* (pp. 213–233). Cheltenham, UK: Edward Elgar.

Darton, D., & Hurrell, K. (2005). *People working part-time below their potential*. Manchester, UK: Equal Opportunities Commission.

Durbin, S., & Tomlinson, J. (2010). Female part-time managers: Networks and career mobility. *Work, Employment and Society, 24*(4), 621–640. doi:10.1177/0950017010380631.

Edwards, C., & Robinson, O. (2004). Evaluating the business case for part-time working amongst qualified nurses. *British Journal of Industrial Relations, 42*(1), 167–183. doi:10.1111/j.1467-8543.2004.00309.x.

Equality and Human Rights Commission (EHRC). (2009). *Financial services inquiry: Sex discrimination and gender pay gap report of the equality and human rights commission*. Equality and Human Rights Commission. http://www.equalityhumanrights.com/publication/financial-services-inquiry-report. Accessed 17 June 2014.

Fagan, C. (2001). Time, money and the gender order: Work orientations and worktime preferences in Britain. *Gender, Work and Organisation, 8*(3), 239–266. doi:10.1111/1468-0432.00131.

Fagan, C., Hegewisch, A., & Pillinger, J. (2006). *Out of time: Why Britain needs a new approach to working-time flexibility*. London: Trades Union Congress.

Finch, N. (2006). Gender equity and time use: How do mothers and fathers spend their time? In J. Bradshaw & A. Hatland (Eds.), *Social policy, employment and family change in comparative perspective* (pp. 13–36). Cheltenham, UK: Edward Elgar.

Gash, V., Mertens, A., & Gordo, L. R. (2012). The influence of changing hours of work on women's life satisfaction. *The Manchester School, 80*(1), 51–74. doi:10.1111/j.1467-9957.2011.02255.x.

Ginn, J., Arber, S., Brannen, J., Dale, A., Dex, S., Elias, P., et al. (1996). Feminist fallacies: A reply to Hakim on women's employment. *British Journal of Sociology, 47*(1), 167–174.

Grant, L., Yeandle, S., & Buckner, L. (2005). *Working below potential: Women and part-time work* (EOC working paper series no 40). Manchester, UK: Equal Opportunities Commission.

Grimshaw, D., & Rafferty, A. (2011). Social impact of the crisis in the United Kingdom: Focus on gender and age inequalities. In D. Vaughan-Whitehead (Ed.), *Inequalities in the world of work: The effects of the crisis* (pp. 525–570). Cheltenham, UK: Edward Elgar.

Hakim, C. (1991). Grateful slaves and self-made women: fact and fantasy in women's work orientations. *European Sociological Review, 7*(2), 101–121.

Hakim, C. (2004). *Key issues in women's work*. London: GlassHouse Press.

Hoque, K., & Kirkpatrick, I. (2003). Non-standard employment in the management and professional workforce: Training, consultation and gender implications. *Work, Employment and Society, 17*(4), 667–690. doi:10.1177/0950017003174004.

Lewis, J., Campbell, M., & Huerta, C. (2008). Patterns of paid and unpaid work in Western Europe: Gender, commodification, preferences and the implications for policy. *Journal of European Social Policy, 18*(1), 21–37. doi:10.1177/0958928707084450.

Lyonette, C., & Crompton, R. (2008). The only way is up? An examination of women's 'underachievement' in the accountancy profession in the UK. *Gender in Management, 23*(7), 506–521. doi:10.1108/17542410810908857.

Lyonette, C., Baldauf, B., & Behle, H. (2010, March). *"Quality" part-time work: A review of the evidence*. Government Equalities Office. http://sta.geo.useconnect.co.uk/publications_and_research/research/quality_part_time_work_eviden.aspx. Accessed 17 June 2014.

McRae, S. (2003). Constraints and choices in mothers' employment careers. *British Journal of Sociology, 54*(3), 317–338.

OECD. (2010, March). *Gender brief*, social policy division. Organisation for Economic Co-operation and Development. http://www.oecd.org/els/family/44720649.pdf. Accessed 17 June 17 2014.

ONS. (2012). *Underemployed workers in the UK, 2012*. Office for National Statistics. http://www.ons.gov.uk/ons/rel/lmac/underemployed-workers-in-the-uk/2012/index.html. Accessed 17 June 2014.

Procter, I., & Padfield, M. (1998). *Young adult women, work, and family: Living a contradiction*. London/Washington, DC: Mansell.

Román, A. (2006). *Deviating from the standard: Effects on labor continuity and career patterns*. Amsterdam: Dutch University Press.

Rubery, J., & Fagan, C. (1994). Does feminization mean a flexible labour force? In R. Hyman & A. Ferner (Eds.), *New frontiers in European industrial relations* (pp. 140–166). Oxford: Blackwell.

Scott, J., & Dex, S. (2009). Paid and unpaid work: Can policy improve gender inequalities? In J. Miles & R. Probert (Eds.), *Sharing lives, dividing assets: An interdisciplinary study* (pp. 41–60). Oxford, UK: Hart.

Smithson, J., Lewis, S., Cooper, C., & Dyer, J. (2004). Flexible working and the gender pay gap in the accountancy profession. *Work, Employment and Society, 18*(1), 115–135. doi:10.1177/0950017004040765.

Thompson, C. A., Beauvais, L. L., & Lyness, K. S. (1999). When work benefits are not enough: The influence of work-family culture on benefit utilization, organizational attachment, and work-family conflict. *Journal of Vocational Behavior, 54*(3), 392–415. doi:10.1006/jvbe.1998.1681.

Thornley, C. (2007). Working part-time for the state: Gender, class and the public sector pay gap. *Gender, Work and Organisation, 14*(5), 454–475. doi:10.1111/j.1468-0432.2007.00360.x.

Tilly, C. (1996). *Half a job: Bad and good part-time jobs in a changing labor market*. Philadelphia: Temple University Press.

Tomlinson, J. (2006). Part-time occupational mobility in the service industries: Regulation, work commitment and occupational closure. *The Sociological Review, 54*(1), 66–86. doi:10.1111/j.1467-954X.2006.00602.x.

Tomlinson, J., Olsen, W., & Purdam, K. (2009). Women returners and potential returners: Employment profiles and labour market opportunities – A case study of the UK. *European Sociological Review, 25*(3), 349–363.

Warren, T. (2003). A privileged pole? Diversity in women's pay, pensions and wealth in Britain. *Gender, Work and Organisation, 10*(5), 605–628. doi:10.1111/1468-0432.00213.

Warren, T. (2008). Universal disadvantage? The economic well-being of female part-timers in Europe. *European Societies, 10*(5), 737–762. doi:10.1080/14616690701757853.

Warren, T., Pascall, G., & Fox, E. (2010). Gender equality in time: Low-paid mothers' paid and unpaid work in the UK. *Feminist Economics, 16*(3), 193–219. doi:10.1080/13545701.2010.499997.

Wheelock, J., & Jones, K. (2002). 'Grandparents are the next best thing': Informal childcare for working parents in urban Britain. *Journal of Social Policy, 31*(3), 441–463. doi:10.1017/S0047279402006657.

Women and Work Commission (WWC). (2006). *Shaping a fairer future. From: Department for culture, media & sport, government equalities office*. Department for Education, Minister for Women and Equalities and others. http://image.guardian.co.uk/sys-files/Guardian/documents/2006/02/27/equality.pdf. Accessed 17 June 17 2014.

Chapter 6
Understanding the Precariousness of the Glass Cliff: An Examination of Social Resources and Global Context

Floor Rink, Michelle K. Ryan, and Janka I. Stoker

Introduction

Despite the fact that men still dominate the upper levels of management in most organisations today (e.g., Acker, 2009; Desvaux, Devillard-Hoellinger, & Baumgarten, 2007), women seem to be breaking slowly through the glass ceiling (Barreto, Ryan, & Schmitt, 2009; Heilman, 2001). For example, over the past six decades, the representation of women on top management boards of United States Fortune 500 largest corporations has steadily increased (Elacqua, Beehr, Hansen, & Webster, 2009). This rise in female executives has motivated researchers and organisations to examine whether women in positions of power still face gender-related barriers in the workplace. Recent findings suggest that they do. Careful analyses of the conditions under which women are appointed to leadership positions demonstrate that women tend to be preferred as leaders when a company is in crisis, whereas men are more likely to achieve leadership positions in times of stability and prosperity (e.g., Ryan & Haslam, 2005, 2007). This discriminatory phenomenon has been labelled the "glass cliff", as it occurs in senior management levels and entails a certain degree of precariousness for the women involved. After all, organisational crises are often attributed to the personal failure of the respective leaders,

F. Rink (✉) • J.I. Stoker
The Faculty of Economics and Business, The University of Groningen,
P.O. Box 800, Groningen, The Netherlands
e-mail: f.a.rink@rug.nl; j.i.stoker@rug.nl

M.K. Ryan
The Faculty of Economics and Business, The University of Groningen,
P.O. Box 800, Groningen, The Netherlands

Social and Organizational Psychology, University of Exeter, Exeter, UK
e-mail: M.Ryan@exeter.ac.uk

R.L. Gervais, P.M. Millear (eds.), *Exploring Resources, Life-Balance and Well-Being of Women Who Work in a Global Context*,
DOI 10.1007/978-3-319-31736-6_6

rather than to circumstances that are beyond their control (Hargie, Stapleton, & Tourish, 2010).

Anecdotally, the current economic crisis certainly underscores the existence of the glass cliff phenomenon. The past few years have brought about several clear examples of women who have been appointed to risky leadership positions within organisations that are going through rough times. For example, in 2008, Lynn Elsenhans was appointed as the first female leader of Sunoco, just after fuel demand was sinking and the company's shares had halved in value. She eventually had to step down after only 4 years in post (Jarrett, 2010). In 2009, it was announced that Rebekah Brooks would become the leader of News International following allegations of phone-tapping and misconduct at newspapers owned by the company. She resigned 2 years later amidst great public controversy and scandal. In 2014, General Motors (GM) appointed Mary Barra as the first female chief executive in the auto industry just before a severe recall crisis broke out. GM is currently threatened with several lawsuits because it had neglected to warn customers about faulty ignition switches to disable airbags in two of their car brands (Trop, 2014).

In this chapter, we provide a nuanced understanding of the glass cliff phenomenon. Based on recent findings, we propose that stereotypical beliefs about leadership and about gender underlie the preferences for female leaders during organisational crisis. Female leaders are expected to be better at establishing acceptance and cooperation among employees than are male leaders, and such leadership skills become more valuable when a company is in crisis. We will summarise a series of studies demonstrating that the availability of social resources during an organisational crisis impacts on the salience of these gendered leadership beliefs. In consequence, the availability of such resources contribute to (a) the appointment of women into leadership positions, (b) the precariousness of these positions, and (c) the way men and women themselves evaluate the positions. Moreover, we review the literature on the appointment of women into precarious leadership positions across national cultures that differ in their endorsement of gendered leadership beliefs. We argue that this difference is best reflected in the degree to which nations' cultures differ in their degree of masculinity. This cultural dimension refers to the extent in which emotional roles and values within the nation are divided among the genders (Hofstede, 1998). So far, no conclusive evidence can be found for the idea that one might expect glass cliff differences on the basis of this cultural dimension, which to our opinion, signals that the phenomenon is complex, subtle and multiple-determined.

Based on the findings and propositions we present, the chapter provides insights in the type of interventions organisations may employ to manage effectively gender-related discrimination at senior levels. Each year, organisations, consultancy firms, and government agencies provide a range of interventions, policy, and practice to ensure that women have the resources they need to fulfil their leader roles to their full potential. However, on this basis of our research, and following a recent report from McKinsey (Women Matter; Devillard, Sancier, Werner, Maller, & Kossoff, 2013), we argue that two interventions should stand out as being particularly useful: strong *top down* commitment to gender diversity, from chief executive officers (CEOs) and top management teams, and a *systematic* inclusion of women in recruitment and promotion pipelines (p. 16). Both interventions create tangible social resources for women in top positions and target prevalent gendered leadership beliefs. The interventions can, therefore, help to combat the glass cliff phenomenon internationally.

We first provide background information on the glass cliff phenomenon and gendered leadership beliefs. We then review the studies showing that the presence of social and financial resources relate to the phenomenon, followed by a discussion of the link between national cultures and the glass cliff. We end the chapter with the two interventions we propose.

The Glass Cliff

In 2003, a newspaper article published in *The Times* (Judge, 2003) concluded that Britain's top 100 companies might be better off without women in top leadership roles because of a negative relationship between the presence of women on boards and share price performance. This conclusion motivated Michelle Ryan and Alex Haslam to investigate whether the casual relationship between women and performance could not be interpreted differently: maybe women were only appointed to leadership positions when companies were performing poorly. Indeed, initial research found evidence for this reverse logic, and introduced the glass cliff phenomenon: while men were generally appointed to a board position when the financial performance of the organisation was stable, women were more likely to be considered for this position after the share price of the organisation had decreased (Ryan & Haslam, 2005).

Over the last 10 years, the glass cliff phenomenon has been replicated in experimental studies, field studies, and in archival data and was observed in business and political samples from the United States, the United Kingdom, Germany, Sweden, Spain, the Netherlands, Australia, the Philippines, and China (for a review see Bruckmüller, Ryan, Rink, & Haslam, 2014; Lam, McGuinness, & Vieito, 2014; Lampitoc & Ignacio, 2014; Mulcahy & Linehan, 2013). Together, these findings suggest that the glass cliff represents a global phenomenon that is relatively robust across sectors and across nations which vary in the degree to which women have been able to break through the glass ceiling.

Mechanisms Underlying the Glass Cliff

The nature of the glass cliff phenomenon troubles many researchers and diversity managers in practice. How can an organisational crisis lead to an increased preference for female leadership? And are these leadership positions indeed always precarious for women? Indeed, to combat gender inequality at the top of an organisation effectively, it is important to know the processes that might underlie this inequality and how pervasive and detrimental it might be (Bruckmüller et al., 2014). While the glass cliff is clearly a multiple-determined phenomenon (Ryan & Haslam, 2007), there are a number of explanatory mechanisms that are particularly relevant for this chapter: the appointment of women as a signal of change, gendered stereotypes of leadership and men and women, and the availability of resources.

Several researchers argue that the glass cliff phenomenon exists because organisations in crisis are compelled to divert from standard practices and can no longer rely on "old" leadership habits (e.g. Brown, Diekman, & Schneider, 2011; see also Diekman & Eagly, 2000). These scholars demonstrate that women are more likely to embody the notions of renewed leadership, while men are generally seen as typical leaders that represent the "status quo" (Brown et al., 2011). There is indeed some evidence that individuals within societies interpret the appointment of women into male-dominated top positions as a signal for change (Bruckmüller & Branscombe, 2010; Ryan, Haslam, & Postmes, 2007).

The most investigated explanation for the glass cliff phenomenon is that women might be appointed to relatively risky leadership positions because of gendered leadership beliefs (Ryan, Haslam, Hersby, & Bongiorno, 2011; see also Bruckmüller & Branscombe, 2010). Individuals within societies generally view and evaluate men and women in light of stereotypical traits. Research consistently demonstrates that men are believed to possess agentic traits, such as being forceful, independent, logical, competitive, resilient, and decisive, whereas women are believed to possess more communal traits, such as being intuitive, spontaneous, caring, cooperative, flexible, emotional, and thorough (Koenig, Eagly, Mitchell & Risthani, 2011). Social role theory posits that these normative beliefs have developed over time, due to the different tasks allocated to each gender and the gendered divisions of work that prevail in society (Eagly & Karau, 2002).

Because the agentic traits commonly associated with men largely overlap with stereotypical beliefs of what it means to be a good leader (e.g., Heilman, 2001), people generally assume that men are better able to fulfil a leadership position than are women (Eagly & Sczesny, 2009). In other words, people tend to hold a "think manager-think male" association (Schein, 1973). Yet research shows that in times of crisis, when organisations face many uncertainties and internal conflicts, this association is weakened (e.g., Pillai, 1996; Ryan et al., 2011). Under these circumstances, people tend to value a communal leadership style that is more characteristic for women, and this explains, at least in part, the appointment of women to such positions (Bruckmüller & Branscombe, 2010; Gartzia, Ryan, Balluerka & Aritzeta, 2012). These findings suggest that women are not only appointed to risky leadership positions to signal change, they are appointed primarily because organisations believe that women possess the leadership skills necessary in times of crisis. In this way, individuals' preference for female leaders in times of crisis is informed by traditional gender-related stereotypes about how women tend to behave and when they tend to excel.

Context Dependency of the Glass Cliff

While gendered leadership beliefs are clearly a central explanation for the glass cliff phenomenon, it is important to note that gendered leadership beliefs are flexible across time and across contexts. In recognition of this, recent research has begun to test the context dependency of the glass cliff phenomenon. These studies show that not all organisational crises are the same, and that some crises are less likely to call for communal leadership traits than others (Bruckmüller & Branscombe, 2010; Ellemers, Rink, Derks, & Ryan, 2012; Ryan et al., 2011).

The glass cliff phenomenon tends to occur when organisations are faced with a crisis which is either characterised by internal struggles and conflicts or requires inward facing management solutions. Here, decision-makers tend to make a think crisis-think female association, favouring female leaders at least in part because they are thought to be most effective in appeasing the parties involved and managing personnel issues (Ryan et al., 2011). Yet, when organisations are confronted with a threatening external business environment or require active external facing management solutions, higher management continues to rely on the "think manager-think male" association, believing that the crisis context requires a directive leader (e.g., Ryan et al., 2011; Van Vugt, De Cremer, & Janssen, 2007).

Continuing this line of research, the chapter discusses two other ways in which to examine the context dependency of the glass cliff. First, we overview a line of research demonstrating that the occurrence of the glass cliff is dependent also on the presence of social resources during an organisational crisis. Second, we propose that the national context in which an organisation crisis takes place may impact on the phenomenon.

Social Resources and the Glass Cliff

Although an organisational crisis may facilitate organisational stakeholders (such as the board or senior management) to be supportive of a new leader so that he or she can change current practices, there is also evidence suggesting that under certain circumstances these stakeholders may be more hesitant about new leadership. For example, research demonstrates that it is difficult to discern the trustworthiness of a new leader (Rink, Kane, Ellemers, & Van der Vegt, 2013). Moreover, stakeholders can fear that new leadership may endanger their own positions and create disturbance (Friedman & Saul, 1991). Although stakeholder support is not the only social resource available to new leaders (they can have employee support); it is highly essential for their effective functioning (e.g., Haslam, Reicher, & Platow, 2011). Leaders who have to implement organisational changes or need to make tough staffing decisions in times of crisis experience more difficulties when these powerful stakeholders are not supportive of these plans (Abrams, de Moura, Marques, & Hutchison, 2008).

On the basis of the literature on gendered leadership beliefs, it can be inferred that the absence of this social resource would augment the occurrence of the glass cliff phenomenon. Any manager or employee who learns that a new leader lacks social resources during the crisis should recognise the importance of a leader with a cooperative attitude and the interpersonal skills to create acceptance among stakeholders. As these are traits that are stereotypically associated with women, these managers and employees should favour a female leader over a male leader in this specific crisis situation. This is less likely to be the case when a new leader does have access to social resources during a crisis, because here stereotypical feminine leadership traits are less needed.

To test these ideas, we conducted a programmatic series of four scenario studies. In a first paper, we conducted two studies among in total $n=261$ Dutch bachelor level degree students in Business and Economics (*M*age=20.51, *SD*=2.35). The first half of the sample was recruited to participate in Study 1 and the other half was subsequently recruited for Study 2. In each study, participants read about the appointment of a leader during a performance crisis, as in the classic glass cliff studies (Rink, Ryan, & Stoker, 2013). Yet they were additionally informed that the leader either could or could not count on the support and confidence from relevant stakeholders and the larger organisational network. The gender of the leader was also manipulated by providing a picture and a name of a man to half the participants, and a picture and the name of a woman to the other half (this manipulation was adopted from Ryan, Haslam, Hersby, Kulich, & Atkins, 2007). All participants received the same brief description of the leader's educational background and work experience. We subsequently measured participants' perceptions of the leader's effective and their beliefs of the leaders' ability to establish acceptance for their position within the company. In the second study, we additionally checked whether participants recognised the importance of social resources for a leader to manage successfully the organisation's crisis (e.g. Pearson & Clair, 1998). In this way, we could compare the precariousness of both leadership positions.

Across both studies, we found strong evidence that the availability of social resources influenced both participants' perceptions of the crisis situation and their beliefs about what constitutes effective leadership. In the crisis situation where social resources were available to the leader, participants in both studies held on to the traditional assumption that the male leader would be more effective than the female leader. Yet in the crisis situation where these resources were absent, the glass cliff phenomenon emerged. In this specific crisis context, the female leader was expected to be more effective than a male leader because the need to build and strengthen relations within the organisation was clearly more urgent. Participants' gender or age did not influence these results.

Importantly, across both studies the results demonstrate that stereotypical beliefs about gender and leadership roles underlie these effects. That is, when social resources were absent, participants evaluated the female leader more positively than the male leader because they expected that she would be better at establishing acceptance. Strikingly, the participants from Study 2 additionally acknowledged that the leadership position was more precarious when social resources were absent than when they were present. This finding confirms that the glass cliff effect can have detrimental consequences for women, as participants considered them for leadership positions that entail a greater risk of personal failure than the positions commonly allocated to men (Ryan & Haslam, 2007).

To advance our research, we additionally tested an alternative possibility for the glass cliff phenomenon that we observed, namely that women are perhaps more willing than men to accept a leadership position in times of crisis because they have so little opportunities to reach the top (Rink, Ryan, & Stoker, 2012). Since the uncovering of the phenomenon, this argument has been raised a number of times by researchers and the media. Research shows that women indeed do not lack ambition compared to men (Stoker, 2007), and evaluate any new job or position as do men. However, it is likely that women's and men's own evaluations of leadership positions could also be informed by gendered leadership beliefs. Indeed, prior research demonstrates that men and women are clearly aware of the existence of gender stereotypes in the workplace. Accordingly, they not only rely on these prevalent gender norms to evaluate others, but also rely on these norms to inform their own behaviour (Koenig & Eagly, 2005). Women themselves thus tend to believe that they are effective leaders when they can establish acceptances, whereas men tend to believe that they are effective leaders when they demonstrate authority and influence (Carli, 1990). Based on this process of self-stereotyping, we proposed that women should *not* be more (or less) attracted to precarious leadership positions than men. Rather, their evaluations of a risky leadership position should also depend on the availability of resources. Whereas women in general should be more motivated to work in a cooperative environment which matches the stereotype of their more communal leadership style, men in general should be more willing to work in an environment that enables them to fulfil the stereotype of their more agentic style.

We conducted another two studies among a total of $n = 280$ Dutch bachelor level degree students in Business and Economics (Mage$=21.72$, $SD = 4.70$). Again, half of this sample was used for Study 1 and the other half for Study 2. This time, participants were asked to imagine that they themselves were working for a large company that had experienced a financial crisis recently. They were offered a leadership position, where they would be in charge of resolving the crisis. As our proposition applied to women *and* men, we not only varied the presence of social resources (i.e., the presence of stakeholder support); we also varied the presence of financial resources (i.e., the presence of financial means to implement change). For one of the studies, the first group of participants read that they would have access to both types of resources, the second group of participants read that they only had access to financial resources (no social resources) and the third group of participants read that they only had access to social resources (no financial resources). We subsequently asked participants to evaluate the leadership positions and measured their beliefs about what skills would be needed to become successful as a leader.

The findings demonstrated that the glass cliff cannot be attributed to the notion that women are more willing than men to accept any kind of leadership role, even risky ones. Comparing across genders, women seemed less likely than men to evaluate any of the risky leadership positions positively. As expected, however, it was also found that women's and men's own evaluations of risky leadership positions were guided by an internalisation of gendered leadership beliefs. Women viewed acceptance from the larger organisational network as a key factor needed to become a successful leader, so they were particularly less likely to accept the position that lacked social resources. Men, on the other hand, believed that access to social resources was less important, and believed that financial means would help them to become a successful leader. They were therefore less inclined to accept the position that lacked financial resources. These effects were again not influenced by students' age.

To conclude, by comparing male and female participants' responses to leadership positions in crisis positions with differential access to important resources, our research across four studies provides further evidence for the context dependency of the glass cliff phenomenon. We demonstrated that the phenomenon only occurred in precarious crisis situations characterised by a lack of social resources. When these resources were present, men were also seen as effective crisis managers. Moreover, we found evidence that the glass cliff phenomenon did not occur because women themselves selected this leadership position. They, in fact, recognised that the position was relatively precarious when it was made clear to them that there were no social resources. Rather, the effect was explained by gendered leadership beliefs; in the crisis situation where social resources were absent, people preferred a female leader over a male leader because they believed that a communal, interpersonal leadership style was needed to solve the crisis. Most likely, women actually end up in these relatively risky leadership positions when the availability of social resources, or lack thereof, is not clearly communicated to them upfront.

Degree of Masculinity and the Glass Cliff

The context dependency of the glass cliff can also be examined by looking at the cultural context in which the phenomenon might occur, whether it is the organisational culture or the national culture. Although the phenomenon has been shown to exist across a range of countries, to date, no studies exist that systematically compared the occurrence of the phenomenon across different nations. Yet given that the glass cliff effect is multiple determined and given our research demonstrating that the context of the crisis matters, we expect the degree to which countries have a masculine culture to impact it as well. Research up until now has demonstrated that the phenomenon prevails in countries where women's participation in the work force is relatively large (e.g., the United States, the United Kingdom, the Netherlands, Australia and Sweden; Bruckmüller et al., 2014) but also in countries were women's position in the labour market is considerably weaker (e.g., the Philippines and China; Lam et al., 2014; Lampitoc & Ignacio, 2014). So it is unlikely that women's position in the labour market in general will simply determine the occurrence of the glass cliff effect. But if we go one step further, there are reasons to suggest, however, that the degree of masculinity within a country or within an organisation will influence *the management level* at which the effect emerges.

Hofstede (2001) argues that a national culture reflects the patterns of thinking and behaving that people from the same social environment share and learned throughout their lifetime. He discovered that the values within national cultures could be classified into five distinct dimensions: Power Distance, Individualism versus Collectivism, Uncertainty Avoidance, Long-term Orientation and Masculinity versus Femininity. While the first four dimensions may inform gender relations within a certain culture, the last dimension directly taps into these relations, as it reflects the existence of traditional gendered-related roles in a society (Hofstede, 1998, 2000). We will therefore focus on this dimension in this chapter.

When a national culture is highly masculine, people tend to value goals concerned with assertiveness, and society at large is relatively competitive (e.g. people are focused on earnings, advancement and respect). More importantly however, the gender roles are clearly distinct; people hold strong stereotypical beliefs that "… men should be assertive, tough and focused on material success, whereas women should be more modest, tender and concerned with the quality of life" (Hofstede, Hofstede, & Minkov, 2010, p. 140). Examples of masculine nations include Japan, the United States, Germany, and Mexico. By contrast, when a national culture is more feminine, people tend to value relationships, and society at large is more consensus-oriented (e.g., people are focused on cooperation and nurturance; Cartwright & Gale, 1995). In these cultures, the gender roles overlap more, such that both men and women are believed to possess agentic as well as communal traits (Hofstede et al., 2010). Feminine nations include Nordic and Northern European nations such as Finland, Sweden and the Netherlands, but they also include Costa Rica and Thailand.

Research suggests that the degree of masculinity within a nation's culture is associated with the extent to which women are faced with career barriers at work and are, thus, able to break through the glass ceiling. The wage gap between men and women is wider in masculine organisations than in feminine organisations (Ward & Mueller, 1985) and the work arrangements are less flexible in masculine organisations than in feminine organisations (Liff & Ward, 2001). Although the causality of this association has not yet been established, Hofstede assumes that the degree of masculinity of a nation's culture should have stronger effects on the position of men and women in the workplace than vice versa. He argues that this cultural dimension is based on the social roles within society at large, not only on labour divisions within the nation. Moreover, Hofstede demonstrates that in masculine cultures, employees (and managers alike) tend to prefer relatively agentic leaders who manage organisational conflicts in assertive ways (e.g., "Let the best man win", Hofstede et al., 2010; see also Van Oostrum & Rabbie, 1995), which tentatively indicates that culture influences people's expectations of others.

Together, the above research suggests that it is more difficult for women to reach top management positions in masculine cultures than in feminine cultures. We therefore propose that a culture of masculinity (either at the level of the organisation or the country) may also represent an important context factor that influences the glass cliff phenomenon. Although it is known that the effect takes place in masculine as well as feminine countries, we expect that it is likely to be more or less prevalent at different management levels. In some masculine countries, which are characterised by distinct gender roles and a preference for agentic leadership, the progression of women into high profile leadership may be so constrained that it is not yet influenced by organisational crises. In such countries, for example, China and Japan, the glass cliff effect may instead occur at lower or mid-management levels where women's suitability for leadership positions is now being considered. Indeed there is evidence in Japan that when faced with a crisis, organisations do not appoint women, but rather, they appoint foreign nationals (Kaplan & Minton, 1994). It should be noted however that some countries classified as masculine, such as the United States, do not conform to this expectation, and it is likely that the other Hofstede dimensions, such as Individualism and Power Distance may play an important role here.

By contrast, in feminine cultures, which are characterised by more equal gender roles and a preference for participative leadership, such as Sweden for example, there is evidence that women are currently breaking through the glass ceiling and gaining more career possibilities. So in these countries, the glass cliff effect may be more prevalent at top management levels.

To conclude, we propose that in masculine contexts, the glass cliff phenomenon conveys yet another career barrier for women to reach the top, whereas in feminine countries, the phenomenon may represent a unique barrier for women once they have achieved a top position. This proposition does not imply that the precariousness of the biased preference for a female leader in times of crisis is culturally determined. Whether women have to lead a team, department or organisation through a crisis, there are always personal risks involved which lower the chances of success. At lower management levels, failure will complicate women's progression into top positions even further; whereas failure in the upper echelons will endanger the positions of women who had been able to reach it.

Discussion

This chapter overviews more recent gains in our understanding of the glass cliff phenomenon. Although men are typically over-represented in leadership positions, women are preferred as leaders in times of crisis. As a result, women tend to be placed in precarious leadership positions in which it is more difficult to succeed. On the basis of existing research and some of our own work, we argued in this chapter that the glass cliff phenomenon is an outcome, at least in part, of gendered leadership beliefs. Men are seen as typical leaders because they are believed to possess the agentic traits commonly associated with effective leadership. However, during organisational crises, women are preferred as leaders because our study participants expected them to be better at solving conflicts and creating cooperation (i.e., to possess communal traits).

Implications

Given that gendered leadership beliefs play a role in the glass cliff phenomenon, we argue that the effect should occur primarily in crisis contexts where these beliefs are highly salient. We presented one clear context in which this is the case; when the decision to appoint a new leader during an organisational crisis was not fully supported by relevant stakeholders. Under these circumstances, the participants in our studies clearly prefer a female leader because she is expected to solve the crisis with her communal leadership style. When, however, a new leader can rely on this important social resource during a crisis, our study participants reverted to their beliefs that a male leader would be more effective in managing the situation. While this finding implies that women are not preferred as leaders in all crises, it shows that women are likely to be appointed as leaders in more precarious crisis situations than men.

On the basis of our findings, we proposed further that the degree of masculinity within which an organisation operates should impact the management level at which the glass cliff effect is most prevalent. The effect should be more visible at mid-management levels in masculine cultures, where there are distinct gender roles and only very few women occupy high-profile leadership positions. Yet in feminine cultures, where there are more equal gender roles and women are increasingly seen as effective leaders, the effect should occur primarily at top-management levels. The possibility that the glass cliff effect emerges at different management levels warrants empirical examination but would explain why the phenomenon has been observed across a range of different nations worldwide. Moreover, this possibility would also provide further evidence that the phenomenon has far reaching consequences for women. It is a common saying that those who climb high can fall hard. Indeed, for women who encounter the phenomenon at top management levels, failure may lead to costly transfers or public resignations. Yet, as said, for women who encounter the phenomenon at lower management levels, failure complicates their career mobility and may result in even greater social isolation.

Interventions

Organisations and diversity executives should be aware that reliance on gender stereotypes in making leadership appointments can be detrimental for women and may lead to glass cliff situations. Based on one of their recent surveys among 1400 managers worldwide (Devillard et al., 2013), McKinsey and Company concluded that the interventions organisations develop to enhance gender diversity in top management have more impact on women's beliefs that they can be successful leaders than their own personal mindsets. The survey also revealed that women *do* want to succeed; they are only less confident than their male counterparts that they will. The report proposes a range of diversity interventions to battle gender discrimination at work, but we consider two of them to be most important: a *systematic* inclusion of women in recruitment and promotion pipelines and strong CEO and *top down* commitment to gender diversity (see page 16 of the McKinsey report).

These two interventions may help overcome gendered leadership beliefs and create resourceful work conditions for women in a number of important ways. For example, the inclusion of women in recruitment and promotion pipelines will reduce the reliance on gender stereotypes during appointment processes and makes it more likely that women will become more involved in succession plans (Van den Brink, Benschop, & Jansen, 2010). Top down commitment towards gender diversity from higher management will ensure the presence of social support from relevant stakeholders to women who are appointed to leadership positions. Moreover, it may create a new tradition of sponsoring, rather than mentoring, women. Ibarra, Carter, and Silva (2010) demonstrated that while more women than men have mentors, men are more likely to advance in their careers because they are actively sponsored. Sponsoring implies pairing mentees with top executives to increase the female talent pool's exposure to these top positions and to ensure that these women have influential advocates for promotion. Clearly, only top management has the power to enable careers, so their commitment to gender diversity is more likely to result in concrete actions to help women's advancement. Finally, the last intervention also makes it more likely that there are sufficient networking opportunities and role models for both men and women. In cases where women are believed to be particularly suitable to manage unsupported leadership positions, these networks may provide them with important alternative social resources to bear upon (Rink, Ryan, & Stoker, 2013).

Conclusion

To conclude, although the glass cliff phenomenon illustrates that women are more likely to be placed in precarious leadership positions than are men, a systematic inclusion of women into promotion committees can prevent this from happening. When the effect does take place, top management support can ensure that both women and men are more likely to see risky leadership offers in times of crisis as a challenge, rather than as a cliff (Rink, Ryan, & Stoker, 2013).

References

Abrams, D., de Moura, G. R., Marques, J., & Hutchison, P. (2008). Innovation credit: When can leaders oppose their group's norms? *Journal of Personality and Social Psychology, 95*, 662–678. doi:10.1037/0022-3514.95.3.662.

Acker, J. (2009). From glass ceiling to inequality regimes. *Sociologie du Travail, 51*, 199–217. http://dx.doi.org/10.1016/j.soctra.2009.03.004.

Barreto, M., Ryan, M., & Schmitt, M. (2009). *The glass ceiling in the 21st century: Understanding barriers to gender equality*. Washington, DC: American Psychological Association.

Brown, E. R., Diekman, A. B., & Schneider, M. C. (2011). A change will do us good: Threats diminish typical preferences for male leaders. *Personality and Social Psychology Bulletin, 37*, 930–941. http://dx.doi.org/10.1177/0146167211403322.

Bruckmüller, S., & Branscombe, N. R. (2010). The glass cliff: When and why women are selected as leaders in crisis contexts. *British Journal of Social Psychology, 49*, 433–451. http://dx.doi.org/10.1348/014466609X466594.

Bruckmüller, S., Ryan, M. K., Rink, F., & Haslam, A. (2014). Beyond the glass ceiling: Exploring and explaining the glass cliff in order to inform organizational policy. *Social Issues and Policy Review, 8*, 202–232. doi:10.1111/sipr.12006.

Carli, L. L. (1990). Gender, language, and influence. *Journal of Personality and Social Psychology, 59*, 941–951. http://dx.doi.org/10.1037//0022-3514.59.5.941.

Cartwright, S., & Gale, A. (1995). Project management: Different gender, different culture? A discussion on gender and organizational culture – Part 2. *Leadership & Organization Development Journal, 16*, 12–16. http://dx.doi.org/10.1108/01437739510089058.

Desvaux, G., Devillard-Hoellinger, S., & Baumgarten, P. (2007). *Women matter: Gender diversity, a corporate performance driver*. New York: McKinsey & Company.

Devillard, S., Sancier, S., Werner, C., Maller, I., & Kossoff, C. (2013). *Women matter 2013. Gender diversity in top management: Moving corporate culture, moving boundaries*. Paris: McKinsey & Company.

Diekman, A. B., & Eagly, A. H. (2000). Stereotypes as dynamic constructs: Women and men of the past, present, and future. *Personality and Social Psychology Bulletin, 26*, 1171–1188. doi:10.1177/0146167200262001.

Eagly, A. H., & Karau, S. J. (2002). Role congruity theory of prejudice toward female leaders. *Psychological Review, 109*, 573–598. http://dx.doi.org/10.1037//0033-295X.109.3.573.

Eagly, A. H., & Sczesny, S. (2009). Stereotypes about women, men, and leaders: Have times changed? In M. Barreto, M. K. Ryan, & M. T. Schmitt (Eds.), *The glass ceiling in the 21st century: Understanding barriers to gender equality* (pp. 21–48). Washington, DC: American Psychological Association.

Elacqua, T. C., Beehr, T. A., Hansen, C. P., & Webster, J. (2009). Managers' beliefs about the glass ceiling: Interpersonal and organizational factors. *Psychology of Women Quarterly, 33*, 285–294. doi:10.1111/j.1471-6402.2009.01501.x.

Ellemers, N., Rink, F., Derks, B., & Ryan, M. K. (2012). Women in high places: When and why promoting women into top positions can harm them individually or as a group (and how to prevent this). *Research in Organizational Behavior, 32*, 163–187. http://dx.doi.org/10.1016/j.riob.2012.10.003.

Friedman, S. D., & Saul, K. (1991). A leader's wake: Organizational members' reactions to CEO succession. *Journal of Management, 17*, 619–643. doi:10.1177/014920639101700306.

Gartzia, L., Ryan, M. K., Balluerka, N., & Aritzeta, A. (2012). Think crisis-think female: Further evidence. *European Journal of Work and Organizational Psychology, 21*, 603–628.

Hargie, O., Stapleton, K., & Tourish, D. (2010). Interpretations of CEO public apologies for the banking crisis: Attributions of blame and avoidance of responsibility. *Organization, 17*, 721–742. doi:10.1177/1350508410367840.

Haslam, S. A., Reicher, S. D., & Platow, M. J. (2011). *The new psychology of leadership: Identity, influence, and power*. New York: Psychology Press.

Haslam, S. A., & Ryan, M. K. (2008). The road to the glass cliff: Differences in the perceived suitability of men and women for leadership positions in succeeding and failing organizations. *Leadership Quarterly, 19*, 530–546. http://dx.doi.org/10.1016/j.leaqua.2008.07.011.

Heilman, M. E. (2001). Description and prescription: How gender stereotypes prevent women's ascent up the organizational ladder. *Journal of Social Issues, 57*, 657–674. doi:10.1111/0022-4537.00234.

Hofstede, G. (1998). *Masculinity and femininity: The taboo dimension of national cultures.* Thousand Oaks, CA: Sage.

Hofstede, G. (2000). Whatever happened to masculinity and femininity? *Cross-Cultural Psychology Bulletin, 34*, 14–19.

Hofstede, G. (2001). *Culture's consequences: Comparing values, behaviors, institutions and organizations across nations* (2nd ed.). Thousand Oaks, CA: Sage.

Hofstede, G., Hofstede, G. J., & Minkov, M. (2010). *Cultures and organizations: Software of the mind: Intercultural cooperation and its importance for survival.* London: McGraw-Hill.

Ibarra, H., Carter, N. M., & Silva, C. (2010). Why men still get more promotions then women. *Harvard Business Review, 88*, 80–85.

Jarrett, C. (2010, September 15). Why are women chosen to lead organizations in a crisis? *The British Psychological Society.* Retrieved from http://bps-research-digest.blogspot.com/2010/09/why-are-women-chosen-to-lead.html

Judge, E. (2003, November 11). Women on board: Help or hindrance? *The Times,* 21.

Kaplan, S., & Minton, B. (1994). Appointments of outsiders to Japanese boards: Determinants and implications for managers. *Administrative Science Quarterly, 37*, 282–301. http://dx.doi.org/10.1016/0304-405X(94)90025-6.

Koenig, A. M., & Eagly, A. H. (2005). Stereotype threat in men on a test of social sensitivity. *Sex Roles, 52*, 489–496. doi:10.1007/s11199-005-3714-x.

Koenig, A. M., Eagly, A. H., Mitchell, A. A., & Ristikari, T. (2011). Are leader stereotypes masculine? A meta-analysis of three research paradigms. *Psychological Bulletin, 137*, 616–642. doi:10.1037/a0023557.

Lam, K. C. K., McGuinness, P. B., & Vieito, J. P. (2014). CEO gender, executive compensation and firm performance in Chinese-listed enterprises. *Pacific-Basin Finance Journal, 21*, 1136fic-B. doi:10.1016/j.pacfin.2012.08.006

Lampitoc, R. R., & Ignacio, L. B. R. (2014). *Women in local legislation*, Antorcha, 1, open access.

Liff, S., & Ward, K. (2001). Distorted views through the glass ceiling: The construction of women's understandings of promotion and senior management positions. *Gender, Work and Organization, 8*, 19–36. doi:10.1111/1468-0432.00120.

Koenig, A. M., Eagly, A. H., Mitchell, A. A., & Ristikari, T. (2011). Are leader stereotypes masculine? A metaanalysis of three research paradigms. *Psychological Bulletin, 137*, 616–642. doi:10.1037/a0023557.

Mulcahy, M., & Linehan, C. (2013). Females and precarious board positions: Further evidence of the glass cliff. *British Journal of Management, 4*, 1–14. doi:10.1111/1467-8551.12046.

Pearson, C. M., & Clair, J. A. (1998). Reframing crisis management. *The Academy of Management Review, 23*, 59–76. http://dx.doi.org/10.2307/259099.

Pillai, R. (1996). Crisis and the emergence of charismatic leadership in groups: An experimental investigation. *Journal of Applied Social Psychology, 26*, 543–562. http://dx.doi.org/10.1111/j.1559-1816.1996.tb02730.x.

Rink, F., Kane, A., Ellemers, N., & Van der Vegt, G. S. (2013). Team receptivity to newcomers: Five decades of evidence and future research themes. *The Academy of Management Annals, 7*, 1–47. doi:10.1080/19416520.2013.766405.

Rink, F., Ryan, M. K., & Stoker, J. I. (2012). Influence in times of crisis: Exploring how social and financial resources affect men's and women's evaluations of glass cliff positions. *Psychological Science, 23*, 1306–1313. doi:10.1177/0956797612453115.

Rink, F., Ryan, M. K., & Stoker, J. I. (2013). Social resources at a time of crisis: How gender stereotypes inform gendered leader evaluations. *European Journal of Social Psychology, 43*(5), 381–392. doi:10.1002/ejsp.1954.

Ryan, M. K., & Haslam, S. (2007). The glass cliff: Exploring the dynamics surrounding the appointment of women to precarious leadership positions. *The Academy of Management Review, 32*, 549–572. doi:10.2307/20159315.

Ryan, M. K., & Haslam, S. A. (2005). The glass cliff: Evidence that women are over-represented in precarious leadership positions. *British Journal of Management, 16*, 81–90. doi:10.1111/j.1467-8551.2005.00433.x.

Ryan, M. K., Haslam, S. A., Hersby, M. D., Kulich, C., & Atkins, C. (2007). Opting out or pushed off the edge? The glass cliff and the precariousness of women's leadership positions. *Social and Personality Psychology Compass, 1*, 266–279. http://dx.doi.org/10.1111/j.1751-9004.2007.00007.x.

Ryan, M. K., Haslam, S. A., Hersby, M. D., & Bongiorno, R. (2011). Think crisis-think female: Glass cliffs and contextual variation in the think manager-think male stereotype. *Journal of Applied Psychology, 96*, 470–484. doi:10.1037/a0022133.

Ryan, M. K., Haslam, S. A., & Postmes, T. (2007). Reactions to the glass cliff: Gender differences in the explanations for the precariousness of women's leadership positions. *Journal of Organizational Change Management, 20*, 182–197. doi:10.1108/09534810710724748.

Schein, V. E. (1973). The relationship between sex role stereotypes and requisite management characteristics. *Journal of Applied Psychology, 57*, 95–100. http://dx.doi.org/10.1037/h0037128.

Stoker, J. I. (2007). Sekse en leiderschap: Over het feminiene voordeel en het masculiene vooroordeel. *M&O, 1*, 5–17.

Trop, J. (2014, April 30). Is Mary Barra standing on a glass cliff? *The New Yorker*. Retrieved from http://www.newyorker.com/online/blogs/currency/2014/04/mary-barra-general-motors-ceo--glass-cliff.html

Van den Brink, M., Benschop, Y., & Jansen, W. (2010). Transparency in academic recruitment: A problematic tool for gender equality? *Organizational Studies, 31*, 1459–1483.

Van Oostrum, J., & Rabbie, J. M. (1995). Intergroup competition and cooperation within autocratic and democratic management regimes. *Small Group Research, 26*, 269–294. http://dx.doi.org/10.1177/1046496495262006.

Van Vugt, M., De Cremer, D., & Janssen, D. P. (2007). Gender differences in cooperation and competition: The male-warrior hypothesis. *Psychological Science, 18*, 19–23. http://dx.doi.org/10.1111/j.1467-9280.2007.01842.x.

Ward, K. B., & Mueller, C. W. (1985). Sex differences in earnings: The influence of industrial sector, authority hierarchy, and human capital variables. *Work and Occupations, 12*, 437–463. http://dx.doi.org/10.1177/0730888485012004003.

Chapter 7
Support for Female Physicians at a University Hospital: What Do Differences Between Female and Male Physicians Tell Us?

Heidi Siller, Angelika Bader, and Margarethe Hochleitner

Support and Career Success

Workplace social support, thus the feeling that a person is valued, cared for and has access to direct or indirect forms of help, can originate from multiple sources such as supervisors, colleagues or the organisation (Kossek, Pichler, Bodner, & Hammer, 2011). Support in this understanding and career success or career satisfaction in women can be interrelated (Ng, Eby, Sorensen, & Feldman, 2005). Per definition, career success consists of subjective or objective aspects. Subjective aspects include, for example, career satisfaction, hence a positive feeling towards one's work-related achievements, whereas objective indices for career success include promotion, positions held and salaries (Ng et al., 2005). Ng et al. (2005) showed in their meta-analysis of career success that support, or as they call it organisational sponsorship, relates positively to career success. Organisational sponsorship was understood to be any kind of assistance provided by the organisation to support career success for its employees. Pachulicz, Schmitt, and Kuljanin (2008) reported that self-efficacy and/or perceptions of success are predictors of career success, especially in female physicians, whereas conflicts between job responsibilities and private life showed a negative relationship with career success. Additionally, they found that women battling with issues in their private life perceive organisational support to a lesser extent than do men; less often hold leadership positions; and have less control over work tasks; with all these findings pointing towards difficulties and hindrances for women in medicine (Pachulicz et al., 2008).

H. Siller (✉) • A. Bader • M. Hochleitner
Women's Health Centre, Medical University of Innsbruck,
Innrain 66, 6020 Innsbruck, Austria
e-mail: Heidi.Siller@i-med.ac.at; angelika.bader@tirol-kliniken.at;
margarethe.hochleitner@i-med.ac.at

R.L. Gervais, P.M. Millear (eds.), *Exploring Resources, Life-Balance and Well-Being of Women Who Work in a Global Context*,
DOI 10.1007/978-3-319-31736-6_7

To promote and support women in their career success, multiple facets have to be taken into account. First of all, it must be asked what support for women in (formerly) male-dominated areas implies. Simultaneously, we have to ask whether support for women in (formerly) male-dominated professions takes a different face than in non-male-dominated professions.

Regarding the work of physicians, it is noteworthy that the profession of physician was formerly male-dominated, whereas now increasing numbers of women have started to enter the medical profession (Levine, Lin, Kern, Wright, & Carrese, 2011; Levinson & Lurie, 2004; Morahan, Rosen, Richman, & Gleason, 2011; Walsh, 2013). However, the mere numerical increase in women in a male-dominated area does not necessarily imply genuine inclusion of women (Showalter, 1999). Genuine inclusion of women comprises equal representation of women at all hierarchical levels, such as senior and leading positions, and equal representation of women in all areas of a profession, e.g. in surgical specialities in the case of physicians. These equal representations are still lacking (Gjerberg, 2001; Ku, 2011; Ozbilgin, Tsouroufli, & Smith, 2011; Rizvi, Raymer, Kunik, & Fisher, 2012; Williams, Pecenco, & Blair-Loy, 2013). The equal representation of women in medical specialities was examined in a Swedish study of medical students in their last year. That study found almost no differences in preferred speciality choice (Diderichsen, Johansson, Verdonk, Lagro-Janssen, & Hamberg, 2013), whereas other studies of physicians have found gender differences in medical specialities (Gour et al., 2011; Ku, 2011; Ozbilgin et al., 2011). Johannessen and Hagen (2013) reported that women were under-represented in medical specialities with longer working hours with the exception of gynaecology, an observation also made by Ku (2011). Ku (2011) showed that speciality choices in first year medical students were as widely gendered as in residents. A difference in speciality choice might result from possibilities but also hindrances or challenges in pursuing such choice, even if preference for specialities is not always prevalent in students (Diderichsen et al., 2013). The definitive decision for a speciality will not only relate to individual interests, but also to other factors such as work-life balance and having a family with children. Along this line, Rizvi et al. (2012) stated in their review that in surgery, emergency medicine and primary care no conflicts between private life (i.e. having children) and professional life were reported, whereas difficulties arose in female physicians who were parents and worked at medical schools. Thus, gender differences in physicians might not necessarily relate to the medical profession in general, but might emerge when pursuing a career in academic medicine.

Barriers for Women in Male-Dominated Areas

Despite the (numerical) increase in women in male-dominated areas, barriers to genuine inclusion of women might exist. Bolton and Muzio (2007) described three major barriers for women in formerly male-dominated areas, taking the legal profession as an example. They describe stratification, thus more difficulties or even no possibility at all for women to enter senior positions; segmentation, such as gender-segmented areas even though the number of women in a specific profession is equal to that of men or even greater, and sedimentation, such as women forming powerful subgroups in an organisation. Segmentation in this context denotes specific knowledge in certain areas that is connected to attributions or traits considered either masculine or feminine. For example, women might more often choose specialties such as paediatrics, general or primary care medicine, whereas women are less often found in surgical specialties or hospital medicine (Gjerberg, 2001; Ozbilgin et al., 2011; Williams et al., 2013). This segmentation is also discussed in terms of working hours and work-family balance (Gjerberg, 2002; Ku, 2011; Ozbilgin et al., 2011) as the balance between professional and private life can be more easily achieved in some areas (e.g., due to shorter working hours), whereas it is more difficult to achieve in others (e.g., due to longer working hours, unpredictable work demands). Stratification and segmentation are two barriers to genuine inclusion of women that consequently lead to sedimentation. When women have conquered specific areas and become more organised to form (powerful) groups or subgroups within the organisation, women also reinforce their position as a subgroup by not adhering to the masculine environment that shaped the given male-dominated profession. Bolton and Muzio (2007) point out that

> [t]he paradox is that, in the process of sedimentation, women may be able to lay claim to an area of special knowledge, but at the same time they reinforce their position as 'other' in relation to the masculine code of the profession overall [...] (p. 59).

In this context it should be discussed whether the accessing, conquering and dominating of specific areas or segments of a profession by women will not result in genuine inclusion in the profession as exercise of the profession is restricted to specific areas. Even by gaining power in a subgroup and as a subgroup itself they remain the "others". The other side of this coin is that by conquering specific areas of one profession, power and influence can be built up step by step and this power can facilitate (other women) to access other areas, consequently resulting in future genuine inclusion in a profession at all levels and in all areas.

The under-representation of women in, for example, math-intensive sciences was in the past mainly attributed to a bias in hiring, funding and a gap in authorship, all to the disadvantage of women (Ceci & Williams, 2011). Ceci and Williams (2011) discussed the cause of this gender gap as a difference in resources and less access to high-quality resources for women. In their review they found no obvious sex discrimination in funding, distribution of grants or hiring procedures and thus Ceci and Williams posed the question "[i]f not discrimination, what is the cause of women's under-representation?" (p. 5). Their article focuses on the aspect of human reproduction and the fact that women might be less productive in science at a time when family and childcare would need more attention, than at times when this is not the case. They also discuss whether it would be better to provide more part-time tenure tracks to meet women's needs during their childcare years.

The increasing number of women and the generational change in the medical profession has also raised questions about work demands and working conditions in this profession. Long working hours, intense work demands and the impossibility to achieve work-life balance are increasingly the subjects of critical probing (Rizvi et al., 2012; Weinstein & Wolfe, 2007). Especially, work and family/private life are seen as hardly compatible with each other. As more women enter the medical profession these issues are raised, because it is still mainly women who do the household chores and care for the children (Siller, Bader, Waldenberger-Steidl, & Hochleitner, 2014; Walsh, 2013). Having a family and being responsible for childcare was also studied in conjunction with a preference for changing working hours, even though results on this issue were inconsistent. Some studies found that female physicians were more likely to state that they wanted to reduce working hours (Diderichsen et al., 2013; Rizvi et al., 2012), especially because of childcare concerns, whereas others found this connection significantly more often in men than in women (Heiligers & Hingstman, 2000). In their review, Rizvi et al. (2012) reported that female physicians felt less supported and experienced more conflicts in balancing working and private life than did their male counterparts. By also referring to the cumbersome progress of women in career advancement, Magrane et al. (2012) described in their *system of career influences model*, a dynamic relationship between individual choices and organisational culture that influences the advancement of women to higher ranks in academic medicine. For example, they stated that organisational culture is not designed for women to have different roles and combine family and work.

Strategies to Promote and Support Women in Their Career Success

By considering these difficulties and hindrances for women in male-dominated areas, strategies for how to best support women in these areas can be shaped at a more concrete level. Hence, support and promotion of women in male-dominated professions, but also in all other professions, cannot be viewed separately from the environment of the profession. The profession developed over centuries, thus including stereotypes, historical and social influences. This implies that the medical profession that was formerly male-dominated is also connected to specific masculine aspects and was not designed with a balance between childcare and work in mind (Magrane et al., 2012). Physicians have to adhere to these masculine aspects in order to be able to perform in this job. Jobs in a hospital setting demand high discipline with long working hours, the inability to predict work demands, the necessity to work weekend and night shifts, being on call (Fuß, Nübling, Hasselhorn, Schwappach, & Rieger, 2008; Gjerberg, 2003; Heiligers & Hingstman, 2000; Walsh, Gold, Jensen, & Jedrzkiewicz, 2005) and also it is compulsory to have an onsite presence (Siller et al., 2014). Additionally, patient care does not recognise public holidays and is a year-round task. These working conditions dominate the balance between working and family/private life and have to be taken into account when offering programmes to support women in their career.

Against this backdrop, support to women is discussed in terms of being better able to integrate personal goals, e.g., starting a family with children, and pursuing a career as a physician, especially at a university hospital, thus combining research and patient care. Almost two decades ago Showalter (1999) reported that despite the existence of crèches and other childcare facilities women less often pursued a career, especially in academic medicine, and less often held senior or leading positions. Lack of mentoring in surgery and urology was reported as a factor for leaving academic medicine (Rizvi et al., 2012). Levine et al. (2011) found in their qualitative study on female physicians that reasons for opting out of their academic career in an institution were lack of role models, lack of support in research activities and frustration with research, also because of competition between research teams and difficulties in raising funding, incompatibility between working and private life as well as an individualistic culture at the institution, where hardly any collaboration was possible, a preference for men and leadership styles.

The ongoing discussions and recommendations surrounding how to best support women in medicine and especially academic medicine have produced a number of approaches. For example, it is recommended that factors related to social, personal and organisational levels be included to achieve gender equality. These levels of support include institutional support in terms of mentoring programmes and policies that focus on gender equality (Carnes, Morissey, & Geller, 2008; Verlander, 2004; Yedidia & Bickel, 2001). Morahan et al. (2011) based their framework for the promotion of women in academic medicine on several questions that mirror the leadership continuum model and the institution-based framework. In this regard they ask whether programmes to support women in their career advancement include equipping women with the skills necessary for leadership roles, providing equal opportunities for career advancement, valuing relational skills and enhancing the visibility of women in all ranks and critically assessing but also revising the work culture, thus also taking organisational change into account. These four areas are always seen in relation to the preparation of women, but also in transition phases. According to Morahan et al. (2011) all steps are necessary for successful advancement of women in academic medicine.

Other factors supporting women include addressing the issue of work-life balance in terms of providing childcare facilities, job security and also addressing the status of women in academic medicine (Carnes et al., 2008; Yedidia & Bickel, 2001). Jagsi, Butterton, Starr, and Tarbell (2007) reported about the implementation of a programme to support female physicians, especially during child-rearing years, by offering financial support for research. This programme aimed at increasing the numbers of female physicians in higher ranks.

Taking these approaches and translating them to this medical university hospital, we see that some steps have already been taken. For example, mentoring programmes for women pursuing *venia docendi* (i.e., in Austria and some other European countries the *venia docendi* is an academic qualification to be pursued after the PhD; by completing the *venia docendi* the applicant shows that she/he is able to fully represent the discipline in research and teaching; e.g., Medizinische Universität Innsbruck, 2007), regulations aimed at having women hold 40 % of positions in all committees and at all hierarchical levels and a regulation regarding hiring staff, i.e., to give priority to female applicants over male applicants in cases of equal qualification, childcare facilities with prolonged opening hours have already been implemented (Medizinische Universität Innsbruck, 2004; Siller et al., 2014).

This study investigated how socio-demographic data such as gender and parenthood relate to research productivity, work strain and support. Research productivity was defined in terms of conducting research, authoring and co-authoring articles, and academic position. Work strain was calculated as working hours, percentage of overall time invested in tasks such as patient care, research, teaching and administration. Support was measured in terms of perceived support by supervisor, physician in the unit, other health care personnel, family/friends and having someone look after one's interests.

As mentioned above, at this medical university hospital support is provided by the organisation in the form of mentoring programmes for female physicians working on their *venia* and childcare facilities for staff employed at the medical university, regulations to achieve that 40 % of positions in all committees and at all hierarchical levels are held by women and a regulation regarding hiring staff, i.e., to give priority to female applicants over male applicants in cases of equal qualification (Medizinische Universität Innsbruck, 2004).

This study looked at whether hospital physicians perceived support provided by the organisation, more specifically by the supervisor, co-workers and other health care staff. It is hypothesised that caring for children exerts an influence on female physicians, but that having children does not exert an influence on male physicians with regard to work strain. Moreover, support provided by others is expected to be perceived differently by women and men. Even though there are activities to support women at this university hospital, women are expected to feel less supported by others and to participate less in research than men do, because of caring for children and other strains (e.g. household choirs, part-time contracts). Differences between women and men in pursuing an academic career in terms of acquiring the *venia docendi* were already found in other studies. It was seen that there was a delay in women in achieving the *venia docendi* (Siller et al., 2014).

Method

This study was part of a project aimed at investigating physicians at university hospitals in seven European countries. The study of "Health and Organisation among University Hospital Physicians in Europe" (HOUPE) is an ongoing project that seeks to investigate career path, work-related health, organisational culture and working conditions in university hospital physicians. The HOUPE project is an international network of researchers. It seeks to investigate national as well as international perspectives on the work and career of university hospital physicians (www.houpe.no).

The survey included instruments to assess psychological and social factors at work, general health, burnout, suicide ideation and the physician's career path. The General Nordic Questionnaire for psychological and social factors at work – QPS Nordic (Lindsträm et al., 1997; Lindsträm et al., 2000), the General Health Questionnaire – GHQ-12 (Goldberg & Williams, 1991), the Oldenburg Burnout Inventory – OLBI (Demerouti, 1999), Questions About Suicidal Ideation and Attempted Suicide (Meehan, Lamb, Saltzman, & O'Carroll, 1992) and the Physician Career Path Questionnaire – PCPQ (Fridner, 2004) were included in the project. An overview of the project, questionnaires and results from other countries can be found elsewhere (Andersen, Aasland, Fridner, & Lövseth, 2010; Fridner et al., 2009; Løvseth & Aasland, 2010; Løvseth, Fridner, Jónsdóttir, Marini, & Linaker, 2013). In this study the focus was set on the Austrian sample to explore the specific situation of university hospital physicians in this country.

The study was conducted as an online survey in English. A sufficient understanding of the English language is needed for research activities, a translation of the questionnaire into German was found to be obsolete. Data collection was centrally administered via the project's website (www.houpe.no), and every participant was given a code to access the questionnaire. The criterion for receiving an invitation to participate in the Austrian HOUPE survey was being employed as a physician at the medical university. This criterion was applied because the study focused on physicians who were engaged in achieving academic qualifications and simultaneously in patient care. Therefore, the intersecting experiences of physicians balancing these equivalent priorities were the main interest in all European countries. Data were collected in Austria from November 2012 to January 2013. Reminders were sent to all participants in order to increase response rate. In total, 111 of 482 physicians completed the questionnaire, giving a response rate of 22%. The project was approved by the Ethics Board of Innsbruck Medical University Hospital in Austria (UN4807).

Instruments

In this study the focus was set on the career path and perceived support of university hospital physicians in relation to parenthood. Thus, only those items that suited the aim of this study were included in analysis. For the analysis six items on work and career as a physician and three items on research activities were taken from the Physician Career Path Questionnaire – PCPQ (Fridner, 2004). For example, items on work as a physician included working hours, or perception of being accurately evaluated by the supervisor. Two items on perception that someone was looking after one's interests were taken from the General Nordic Questionnaire for psychological and social factors at work – QPS Nordic (Lindsträm et al., 1997; Lindsträm et al., 2000; Lindsträm, Peterson, Åsberg, Nygren, & Gustavsson, 2009) and three items on social support from others (Løvseth & Aasland, 2010; Løvseth et al., 2013) were included. The items on support were measured using a 5-point Likert scale ranging from not at all (1) to very much (5), whereby the other items were dichotomous and coded with no (0) or yes (1).

Statistical Analysis

Due to the small groups and the non-normal distribution of the sample non-parametric tests were used. Group comparisons were made with the Mann-Whitney *U* Test. Additionally Pearson's chi-square, Fisher's Exact Test, logistic regression analysis and loglinear analysis were used to assess the relationships between variables. Significance was tested on a .05 level, if not otherwise stated. Division into groups was based on being male or female and/or being a parent in order to assess specific experiences of subgroups among the participating physicians.

Participants

The sample consisted of 111 participants (44 women and 67 men). As mentioned previously 111 out of 482 (22 %) eligible physicians participated in the Austrian HOUPE survey. Female physicians were between 35 and 39 years of age, male physicians between 40 and 44 years. Of the female physicians 52 % lived with a partner and 23 % were in a partnership but did not live with the partner. Of the male physicians 74 % lived with a partner and only 9 % were in a partnership but did not live with the partner. Of the men 36 % and of the women 61 % were childless. Mothers had on average 2.5 children, fathers 3.1 children. Of the women 77 % took parental leave for their children as compared to 7 % of the men.

Results

Total Working Hours/Week and Tasks

Total working hours were calculated by adding working hours in hospital, private practice and other paid work. When looking at total working hours per week, the Mann-Whitney *U* Test revealed that men worked significantly more hours than did women. On average, men worked 57.5 h ($SD=16.4$), whereas women stated that they worked 48.9 h ($SD=25.5$), ($U=865.0$, $z=-3.5$, $p<.001$, 1-tailed, $r=-.34$).

Tasks performed by women and men revealed more similarities than differences. Women and men were equally engaged in patient care (mean percentage of time invested: men: 58 %, $SD=24$ %; women: 58 %, $SD=24.2$ %), research (mean percentage of time invested: men: 19 %, $SD=19.2$ %; women: 17 %, $SD=20.3$ %)

and teaching (mean percentage of time invested: men: 9 %, $SD=4.9$ %; women: 8 %, $SD=4.7$ %). Taking into account the fact that children could have an effect on distribution of tasks, it was obvious that the only effect was seen on women having children or not. Comparing women with and without children, it was found that mothers spent more time on patient care ($U=113.5$; $z=-2.3$; $p=.01$, 1-tailed, $r=-.36$), less time on research ($U=97$, $z=-2.3$, $p=.009$, 1-tailed, $r=-.37$) and less time on administrative tasks ($U=128$, $z=-2.0$, $p=.022$, 1-tailed, $r=-.31$), than did female physicians without children.

Clinical & Academic Position

A difference in clinical and academic positions was expected as medicine was formerly male-dominated and hierarchical structures in hospitals were not expected to fit women's multiple roles (e.g., being a mother and having a leading position). It was evident that the percentage of women and men was not significantly different with regard to holding clinical positions, being a specialist (men 42 %; women 39 %), being a resident doing specialist training (men 22 %; women 36 %), or being a chief physician (men 27 %; women 11 %). This finding is also in concordance with Rizvi et al. (2012). Due to the sample size, we clustered academic positions into four categories: none, PhD student, lecturer, and adjunct or full professor. It was found that women and men significantly differed in academic positions regarding being an adjunct or full professor (58 % men, 28 % women) ($\chi^2(3)=9.9$, $p=.02$). They did not differ in having a PhD (men 15 %; women 18 %) or being a PhD student (men 14 %, women 18 %).

These findings might indicate that gender differences in positions held, resulting from hierarchical structures and male-dominance in medicine, are not experienced in clinical positions, but seem to be an issue related to academia and research.

Women and men indicated similar research activities regarding collecting data (75 % of men, 75 % of women), analysing data (63 % of men, 64 % of women), writing articles (75 % of men, 59 % of women), being a project leader (37 % of men, 23 % of women), applying for funding (39 % of men, 36 % of women), supervising (46 % of men, 32 % of women) and being a formal responsible (30 % of men, 16 % of women). However, significant differences were found with regard to being a research leader (48 % of men, 23 % of women $\chi^2(1)=7.1$, $p=.009$). Additionally, being a research leader was less often true for mothers (χ^2 $(1)=8.9$, $p=.004$) compared to fathers (18 % of mothers, 61 % of fathers), whereas no difference between men and women without children (25 % of men, 26 % of women) was seen. The three-way loglinear analysis showed that all effects were retained. Thus, the likelihood ratio was χ^2 $(0)=0$, $p=1$, showing a significant highest order interaction (parent × research leader × sex, χ^2 $(1)=4.7$, $p=.03$). As reported above separate chi-square tests were performed for parents, women and men with regard to being a research leader. Also in terms of authoring articles, women stated that they less often authored an article in a scientific peer-reviewed journal (*Fisher's Exact Test*, $p = .001$) and they had less often co-authored an article as first or last author (above 51 articles, *Fisher's Exact Test*, $p = .02$) than did their male counterparts. Again, it was evident in parents that mothers had less often authored or co-authored peer-reviewed scientific articles, when it came to 100 or more articles (*Fisher's Exact Text*, $p = .001$), as compared to fathers.

Social Support

Except for not receiving support from anyone, no significant differences were seen in how respondents felt their interests were being looked after by others, whether supervisors, mentors, colleagues and/or labour unions.

A logistic regression was performed to ascertain the effects of gender and leadership support on the likelihood that participants feel supported by no one. The logistic regression model was statistically significant ($\chi^2(2) = 23.6$, $p < .001$). The model explained 27 % (*Nagelkerke* R^2) of the variance in support by no one and correctly classified 74 % of cases. Men were 3.2 times more likely to report not receiving support from anyone than were women. Increasing leadership support was associated with a reduction in the likelihood of not being supported by anyone.

Evaluation of Competence

To investigate the relationship between evaluation of competence and support, differences in feeling accurately evaluated by the supervisor were sought. Women and men felt their competence was evaluated accurately by their supervisor (52 % men; 54 % women), and ethnicity, sexual orientation and religion did not interfere. Gender, on the other hand, was perceived as interference in evaluation of competence by women (22.7 %), but not by men (0 %) (*Fisher's Exact Test*, $p < .001$).

Taking into account the fact that approximately half of the participating women and men felt they were accurately evaluated by their supervisor, the relationship between perceived accurate evaluation and perceived support by supervisor, other physician, health care personnel, spouse/partner and friends was analysed. The Mann-Whitney U Test revealed that those who felt accurately evaluated by their supervisor also stated that they felt supported by their supervisor ($U = 870.5$, $z = -3.9$, $p < .001$, 1-tailed, $r = -.37$) and other physicians in their unit ($U = 1050.0$, $z = -2.8$, $p = .002$, 1-tailed, $r = -.27$), whereas no significant differences for support from other health care personnel, spouse/partner and friends were found.

Splitting the sample by gender revealed that men felt more supported by their supervisor ($U = 275.5$, $z = -3.6$, $p < .001$, 1-tailed, $r = -.45$), by other physicians in their unit ($U = 296.0$, $z = -3.4$, $p < .001$, 1-tailed $r = -.42$) and by other health care personnel ($U = 330.5$, $z = -2.9$, $p = .001$, 1-tailed, $r = -.36$) when feeling accurately evaluated by their supervisor. Women felt supported by other health care personnel when not feeling accurately evaluated by their supervisor ($U=150.5$, $z=-2.0$, $p=.024$, 1-tailed, $r=-.31$). Feeling supported by others in general did not reveal any significant differences between women and men. Feeling supported by other health care personnel was true for mothers but not for female physicians without children ($U=143.5$, $z=-2.1$, $p=.016$, 1-tailed, $r=-.32$). A similar finding was revealed when performing a Mann-Whitney *U* Test on differences between mothers and fathers with regard to perceived support by others. Mothers felt more supported by other health care personnel ($U=238$, $z=-2.1$, $p<.015$, 1-tailed, $r=-.28$) than did fathers. This was a significant difference only between parents and was not significant when comparing women and men in general.

Discussion

Support of women in their career in medicine must take several issues into account. The male domination in this area is still noticeable, especially when taking into account the barriers mentioned by Bolton and Muzio (2007). Women in medicine are unevenly distributed in medical specialities and at hierarchical levels. However, this is noticeable in academic positions, but not in clinical positions, as was seen in the findings of the Austrian HOUPE survey and has also been discussed in other studies (Rizvi et al., 2012). The under-representation of women in higher ranks might thus refer to academic positions but not clinical positions. Thus, the question arises whether this is an effect of academia and science or of the medical profession as such.

Women and men did not differ in the amount of time they invested in patient care, research, teaching and administrative tasks, but when comparing only women with and without children it was also found that mothers spent more time on patient care and less on other tasks. This effect was not observed in men. These findings might point towards the greater responsibility of women in childcare, thus affecting their academic ambitions to a greater extent than those of their male counterparts. Childcare seems to be a female task because women report a greater responsibility in childcare and more time invested in childcare (Siller et al., 2014; Walsh, 2013). Therefore it is hardly surprising that programmes to support women in medicine also address the issue of childcare. Women are still affected by having children, but in terms of support in career advancement the study findings do not reveal whether it is still necessary to expand childcare facilities (e.g. opening hours, nationwide facilities, and financial support for fees) or whether the issue is a different one, namely independent of childcare.

Interestingly, women perceived that gender contributed to an inaccurate evaluation by their supervisor. Thus, it can be hypothesised that gender issues in promotion of women and the status of women in medicine are noticeable at this university hospital. This might stem from numerous activities surrounding these issues at this university hospital and might result in women having a greater awareness for the influence of gender on the perception of performance. This might possibly explain why men are more likely than women to report that they feel supported by no one because programmes for women and strategies to support women are more visible.

It was evident that even though on a general level no differences were found between women and men in time invested in patient care, research and administrative tasks, a difference was observed between mothers and women without children. Mothers spent more time on patient care and less time on research. A similar pattern was shown regarding being a research leader. It can be hypothesised that mothers might have less time to engage in research or in being a research leader as these tasks can also involve investing additional time in evenings, on weekends, for example because of deadlines to finish projects, preparation of project proposals, collection and analysis of data, meetings with colleagues or members of the specific research team, attending several international conferences and so forth. This additional time might have to be invested at the expense of spending time with children and therefore it is less possible for mothers to take on these tasks.

Additionally, mothers felt less supported by their supervisor than did women without children, and men, and felt more supported by other health care personnel. From this it is not possible to deduce whether this perceived support from other health care personnel stems from the larger number of women in nursing staff as well as the (possibly) larger number of mothers in nursing staff and thus the perceived support is connected to the shared characteristic of being a mother. It could also be the case that more time spent with other health care staff because of more time invested in patient care and less time spent with physicians from the same unit and the supervisor on research tasks results in greater perceived support from people with whom more time is spent.

The findings in this survey suggest that children affect women's careers. However, the small sample size did not permit further analysis of parents and the effect of children. Therefore, the findings have to be interpreted with care. The small sample size and the non-normal distribution of the sample limited analysis of all subgroups in the sample. Comparison should not only include women and men, but also parents, women with and without children, age groups and so forth. It is necessary to find groups that share the most characteristics with each other (e.g., age, with/without children, etc.) and to look for similarities and differences. From these findings it can be hypothesised that differences in conduct of research, work strain and support do not result from being male or female, but instead from having children, particularly in women.

Children exert an effect on a person's career, especially in women and in particular in academic medicine. It should not be the case that childlessness is a perquisite for a career in academic medicine. However, providing childcare facilities is evidently not enough (Showalter, 1999; Siller et al., 2014). Mentoring programmes, providing role models and financing research projects for women should be included as support for women wishing to engage in a successful career. Support of women resulting in programmes and strategies should include (1) childcare facilities (e.g., longer opening hours, nationwide offers, and financial support); (2) access to resources for women in academic medicine (e.g., access to research facilities during parental leave, sufficient number of staff, sufficient financial support for international conferences and the conduct of research, staff to assist in administrative tasks); (3) role models, mentoring, hiring procedures; (4) access to networks that include the supervisor and other physicians in order to enhance the likelihood of collaboration; (5) persistent progress in organisational development in order to facilitate women's various roles (e.g., being a mother, holding a leading position, engaging in research). In the long run women will genuinely be included in formerly male-dominated professions. Inclusion not only means a numerical increase in the number of women in medicine, but also in involvement in decision-making processes and ensuring that women are present in all ranks and positions.

Acknowledgments We would like to thank all participants in the study and the international project coordinator Lise Tevik Løvseth, PhD and the senior international project coordinator associate professor Ann Fridner, PhD for initiating the HOUPE study.

References

Andersen, G. R., Aasland, O. G., Fridner, A., & Lövseth, L. T. (2010). Harassment among university hospital physicians in four European cities. Results from a cross-sectional study in Norway, Sweden, Iceland and Italy (the HOUPE study). *Work: Journal of Prevention, Assessment & Rehabilitation, 37*(1), 99–110.

Bolton, S. C., & Muzio, D. (2007). Can't live with 'em; Can't live without 'em: Gendered segmentation in the legal profession. *Sociology, 41*(1), 47–64.

Carnes, M., Morissey, C., & Geller, S. E. (2008). Women's health and women's leadership in academic medicine: Hitting the same glass ceiling? *Journal of Women's Health, 17*(9), 1453–1462.

Ceci, S. J., & Williams, W. M. (2011). Understanding current causes of women's underrepresentation in science. *PNAS Proceedings of the National Academy of Sciences of the United States of America, 108*(8), 3157–3162.

Demerouti, E. (1999). Burnout. Eine Folge konkreter Arbeitsbedingungen bei Dienstleistungs- und Produktionstätigkeiten. [*Burnout. A consequence of specific working conditions among human service and production tasks*]. Frankfurt a.M.: Lang.

Diderichsen, S., Johansson, E. E., Verdonk, P., Lagro-Janssen, T., & Hamberg, K. (2013). Few gender differences in specialty preferences and motivational factors: A cross-sectional Swedish study on last-year medical students. *BMC Medical Education, 13*(39), 1–8. doi:10.1186/1472-6920-13-39.

Fridner, A. (2004). *Career paths and career patterns among physicians with a PhD.* Doctoral Dissertation, Department of Psychology, Uppsala University.

Fridner, A., Belkic, K., Marini, M., Minucci, D., Pavan, L., & Schenck-Gustafsson, K. (2009). Survey on recent suicidal ideation among female university hospital physicians in Sweden and Italy (The HOUPE Study): Cross-sectional associations with work stressors. *Gender Medicine, 6*(1), 314–328.

Fuß, I., Nübling, M., Hasselhorn, H.-M., Schwappach, D., & Rieger, M. A. (2008). Working conditions and work-family conflict in German hospital physicians: Psychosocial and organisational predictors and consequences. *BMC Public Health, 8*, 353–369.

Gjerberg, E. (2001). Medical women – Towards full integration? An analysis of the specialty choices made by two cohorts of Norwegian doctors. *Social Science & Medicine, 52*, 331–343.

Gjerberg, E. (2002). Gender similarities in doctors' preferences – And gender differences in final specialisation. *Social Science & Medicine, 54*(4), 591–605.

Gjerberg, E. (2003). Women doctors in Norway: The challenging balance between career and family life. *Social Science & Medicine, 57*, 1327–1341.

Goldberg, D., & Williams, P. (1991). *A user's guide to the general health questionnaire*. London: Nfer-Nelson.

Gour, N., Srivastava, D., Adhikari, P., Shahi, A., Sharma, M., & Mahajan, P. (2011). Specialty preference among medical students and factors affecting it. *Online Journal of Health and Allied Sciences, 10*(2). doi: http://www.ojhas.org/issue38/2011-2-12.htm

Heiligers, P. J. M., & Hingstman, L. (2000). Career preferences and the work-family balance in medicine: Gender differences among medical specialists. *Social Science & Medicine, 50*(9), 1235–1246.

Jagsi, R., Butterton, J. R., Starr, R., & Tarbell, N. J. (2007). A targeted intervention for the career development of women in academic medicine. *Archives of Internal Medicine, 167*(4), 343–3451.

Johannessen, K.-A., & Hagen, T. P. (2013). Individual and hospital-specific factors influencing medical graduates' time to medical specialization. *Social Science & Medicine, 97*, 170–175. doi:10.1016/j.socscimed.2013.08.026.

Kossek, E. E., Pichler, S., Bodner, T., & Hammer, L. B. (2011). Workplace social support and work–family conflict: A meta-analysis clarifying the influence of general and work–family-specific supervisor and organizational support. *Personnel Psychology, 64*(2), 289–313.

Ku, M. C. (2011). When does gender matter? Gender differences in specialty choice among physicians. *Work and Occupations, 38*(2), 221–262.

Levine, R. B., Lin, F., Kern, D. E., Wright, S. M., & Carrese, J. (2011). Stories from early-career women physicians who have left academic medicine: A qualitative study at a single institution. *Academic Medicine, 86*(6), 752–758.

Levinson, W., & Lurie, N. (2004). When most doctors are women: What lies ahead? *Annals of Internal Medicine, 141*, 471–474.

Lindsträm, I., Peterson, U., Åsberg, M., Nygren, Å., & Gustavsson, J. P. (2009). Psychometric properties of scales in the general Nordic questionnaire for psychological and social factors at work (QPSNordic): Confirmatory factor analysis and prediction of certified long-term sickness absence. *Scandinavian Journal of Psychology, 50*(3), 231–244. doi:10.1111/j.1467-9450.2008.00697.x.

Lindsträm, K., Dallner, M., Elo, A. L., Gamberale, F., Knardahl, S., Skogstad, A., et al. (1997). *Review of psychological and social factors at work and suggestions for the general Nordic questionnaire (QPSNordic): Description of the conceptual and theoretical background of the topics selected for coverage by the Nordic questionnaire*. Copenhagen, Denmark: Nordic Council of Ministers.

Lindsträm, K., Elo, A., Skogstad, A., Dallner, M., Gamberale, F., Hottinen, V., et al. (2000). *User's guide for the QPSNordic: General Nordic questionnaire for psychological and social factors at work*. Copenhagen, Denmark: Nordic Council of Ministers.

Løvseth, L. T., Fridner, A., Jónsdóttir, L. S., Marini, M., & Linaker, O. M. (2013). Associations between confidentiality requirements, support seeking and burnout among university hospital physicians in Norway, Sweden, Iceland and Italy (the HOUPE study). *Stress & Health: Journal of the International Society for the Investigation of Stress, 29*(5), 432–437. doi:10.1002/smi.2479.

Løvseth, L., & Aasland, O. (2010). Confidentiality as a barrier to social support: A cross-sectional study of Norwegian emergency and human service workers. *International Journal of Stress Management, 17*(3), 214–231.

Magrane, D., Helitzer, D., Morahan, P., Chang, S., Gleason, K., Cardinali, G., et al. (2012). Systems of career influences: A conceptual model for evaluating the professional development of women in academic medicine. *Journal of Women's Health (15409996), 21*(12), 1244–1251. doi:10.1089/jwh.2012.3638.

Medizinische Universität Innsbruck. (2004, April 16). Frauenförderungsplan der Medizinischen Universität [Plan for the promotion of women at the Medical University]: Mitteilungsblatt der Medizinischen Universität Innsbruck, 21. Stück.

Medizinische Universität Innsbruck. (2007, May 2). 133. Satzungsteil Habilitationsordnung der Medizinischen Universität Innsbruck [Statutes for venia docendi at the Medical University Innsbruck]. Mitteilungsblatt der Medizinischen Universität Innsbruck, 20. Stück.

Meehan, P. J., Lamb, J. A., Saltzman, L. E., & O'Carroll, P. W. (1992). Attempted suicide among young adults: Progress toward a meaningful estimate of prevalence. *American Journal of Psychiatry, 149*(41–44).

Morahan, P. S., Rosen, S. E., Richman, R. C., & Gleason, K. A. (2011). The leadership continuum: A framework for organizational and individual assessment relative to the advancement of women physicians and scientists. *Journal of Women's Health, 20*(3), 387–396.

Ng, T. W. H., Eby, L. T., Sorensen, K. L., & Feldman, D. C. (2005). Predictors of objective and subjective career success. A meta-analysis. *Personnel Psychology, 58*(2), 367–408.

Ozbilgin, M. F., Tsouroufli, M., & Smith, M. (2011). Understanding the interplay of time, gender and professionalism in hospital medicine in the UK. *Social Science & Medicine, 72*(10), 1588–1594. doi:10.1016/j.socscimed.2011.03.030.

Pachulicz, S., Schmitt, N., & Kuljanin, G. (2008). A model of career success: A longitudinal study of emergency physicians. *Journal of Vocational Behavior, 73*(2), 242–253.

Rizvi, R., Raymer, L., Kunik, M., & Fisher, J. (2012). Facets of career satisfaction for women physicians in the United States: A systematic review. *Women & Health, 52*(4), 403–421. doi:10.1080/03630242.2012.674092.

Showalter, E. (1999). Improving the position of women in medicine, Editorial. *BMJ: British Medical Journal (International Edition)*, 71–72. Retrieved from http://search.ebscohost.com/login.aspx?direct=true&db=aph&AN=1483169&site=ehost-live

Siller, H., Bader, A., Waldenberger-Steidl, B., & Hochleitner, M. (2014). Female and male physicians in academic medicine: Is work-life balance still an issue? In B. Thege, S. Popescu-Willigmann, R. Pioch, & S. Badri-Höher (Eds.), *Paths to career and success for women in science. Findings from international research* (pp. 191–206). Wiesbaden, Germany: Springer VS.

Verlander, G. (2004). Female physicians: Balancing career and family. *Academic Psychiatry, 28*(4), 331–336.

Walsh, A., Gold, M., Jensen, P., & Jedrzkiewicz, M. (2005). Motherhood during residency training. Challenges and strategies. *Canadian Family Physician, 51*, 991–997.

Walsh, J. (2013). Gender, the work-life interface and wellbeing: A study of hospital doctors. *Gender, Work & Organization, 20*(4), 439–453. doi:10.1111/j.1468-0432.2012.00593.x.

Weinstein, L., & Wolfe, M. (2007). The downward spiral of physician satisfaction. *Obstetrics & Gynecology, 109*(5), 1181–1183.

Williams, S. J., Pecenco, L., & Blair-Loy, M. (2013). *Medical professions: The status of women and men*. Retrieved June 27, 2014, from http://crgp.ucsd.edu

Yedidia, M., & Bickel, J. (2001). Why aren't there more women leaders in academic medicine? The views of Clinical Department Chairs. *Academic Medicine, 76*(5), 453–465.

Part IV
Balancing Work: Women's Choices and Their Lives Outside Work

Chapter 8
Managing the Work-Home Interface: The Experience of Women Academics

Gail Kinman

Roles, Work-Life Conflict and Well-Being

There is increasing concern about the ability of the workforce to manage the competing demands of work and personal life. Occupying multiple roles in life can have many psychological benefits; the acquisition of skills, resources and positive experiences in one role can improve the quality of life in other domains. Work-life facilitation is where resources provided in one domain contribute to enhanced functioning in another, whereas work can enrich other life domains by engendering feelings of fulfilment and satisfaction (Greenhaus & Powell, 2006; Wayne, Grzywacz, Carlson, & Kacmar, 2007). Nonetheless, there is strong evidence that the demands and expectations attached to different life roles have the potential to conflict. 'Role conflict' has been defined as a "situation in which differing role expectations result in incompatible role pressures, leading to psychological conflict for an individual as the pressures and role forces compete and conflict" (Korabik, Lero, & Whitehead, 2008).

Role conflict takes two forms: *intra-role conflict*, referring to incompatible requirements within the same role; and *inter-role conflict*, which is a clash between the demands of two or more roles (Katz & Kahn, 1978). Work-life conflict is a form of inter-role conflict; it draws upon resource-drain theory which maintains that personal resources (such as time, attention and physical and psychological energy) are limited, so fulfilling the requirements of one role will deplete the resources available to meet the demands of other roles (Edwards & Rothbard, 1999). This is discussed further below. Work-life conflict can be bi-directional in that work-related demands can interfere with responsibilities and activities outside work and the demands of

G. Kinman (✉)
Department of Psychology, University of Bedfordshire, Luton, UK
e-mail: Gail.Kinman@beds.ac.uk

R.L. Gervais, P.M. Millear (eds.), *Exploring Resources, Life-Balance and Well-Being of Women Who Work in a Global Context*,
DOI 10.1007/978-3-319-31736-6_8

personal life can conflict with the job role (Grzywacz & Marks, 2000). Nonetheless, there is evidence that work exerts a more powerful negative impact on non-working life than vice versa (Grzywacz & Demerouti, 2013; Kinman & Jones, 2001). The job role has the potential to 'spill over' into non-working life in several different ways (Netemeyer, Boles, & McMurrian, 1996):

- *Time-based conflict* occurs when the time spent in one role limits that available for other activities. For example, a heavy workload requires long working hours, which will limit the time available to recover from work demands and engage in family and social activities.
- *Strain-based conflict* arises when negative emotional reactions to work manifest themselves in personal life. This may lead to people feeling anxious, irritable or emotionally depleted outside work. They may also withdraw from personal relationships in an attempt to recover their psychological, physical and cognitive energy.
- *Behaviour-based conflict* is where problem-solving behaviours that are functional in one role are incompatible with those required in another. This type of conflict is thought to be more common in jobs requiring a high level of interdependency and responsibility for others (Dierdorff & Ellington, 2008).

There is also evidence that work can intrude cognitively into non-working life where people ruminate about work when in non-working environments. Excessive preoccupation with work-related concerns limits opportunities to detach from the job role by engaging fully in family life and leisure (Querstret & Cropley, 2012).

The various forms of work-life conflict can have a wide-ranging impact on well-being and functioning in both the work and personal domains (Michel, Clark, & Beiler, 2013). Employees may experience psychological symptoms including depression, anxiety and emotional exhaustion; they are also at increased risk of insomnia and physical health problems ranging from headaches to cardiovascular disease (Allen, Herst, Bruck, & Sutton, 2000). Conflict between work and non-working life can also encourage negative health behaviours such as poor eating habits and physical inactivity, as well as increased alcohol consumption in an attempt to reduce work-related tension (Payne, Kinman, & Jones, 2012). Evidence is also accumulating that people who experience chronic work-life conflict are at greater risk of raised cholesterol levels, and increased body mass index with clear implications for long term health status (Allen & Armstrong, 2006; Van Steenbergen & Ellemers, 2009).

Work-life conflict can impact on personal relationships and work-related functioning as well as health. Employees who experience more conflict tend to be less satisfied with their relationships with family and friends (Kinman & Jones, 2001). An employee's job-related stress can also 'cross over' to engender anxiety and depression in partners and children (Crossfield, Kinman, & Jones, 2005; Kinnunen, Rantanen, & Mauno, 2013). Conflict between work and non-working life has also been linked to key work-related outcomes such as lack of commitment, absenteeism and turnover (Eby, Casper, Lockwood, Bordeaux, & Brinley, 2005; Wayne, Casper, Matthews, & Allen, 2013). Limited opportunities to recover from job demands and concerns can also impair job performance by weakening cognitive abilities such as memory, attention and concentration (MacEwen & Barling, 1991; Odle-Dusseau, Britt, & Greene-Shortridge, 2012).

Work-Life Conflict: Job Type and Gender

A recent survey of medium and large employers in the United Kingdom (UK) indicated that poor work-life balance was considered a more serious threat to organisations than stress and mental health problems (Group Risk Development [GRiD], 2012). There is evidence that knowledge workers such as academic employees, who typically encounter high demands and lack firm boundaries between domains, may be particularly vulnerable to work-life conflict (Albertsen, Persson, Garde, & Rugulies, 2010; Lewis & Cooper, 2005). A review of the research findings from several countries suggests that academic work encompasses many of the characteristics associated with aspects of work-life conflict, such as high demand, role overload and long working hours (Doyle & Hind, 1998; Kinman, 2014; Kinman, Jones, & Kinman, 2006; Kinman & Wray, 2013; Kotecha, Ukpere, & Geldenhuys, 2014; Mark & Smith, 2012; Watts & Robertson, 2011; Winefield, Boyd, & Winefield, 2014; Winefield, Boyd, Saebel, & Pignata, 2008). Several studies suggest also that levels of psychological distress in the higher education sector are higher than those reported by many other occupational groups and community samples (Kinman et al., 2006; Winefield et al., 2008). Work-life conflict has been found to be a key predictor of psychological distress in the sector as well as other outcomes such as job dissatisfaction and leaving intentions (Kinman & Jones, 2009).

A recent survey of over 14,000 academic employees working in the UK (55 % female) found that almost two-thirds of the sample (65 %) indicated that they frequently neglected their personal needs because of the competing demands of their work and home life (Kinman & Wray, 2013). Although there is evidence that work can be beneficial for non-working life even where role conflict is high (Morganson, Culbertson, & Matthews, 2013), little evidence of work-life facilitation was found in this study; for example, only 8 % of the sample reported that their work enhanced their mood at home and a similar proportion (7 %) indicated that their job gave them energy to pursue activities outside work that were important to them.

Research that has examined gender differences in self-reported levels of work-life conflict has yielded mixed findings. Several studies find no evidence that women report greater conflict between work and home life than men (Frone, 2003; Grandey & Cropanzano, 1999). Nonetheless, it has been argued that men and women experience and react to work-life conflict differently (Galinsky, Kim, & Bond, 2001; Wharton & Blair-Loy, 2006). As even professional women tend to shoulder the burden of housework and child and elder care (Baxter & Chesters, 2011), it is unsurprising that some studies show that women engage in more work-family multitasking than men and find it more difficult to maintain boundaries between domains Rothbard, 2001). There is also evidence that women feel more guilt and distress when their job demands interfere with their home responsibilities (Glavin, Schieman, & Reid, 2011). Such reactions are likely to be attributable to societal assumptions of traditional gender roles which continue to influence men's and women's attitudes towards work and home responsibilities (Brough & O'Driscoll, 2005). Nonetheless, women academics also experience work-life balance challenges from organisational cultures, structures and stereotypes where the norm is to prioritise work above all other life roles (Beninger, 2010; King, 2008). Currie, Harris, and Thiele (2000) have utilised the concept of the 'greedy institution' to describe the personal sacrifices academics frequently make to comply with the unreasonable expectations of their university. Attempting to reconcile the demands of a greedy working environment with those of personal life is likely to make a strong contribution to the increasing levels of work-life conflict experienced by academic women.

Women Academics and the Work-Home Interface

Studies of the higher education sector have found that women academics tend to report higher levels of work-life conflict than their male counterparts (Hogan, Carlson, & Dua, 2002; Kinman & Wray, 2013; Varner, 2000; Weinrib et al., 2013). The findings of a study of 16 female academic managers conducted by Woodward (2007) revealed high workloads and long working hours, which left little time for recovery or to fulfil the demands of other life roles. Although some participants had established rigid boundaries between their work and home (generally for self protection purposes), they were frequently eroded to accommodate work demands.

This chapter will now discuss research that has explored women's experiences of the work-home interface and the factors that might help or hinder them in achieving balance between the competing demands of their work and non-working life. Focus is placed on characteristics of the working environment (such as demands, control and support and a perceived imbalance between efforts and rewards), the boundary management behaviours women utilise to balance the demands inherent in their work and non-working roles and personal features such as absorption in the job role. The findings and implications of research that has been conducted by the author of this chapter and colleagues will be considered, together with the literature more generally.

Work-Life Conflict and Facilitation

Research has examined levels of work-life conflict and facilitation in the university sector in the UK, together with the features of work that are the strongest predictors of these outcomes. Based on a sample of nearly 8000 women academics, Kinman and Wray (2013) found high levels of time-based and strain-based work-life conflict (see Fig. 8.1).

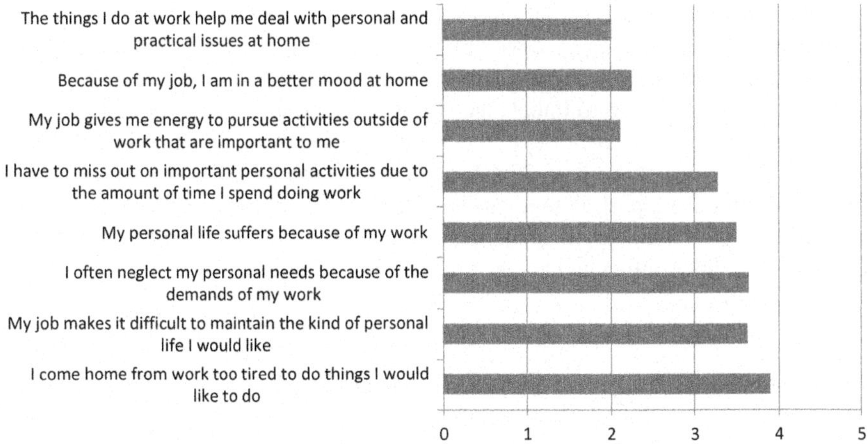

Fig. 8.1 Work-life conflict and facilitation reported by women academics (Mean scores for each item)

Comparisons of mean scores reported by male and female academics showed that women reported higher levels of all of the aspects of work-life conflict shown in Fig. 8.1. As can be seen from these figures, levels of work-life facilitation were low. Few gender differences emerged in the extent to which work benefited home life, but women were significantly more likely to indicate that the things they do at work help them manage personal and practical issues in their non-working life.

In order to develop precisely-targeted interventions to enhance work-life balance it is crucial to identify the factors that underpin work-life conflict and the resources that might alleviate it. The job demands resources model (JDR: Bakker & Demerouti, 2007) can be useful in highlighting these effects. This model stipulates that all job characteristics can be classified as either demands or resources. Demands are aspects of the job requiring sustained mental and/or physical effort that have the potential to impair well-being (such as working hours, workload and work pace), whereas resources help employees achieve work goals, reduce the negative impact of demands and/or stimulate personal development. It is argued that strain, such as work-life conflict, develops when demands are high and resources are limited.

Analysis of data obtained from over 7000 women academics indicated that the JDR model explained 57 % of the variance in work-life conflict. Sixty three per cent of the sample worked more than 40 h in an average week and 24 % in excess of 50 h. Weekly working hours and job-related demands were found to be strong predictors of conflict, but peer support, positive working relationships and effective change management emerged as protective resources. Women who reported greater autonomy and role clarity at work also tended to report less conflict under conditions of high work demand. No evidence was found that support from managers helped women balance the demands of their work and home lives. It should be emphasised, however, that the overall level of satisfaction with manager support was low. The important role played by the line manager in alleviating work-life conflict is discussed further in this chapter.

This research provided useful insight into the work-related factors that help and hinder women academics in developing an effective work-life balance. Other studies have identified a discrepancy between job demands and autonomy and perceptions of effort-reward imbalance as important predictors of work-life conflict and other strain outcomes in the higher education sector (Kinman & Jones, 2008; McClenahan, Giles, & Mallett, 2007). The next section focuses on the role played by organisational support, with a particular focus placed on schedule flexibility as well as individual boundary management behaviours and job involvement in underpinning work-life conflict and balance in women academics.

Organisational Support: Schedule Flexibility

Research conducted by Kinman and Jones (2009) examined also academics' perceptions of organisational support available for work-life balance. When asked to rate the extent their institutions helped employees achieve a balance between their work demands and their family responsibilities, almost half (48 %) said 'not at all', and a further 39 % indicated 'a little'. Levels of satisfaction with the manner in which institutions addressed the work and personal needs of employees was similarly low with 43 % indicating that they were 'not at all' satisfied. In respect of organisations providing women with required resources see also Siller, Bader, and Hochleitner (2016), who explored the resources that are available to women within a medical setting and their impact on the women's career advancement. Schedule flexibility is the most common initiative provided by organisations to help their employees balance competing role demands. The extent to which employees are able to adapt their working hours and locations to meet changing personal or family needs can help them create a work-life balance that fits their needs. Flexibility can also be used for career advancement. A study of American academics conducted by Shockley and Allen (2007) found that both women and men used flexible working policies to manage the competing demands at the work-home interface, but women were more likely than men to use flexibility to boost their productivity.

The degree of schedule flexibility perceived by academics and the extent to which it helps them manage the work-home interface has been examined. The majority of academic women (66 %) felt that the degree of flexibility in their working schedule met their own needs and 57 % indicated that the needs of their family were met. Although participants who reported more flexibility in their work role tended to have a better work-life balance (Kinman & Jones, 2008), no evidence was found that it protected academics from the negative impact of job demands. Several explanations could be provided for this finding. It has been argued that the intra-role demands central to academic work might outweigh the advantages conferred by schedule flexibility in other types of organisations (Anderson, Coffey, & Byerly, 2002). Moreover, as academics expect high levels of autonomy (Winefield & Jarrett, 2001), they may see schedule flexibility as an intrinsic part of the job role rather as a work-life balance benefit provided by their employers. Finally, self regulation of working hours might lead to work intensification, where employees "choose" to work longer and harder to fulfil the demands placed upon them (Kelliher & Anderson, 2010; Major & Germano, 2006). Academics who are more absorbed in the job role may find that schedule flexibility enables them to spend more time on the job role, rather than help them balance the demands of work and family life. This is discussed in the next section.

Job Involvement and Commitment

Job involvement is defined as the degree to which a person identifies psychologically with the job, and its importance to their self-concept (Higgins, Duxbury, & Irving, 1992). There is evidence that academics tend to be highly absorbed in their work, and attach considerable psychological significance to it (Hogan, Hodgins, & Hogan, 2014). Qualitative research with female academics from several countries conducted by Beninger (2010) found that participants considered work to be crucial to their identity, with many being unable to (and often unwilling to) make a clear distinction between their work and home lives. Questionnaire-based research conducted by Kinman and Jones (2008) also found high levels of job involvement and strong evidence of over-commitment to the job role. This is illustrated by 85 % of female respondents reporting that they were very much personally involved in their work and 38 % indicating that most of their interests were centred on their work.

There is some evidence that engagement in the work role can promote positive work-family experiences (Culbertson, Mills, & Fullagar, 2012). Nonetheless, Kinman and Jones found that women who were more deeply involved in the job role tended to experience higher levels of work-life conflict as well as poorer psychological and physical health. The impact on personal life was further emphasised by the finding that 61 % of participants disclosed that their family and friends believed they make too many personal sacrifices for their work. The authors argued that job involvement may weaken boundaries between work and home in two ways: firstly, the amount of time devoted to the work role may make it difficult to fulfil the physical requirements of other life roles; secondly, preoccupation with the work role may lead to psychological unavailability in other roles. Daily diary research with a sample of Irish academics conducted by Hogan et al. (2014) fund that excessive involvement in work limited recovery and detachment opportunities with implications for health. It is concluded, therefore, that job involvement at moderate levels is likely to be beneficial for non-working life, but over-involvement and over-commitment can pose a considerable threat to work-life balance and well-being more generally due to lack of opportunity and motivation to recover from work concerns. The implications of limited opportunities to detach from work concerns for job performance over the long term are also clear.

Work-Life Balance Behaviours

Like other knowledge workers, academics frequently engage in 'boundary-spanning' activities. Ways in which employees construct boundaries between work and their personal life will facilitate or restrict opportunities to engage with family and leisure. This section discussed research that has explored the strength of boundaries between the work and home and the boundary spanning behaviours in which women academics engage. The implications of working at home and using information communication technologies (ICTs) outside traditional working hours will be considered.

Boundary theory maintains that the borders between work and non-work roles form a continuum from integration to segmentation (Nippert-Eng, 1996). Boundaries between roles are also conceptualised in terms of their flexibility (referring to the extent to which a role can be enacted in different contexts and times) and permeability (representing the degree to which an individual can be "physically located in one role domain but psychologically and/or behaviourally involved in another role"; Ashforth, Kreiner, & Fugate, 2000, p. 474). Two roles are integrated when the boundary between them is flexible and permeable, and segmented if it is inflexible and impermeable.

The importance of disengagement from job demands for employee well-being has been emphasised. Indeed, longitudinal research has demonstrated that respite from work is essential in order to replenish personal resources and maintain well-being and productivity (Flaxman, Bond, Menard & Kinman, 2012). It could be argued that employees who are better able to compartmentalise their work and home roles will experience less conflict between life domains. In contrast, a high level of integration between work and home roles might facilitate role transition and enhance work-life balance, particularly for women.

There is some evidence that employees who lack clear boundaries between their work and home roles report more work-life conflict (e.g., Desrochers, Lehoux, Halpern, & Riggio, 2004). A review of the literature conducted by Sullivan and Lewis (2006) concluded that neither integration nor segmentation have uniformly positive effects on employee well-being and family outcomes. Research findings indicate that, for many academics, the work and person domains are highly integrated (Kinman & Jones, 2009; Kinman & Wray, 2013). More than a quarter of the women academics surveyed (26 %) indicated that there was no clear work-home boundary and a further 42 % stated that the boundary was weak. Those whose work and home lives were less enmeshed tended to report lower levels of conflict between domains and less psychological distress, but the degree of work-life integration that was deemed acceptable varied considerably. On average, levels of strain rose as the discrepancy between actual and ideal levels of work-life integration widened. Indeed the "fit" between the extent of integration between work and home roles was a stronger predictor of work-life conflict and distress than the degree of integration itself.

These findings highlight the importance of examining the extent to which employees *wish* to integrate or segment their working and non-working lives, rather than focusing on their current situation. Professionals who are deeply involved in their work, or who consider that integration is an effective way of managing their work and non-working roles, might desire little separation between their work and home lives, whereas others might prefer to construct a firm physical and/or psychological boundary between domains. Adopting a 'person-environment fit' approach to work-life integration has important implications for the development of interventions to enhance work-life balance which is discussed further in the chapter.

Working at Home

Although formal policies have not yet been introduced across the sector, most UK universities encourage academic employees to work at home at least occasionally (Ridgley, Scott, Hunt, & Harp, 2005). The widespread introduction of open-plan offices by many universities has resulted in reports of increased interruptions and lack of privacy, which may have made working at home a more attractive option (Baldry & Barnes, 2012). Working at home is frequently promoted as a way for employees to enhance their productivity and achieve a more effective balance between work and family responsibilities. Although there is evidence that working at home may help employees manage multiple role demands (Hill, Hawkins, & Miller, 1996), it has the potential to erode the boundaries between domains, reduce opportunities for detachment from work concerns and therefore increase the potential for work-life conflict (Desrochers, Hilton, & Larwood, 2005; Sonnentag, Kuttler, & Fritz, 2010).

Research conducted by Kinman and Jones (2004, 2009) indicated that academic employees work at home on a frequent basis. More than half of the sample (55 %) did more than one quarter of their overall workload at home. Analysis of the data for women academics found a significant positive relationship between working at home and work-life conflict. Participants indicated that they worked at home for several reasons: to increase their productivity, especially their research output; to allow them to use their time more efficiently; to avoid the interruptions and competing demands that frequently occurred in their place of work; and to juggle the demands of work and family and other commitments more effectively. Women who were more absorbed in the job role tended to work at home more frequently, further emphasising that this practice is not only used to tackle work overload. The risks of working at home disrupting family life and leisure activities were recognised.

Use of Information Communication Technology

The development of Information Communication Technology (ICT) has led to a profound reconfiguration of working time and space. Like other knowledge workers, academics frequently use ICTs for work purposes in other life domains

(Menzies & Newson, 2007). ICTs have the potential to help employees manage the competing demands of their work and home lives; it is nonetheless recognised that this boundary-spanning practice can lead to work "colonising" other life domains and engender conflict rather than harmonisation between work and home roles (Boswell & Olson-Buchanan, 2007). The use of ICTs is likely to be a particular problem for employees who use them to remain connected with work beyond traditional hours (Golden, 2011). This practice is also likely to increase expectations regarding the availability of employees, further increasing the likelihood of work encroaching on family life and recovery time (Major & Germano, 2006).

Ethnographic research with female academics conducted by Araujo (2008) highlights the positive and negative implications of using ICTs as a boundary-spanning activity. Although using ICTs away from the workplace was generally considered by academics to be an effective way to help balance work demands with family needs (often simultaneously), the lack of differentiation between "work" and "personal" time resulting from frequent engagement with technology, and the feelings of guilt and resentment engendered by this, was a cause for concern. It is perhaps unsurprising that positive associations have been found between ICT use by academics, work-life integration and perceptions of work-life conflict (Kinman & Jones, 2004).

These findings suggest that boundary-spanning activities, such as working at home and ICT use, have the potential to increase rather than reduce work-life conflict. Although considerable variation exists in the extent to which academics wish their work and home lives to be integrated, guidance based on research evidence should be provided for academic employees regarding 'healthy' boundary spanning activities and effective ways to manage intrusions.

Personal Strategies Used to Achieve Work-Life Balance

Content analysis of qualitative data obtained from open-ended questions highlights a range of strategies used by women academics to manage the competing demands of their work and personal life. The findings are summarised below:

- *Forward planning and time management*

This category encompasses various behaviours designed to maximise time for personal life. Some women stop work at a set time each day regardless of the volume or urgency of work left undone, others work early in the morning or late at night to spend time with family. Women also commonly "ring fence" time: for example, they might work longer hours on weekdays in order to keep weekends free.

- *Negotiating (and Re-negotiating) leisure and family time*

Women academics, especially those with young children, wrote about the complex arrangements that were required to ensure role expectations in each domain were met. One woman described preparing a spreadsheet which sets out her children's school and leisure activities to avoid clashes with work obligations. Academics frequently encountered difficulties maintaining their meticulously planned time management strategies in the face of heavy and unpredictable work demands. Women also highlighted the need to re-negotiate plans in response to changing family circumstances such as a sick child or parent.

- *Attempting to maintain boundaries between domains*

Participants described their attempts to segment their work and non-working life, whereby the job was prioritised during 'normal' working hours and personal life outside these times. Separating life domains also involved formulating firm 'rules of engagement' for the use of ICTs, especially e-mail, in order to limit the intrusion of work-related issues. Women frequently commented, however, that checking e-mail when they were 'off duty' helped them feel in control, and meant that they could focus on more pressing tasks during 'official' work time.

- *Gaining a 'breathing space'*

Many women academics indicated that they failed to take their full annual leave allocation due to pressure of work. Some disclosed that they frequently took annual leave to fulfil pressing work deadlines rather than spend time on leisure activities. Some academics also remarked that they took sick leave in an attempt to gain a 'breathing space' to catch up with work demands or reduced the number of hours that they slept. Such strategies are likely to take their toll on health as well as work-life balance, as adequate time for respite and recovery is vital in order to replenish personal and professional resources (Sonnentag et al., 2010).

- *Relying on support from family and friends*

Many women remarked upon the high level of support that they obtained when faced with work difficulties. The need for family and friends to appreciate the heavy and often unpredictable nature of academic work, and the strain that it can engender, was emphasised. For those who were married or cohabiting, a good level of communication between partners was considered to be an important factor in developing an effective work-life balance. A number of respondents (most notably those with partners who were also academics) revealed that they had mutually to restrict discussions about work during evenings, weekends or holidays. The risks and benefits for work-life balance of being married to or cohabiting with a fellow academic have been previously identified (Kinman, 2012).

- *Re-evaluating personal and work priorities*

Participants frequently described attempting to reduce their workload by refusing to take on additional work, letting the quality of their work decline, or leaving some tasks undone. The costs to self esteem, professional identity and relationships with colleagues when re-evaluating work priorities and reducing effort were, however, highlighted. Women also disclosed feelings of guilt for refusing to take on additional work when they knew colleagues would be required to do it and for not fulfilling their perceived obligations to their students. The implications of reducing the volume and quality of work for promotion was also widely emphasised, as evenings and weekends were commonly considered the only time available to engage in research. In an attempt to gain an acceptable balance between their work and home lives, a few respondents reported that they had formally reduced their contracted hours. The financial costs of this practice were, however, highlighted.

Work-Life Balance Interventions

The findings of several studies, including the research presented in this chapter, indicate that support for work-life balance may be poorer in universities than in many other types of organisation (Austin & Pilat, 2000; Jacobs & Winslow, 2004). It has been suggested that assumptions about the inherent flexibility of academic work may mean that universities have made little effort to develop interventions beyond basic compliance with legislation (Winefield et al., 2008). The important role of job control and flexibility in helping academics managing the work-home interface has been highlighted. Nonetheless, multi-level interventions are required to help academics balance the demands of their work and personal lives more effectively. Interventions are needed at the level of the sector, the institution, the line manager, the work-group and the individual employee.

Sector Level Greater insight is required into how the multiple demands inherent in academic work can combine and conflict with duties and obligations in the personal domain, how this can constrain opportunities for respite and recovery and the implications for personal and professional functioning over the long term. As discussed in this chapter, to some extent the precipitating factors and outcomes of work-life conflict are likely to be context and gender specific. Knowledge gained will help create the working conditions that will help academics navigate the boundaries between work and personal life more effectively with clear benefits for all stake-holders.

Institutional Level Knowledge is needed of the work-life balance culture of individual universities; more specifically, the initiatives that are available, their acceptability to employees and whether they are distributed equitably. Organisational culture can strongly influence the uptake of work-life balance programmes (Thompson, Beauvais, & Lyness, 1999). Whether there are any barriers to the utilisation of such initiatives at an institutional level by male and female academics should also be explored.

It has been recognised that line managers' behaviours are crucial in helping employees manage the interface between work and personal life. The research discussed above shows that autonomy, respect and fair treatment from managers, in particular, can protect employees from the negative impact of even heavy job demands on non-working life (Kinman, 2014). Hammer, Kossek, Zimmerman, and

Daniels's (2007) conceptualisation of family supportive supervisor behaviours has great potential in maximising organisational support for work-life balance. This encompasses a range of competencies such as *emotional support* (learning about work-life balance needs and listening to problems); *instrumental support* (helping employees avoid work-life conflict); *role modelling* (demonstrating effective work-life balance behaviours) and *creative work-life balance management* (using novel solutions to reduce conflict). Hammer and colleagues have developed a training programme to enhance these behaviours in managers with demonstrable benefits. Of particular relevance to academics, management behaviours that endeavour to accommodate employees' preferences for work-life integration or segmentation have been found to facilitate role transitions and achieve an optimum work-life balance fit (Hammer, Kossek, Anger, Bodner, & Zimmerman, 2011). It should be acknowledged, however, that line managers will require support to manage their own work-life balance.

Individual As discussed above, there is considerable variation in the extent to which academics prefer their work and home lives to be integrated. Based on extensive research, Kossek and Lautsch (2007) have identified three distinct boundary management styles: separators, integrators and volleyers (who alternate between periods of separation and integration). The consequences of each of these styles for functioning and well-being is dependent upon whether employees feel in control and satisfied with their current work-life balance 'fit', or out of control and dissatisfied. Using Kossek and Lautsch's typology to help employees gain insight into their boundary management styles will help them develop a work-life balance that meets their preferences.

The potential risks of excessive commitment to the job role for the work-life balance of academics have been identified above. While a high degree of involvement could be seen as pre-requisite for success in academia, awareness of its long-term implications for recovery, functioning in personal roles, well-being and, ultimately, job performance should be highlighted. The benefits and risks of schedule flexibility, working at home and the use of ICTs as boundary management tools should also be widely communicated and information provided on how to safeguard work-life balance, even where people prefer the domains to be highly integrated. Grawitch, Barber, and Justice's (2010) personal resource allocation framework could be utilised to gain insight into how academics juggle the demands of work and home roles. This could result in interventions to help employees allocate appropriate time and physical and psychological energy across life domains.

Conclusion

This chapter has examined some of the work-related factors that might help or hinder academic women in achieving an acceptable balance between the wide-ranging, and frequently excessive, demands of their job with their personal lives. Interventions to enhance work-life balance in the sector, especially for women academics, are urgently required. Each of the interventions recommended above cannot work in isolation. They should be firmly embedded within a broader culture where all academic employees, regardless of gender, caring responsibilities or life stage, are helped to achieve a work-life balance that meets their current needs and the benefits for personal well-being and job performance are recognised.

References

Albertsen, K., Persson, R., Garde, A. H., & Rugulies, R. (2010). Psychosocial determinants of work to family conflict among knowledge workers with boundaryless work. *Applied Psychology: Health and Well Being, 2*(2), 160–181. doi:10.1080/15402002.2012.636272.

Allen, T. D., & Armstrong, J. (2006). Further examination of the link between work-family conflict and physical health: The role of health-related behaviors. *American Behavioral Scientist, 49*, 1204–1221. doi:10.1177/0002764206286386.

Allen, T. D., Herst, D. E. L., Bruck, C. S., & Sutton, M. (2000). Consequences associated with work-to-family conflict: A review and agenda for future research. *Journal of Occupational Health Psychology, 5*, 278–308. doi:10.1037/1076-8998.5.2.278.

Anderson, S. E., Coffey, B. S., & Byerly, R. T. (2002). Formal organizational initiatives and informal workplace practices: Links to work-family conflict and job-related outcomes. *Journal of Management, 28*(6), 787–810. doi:10.1177/014920630202800605.

Araujo, E. R. (2008). Technology, gender and time: A contribution to the debate. *Gender, Work and Organization, 15*(5), 477–503. doi:10.1111/j.1468-0432.2008.00414.

Ashforth, B. E., Kreiner, G. E., & Fugate, M. (2000). All in a day's work: Boundaries and micro role transitions. *Academy of Management Review, 25*, 472–491. doi:10.5465/AMR.2000.3363315.

Austin, A., & Pilat, M. (2000). Tension, stress and the tapestry of faculty lives. *Academe, 76*(1), 38–42.

Bakker, A. B., & Demerouti, E. (2007). The job demands-resources model: State of the art. *Journal of Managerial Psychology, 22*(3), 309–328. doi:10.1108/02683940710733115.

Baldry, C., & Barnes, A. (2012). The open-plan academy: Space, control and the undermining of professional identity. *Work, Employment & Society, 26*(2), 228–245. doi:10.1177/0950017011432917.

Baxter, J., & Chesters, J. (2011). Perceptions of work-family balance: How effective are family-friendly policies? *Australian Journal of Labour Economics, 14*(2), 139–151.

Beninger, A. (2010). *Women in Academia: a Cross-Cultural Perspective on Work/life Balance*. Unpublished research report. London School of Economics, UK – http://www.claremontmckenna.net/berger/pdf/BeningerDissertationWomeninAcademia.pdf

Boswell, W. R., & Olson-Buchanan, J. B. (2007). The use of communication technologies after hours: The role of work attitudes and work-life conflict. *Journal of Management, 33*(4), 592–610. doi:10.1177/0149206307302552.

Brough, P., & O'Driscoll, M. (2005). Work-family conflict and stress. In *Research Companion to Organizational Health Psychology*. Cheltanhalm, UK: Edward Elgar.

Crossfield, S., Kinman, G., & Jones, F. (2005). The spillover of stressors in full-time working couples. *Work, Community and Family, 8*(2), 211–232. doi:10.1080/13668800500049779.

Culbertson, S. S., Mills, M. J., & Fullagar, C. J. (2012). Work engagement and work-family facilitation: Making homes happier through positive affective spillover. *Human Relations, 65*(9), 1155–1177. doi:10.1177/0018726712440295.

Currie, J., Harris, P., & Thiele, B. (2000). Sacrifices in greedy universities: Are they gendered? *Gender and Education, 12*(3), 269–291. doi:10.1080/713668305.

Desrochers, S., Hilton, J., & Larwood, L. (2005). Preliminary validation of the work-family integration blurring scale. *Journal of Family Issues, 26*, 442–466. doi:10.1177/0192513X04272438.

Desrochers, A., Lehoux, M., Halpern, D., & Riggio, H. (2004). *The complex relationship between wellbeing and level of work-family blurring in two local organisations.* Retrieved from http://berger.research.claremontmckenna.edu/research/workfamblur/

Dierdorff, E. C., & Ellington, J. K. (2008). It's the nature of the work: Examining behaviour-based sources of work-family conflict across occupations. *Journal of Applied Psychology, 93*(4), 883–892. doi:10.1037/0021-9010.93.4.883.

Doyle, C., & Hind, P. (1998). Occupational stress, burnout and job status in female academics. *Gender, Work and Organisation, 5*(2), 67–82. doi:10.1111/1468-0432.00047.

Eby, L., Casper, W., Lockwood, A., Bordeaux, C., & Brinley, A. (2005). Work and family research in IO/OB: Content analysis and review of the literature (1980–2002). *Journal of Vocational Behavior, 66*(1), 124–197. doi:10.1016/j.jvb.2003.11.003.

Edwards, J. R., & Rothbard, N. P. (1999). Work and family stress and well-being: An examination of person-environment fit in the work and family domains. *Organizational Behavior and Human Decision Processes, 77*(2), 85–129. doi:10.1006/obhd.1998.2813.

Flaxman, P. E., Ménard, J., Bond, F. W., & Kinman, G. (2012). Academics' experiences of a respite from work: Effects of self-critical perfectionism and perseverative cognition on post-respite well-being. *Journal of Applied Psychology, 97*(4), 854. doi:10.1037/a0028055.

Frone, M. (2003). Work-family balance. In J. C. Quick & L. E. Tetrick (Eds.), *Handbook of occupational health psychology* (pp. 143–162). Washington, DC: American Psychological Association (APA) Books.

Galinsky, E., Kim, S. S., & Bond, J. T. (2001). *Feeling overworked: When work becomes too much.* New York, USA: Families and Work Institute.

Glavin, P., Schieman, S., & Reid, S. (2011). Boundary-spanning work demands and their consequences for guilt and psychological distress. *Journal of Health and Social Behavior, 52*(1), 43–57. doi:10.1177/0022146510395023.

Golden, T. D. (2011). Altering the effects of work and family conflict on exhaustion: Telework during traditional and non-traditional work hours. *Journal of Business and Psychology, 27*(3), 255–269. doi:10.1002/job.652.

Grandey, A. A., & Cropanzano, R. (1999). The conservation of resources model applied to work–family conflict and strain. *Journal of Vocational Behavior, 54*(2), 350–370. doi:10.1006/jvbe.1998.1666.

Grawitch, M. J., Barber, L. K., & Justice, L. (2010). Rethinking the work-life interface: It's not about balance, it's about resource allocation. *Applied Psychology: Health and Well Being, 2*(2), 127–159. doi:10.1111/j.1758-0854.2009.01023.

Greenhaus, J. H., & Powell, G. N. (2006). When work and family are allies: A theory of work-family enrichment. *Academy of Management Review, 31*, 72–92. doi:10.5465/AMR.2006.19379625.

Group Risk Development [GRiD]. (2012). 2011 *Employer research. Summary of findings.* Available from www.grouprisk.org.uk

Grzywacz, J., & Demerouti, E. (2013). *New Frontiers in work and family research.* London: Psychology Press.

Grzywacz, J., & Marks, N. (2000). Family, work, work-family spillover and problem drinking during midlife. *Journal of Marriage and the Family, 62*(2), 336–349. doi:10.1037/1076-8998.5.1.111.

Hammer, L. B., Kossek, E. E., Anger, W. K., Bodner, T., & Zimmerman, K. L. (2011). Clarifying work–family intervention processes: The roles of work-family conflict and family-supportive supervisor behaviors. *Journal of Applied Psychology, 96*(1), 134–150. doi:10.1037/a0020927.

Hammer, L., Kossek, E., Zimmerman, K., & Daniels, R. (2007). Clarifying the construct of family supportive supervisory behaviors: A multilevel perspective. In P. Perrewe & D. Ganster (Eds.), *Research on occupational stress and well-being* (pp. 165–204). Greenwich, CT: Elsevier Press.

Higgins, C. A., Duxbury, L. E., & Irving, R. H. (1992). Work-family conflict in the dual-career family. *Organizational Behavior and Human Decision Processes, 51*(1), 51–75. doi:10.1016/0749-5978(92)90004-Q.

Hill, J., Hawkins, A. J., & Miller, B. C. (1996). Work and family in the virtual office: Perceived influences of mobile telework. *Family Relations, 45*, 293–301.

Hogan, J. M., Carlson, J. G., & Dua, J. (2002). Stress and stress reactions among university personnel. *International Journal of Stress Management, 9*(4), 289–310. doi:10.1023/A:1019982316327.

Hogan, V., Hodgins, M., & Hogan, M. (2014, April). Workaholism, recovery and detachment from work among Irish academics. In *Proceedings of the European academy of occupational health psychology conference*, London.

Jacobs, J. A., & Winslow, W. E. (2004). Overworked faculty: Job stresses and family demands. *The Annals of the American Academy of Political and Social Science, 596*, 104–129. doi:10.1177/0002716204268185.

Katz, D., & Kahn, R. L. (1978). *The social psychology of organizations* (2nd ed.). New York: Wiley.

Kelliher, C., & Anderson, D. (2010). Doing more with less? Flexible working practices and the intensification of work. *Human Relations, 63*(1), 83–106. doi:10.1177/0018726709349199.

King, E. B. (2008). The effect of bias on the advancement of working mothers: Disentangling legitimate concerns from inaccurate stereotypes as predictors of advancement in academe. *Human Relations, 61*(12), 1677–1711. doi:10.1177/0018726708098082.

Kinman, G. (2012, January). Work-linked couples and work-life balance – Resource or liability? In *Proceedings of the BPS division of occupational psychology conference*, Chester.

Kinman, G. (2014). Doing more with less? Work and wellbeing in academics. *Somatechnics, 4*(2), 219–235.

Kinman, G., & Jones, F. (2001). The work-home interface. In F. Jones & J. Bright (Eds.), *Stress: Myth, theory and research*. London: Prentice Hall.

Kinman, G., & Jones, F. (2004). *Working to the limit*. London: AUT Publications.

Kinman, G., & Jones, F. (2008). Effort-reward imbalance, over-commitment and work-life conflict: Testing an expanded model. *Journal of Managerial Psychology, 23*(3), 236–251. doi:10.1108/02683940810861365.

Kinman, G., & Jones, F. (2009). A life beyond work? Job demands, work-life balance and wellbeing in UK academics. In D. Buckholdt & G. Miller (Eds.), *Faculty stress*. New York: Routledge.

Kinman, G., Jones, F., & Kinman, R. (2006). The wellbeing of the UK Academy. *Quality in Higher Education, 12*(1), 15–27. doi:10.1080/13538320600685081.

Kinman, G., & Wray, S. (2013). *Higher stress: A survey of stress and well-being among staff in higher education*. UCU available at https://www.ucu.org.uk/media/5911/Higher-stress-a-survey-of-stress-and-well-beingamong-staff-in-higher-education-Jul-13/pdf/HE_stress_report_July_2013.pdf

Kinnunen, U., Rantanen, J., & Mauno, S. (2013). Crossover and spillover between family members and work and family roles. In *Handbook of work-life integration among professionals: Challenges and opportunities* (pp. 77–92). Cheltenham, UK: Edward Elgar Publishing.

Korabik, K., Lero, D., & Whitehead, D. (2008). *Handbook of work-family integration*. Amsterdam: Academic Press/Elsevier.

Kossek, E. E., & Lautsch, B. (2007). *CEO of Me: Creating a life that works in the flexible job age*. Upper Saddle River, NJ: Prentice Hall.

Kotecha, K., Ukpere, W., & Geldenhuys, M. (2014). Technology and work-life conflict of academics in a South African Higher Education Institution. *Mediterranean Journal of Social Sciences, 5*(2), 629–641. doi:10.5901/mjss.2014.v5n2p629.

Lewis, S., & Cooper, C. (2005). *Work-life integration: Case studies of organizational change*. Hoboken, NJ: Wiley.

MacEwen, K. E., & Barling, J. (1991). Effects of maternal employment experiences on children's behavior via mood, cognitive difficulties, and parenting behavior. *Journal of Marriage and the Family, 53*(3), 635–644.

Major, D. A., & Germano, L. M. (2006). The changing nature of work and its impact on the work-home interface. In F. Jones, R. Burke, & M. Westman (Eds.), *Work-life balance: A psychological perspective* (pp. 13–38). London: Psychology Press.

Mark, G., & Smith, A. P. (2012). Effects of occupational stress, job characteristics, coping, and attributional style on the mental health and job satisfaction of university employees. *Anxiety, Stress & Coping, 25*(1), 63–78. doi:10.1080/10615806.2010.548088.

McClenahan, C. A., Giles, M. L., & Mallett, J. (2007). The importance of context specificity in work stress research: A test of the demand-control-support model in academics. *Work & Stress, 21*(1), 85–95. doi:10.1080/02678370701264552.

Menzies, H., & Newson, J. (2007). No time to think: Academics' life in the globally wired university. *Time and Society, 16*(1), 83–98. doi:10.1177/0961463X07074103.

Michel, J. S., Clark, M. A., & Beiler, A. A. (2013). Work-life conflict and its effects. In D. A. Major & R. J. Burke (Eds.), *Handbook of work-life integration among professionals: Challenges and opportunities* (pp. 58–76). Cheltenham, UK: Edward Elgar Publishing Limited. doi:10.4337/9781781009291.00012.

Morganson, V. J., Culbertson, S. S., & Matthews, R. A. (2013). Individual strategies for navigating the work-life interface. In D. A. Major & R. J. Burke (Eds.), *Handbook of work-life integration among professionals: Challenges and opportunities* (pp. 205–224). Cheltenham, UK: Edward Elgar Publishing Limited. doi:10.4337/9781781009291.

Netemeyer, R. G., Boles, J., & McMurrian, R. (1996). Development and validation of work-family conflict and family-work conflict scales. *Journal of Applied Psychology, 81*, 400–410. doi:10.1037/0021-9010.81.4.400.

Nippert-Eng, C. (1996). *Home and work: Negotiating boundaries through everyday life*. Chicago: University of Chicago Press.

Odle-Dusseau, H. N., Britt, T. W., & Greene-Shortridge, T. M. (2012). Organizational work-family resources as predictors of job performance and attitudes: The process of work-family conflict and enrichment. *Journal of Occupational Health Psychology, 17*, 28–40. doi:10.1037/a0026428.

Payne, N., Kinman, G., & Jones, F. (2012). Work stress and health behaviour: Evidence and potential mechanisms. In J. Houdmont & S. Leka (Eds.), *Contemporary occupational health psychology (Vol. 2): Global perspectives on research and practice*. Chichester, UK: Wiley Blackwell.

Querstret, D., & Cropley, M. (2012). Exploring the relationship between work-related rumination, sleep quality, and work-related fatigue. *Journal of Occupational Health Psychology, 17*(3), 341–353. doi:10.1037/a0028552.

Ridgley, C., Scott, J., Hunt, A., & Harp, C. (2005) *Homeworking: A guide to good practice*. The FEO project/Staffordshire University, UK. http://www.staffs.ac.uk/feo/documents/homeworking_goodpractice.pdf

Rothbard, N. P. (2001). Enriching or depleting? The dynamics of engagement in work and family roles. *Administrative Science Quarterly, 46*(4), 655–684. doi:10.2307/3094827.

Shockley, K. M., & Allen, T. D. (2007). When flexibility helps: Another look at the availability of flexible work arrangements and work-family conflict. *Journal of Vocational Behavior, 71*, 479–493. doi:10.1016/j.jvb.2007.08.006.

Siller, H., Bader, A., & Hochleitner, M. (2016). Support for female physicians at a University Hospital: What do differences between female and male physicians tell us? In R. L. Gervais, & P. M. Millear (Eds.), *Exploring resources, life-balance and well-being of women who work in a global context* (pp. 109–123). Cham, Switzerland: Springer International Publishing Switzerland.

Sonnentag, S., Kuttler, I., & Fritz, C. (2010). Job stressors, emotional exhaustion, and need for recovery: A multi-source study on the benefits of psychological detachment. *Journal of Vocational Behavior, 76*, 355–365. doi:10.1016/j.jvb.2009.06.005.

Sullivan, C., & Lewis, S. (2006). Relationships between work and home life. In F. Jones, R. Burke, & M. Westman (Eds.), *Managing the work-home interface: A psychological perspective*. London: Taylor & Francis.

Thompson, C. A., Beauvais, L. L., & Lyness, K. S. (1999). When work–family benefits are not enough: The influence of work–family culture on benefit utilization, organizational attachment, and work–family conflict. *Journal of Vocational Behavior, 54*(3), 392–415. doi:10.1006/jvbe.1998.1681.

Van Steenbergen, E., & Ellemers, N. (2009). Feeling committed to work: How specific forms of work-commitment predict work behavior and performance over time. *Human Performance, 22*, 410–431. doi:10.1080/08959280903248385.

Varner, A. (2000). *The consequences and costs of delaying attempted childbirth for women faculty*. Department of Labor Studies and Industrial Relations, Penn State University.

Watts, J., & Robertson, N. (2011). Burnout in university teaching staff: A systematic literature review. *Educational Research, 53*(1), 33–50. doi:10.1080/00131881.2011.552235.

Wayne, J. H., Casper, W. J., Matthews, R. A., & Allen, T. D. (2013). Family-supportive organization perception and organizational commitment: The mediating role of work-family conflict and enrichment and partner attitudes. *Journal of Applied Psychology, 98*, 606–622. doi:10.1037/a0032491.

Wayne, J. H., Grzywacz, J. G., Carlson, D. S., & Kacmar, K. M. (2007). Work–family facilitation: A theoretical explanation and model of primary antecedents and consequences. *Human Resource Management Review, 17*, 63–76. doi:10.1016/j.hrmr.2007.01.002.

Weinrib, J., Jones, G. A., Metcalfe, A. S., Fisher, D., Gingras, Y., Rubenson, K., et al. (2013). Canadian university academics' perceptions of job satisfaction: "The future is not what it used to be". In *Job Satisfaction around the Academic World* (pp. 83–102). Dordrecht, The Netherlands: Springer.

Wharton, A. S., & Blair-Loy, M. (2006). Long work hours and family life a cross-national study of employees' concerns. *Journal of Family Issues, 27*(3), 415–436. doi:10.1177/0192513X05282985.

Winefield, A. H., Boyd, C. M., Saebel, J., & Pignata, S. (2008). Update on national university stress study. *Australian Universities Review, 50*, 20–29. doi:10.1111/j.1464-0597.2010.00429.

Winefield, A. H., & Jarrett, R. (2001). Occupational stress in university staff. *International Journal of Stress Management, 8*(4), 285–298. doi:10.1023/A:1017513615819.

Winefield, H. R., Boyd, C., & Winefield, A. H. (2014). Work-family conflict and well-being in university employees. *The Journal of Psychology, 148*(6), 683–697.

Woodward, D. (2007). Work-life balancing strategies used by women managers in British "modern" universities. *Equal Opportunities International, 26*(1), 6–17. doi:10.1108/02610150710726507.

Chapter 9
Working It Out: Balancing Work and Care After the Birth of a First Child

Wendy Boyd, Prudence M. Millear, Karen L. Thorpe, and Sue Walker

Introduction

Australia, like most western developed economies, has witnessed a continual increase in maternal employment in recent decades (Baxter, 2014). This ongoing trend has been in response to public and private economic demands and changing social values that view the combination of paid work and motherhood as increasingly acceptable or, at least, necessary (Huerta et al., 2011). Yet the decisions regarding the balancing of paid employment and the selection of childcare remain intensely personal and present a major concern in the Australian context (Charlesworth & Chelmers, 2005; Craig, 2007; Pocock, 2005). For many women, investment in a career, contribution to family finances, and financial independence are personal incentives to engage in paid work while home responsibilities and the level of apprehension about the use of non-parental care for their child serve to set

W. Boyd (✉)
School of Education, Southern Cross University, Lismore, NSW 2480, Australia
e-mail: wendy.boyd@scu.edu.au

P.M. Millear
School of Social Sciences, University of the Sunshine Coast,
Locked Bag 4, Maroochydore DC, QLD 4558, Australia
e-mail: pmillear@usc.edu.au

K.L. Thorpe
School of Psychology and Counselling, Queensland University of Technology,
Victoria Park Rd, Kelvin Grove, QLD 4058, Australia
e-mail: k.thorpe@qut.edu.au

S. Walker
School of Early Childhood, Queensland University of Technology,
Victoria Park Rd, Kelvin Grove, QLD 4058, Australia
e-mail: sue.walker@qut.edu.au

R.L. Gervais, P.M. Millear (eds.), *Exploring Resources, Life-Balance and Well-Being of Women Who Work in a Global Context*,
DOI 10.1007/978-3-319-31736-6_9

the boundaries of a woman's decisions about the quantity, timing and flexibility of employment in which she is able to engage. The Australian Bureau of Statistics (2013) indicate that 54 % of Australian mothers engage in paid work with children under 4 years of age, most working part-time.

Policies that support women's choices for satisfying employment and care arrangements have been identified as significant in optimising economic productivity and enhancing social well-being (Organisation for Economic Development, [OECD], 2007). Such policies include family friendly employment arrangements, paid parental leave, and provision of high quality and affordable childcare. In countries such as Denmark, France and Sweden, the recognition of the value of maternal workforce participation is reflected in public policy that ensures comprehensive support for maternal employment through funded parental leave and publicly subsidised child care (Craig & Mullan, 2010; Krapf, 2009; OECD, 2007). In these countries, maternal workforce participation is high both in number of participants and the hours each woman works (Krapf, 2009; OECD, 2007). In contrast, in Australia, there are not comprehensive and coherent policies on work and family. For Australian mothers, part-time paid work is usually combined with responsibility for unpaid work in the home including household tasks and care of the child. Women take a greater share of the non-paid work than their male partners. The reasons offered for this ongoing unequal division of unpaid work are economic limitations on partner participation in care and traditional gender ideology (Craig & Mullan, 2010). The balancing of work and care duties remains largely a matter for women and is centred in the private domain.

The Private Context of Balancing Paid Work and Care in Australia

Care for the child enables mothers to engage in paid work, and when of high quality provides positive early educational experiences for children (Thorpe, Cloney, & Tayler, 2010). The personal decisions a mother makes regarding engagement in paid work are, therefore, important not only for her family's economic well-being and the child's learning and development, but can also have a profound effect on her own well-being (DeMeis, Hock, & McBride, 1986; Killien, 2005).

Research examining maternal mental health following the birth of a child has identified participation in the workforce as a protective factor associated with reduced risk of maternal depression (Hock & DeMeis, 1990; Pungello & Kurtz-Costes, 2000). The now classic study conducted by Hock and DeMeis in the late 1980s (Hock & DeMeis, 1990) examined women's preference for a return to work against their actual work participation behaviour. In this study, as expected, those whose work behaviour matched preference were least likely to be depressed. More importantly, of those not able to take up their preference, women returning to work were less likely to experience depression than those not working (Hock & DeMeis, 1990). This finding suggests women adjust to working, and has positive well-being outcomes. The longitudinal study of Pungello and Kurtz- Costes (2000) provides further insight into this finding. This longitudinal study tracked women's workforce participation from pregnancy across the first year postpartum obtaining preferences and documenting the dynamics of their decision-making. The study attests to women's adjustment to their circumstances, even if against preference, and the acknowledgement of the benefits of workforce participation in which personal factors such as career maintenance and financial and personal independence feature alongside the financial support of the family.

A key factor supporting positive workplace participation, identified in this study and many others, is the security of alternative care provision for the child. Care that is of an acceptable quality to the mother has been found to impact positively on maternal well-being in the workplace (Craig, 2007) and is a key factor in facilitating and maintaining workforce participation (Coffey, 2004). Conversely, concerns about quality of childcare have been reported as being an emotional barrier to women's workforce engagement (Boyd, Walker, & Thorpe, 2013; Harris, 2008). In an Australian study, Harris (2008) reported that women felt emotionally torn by the decision to support their family financially at the cost of placing a child in a non-parental care setting that they deemed as unacceptable. In the Australian context, the questioning of the quality of formal early childhood care services, and hypothesised harmful effects for young children, have been prevalent in the popular media across the last decade (for example, Biddulph, 2005; Clausen, 2006; Manne, 2005), which has fuelled further these concerns. Given these circumstances, it is perhaps not surprising that Australian women have a preference for informal care with a relative or friend in the infancy period, and those using formal group-based care often do so insecurely (Boyd, 2014). Reasons for this care preference was the trustworthiness of, and familiarity with the caregiver, while those women using formal child care often did so insecurely, owing to their child being constantly ill, and that they felt guilty about leaving the child.

Additionally, how women feel about their own employment and its effects on their children had impacts on their mental health; the mother's role; and their children's development. Attitudes towards maternal employment were predictors of mental health of employed mothers in separate analyses of the National Institute of Child, Health and Development (NICHD) Study of Early Child Care, which followed a large sample of mothers and their healthy infants from birth to 36 months of age (Holmes, Erickson, & Hill, 2012). Positive attitudes towards maternal employment (measured as perceiving less costs and more benefits for children) were strong predictors of improved psychological well-being for consistently employed mothers. These mothers also reported less depression and less parenting stress and greater satisfaction with the mothering role. Interestingly, this was not the case for mothers who were not employed, indicating that actual employment status impacts on mothers' well-being. In all mothers however, better mental health for mothers was associated with children who displayed greater social competence at 36 months of age (Chang, 2013). In a separate, expanded analysis, Holmes et al. (2012) found that where mothers perceived employment as costly for their child; where they felt a lack of social support, a mismatch of ideal and actual work situations, had less education and were single; they were more likely to report higher levels of depression. Perceived costs of maternal employment was also a significant predictor of parenting stress, as did having more children and a lack of social support (Holmes et al., 2012). In the current study, the prospective design allows the mothers' changing beliefs about the balance of costs and benefits of their employment to be understood, in the context of their employment decisions.

Examining Australian Women's Resilience in the Public Context of Return to the Workforce

In a national economic environment requiring the skill and productivity brought by women to the workforce (OECD, 2006), decisions about return to paid work after the birth of a child is often a precarious balance of meeting the dual challenges of career and economic sustenance and providing good, or at least acceptable, levels of care. The research presented in this chapter, conducted in Australia across 2007 and 2008, tracked women's intentions, work and care decisions following the birth of their first child. The women made these intensely personal decisions against the challenging and changing public context of the economic and family policies of that period. At the time of data collection, paid parental leave was not available as a statutory right in Australia, but rather was associated with specific employment sectors. As a consequence, some of the women in our sample had paid leave provision while others did not. The data provided the opportunity therefore to examine the effects of paid leave. Across the same period, childcare provisions were a major focus of attention for governments. A new Australian Federal Government was elected in 2007 and directed the creation of policies to raise the quality standards for childcare in Australia, but so doing also highlighted existing inadequacies. At the time of data collection, national quality standards for childcare were focussed on attainment of minimum criteria, with the change to aspirational standards occurring in 2011. In addition, the financial collapse of Australia's largest private childcare provider (ABC Developmental Learning Centres) had further heightened social interest in child care provision and quality.

This study examined Australian women's negotiations of decisions regarding return to the workforce against this complex background of public and personal judgement. The study sought to identify salient factors in decision-making and how the mothers' adjusted to these decisions, through impacts on their well-being, satisfaction with motherhood, and how they perceived the personal costs and benefits of paid work.

Method

Research Design and Significance

This research was designed to capture expectant first-time mothers' preferred options for engaging in paid work and the care of their child, and to investigate their actual decisions made at 6, 12 and 18 months postpartum. To capture preferred options, decisions and outcomes of decisions regarding paid work and care of the child a prospective longitudinal research design was utilised. This design had three important components that addressed key limitations in the extant literature. First the research commenced in pregnancy, in order to investigate preferences and beliefs about paid work and care and to examine baseline data that may influence decisions made as the women returned to paid work. Second the research involved longitudinal tracking from the antenatal time point to 6, 12 and 18 months postpartum in order to identify the patterns and salient influences on decisions made. Third the research measured mental health and cost-benefit outcomes resulting from their decisions at each time point.

Participants and Recruitment Procedure

First-time mothers ($n=124$) were recruited in the final trimester of their pregnancies, using two methods. A direct approach was made to expectant mothers in hospital ante-natal classes across Brisbane, Queensland (80 respondents) and clinics conducted by Regional Health Authorities in northern New South Wales (19 respondents). The second approach was a request for volunteers accessed through the media of a Queensland university's online news and a national parent magazine (25 respondents mostly from Brisbane). Recruitment began in late May 2007 and continued until November 2007. The participants were surveyed for the second time when their child was 6 months old (January to July 2008), 12 months (June to December 2008) and 18 months postpartum (January to July 2009). The sample reduced across the four data collection phases (see Table 9.1). The total retention rate of the sample at 18 months postpartum from the antenatal point was 60 %. This study focussed on the women who completed all four surveys ($n=74$). For this group, the mothers' age ranged from 19 to 39 years ($M=30.2$, $SD=4.4$) at the

Table 9.1 The education, work status and income of the mothers and their partners

	Before birth		At 6 months		At 12 months		At 18 months	
	Mother	Partner	Mother	Partner	Mother	Partner	Mother	Partner
	$N=124$	$N=116$	$n=98$	$n=92$	$n=93$	$n=87$	$n=74$	$n=70$
	n (%)	*n* (%)	*n* (%)	*n* (%)	*n* (%)	*n* (%)	*n* (%)	*n* (%)
Educational status: Year 12	27 (22)	27 (23)	20 (20)	18 (20)	18 (19)	17 (20)	13 (18)	14 (20)
Diploma	35 (28)	48 (41)	25 (25)	37 (40)	22 (24)	32 (37)	15 (21)	22 (31)
University	62 (50)	42 (36)	54 (55)	37 (40)	53 (57)	37 (43)	44 (61)	34 (49)
Work status: Self-employed	9 (7)	12 (10)	8 (8)	12 (13)	6 (6)	12 (14)	5 (7)	5 (7)
Casual	25 (20)	26 (22)	26 (27)	17 (18)	27 (29)	13 (15)	15 (21)	16 (23)
Permanent	82 (66)	76 (66)	36 (37)	63 (69)	39 (40)	57 (65)	49 (68)	50 (70)
Not working	9 (7)	10 (9)	26 (27)	0	23 (25)	5 (6)	3 (4)	0
Household income per annum								
< $60,000 pa	47 (38)		34 (35)		31 (33)		26 (38)	
≥ $60,000 pa	77 (62)		64 (65)		62 (67)		43 (62)	

baseline data collection in third trimester of pregnancy (M = 32.5, SD = 3.2 weeks). At this time their partners' age ranged from 21 to 48 years (M = 31.8, SD = 5.5 years). Before the birth of the children, most of the women were in permanent, full-time employment (in Australia full-time employment is a minimum of 35 h per week), a few were self-employed, in casual or contract positions, or unemployed (See Table 9.1). At this time their partners were also mostly in permanent full-time employment. The education of parents varied widely, as shown in Table 9.1. Most mothers with university degrees returned to work in the first post-partum year, whereas among the group with lower levels of education, fewer had returned to work. Families' combined incomes also varied (see Table 9.1), depending on whether the mother returned to work (χ^2 = 28.5 (df = 12, n = 69), p = .005). Where the mothers did not return, there were significantly fewer families with combined incomes over $60,000, compared to where mothers would later be working, although at later times, household incomes were similar across the families.

Materials and Measures

Paid Work and Leave Entitlements At Time 1 (third trimester of pregnancy), the mothers reported their maternity leave provisions (number of weeks of paid and unpaid maternity leave available), their type of work (not working; self-employed; casual or contract; permanent), and if working, how many hours they were currently working each week (<24 h/week; 25–35 h/week, >35 h/week). The women also indicated if they intended to return to work (Yes [Y] or No [N]) and then at Time 2 (6 months post-partum), Time 3 (12 months post-partum) and Time 4 (18 months post-partum), they were asked if they were working (Yes [Y] or No [N]) at that time.

Work Engagement The women's feelings about work were measured at each time with two items, 'Paid work gives me a great sense of satisfaction' and 'Paid work gives me a sense of personal enjoyment', rated on a Likert scale, 1 = strongly disagree to 5 = strongly agree. The range of Cronbach's alpha values from Time 1 to Time 4 was .72 to .92.

Views About Motherhood The women's views on motherhood were measured with single items, which rated how much the women were satisfied with and enjoyed motherhood, found motherhood difficult, and if they felt they could combine motherhood with paid work. Each item was rated on a 5-point Likert scale, from 1 = strongly disagree to 5 = strongly agree.

Beliefs About Maternal Employment Beliefs around maternal employment were measured with an adaptation of the Beliefs and Consequences of Maternal Employment for Children (BACMEC; Greenberger, Goldberg, Crawford, & Granger, 1988) scale. Initially the BACMEC was used as a guide to write a 43-item measure for the antenatal questionnaire. The original BACMEC scale has 24 items, however some items were rewritten to modernise the scale and additional questions added that measured the benefits and costs for the mother of engaging in paid work as well as the mother's perspective on how it affected her child. Subsequent surveys used 26 items for the scale, following factor analysis of the newly devised scale to check its performance in this sample and only mean scale scores were used in all analyses to ensure equivalence between measurement times. A sample item for Costs of Maternal employment is 'children whose mothers are more likely to have behaviour problems'. The range of Cronbach's alpha values from Time 1 to Time 4 were .93 to .94. A sample item for Benefits of Maternal Employment is 'children whose mothers work are more respectful of their mothers', with the range of Cronbach's alpha values, from Time 1 to Time 4 was .86 to .92. All items were rated on a Likert scale from 1 = strongly disagree to 5 = strongly agree.

Depression Maternal depression was measured with the 10-item Edinburgh Postnatal Depression Scale (Cox, Holden, & Sagovsky, 1987), from which a sample item is, 'I have been so unhappy that I have been crying (reversed-scored)'. The range of Cronbach's alpha values from Time 1 to Time 4 was .81 to .87. Items were rated on a scale, from '1= Yes, most of the time; 2= Yes, quite often, 3= Not very often, 4= No, not at all', with high scores indicating higher levels of maternal depression.

Analytic Strategy

The sample size for those completing all four surveys did not provide sufficient power to conduct regression analyses. Therefore, Mixed Methods ANOVA (Analyses of Variance) were used to explore the data, with the mothers' Work Patterns used as the Between Group factor and the mothers' responses for each variable at baseline (pregnancy), 6 months, 12 months, and 18 months post-partum as the Within Group factor, Time.

Results

Work and Care Decisions

Return to Work Patterns

Before birth, nearly all the mothers intended to return to work (n=66, 90.4 %). However only half were working at Time 2 (n=36, 49.3 %), with the numbers rising at Time 3 (n=53, 72.6 %) to be steady at Time 4 (n=51, 69.9 %). For the purposes of the current analyses, mothers were allocated to groups based on their work patterns following the birth of the children, regardless of whether they had intended to return to work at Time 1. Using employment status at Times 2, 3, and 4 (Y or N), cross-tabs was then used to allocate the women to four Work Pattern groups. Group 1, At Work by 6 months (YYYY or NYYY, $n=33$); Group 2, At Work by 12 months (YNYY, or NNYY, $n=14$), Group 3, Variable Work Patterns ($n=10$); and Group 4, Not Returned to Work (YNNN [$n=11$] or NNNN [$n=4$], $n=15$). For example, mothers in the Variable Work Pattern group may have worked when their children were 6 months old, not at 12 months, and be working again at 18 months, or another combination of entry and exit from employment.

Factors Associated with Return to Work

Provisions for Maternity Leave First, did those who return to work more quickly have less paid maternity leave? Less than half of the total sample reported having paid maternity leave ($n=31$, 42.5 %). The availability of paid maternity leave did impact significantly on return to work ($F(3,27)=4.00$, $p=.018$, $\eta^2=.31$), with pair-wise comparisons (with Bonferonni adjustments) finding that mothers with Variable Working Patterns had significantly longer maternity leave ($M=19.0$ weeks, $SD=8.1$) than mothers who were At Work at 6 months ($M=9.4$ weeks, $SD=3.9$). Just over half the mothers ($n=45$, 62.5 %) were able (or planned) to take unpaid maternity leave, although there were no differences in this respect between the women's different work patterns ($F(3,37)=0.38$, $p=.768$, $\eta^2=.03$). Cross-tabulations found that mothers without the provision for paid maternity leave (i.e., had 6 weeks or less leave available) planned to take more than 26 weeks unpaid maternity leave.

Work and Care Personal Impacts

Maternal Satisfaction

The means and standard deviations for the mothers' satisfaction and enjoyment of motherhood and how difficult they rated motherhood are shown in Table 9.2. The ANOVA results for all comparisons are shown in Table 9.3. The mothers did not differ on their satisfaction with motherhood, regardless of the age of their child, their work pattern, or as the interaction between age of child and work pattern. Similarly, the mothers did not differ in their enjoyment of motherhood, regardless of age of their child, across work patterns, or in the interaction between age of the child and work pattern.

Interestingly, how difficult motherhood was considered, did change over time for all mothers, but this was best explained by a quadratic trend as an inverted U shape. Motherhood was rated less difficult when the children were 6 and 12 months compared to before birth, but was considered to increasingly difficult again when

Table 9.2 Means and standard deviations for the ratings about motherhood, over time and based on their work patterns

	Satisfaction with motherhood							
	Before birth		At 6 months		At 12 months		At 18 months	
Mothers' work pattern	M	(SD)	M	(SD)	M	(SD)	M	(SD)
Not worked after birth	4.55	(0.69)	4.82	(0.41)	4.64	(0.51)	4.73	(0.47)
Variable working pattern	4.33	(1.12)	4.89	(0.33)	4.89	(0.33)	4.67	(0.50)
Working by 12 months	4.31	(0.63)	4.15	(0.90)	4.38	(0.65)	4.23	(0.93)
Working by 6 months	4.50	(0.67)	4.25	(1.05)	4.72	(0.52)	4.66	(0.55)
	Enjoyment of motherhood							
	Before birth		At 6 months		At 12 months		At 18 months	
Mothers' work pattern	M	(SD)	M	(SD)	M	(SD)	M	(SD)
Not worked after birth	4.45	(0.69)	4.82	(0.41)	4.73	(0.47)	4.73	(0.47)
Variable working pattern	4.89	(0.33)	4.89	(0.33)	4.89	(0.33)	4.67	(0.50)
Working by 12 months	4.38	(0.65)	4.46	(0.66)	4.54	(0.66)	4.46	(0.66)
Working by 6 months	4.59	(0.62)	4.50	(0.80)	4.72	(0.46)	4.66	(0.48)
	'Motherhood is difficult'							
	Before birth		At 6 months		At 12 months		At 18 months	
Mothers' work pattern	M	(SD)	M	(SD)	M	(SD)	M	(SD)
Not worked after birth	3.73	(0.88)	3.53	(1.25)	3.67	(0.98)	4.00	(0.93)
Variable working pattern	4.33	(0.71)	3.85	(0.78)	4.00	(0.87)	4.22	(0.44)
Working by 12 months	4.00	(0.39)	4.00	(0.96)	3.71	(1.20)	4.07	(0.73)
Working by 6 months	4.00	(0.74)	3.57	(1.15)	3.53	(1.13)	3.74	(1.05)

Table 9.3 Results of ANOVAs that compared the outcomes, based on mothers' work patterns and child age

	Mothers' work pattern		Age of child		Work pattern × Age of child	
Outcomes	F(3,61)	η^2	F(3,204)	η^2	F(9,204)	η^2
Satisfaction with motherhood	1.77	.08	1.59	.03	1.52	.07
Enjoyment of motherhood	1.40	.07	0.88	.01	0.81	.03
'Motherhood is difficult'	0.83	.03	3.18*	.05	0.64	.05
Maternal depression	0.26	.01	2.34†	.03	1.88†	.08
Costs of maternal employment	3.70*	.14	2.71*	.04	1.01	.04
Benefits of maternal employment	3.82*	.14	0.30	.01	1.03	.04
Work engagement	0.28	.01	9.34***	.13	1.03	.05
Combining motherhood & paid work	4.69**	.19	0.84	.01	2.09*	.09

† $p<.10$, * $p<.05$, ** $p<.01$, *** $p<.001$
Note. 'Age of child': measurements taken before birth, and when the children were 6 months, 12 months, and 18 months old

the children were 18 months (i.e., change from 12 months to 18 months, $t(71)=2.7$, $p=.051$). However, whether motherhood was considered difficult did not vary between the work pattern groups, or as the interaction between work pattern and age of child.

Table 9.4 Means and standard deviations of the costs and benefits of maternal employment and levels of depressive symptoms over time and by work pattern

	Costs of maternal employment							
	Before birth		At 6 months		At 12 months		At 18 months	
Mothers' work pattern	M	(SD)	M	(SD)	M	(SD)	M	(SD)
Not worked after birth	2.75	(0.65)	2.69	(0.53)	2.86	(0.58)	2.59	(0.81)
Variable working pattern	2.43	(0.74)	2.22	(0.89)	2.27	(0.84)	2.15	(0.76)
Working by 12 months	2.16	(0.37)	2.08	(0.52)	2.00	(0.57)	2.11	(0.62)
Working by 6 months	2.54	(0.57)	2.39	(0.59)	2.22	(0.60)	2.24	(0.60)
	Benefits of maternal employment							
	Before birth		At 6 months		At 12 months		At 18 months	
Mothers' work pattern	M	(SD)	M	(SD)	M	(SD)	M	(SD)
Not worked after birth	2.77	(0.55)	2.66	(0.59)	2.68	(0.51)	2.75	(0.77)
Variable working pattern	2.79	(0.75)	2.73	(0.61)	2.64	(0.76)	2.58	(0.59)
Working by 12 months	2.93	(0.45)	3.12	(0.57)	3.25	(0.48)	3.20	(0.59)
Working by 6 months	2.98	(0.62)	3.11	(0.53)	3.13	(0.52)	3.14	(0.56)
	Depression							
	Before birth		At 6 months		At 12 months		At 18 months	
Mothers' work pattern	M	(SD)	M	(SD)	M	(SD)	M	(SD)
Not worked after birth	17.64	(4.45)	17.64	(4.43)	16.07	(4.62)	15.57	(3.37)
Variable working pattern	17.56	(3.57)	17.44	(4.61)	14.78	(2.91)	16.00	(3.39)
Working by 12 months	15.79	(4.32)	17.64	(3.79)	17.07	(3.71)	19.21	(5.81)
Working by 6 months	16.64	(3.77)	16.94	(4.70)	16.00	(4.91)	16.33	(4.47)

Maternal Depression

The means and standard deviations for the mothers' ratings on the Edinburgh Post-Natal Depression scale are shown in Table 9.4. An examination of the means shows that there was considerable variability in the scores, with some increasing and some decreasing over time. The interaction between work pattern and time approached significance, as did the effect of the age of the child. The effect of the child's age was best explained as a cubic trend, with significant differences between the highest level of depressive symptoms (at 6 months) and the least (at 12 months; $t(69)=2.98$, $p=.024$) and similar levels before birth and at 18 months when all mothers were combined. The level of depression overall did not vary with the mothers' pattern of work. Although the interaction between work and age of the children did not quite reach significance, examination of the means indicated considerable variability amongst the mother's levels of depressive symptoms. Simple main effects for the interactions between age of children and work pattern group showed that only mothers in the Working at 12 Months group ($F(3,64)=2.97$, $p=.0$, $\eta^2=.12$) reported an increase in depressive symptoms over time and this increase was significant only from before birth to when the child was 18 months old ($t(69)=2.74$, $p=.008$).

Costs and Benefits of Maternal Employment

The means and standard deviations for the mothers' belief about the cost and benefits of maternal employment at each time point are shown in Table 9.4. Mothers differed on how they perceived the costs of maternal employment based on both their work pattern and the age of their children. With regards to perceived costs between the mothers in the work pattern groups, pairwise comparisons, with Bonferroni adjustments, found that mothers who had returned to work by 12 months saw significantly fewer costs of maternal employment than mothers who had not worked after the birth of their child, $t(26)=3.23$, $p=.011$, with the other comparisons not reaching significance. With regards to the age of the children, there was a decrease in perceived costs across all mothers, with the difference approaching significance (after the Bonferroni adjustment) from before birth to when the child was 18 months old, $t(72)=2.56$, $p=.075$. The interaction between work pattern and the age of the children was not significant.

When the benefits of maternal employment were considered, the mothers' work patterns were important differences, as pairwise comparisons (with Bonferroni adjustment) showed that overall, mothers who were not working perceived fewer benefits than mothers who had returned to work by 6 months, $t(42)=2.53$, $p=.082$. Within the work pattern groups, the mothers' attitudes remained constant as their children grew older, and the interaction between work pattern and age of children was not significant.

Engaging with Work and Combining Work and Family

The means and standard deviations for the mother's engagement with their jobs and how they felt about combining with their work and family roles are shown in Table 9.5. The mothers' satisfaction and enjoyment in work changed significantly over time, which was best explained as a quadratic trend of an inverted U shape. There were no differences between the work patterns or for the interaction between age of child and work pattern. The pair-wise comparisons (with Bonferroni adjustments) found that all times after birth were less than before birth (at 6 months, $t(67)=4.02$, $p=.001$; at 12 months, $t(67)=4.47$, $p<.001$), although work engagement was closer to pre-birth levels when the children were 18 months old ($t(67)=2.99$, $p=.023$).

When the mothers rated how well they believed they could combine work and family, the interaction between work pattern and age of the children was significant and showed substantial variation depending on work pattern, whilst age of child did not affect this belief. Mothers who had not returned to work believed they would be less able to combine work and motherhood than all the other mothers (versus Variable Work Pattern, $t(18)=2.63$, $p=.065$; versus Working at 12 months, $t(22)=3.06$, $p=.020$; versus Working at 6 months, $t(42)=3.56$, $p=.004$). The greatest differences were when the children were 6 months old (versus Variable

Table 9.5 Means and standard deviations for the ratings about work, over time and based on their work patterns

	Work engagement							
	Before birth		At 6 months		At 12 months		At 18 months	
Mothers' work pattern	M	(SD)	M	(SD)	M	(SD)	M	(SD)
Not worked after birth	4.12	(0.58)	3.81	(0.33)	3.62	(0.87)	3.92	(0.45)
Variable working pattern	4.31	(0.46)	3.94	(0.90)	3.81	(0.59)	4.06	(0.68)
Working by 12 months	4.43	(0.62)	3.89	(0.88)	3.61	(1.15)	3.86	(0.63)
Working by 6 months	3.94	(0.75)	3.76	(0.87)	3.74	(0.88)	3.88	(0.66)
	Combining motherhood and paid work							
	Before birth		At 6 months		At 12 months		At 18 months	
Mother's work pattern	M	(SD)	M	(SD)	M	(SD)	M	(SD)
Not worked after birth	3.64	(0.92)	3.36	(0.92)	3.64	(0.92)	3.64	(1.29)
Variable working pattern	4.22	(0.67)	4.33	(0.71)	4.11	(0.60)	4.11	(0.60)
Working by 12 months	4.46	(0.66)	3.77	(0.83)	4.38	(0.51)	4.31	(0.75)
Working by 6 months	3.94	(0.75)	4.30	(0.59)	4.30	(0.77)	4.36	(0.60)

Work Pattern, $t(18)=3.01$, $p=.004$; versus Working at 6 Months, $t(42)=3.77$, $p<.001$). Women who were working by 12 months also reported a dip in their confidence of combining work at family when their children were 6 months old, compared to before birth ($t(12)=3.05$, $p=.003$) and when the children were 12 months old ($t(12)=2.96$, $p=.004$).

Discussion

The circumstances that challenge us are those in which resilience can be observed. The data presented in this chapter focussed on the significant challenge of women's return to work following the birth of their first child against a context where public policy provided limited support and social values regarding work and motherhood were ambivalent. We examined the decision women made regarding timing of return to paid work and the impact of these decisions on their well-being, satisfaction with motherhood, assessment of the personal costs and benefits of paid work.

Although the timing of re-entry and hours of participation varied by 18 months after the birth of their first child, the large majority of women had returned to the workforce, albeit with some returning earlier than anticipated. For those who had entitlement for paid maternity leave, their return to the workforce was significantly later; suggesting financial circumstances drive the decisions of the timing of a return. The data provide important insight into how paid parental leave can provide women with the opportunity to maximise time with their infant in the crucial first year of the child's development. Women also reported that they would take unpaid leave, where paid leave was not available. While our sample size did not permit complex multivariate analyses the emerging significance of these two factors suggests that return to work is more possible and less anxiety provoking when women leave their infants in circumstances of care with which they feel secure. For most this was care with relatives. Qualitative data from two Australian studies (Boyd et al., 2013; Harris, 2008) align with this proposition, reporting that insecurity with quality of care limited workforce participation while known and trusted care facilitated return to the workforce and maintenance of employment. Alongside the availability of known and trusted care, reduced separation anxiety for mothers predicted their return to work (Boyd, 2014).

The majority of women not only returned to work within the first 18 months after giving birth but adapted well to their circumstances. Regardless of the decision that had made about returning, there were no differences amongst the mothers with regard to their feeling about motherhood. All reported positively on their experience of motherhood as being satisfying and enjoyable. Interestingly, whether they regarded motherhood as 'difficult' did change, but this was linked to their child's age. Perhaps the increase in perceived difficulty when the children were 18 months old was associated with normal developmental changes, as the child is becoming more mobile, inquisitive, and independent. These behavioural changes may present a challenge for any mother, whether or not she is working.

The mothers, however, did vary on how they perceived the costs and benefits of maternal employment; with the mothers who did not return being more negative about the effects of working, reporting that they felt there were fewer benefits and more costs for children when mothers worked. Notably, among women who returned to work, the benefits of maternal employment were more highly rated, while how they perceived the costs of work reduced across time. Though the design of this study is different from that of Hock and DeMeis (1990), the increased perception of benefits of work across time may reflect the personal and mental health benefits of paid work previously reported in this study. This and other studies report significantly greater well-being of women returning to work compared with those outside employment, but who would prefer to engage in paid work (Hock & DeMeis, 1990; Pungello & Kurtz- Costes, 2000). The results for the levels of postnatal depression were more varied and more difficult to interpret; given the sample size and that the results only approached significance. It is likely that the variability may reflect the mothers' feelings about becoming accustomed to and settling into their new roles. It is interesting that work patterns did not affect levels of depressive symptoms, which would indicate that employment per se did not impact on the mother's mental health. However, the current study only included mothers until their children reached 18 months of age and the widening gap between perceived costs and benefits for working mothers between the working and non-working mothers in this sample however may influence future well-being. Previous research on large samples that followed mothers and their children up to 3 years of age found that where mothers perceived greater costs of maternal employment and a mismatch between actual and ideal employment, they were more likely to be depressed and feel maternal stress (Chang, 2013; Holmes et al., 2012). Should the 'cost' of work continue to grow however, then mothers who remain out of the workforce could be at risk of poorer mental health and becoming disengaged from their pre-birth occupations and future career opportunities.

While each woman found different ways to balance work and care, paid work did seem to have increased benefits across time. When asked specifically about combining work and motherhood, the mothers who had not returned to work were much less confident that they could combine work and motherhood, particularly in the months after birth. Interestingly, amongst the mothers who had returned to work when their children were 12 months, also reported a dip in this confidence immediately after birth, but this had increased again at the time when they were actually doing so. It is likely that the lived experience of combining work and mothering gave the women confidence that the combination could be 'successful' for them and their children and that the costs of this arrangement were manageable.

The data provided in this chapter have considerable strength. The focus on a community sample, commencement in pregnancy and the prospective longitudinal design all allow an understanding of the dynamics of decision making and associations with outcomes. There are, however, limitations relating to attrition of sample that limited sophistication of statistical analyses. Our data, like prior studies (Hock & DeMeis, 1990; Pungello & Kurtz- Costes, 2000) attest to women's ability to adjust to and thrive in the workplace after the birth of a child. The circumstances of the women in our study provide a further example in contemporary Australian society.

In conclusion, our study showed that there are two external forces that can support a balance between their personal needs and roles as mothers and employee. First, government regulations that support and encourage the workplace provision of maternity leave as an explicit societal goal that will benefit all of our society. Second, the provision of quality care that is trusted, familiar, and available and not a significant financial burden, is vital for mothers to accommodate the challenge of combining their family and occupational roles.

References

Australian Bureau of Statistics. (2013). *Australian social trends data: Work*. Retrieved from www.abs.gov.au

Baxter, J. (2014). *Child care participation and maternal employment trends in Australia*. Retrieved from http://www.aifs.gov.au/institute/pubs/resreport26/rr26a.html

Biddulph, S. (2005). *Raising babies. Should under 3s go to nursery?* London: Harper Thorsons.

Boyd, W. (2014). Parents' choices of child care in Australia. *NZ Research in Early Childhood Education, 17*, 51–69.

Boyd, W., Walker, S., & Thorpe, K. (2013). Choosing work and choosing care: Four Australian women negotiating return to paid work in the first year of motherhood. *Contemporary Issues in Early Childhood, 14*(2), 168–178.

Chang, Y. E. (2013). The Relation between mothers' attitudes toward maternal employment and social competence of 36-month-olds: The roles of maternal psychological well-being and sensitivity. *Journal of Child and Family Studies, 22*(7), 987–999. doi:10.1007/s10826-012-9660-7.

Charlesworth, S., & Chelmers, J. (2005). Studies in 'quality' part-time employment. *Labour & Industry, 15*(3), 1–6.

Clausen, L. (2006, March 13). Who's minding the kids? *Time Magazine, 13th March, 2006.*

Coffey, A. (2004). *Reconceptualising social policy*. Berkshire, UK: Open University Press.

Cox, J. L., Holden, J. M., & Sagovsky, R. (1987). Detection of postnatal depression. Development of the 10 item Edinburgh postnatal depression scale. *The British Journal of Psychiatry, 150*(6), 782–786.

Craig, L. (2007). *Contemporary motherhood: The impact of children on adult time*. Aldershop, UK: Burlington.

Craig, L., & Mullan, K. (2010). Parenthood, gender and work-family time in the United States, Australia, Italy, France, and Denmark. *Journal of Marriage and the Family, 72*, 1344–1361.

DeMeis, D. K., Hock, E., & McBride, S. L. (1986). The balance of employment and motherhood: Longitudinal study of mothers' feelings about separation from their first-born infants. *Developmental Psychology, 22*(5), 627–632.

Greenberger, E., Goldberg, W. A., Crawford, T. J., & Granger, J. (1988). Beliefs about the consequences of maternal employment for children. *Psychology of Women Quarterly, 12*, 35–59. doi:10.1111/j.1471-6402.1988.tb00926.x.

Harris, N. (2008). Women's reflections on choosing quality long day care in a regional community. *Australian Journal of Early Childhood, 33*(3), 42–49.

Hock, E., & DeMeis, D. K. (1990). Depression in mothers of infants: The role of maternal employment. *Developmental Psychology, 26*(2), 285–291.

Holmes, E. K., Erickson, J. J., & Hill, E. J. (2012). Doing what she thinks is best: Maternal psychological well-being and attaining desired work situations. *Human Relations, 65*(4), 501–522. doi:10.1177/0018726711431351.

Huerta, M. C, Adema, W., Baxter, J., Corak, M., Deding, M., Gray, M., Han, W., & Waldfogel, J. (2011). *Early maternal employment and child development in five OECD countries*. Retrieved from oecd.org

Killien, M. G. (2005). The role of social support in facilitating postpartum women's return to employment. *Journal of Obstetric, Gynecologic, & Neonatal Nursing, 34*(5), 639–646.

Krapf, S. (2009). *Childcare and family ideology in Sweden*. Rostock, Germany: Max Planck Institute for Demographic Research.

Manne, A. (2005). *Motherhood*. Crows Nest, Australia: Allen & Unwin.

Organisation for Economic Co-operation and Development (OECD). (2006). *Starting strong II*. Paris: OECD.

Organisation for Economic Co-operation and Development (OECD). (2007). *Babies and bosses. Reconciling work and family life*. Paris: OECD.

Pocock, B. (2005). Work/care regimes: Institutions, culture and behaviour and the Australian case. *Gender, Work & Organization, 12*(1), 32–49.

Pungello, E. P., & Kurtz- Costes, B. (2000). Working women's selection of care for their infants: A prospective study. *Family Relations, 49*, 245–255.

Thorpe, K., Cloney, D., & Tayler, C. (2010). Rethinking early childhood education and care: Implications for research and evaluation. In *Encyclopedia of education* (3rd ed.). Oxford, UK: Elsevier.

Chapter 10
Building Capacity for Positive Communication: A Web-Based Mother-Daughter Communication Resource to Support Work-Family Balance

Mary Katsikitis, Christian Jones, Melody Muscat, and Kate Crawford

Introduction

This chapter focuses on one method of supporting women through their lives by providing a resource that supports simple and easy to embrace strategies to improve and sustain open and positive communication, which the family can adopt on a daily basis. This chapter has one simple message and that is, if effective communication strategies for women can be initiated and nurtured at home, then women will take these strategies into any other forum they encounter (e.g., other relationships, work). In fact, it was the early theorising of Bowlby that hypothesised that early positive relationships between a child and her/his parents set the scene, and act as prototypes, for all relationships later in life (Bowlby, 1969). This was followed by the work of Papousek and Papousek (1997) which highlighted the role of communication, in particular, learning to communicate, as the most important learning in human development.

The theoretical foundation of this work sits firmly in the positive psychology literature and the clinical psychology literature which highlights the importance of early positive modelling experiences and relationships on the future well-being and resilience of all individuals (Dekovic & Meeus, 1997; Raudino, Fergusson, & Horwood, 2013).

M. Katsikitis (✉) • C. Jones • M. Muscat
Discipline of Psychology and the Engage Laboratory, University of the Sunshine Coast, Maroochydore, QLD 4558, Australia
e-mail: mkatsiki@usc.edu.au; cmjones@usc.edu.au; mmuscat@usc.edu.au

K. Crawford
Eviva Pty Ltd, Kuranda, QLD, Australia
e-mail: Kate@eviva.com.au

R.L. Gervais, P.M. Millear (eds.), *Exploring Resources, Life-Balance and Well-Being of Women Who Work in a Global Context*,
DOI 10.1007/978-3-319-31736-6_10

Happiness and well-being in life have taken over our lexicon in recent years and more evidence points towards the existence and scientific measurement of these concepts (Diener, 2000; Lyubomirsky & Lepper, 1999). These topics of discussion take pride of place in the positive psychology literature and are preferred over research covering disease and interventions which are aimed primarily at the treatment of illnesses. Positive psychology focuses on the science of well-being and the quest to support sustained flourishing of individuals from all walks of life and throughout the lifespan. The five pillars of Seligman's theory of well-being: positive emotion, engagement, relationships, meaning, and accomplishment (PERMA) have been used here for the development and establishment of a positive psychology intervention for mothers and their adolescent daughters (Seligman, 2011). In particular, our focus on positive relationships draws our attention to one of the five PERMA pillars, and in this chapter, we use communication skills, conflict resolution skills and parenting style as firstly, acknowledged mediators for healthy relationships (Egan, 2012; Papousek & Papousek, 1997), and secondly, simple and straightforward skills to teach to both the mothers and their daughters in a non-therapeutic, and non-invasive environment, that is, in the family home.

This chapter introduces a positive communication intervention strategy designed to bring mothers and daughters together to discuss and explore several issues, including interpersonal communication and parenting style, and conflict resolution. The project had two stages. Stage 1 consisted of conducting two separate focus groups, one with mothers, and a separate one with their adolescent daughters. The purpose of the focus group meetings was to enquire with each group separately, as to their relationship (positive or otherwise) with their daughters (mothers' focus group) and with their mothers (daughters' focus group), and how well they felt they communicated in this relationship. We also posed some questions about their confidence with technology use, as we were anticipating that our intervention would take on a web-based and Short Message Service (SMS) design, developed for mothers and daughters to work independently at times (as well as together for much of the time), hence some level of competence in this domain was important. In Stage 2, we designed a web-based intervention, using technologies such as Facebook and SMS to support our programming (Katsikitis, Jones, Muscat, & Crawford, 2014). The intervention provides a new opportunity to provide supportive, positive experiences that meet the developmental needs of both groups. The intervention involves activities that mothers and daughters do together, once a week, for a period of three weeks. The targeted outcome variables in the intervention include mother-daughter communication, parenting style, parental confidence in parenting, and self-esteem of both parties.

Much of the focus of mother-daughter relationships in the literature has been on strategies to manage and deal with negative adolescent behaviour such as identity and attachment issues (Benson, Harris, & Rogers, 1992), conflict (Steinberg, 1990), violence (Caprara, Regallia, & Bandura, 2002), parental satisfaction (Erel & Burman, 1995), divorce and remarriage (Orbuch, Thornton, & Cancia, 2000), and antisocial behaviour (Loeber, Farrington, Stouthamer-Loeber, & Van Kammen,

1998). This deficit-based approach has been replaced in recent times by the strengths-based approach of positive psychology and is the focus of this paper.

There is a substantial body of evidence endorsing the mother-daughter relationship and the influence that a positive, stable bond has on females throughout their lives (Boyd, 1989; Herman, 1989). The research evidence also suggests that it is the quality of the relationship and interactions between mother and daughter and positive parenting practices that contribute to the psychosocial adjustment of the adolescent girl (Barber, Bolitho, & Bertrand, 2001). In a survey of parent-adolescent dyads, Barber et al. found that adolescents showed better emotional adjustment when a parent shared similar views of the adolescent's psychological state. In another study, positive parent-adolescent relationships were shown to contribute to better mental well-being and less delinquency in the adolescent (Hair, Moore, Garrett, Ling, & Cleveland, 2008). Positive effects of the parent-adolescent relationship were seen in adolescents who perceived their parents to have good awareness of their peer friendships and activities, engaged in routine family activities (e.g., eating dinner together or doing a fun activity together), and perceived higher parental supportiveness (Hair et al., 2008). Although adolescence marks a time of increasing independence from parents, the research indicates a continuing role of parent-child interactions in improving adolescent outcomes. This suggests that adolescent adjustment and well-being are enhanced when mothers and daughters communicate well and share understanding.

The effects of positive mother-daughter communication can also be seen for mothers in the workplace. Balancing work commitments with family life can be difficult. Despite cultural changes over the past decades, for many women with children, the concept that "good mothering" is important to a woman's femininity remains prevalent (Maher & Saugeres, 2007). Some mothers may experience challenges attempting to fulfil this traditional role, whilst also maintaining career progression (Raskin, 2006). Positive relationships can be viewed as psychosocial resources enabling resilience (Moen & Erickson, 1995). Relationships within the family can be considered a particularly potent resource due to their proximity and positive mother-daughter relationships would provide a resource to support mothers undertaking these multiple roles. Indeed, research has shown that working mothers who reported rewarding experiences with their partner or children were buffered against negative effects of poor job experiences (Barnett, 1994). Other research has shown that working mothers experience greater negative home-to-work spillover than do working fathers (Long Dilworth, 2004). In particular, family life satisfaction was shown to be a strong predictor of whether home interactions were perceived as detrimental to work performance (Long Dilworth, 2004). Conditions in the family appear to spillover into the workplace, whether to reduce a mother's capacity to work well or to buffer against negative work experiences. Millear (2016) discusses these multiple roles a woman faces in her lifetime and suggests that these experiences have indeed had a positive effect on women's parenting, creating a sense of resourcefulness and less anxiety. Overall, the research evidence would suggest that an intervention designed to improve mother-daughter communication may produce benefit for both psychosocial adjustment during adolescence and work outcomes for mothers. Furthermore, following and adding an observation to Millear's research, if we can achieve a sense of parent-child engagement that is sustained throughout life, then mothers and their children can reach a state of relaxation earlier (and not just in the adult years).

It is necessary to consider that a child's entry into adolescence leads to many changes within a family that affect the capacity for positive mother-daughter communication. Social relationships between parents and their children change as part of the developmental stage of the child (Belsky, 1984; Ben-Zur, 2003). Indeed as children pass through middle childhood and enter adolescence, the cognitive and emotional changes that occur at this stage, leave many parents reeling and questioning their own skills for successful adjustment through this transitional period. Belsky noted that it is those parents who are able to remain flexible in their approach to parenting, that adapt more positively to the changes occurring within the family at this time. Although the quest for independence is a rite of passage for adolescents, parents continue to remain a significant and influential part of their children's lives (Furnham & Cheng, 2000).

The emotional climate within the family home is also an important indicator of adolescent well-being. Montemayor (1986) found that there was significant family variation in parenting during times of stress and also marked parent-adolescent differences in their degree of conflict. This work identified four ways to minimise conflict between mother and daughters: (1) improve the interaction style so that it is more positive; (2) hone the parenting techniques used to manage adolescent behaviour; (3) practice active problem solving; and (4) use positive communication skills. These findings overlap with our work presented below, utilising focus groups with mothers and daughters regarding their current positives and conflicts.

Stocker, Richmond, Rhoades, and Kiang (2007) supported the consideration of the emotional climate for adolescent well-being. In their work, they suggested that parents maintain an active support role for their adolescent's emotional experiences and that they use these times as opportunities for building intimacy and trust. Furthermore, they found that adolescent psychological well-being was associated with appropriate validation, openness of parental communication and empathy to their emotional experiences. Other research has shown that positive communication skills training involves empathic understanding, clarity and congruence of the message, good problem solving skills and the ability to use language and emotion effectively in communication (Cole, Martin, & Dennis, 2004; Olson, Russell, & Sprenkle, 1983).

The complex biological transition of adolescence occurs at the same time as most mothers reach middle age. For adolescents the change represents the beginning of adult sexuality and independence. For mothers, it is the beginning of the end of a period of life in which parenting was a priority activity. Thus both mothers and daughters have the need for support and nurturing through this transition period. Research has suggested that it is the quality of the relationship with parents as well as the activities with friends that are the best indicators of risk taking behaviours such as alcohol abuse. In particular, authoritative parenting appears to provide young people with a better family based support for managing personal risks and safety, as opposed to permissive or authoritarian parenting (Donnelly, Young, Pearson, Penhollow, & Hernandez, 2008), and as well, it is difficult for adults who are uncertain of their role or capability to be authoritative (Guilamo-Ramos, Jaccard, Dittus, & Bouris, 2006).

Stage 1

Method

The research for Stage 1 of this project was carried out using a small group of mother and daughter dyads. Two focus groups were formed, one each for daughters ($n=4$) and mothers ($n=4$). It was anticipated that separate focus groups would improve the honesty of answers. In addition, a combined focus group may have increased the potential for mother-daughter conflicts and was thus avoided. Daughters were aged between 12 and 13 years. The participants were volunteers recruited from a school in the local region and they had already been informed of the purpose of the focus groups through a school flyer. The recruitment process targeted both mothers and daughters, who then ask their respective child or mother whether they would like to participate. Parents had also given their consent for daughters (daughters also gave consent) to participate. This research was approved and supported by the Human Research Ethics Committee at the University of the Sunshine Coast (A10223).

At the beginning of the session, both groups were again given a brief scripted explanation of the purpose and aims of the discussion and what was expected of the participants in each of the focus groups. The voluntary nature of their participation and the privacy issues were emphasised once more. Each focus group lasted approximately one hour and had two facilitators present. The focus group discussions were recorded and transcribed. The two focus groups; one for mothers and one for daughters, and members of each group were separately guided through a discussion using the following questions as stimuli:

1. What can you tell us about your current communication experiences with your mum/ daughter?, e.g., time spent communicating, style of the communication, types of technologies used in your communication, confidence in using these technologies?
2. Have you noticed any change in your communication experience with your mum/daughter recently?, and, if any, what kinds of change?
3. What sorts of things do you talk to your mum/daughter about?
4. How do you feel about talking things over with your mum/daughter?, e.g., does she always listen to you?, do you listen to her?, do you spend the time it takes to be heard?
5. Do you have established ground rules at your place and what are they?, e.g., time home from school/ outings, privacy, showing respect, knowing friends or friends' parents?, and, how do you discuss and negotiate the ground rules together?

6. Do you always agree? e.g., areas of agreement?, what happens?, areas of disagreement?, what happens?, how do you feel about your reactions? (in control, out of control, reasonable?), and, do you resolve your disagreements?, if so, how?
7. Is there anything else you think is important for us to discuss at this session?

The focus group transcripts were analysed using a phenomenographic method. Responses were noted as involving "key consensus", "general agreement", or "more individual responses". Sequences of conversation with explicit group agreement were most heavily weighted, whereas those with implied agreement were weighted at a medium level. Individual responses were included to indicate the scope of responses within the group. The resulting analysis contrasted the perspectives of mothers and daughters.

Results and Discussion

One important result from the small focus group discussions was that they generally aligned with the research literature on relationships and expectations between mothers and pre-adolescent daughters. The two groups confirmed that relationships between mothers and daughters at this stage are already emotionally intense on both sides and clearly centre on talking, fighting, and making up. The communication is considered important by both groups. The conflict is generally considered shameful by both groups, to be avoided, and a cause of stress, guilt and anxiety.

Fighting from the daughters' perspectives was shown through verbatim comments such as, "*Me and my mum fight because I answer her back*" and "*Yeah we don't really fight we just, yeah we fight, argue little a bit*", and,

> Me and my mum have like short sharp bickers. Like she might shout at me for doing something so I'll annoy her and then she'll shout at me for doing it and then I'll get upset, more upset and she'll like "Well why'd you do that ?" and then it's over.

The mothers' discussion group revealed the level of emotional intensity for them in the conflict and their anxiety and helplessness about the kind of role model they were being.

> So yeah, something that would kind of normalise the behaviour and make you kind of keep yourself in check I suppose. And stop yourself repeating the mistakes that people have repeated. I mean when we were talking about communication, I often, I mean I don't hit M....., I don't believe that using violence is a good way of teaching your child, "Oh don't do that or I'll thump you" because what is that teaching them. But equally like you were saying about the shouting, it's the same, you know, I'm teaching her "Don't do that or I'll yell in your face" so ... I know that's not good. I know that, I'd prefer it to hitting her, I'd be honest, but it's still not good and I'd like something, an alternative that would keep me calm but it is difficult.

> It feels like we do lots of shouting except now there is lots [sic] more shouting coming from her side as well. I can feel that the shouting is building up in the house. I just think sometimes when the windows are open, "What must my neighbours be thinking?"

The focus group with mothers also highlighted their strong sense of normative social expectations about the role as a parent, and in particular, a mother, as a model and support for their daughters. Mothers are keenly aware of what the neighbours or school will think of their parenting capabilities. There is general agreement in both groups that conflict, or '*fighting*' is bad but the daughters sense a need for it, whereas mothers feel helpless in avoiding conflict. The quote above from the mothers' focus group illustrates their emotional intensity as well as their sense of vulnerability in the face of neighbours' negative judgements.

Many of the daughters' comments suggested a real sense that they were aware the mothers felt they needed to be a good mother and made a real effort. This was evident in a particular exchange, "*But she makes sacrifices to let you do what you want so* ..." [a facilitator noted that all looked embarrassed] (Several) "*Yeah*". "*If she has to sacrifice something, she'll do it just to be with you*".

There is also a strong sense by the daughters of using conflict to actively contest issues and that the need to do this is growing. One daughter said:

> Well I suppose a lot of the time we have conflict it's not very cool, it's that whole conflict, because it projects in something which we probably could a couple years ago minimise but I think now this age I don't really want to be told to, that she's right, I suppose and I always think that I am and so that ends up in conflict.

In contrast, the daughters also appeared concerned and guilty about the fact that their mothers are hurting as they seek more privacy and independence. Typically there was also a sense that the conflict is their fault. The daughters were very aware of the emotional spirals that are set in motion. One group discussion is presented below.

> "And you take it personally."
> "And you always think that it's your fault."
> "Like the end of the world."
> "You always seem like you've made them feel like such a big part of your life and if it's the end it's going to hurt really badly so you like get really sad and anxious."
> "And then if you get all sad it makes them feel bad and then you feel bad and then you all feel bad."
> "Yeah!"

For mothers, there was a strong sense that the tensions reflect on their capabilities, are bad and frowned upon by their neighbours. The mothers would like better strategies to deal with the changing relationships. An alternate view is that the 'behaviour' of their daughters should be normalised so there is less blame for them.

The focus groups also confirmed the importance of body image and sexuality as large issues for both mothers and daughters. Daughters were anxious and getting messages about the trouble sexuality will cause them. Mothers in this group strongly avoided discussing the issue. There is ambivalence about body image for both groups in several ways. The daughter comment below illustrates the sensitivity of the issue.

> The other day my mum was shopping for a bikini, like a new one, like she came out with this really skimpy one and I'm like "Well … Um …" and I didn't want to offend her and then she goes "Think it's skimpy ?" and I'm like "Well dah!" [sic] and she goes "Hmf" and I'm like "No!"

This comment illustrates a mother's perspective on emerging sexuality:

> I'm just going to be like "Oh no" because how do you see them through that because I can even remember that still, even as old as I am. I can remember sitting in my bedroom and thinking that it was the end of the world that this boy didn't like me anymore and I think because of that I keep trying to drum into her, you know how it can be when you're grown up, how you can think that you really do like somebody but you might really like 5 or 6 or 7 or 8 people as you go along and that boys can put pressure on you to do things that you don't want to do, so I'm trying to like gear her up for all that. No one had that talk with me so my first boyfriend told me that everybody was having sex, I believed him.

The blooming sexuality of their daughters was a cause for anxiety as the mothers are expecting a '*rough ride*' and the daughters were also ambivalent about their physical maturity. There is ample evidence in these discussions that mothers and daughters do talk about sexuality. Mothers in general tried to pass on their experience. However, the quality of the discussion is generally in terms of authoritative warnings by mothers. Their anxiety for their daughters was evident in the mothers' focus group.

The daughters were generally anxious about adolescence, sexuality and boys because of what their mothers were telling them. However the daughters were also excited at the prospect of the change.

Both groups liked communicating and doing '*girlie*' things together. However, in the busy lives of the twenty-first century both needed to plan to spend leisure time together to go shopping, straighten hair or walk and talk. One participant described her family's process of arranging '*mummy dates*' and '*daddy dates*' to ensure that children had time with parents.

The focus group confirmed the generational differences (Prensky, 2001a, 2001b) in attitude to, knowledge about, and capability to use communication technologies. Again this is not well researched in the public health literature as an issue that potentially causes greater stresses and alienation between generations as adolescents switch from having parents as their closest relationships to a greater focus on, and attachment to, their peers (Vellerman, 2009a). Mothers were essentially uninterested in the use of communication technologies to keep in touch and still viewed communication in terms of the face to face interactions in the intimacy of the family. The mothers joked about needing control technologies such as "*microchips*" and "*tracking devices*" when asked about using communication technologies. In contrast most of the daughters had mobile phones.

The daughters were aware of their mothers' limited knowledge but both groups use mobile phones to monitor or keep in touch. The daughters reported assisting their mothers to learn to use a new phone. One daughter said, "*when my mum gets a new phone she usually doesn't know how to use it, [laughter] and it's like ok, you do this and this and then she'll just be like 'what'. Like, what was that again?*"

The daughters reported having access to computers, phones, television (TV), and Wii (video game console) games. However, for them even at 11 and 12 years of age, phones were clearly becoming important ways to keep in touch with their mothers from school, when visiting fathers and friends. Even if they did not have credit on their phone they used better organised friend's phones to stay in touch or to organise their lives. The girls reported also that phone calls and text messages were a good way to discuss edgy or difficult topics with their mothers.

> It's kind of weird. When we're just, like together sometimes we don't actually communicate very well, like back and forward, back and forward. I think that's just a girl thing. But when I'm on the phone, there's [sic] no awkward silences, you just go blah, blah, blah, blah. You just keep on going. 'Cos [sic] they can't really see you.

The focus groups also confirmed a pre-adolescent desire for continuing authoritative, supportive and nurturing relationships with their mothers though they expected that this might change in the near future.

'*Making up*', when there were fights, was very important for both groups. Results from the focus groups strongly supported the work of Schinke, Cole, and Fang (2009) in developing conflict resolution skills. However, the discussion suggests a greater focus on conflict resolution for parents and other young adults as a form of resilience or psychological capital development in the face of changing relationships and changing conditions.

There was consensus among the daughters, in this study, that they needed their mothers even though they also needed more independence, more self-expression and more privacy than they did when they were younger. The daughters were generally optimistic about their mothers' continued support.

> How we, how you get along with your mum and if you take silly choices when you're a teenager, like you hear of people that run away and things like that because of the raging hormones but you know that you'll get through thick and thin with your mum. You know, she'll always be there for you no matter what.

In contrast, the mothers were generally very sad at the prospect of '*losing*' their daughters as they grew up. The mothers also appeared to be reporting fairly authoritarian ways of giving instructions in the past and a strong pressure towards more authoritative methods of parenting at the same time as they sense their authority as a parent was diminishing. In contrast to the daughters, the mothers appeared to have little vision of the future and their relationship with an adult daughter. Perhaps this reflects the rarity of close intergenerational relationships and co-housing in the era and the additional intensity of relationships in single parent and nuclear families.

> I mean up until now I've felt that she's very much part of me. She is an extension of me and now it's that move away from your parent and become your own person and being your own individual. And that's difficult when someone's been an extension of you and agreed with everything you've said and thought you were wonderful and I think it's that. It's kind of kicking against that. I mean, I can remember it myself from being her age, of just looking at my mum and thinking, oh, you're such an idiot and I can feel it coming. It's not there yet

> but I can see her looking at me sometimes when I'm going on, going "mm, mm, mm" and she's really thinking "You idiot".

To summarise the findings of the focus group discussions, the issues of communication style, parenting style, and conflict resolution style were all identified as pivotal to the mother-daughter relationship at this stage of the developmental cycle (for both mothers and daughters). These are the three key issues that we have focused on to build a positive intervention via a web-based and Short Message Service (SMS) platform in Stage 2 of this project. The aim of Stage 2 is to provide a positive communication game via the medium of web-based cartoon characters and text messaging to inform mothers and daughters about positive communication, relationship building, and minimisation of risky behaviours. The 'Knowing you, Knowing me' or the KYKM project has been developed as a multimedia gaming and mobile resource to increase the positive communication skills of adolescent females and their mothers during this time of developmental transition.

Stage 2

Introduction

Successful intervention programmes meet the needs of parents as well as their children with the best impact being for mothers and daughters in programmes that facilitate interaction between dyads to raise communication and conflict resolution skills and support positive longer term relationships (Schinke et al., 2009; Vellerman, 2009b). Early intervention that involves both groups provides the best results (Koning et al., 2009).

New communication technologies such as KYKM are now being used to support these programmes (Newton, Vogl, Teeson, & Andrews, 2009a, 2009b; Schinke et al., 2009). They are attractive to adolescents and in the case of KYKM, are out-of-school activities; therefore they provide a cost effective way to deliver alternate experiences and information to adolescents. They also provide a new opportunity to design supportive, attractive and nurturing experiences that meet the developmental needs of both groups and lead to better outcomes for participants. Research suggests that web-based programmes can build social capital in terms of hope, resilience, optimism and efficacy (Luthens, Avy, & Patera, 2008). Finally, the revolution in communication technologies has been driven by the fact that these technologies are used to meet real needs. New forms of networked technologies and the underpinning networked relationships now offer new ways for people to manage the emotional risks of negotiating boundaries, privacy and shared intimacy (De Vulpian, 2005).

The rapid growth and uptake of social networking communication technologies in the twenty-first century, has highlighted that there are new needs for better communication technologies. One result of the rate of change is a very large generation gap in knowledge, experience and capabilities to use these technologies (Prensky, 2001a, 2001b). However, from a positive psychology point of view, one opportunity presented by these developments is the emergence of a new form of intergenerational support and nurturing as mothers and daughters build their shared psychological capital through the maintenance of strong communication links using these new technologies together (Luthens et al., 2008).

Multimedia gaming resource interventions offer a portable mode of delivery that is appealing to young people. Text messaging by phone or online chat is an effective method to communicate about emotionally charged issues or to coordinate shared activities effectively (Fukkink & Hermas, 2009). Similarly, motion cartoon characters and home-made short videos (Schinke et al., 2009) have been used successfully by mothers and their daughters to amplify the emotional content and risks of situations in ways that can be accepted, discussed, thought about, and learned from.

Method

The KYKM project is a gender specific programme that has been developed to meet the needs of adolescent females and their mothers and allow them to engage in shared activities. In addition, this form of delivery advocates for a consistent approach to ensuring all recipients receive the same messages. One of the advantages in the delivery of this project is that it does not rely on the school system and its overcrowded curricula or a funded community programme, for its implementation. The limitations of available time of teachers, training required, and availability of facilitators and youth workers to deliver prevention programmes, are often barriers for dissemination to the wider community.

Knowing you, Knowing me is an online, social media environment, built with a similar style and functionality to Facebook, but automated so that the mother and daughter interact with a virtual character, called Rose, who leads them through the intervention. The project has utilised a fairy-tale-style of media and taken advantage of the immensely successful Hollywood interest in "fairy-tale" characters as protagonists. In KYKM, Rose is a fairy and is presented as a 'talk show' host using animated webisodes (short video episodes ranging from 2.6 to 6 min, depending on the level). The decision to use an ethereal character such as a fairy to facilitate the game was an opportunistic way of capitalising on the engagement that adolescent girls have with such fairy-tale characters on the big screen and television (e.g., Twilight, Harry Potter, Once Upon a Time, etc.). Using a fairy as the "director" of the game means that there are not two adult authority figures in the frame of the screen which could overwhelm the daughter with their advice. This is a distinct point of difference between KYKM and other such games, for example, as described by Schinke et al. (2009).

From Fig. 10.1, it can be seen that Rose is joined by a mother and her daughter, Claire and Lucy respectively, who discuss key themes of the game and provide both mother and daughter perspectives. Through the social media wall, Rose asks the

Fig. 10.1 Webisode from the Knowing you, Knowing me, talk show with Rose (*right*), and daughter, Lucy (*left*) and mother, Claire (*middle*)

participating mother and daughter to post to her wall to reflect on webisodes and to also plan activities together to practise skills (see Fig. 10.2).

Mothers and daughters can upload images of themselves, individually and together, which are displayed alongside their posts, and can also share images in a gallery. They complete the levels together at one screen, but can also return and converse online through the programme.

Participants engage in games and activities in Knowing you, Knowing me designed to integrate the educational content into their relationships. Importance is placed on the mother and the daughter listening to one another, spending time together, understanding each other's point of view, negotiating through conflict toward mutually agreeable outcomes and giving one another encouragement, support, compliments and personal favours.

The three levels (modules) in the game are:

1. Participate in effective communication,
2. Develop healthy relationships, and
3. Manage risky behaviour in the social environment.

The Knowing you, Knowing me environment is built using Drupal (open source content management platform, www.drupal.org) and is fully scalable and flexible. The administration environment allows the research team to directly modify what, when, and how Rose discusses with the mother and daughter participants, including automatically triggering of conversations, SMS messages (sent 1–5 days after

Fig. 10.2 Screenshot of Rose's Knowing you, Knowing me, social media wall, with posts from mother and daughter participants

completing a level), questions, weblinks, webisodes, diaries (see Figs. 10.3 and 10.4) and unlocking of levels and new levels and content can be easily added without rebuilding the system. The research team can also track the progress of the mother-daughter pair and contact participants through the site should there be concerns with progress. The researchers propose to build other positive psychology intervention modules using the core environment and updated style sheets.

Conclusions and Future Implications

The Knowing you, Knowing me game contains information to develop healthy interpersonal communication, respect, trust, negotiation setting limits, values, and analysing situations. The game provides opportunities to personalise information by having mothers and daughters identify their own strengths in themselves and their relationship and identify their personal values. Additionally, there are opportunities to recognise social pressures and influences by having mothers and daughters examine images and messages used to define for example, gender identity, mother-daughter relationships, and female alcohol use and demonstrate how to be resilient

Fig. 10.3 Screenshot of mother's mobile phone showing two SMS messages and new level unlocked message

to these pressures. The game provides consistent reinforcement of positive norms through the use of process praise rather than personal praise, and opportunities to learn and practice skills including refusal skills and delaying skills.

The skills KYKM aims to develop relate to the pillars of the PERMA model, in particular positive emotions, relationships, meaning, and accomplishment (Seligman, 2011). The game guides participants to experience positive activities that also help to bolster the mother-daughter relationship. For both mother and daughter, the relationship can be a source of perspective and an additional coping resource. Furthermore, for the mother, raising a family can be a source of meaning. Thus, investing extra time in this domain can increase the mother's sense of personal value. Accomplishment comes from progressing towards the goals set in the game, whether these goals involve spending more time with the family member or improving on the understanding of the family member's needs.

Knowing you, Knowing me has major implications for families everywhere. The information and activity contained in the game offers mothers and daughters a "toolbox" for handling a variety of domestic situations, from the most basic communication skills (such as listening and responding in a timely manner) to the more difficult and complex communication tasks of conflict resolution and negotiation within the scope of the problem. This toolbox can be used by both mother and

Fig. 10.4 Knowing you, Knowing me diary page with posting from mother and daughter reflecting on their experience during the week

daughter to manage other areas of their lives, for example, work issues and other relationships. The skills developed in KYKM are fundamental to all interpersonal relationships and thus would be expected to transfer into other spheres of life, such as the mothers' current and daughters' future work roles.

Furthermore, KYKM has the capacity to grow into many different areas beyond two of its initial foci: communication skills and alcohol use in adolescence. In Stage 1 of this project, the focus groups of mothers and daughters, valuable information was shared with the investigators with regard to future topics for Claire, Lucy, and Rose to tackle (e.g., bullying, body image, friendships, etc.). In addition, young adolescent boys and the relationship they have with their fathers (and/or their mothers) is also worthy of consideration. The authors recommend that this game be used as a positive psychology "intervention" in future studies so as to evaluate its properties and utility beyond the gaming circles, and investigate the possibility that KYKM may be useful in health promotion.

As a final note to this chapter, in our attempt to engage mothers and daughters for Stage 2 of the project, we encountered one major obstacle. During the recruitment phase of the intervention, mothers were identified as a main barrier to participation. While many daughters expressed interest in participating in the intervention, mothers often declined, noting a lack of time. In current society, mothers are encouraged to be the "super mum", excelling in career, family, and social spheres of life. It may be that time spent struggling to accomplish this high standard, comes at the price of investing in any one of the domains. Even though the KYKM intervention requires less than 20 min a week and the mother-daughter relationships is recognised as important to mothers and daughters, this time investment may be a challenge for mothers in our society who are dealing with an overburdened workload. The Australian Bureau of Statistics (2014) reported that 36 % of mothers with a child aged 6–14 years also worked full-time, with a further 42 % working part-time. A challenge for future research is not only to provide effective means of intervention, but also to convince mothers that these interventions are valuable and worth their time investment.

Acknowledgements The authors acknowledges the funding support for this project from Queensland Health, DRUG-ARM Australasia, .auDA Foundation, Drink Safe Coalition, Sunshine Coast Youth Partnership and Project support from the following organisations: Various Artists and Virtual Obsession.

References

Australian Bureau of Statistics. (2014). *Gender indicators* (Cat. No. 4125.0). Retrieved from http://www.abs.gov.au/ausstats/abs@.nsf/Lookup/by%20Subject/4125.0~Feb%202014~Main%20Features~Contents~1

Barber, J. G., Bolitho, F., & Bertrand, L. (2001). Parent-child synchrony and adolescent adjustment. *Child and Adolescent Social Work Journal, 18*, 51–69. doi:10.1023/A:1026673203176.

Barnett, R. C. (1994). Home-to-work spillover revisited: A study of full-time employed women in dual-earner couples. *Journal of Marriage and Family, 56*, 647–656. doi:10.2307/352875.

Belsky, K. (1984). The determinants of parenting: A process model. *Child Development, 55*, 83–96. doi:10.2307/1129836.

Ben-Zur, H. (2003). Happy adolescents: The link between subjective well-being, internal resources, and parental factors. *Journal of Youth and Adolescence, 32*, 67–79. doi:10.1023/A:1021864432505.

Benson, M. J., Harris, P. B., & Rogers, C. S. (1992). Identity consequences of attachment to mothers and fathers among late adolescents. *Journal of Research on Adolescence, 2*, 187–204. doi:10.1207/s15327795jra0203_1.

Bowlby, J. (1969). *Attachment* (Vol. 1). New York: Basic Books.

Boyd, C. J. (1989). Mothers and daughters: A discussion theory and research. *Journal of Marriage and Family, 51*, 291–301. doi:10.2307/352493.

Caprara, G. V., Regallia, C., & Bandura, A. (2002). Longitudinal impact of perceived self-regulatory efficacy on violent conduct. *European Psychologist, 7*, 63–69. doi:10.1027//1016-9040.7.1.63.

Cole, P. M., Martin, S. E., & Dennis, T. A. (2004). Emotional regulation as a scientific construct: Methodological challenges and directions for child development research. *Child Development, 75*, 317–333. doi:10.1111/j.1467-8624.2004.00673.x.

Dekovic, M., & Meeus, W. (1997). Peer relations in adolescence: Effects of parenting and adolescents' self-concept. *Journal of Adolescence, 20*, 163–176. doi:10.1006/jado.1996.0074.

De Vulpian, A. (2005). *Listening to ordinary people*. Paper presented at The International Conference for Organizational Learning, Vienna, September, 13–16.

Diener, E. (2000). Subjective well-being: The science of happiness and a proposal for a national index. *American Psychologist, 55*, 34–43. doi:10.1037/0003-066X.55.1.34.

Donnelly, J., Young, M., Pearson, R., Penhollow, T., & Hernandez, A. (2008). Area specific self-esteem, values and adolescent substance abuse. *Journal of Drug Education, 38*, 389–403. doi:10.2190/DE.38.4.f.

Egan, G. (2012). *The skilled helper*. Belmont, CL: Brooks/Cole.

Erel, O., & Burman, B. (1995). Interrelatedness of marital relations and parent-child relations: A meta-analytic review. *Psychological Bulletin, 118*, 108–132. doi:10.1037/0033-2909.118.1.108.

Fukkink, R., & Hermas, J. (2009). Counselling children on a help line chatting or calling. *Journal of Community Psychology, 37*, 939–948. doi:10.1002/jcop.20340.

Furnham, A., & Cheng, H. (2000). Perceived parental behaviour, self-esteem and happiness. *Social Psychiatry and Psychiatry Epidemiology, 35*, 463–470. doi:10.1007/s001270050265.

Guilamo-Ramos, V., Jaccard, J., Dittus, P., & Bouris, A. M. (2006). Parental expertise, trustworthiness, and accessibility: Parent-adolescent communication and adolescent risk behaviour. *Journal of Marriage and Family, 68*(5), 1229–1246. doi:10.1111/j.1741-3737.2006.00325.x.

Hair, E. C., Moore, K. A., Garrett, S. B., Ling, T., & Cleveland, K. (2008). The continued importance of quality parent-adolescent relationships during late adolescence. *Journal of Research on Adolescence, 18*, 187–200. doi:10.1111/j.1532-7795.2008.00556.x.

Herman, N. (1989). *Too long a child: The mother-daughter dyad*. London: Free Association Books.

Katsikitis, M., Jones, C., Muscat, M., & Crawford, K. (2014). Knowing You, Knowing Me (KYKM): An interactive game to address positive mother-daughter communication and relationships. *Frontiers in Psychology, 11*, 721. doi:10.3389/fpsyg.2014.00721.

Koning, I. M., Vollebergh, W. A. M., Smit, F., Verdurmen, J. E. E., Van Den Eijnden, R. J. J. M., Ter Bogt, T. F. M., et al. (2009). Preventing heavy alcohol use in adolescents (PAS): Cluster randomised trial of parent and student intervention offered separately and simultaneously. *Addiction, 104*, 1669–1678. doi:10.1111/j.1360-0443.2009.02677.x.

Loeber, R., Farrington, D. P., Stouthamer-Loeber, M., & Van Kammen, W. B. (1998). *Antisocial behaviour and mental health problems: Explanatory factors in childhood and adolescence*. Mahwah, NJ: Lawrence Erlbaum.

Long Dilworth, J. E. (2004). Predictors of negative spillover from family to work. *Journal of Family Issues, 25*, 241–261. doi:10.1177/0192513X03257406.

Luthens, F., Avy, J., & Patera, J. (2008). Experimental analysis of a web-based training intervention to develop positive psychological capital. *Academy of Management Learning and Education, 7*, 209–221. doi:10.5465/AMLE.2008.32712618.

Lyubomirsky, S., & Lepper, H. S. (1999). A measure of subjective happiness: Preliminary reliability andconstructvalidation.*SocialIndicatorsResearch,46*,137–155.doi:10.1023/A:1006824100041.

Maher, J., & Saugeres, L. (2007). To be or not to be a mother? Women negotiating cultural representations of mothering. *Journal of Sociology, 43*, 5–21. doi:10.1177/1440783307073931.

Millear, P. M. (2016). Age and experience: A comparison of work and family demands across the lifespan. In R. L. Gervais & P. M. Millear (Eds.), *Exploring resources, life-balance and well-being of women who work in a global context* (pp. 179–197). Cham, Switzerland: Springer International Publishing Switzerland.

Moen, P., & Erickson, M. A. (1995). Linked lives: A transgenerational approach to resilience. In P. Moen, G. H. Elder, & K. Luscher (Eds.), *Examining lives in context: Perspectives on the ecology of human development* (pp. 169–210). Washington, DC: American Psychological Association.

Montemayor, R. (1986). Family variation in parent-adolescent storm and stress. *Journal of Adolescent Research, 1*, 15–31. doi:10.1177/074355488611003.

Newton, N. C., Vogl, L. E., Teeson, M., & Andrews, G. (2009). CLIMATE schools: Alcohol module: Cross validation of a school-based prevention programme for alcohol misuse. *Australian and New Zealand Journal of Psychiatry, 43*, 201–207. doi:10.1080/00048670802653364.

Newton, N. C., Andrews, G., Teeson, M., & Vogl, L. (2009). Delivering prevention for alcohol and cannabis using the internet: A cluster randomised controlled trial. *Preventative Medicine, 48*, 579–584. doi:10.1016/j.ypmed.2009.04.009.

Olson, D. H., Russell, C. S., & Sprenkle, D. H. (1983). Circumplex model of marital and family systems: IV. Theoretical update. *Family Process, 22*, 69–83. doi:10.1111/j.1545-5300.1983.00069.x.

Orbuch, T. L., Thornton, A., & Cancia, J. (2000). The impact of marital quality, divorce, and remarriage on the relationships between parents and their children. *Marriage and Family Review, 29*, 221–246. doi:10.1300/J002v29n04_01.

Papousek, H., & Papousek, M. (1997). Fragile aspects of early social integration. In L. Murray & P. J. Cooper (Eds.), *Postpartum depression and child development* (pp. 35–53). New York: Guilford Press.

Prensky, M. (2001a). Digital natives, digital immigrants. *On the Horizon, 9*(5), 1–6. doi:10.1108/10748120110424816.

Prensky, M. (2001b). Digital natives, digital immigrants, part II: Do they really *think* differently? *On the Horizon, 9*(6), 1–6. doi:10.1108/10748120110424843.

Raskin, P. M. (2006). Women, work, and family: Three studies of roles and identity among working mothers. *American Behavioral Scientist, 49*, 1354–1381. doi:10.1177/0002764206286560.

Raudino, A., Fergusson, D. M., & Horwood, L. J. (2013). The quality of parent/child relationships in adolescence is associated with poor adult psychosocial adjustment. *Journal of Adolescence, 36*, 331–340. doi:10.1016/j.adolescence.2012.12.002.

Schinke, S., Cole, K., & Fang, L. (2009). Gender specific intervention to reduce underage drinking among early adolescent girls: A test of a computer-mediated, mother-daughter program. *Alcohol and Drugs, 70*, 70–77. Retrieved from http://www.jsad.com/jsad/article/GenderSpecific_Intervention_to_Reduce_Underage_Drinking_Among_Early_Adoles/4289.html

Seligman, M. (2011). *Flourish: A visionary new understanding of happiness and well-being*. New York: Free Press.

Steinberg, L. (1990). Autonomy, conflict, and harmony in the family relationship. In S. S. Feldman & G. R. Elliot (Eds.), *At the threshold: The developing adolescent* (pp. 255–276). Cambridge, MA: Harvard University Press.

Stocker, C. M., Richmond, M. K., Rhoades, G. K., & Kiang, L. (2007). Family emotional processes and adolescents' adjustment. *Social Development, 16*, 310–325. doi:10.1111/j.1467-9507.2007.00386.x.

Vellerman, R. (2009a). *Influences on how children and young people learn about and behave towards alcohol*. York: Joseph Rowntree Foundation. Retrieved from http://www.jrf.org.uk/pulications

Vellerman, R. (2009b). *Alcohol prevention programs, review of the literature for the Joseph Rowntree Foundation (part two)*. York: Joseph Rowntree Foundation. Retrieved from http://www.jrf.org.uk/publications

Chapter 11
Age and Experience: A Comparison of Work and Family Demands Across the Lifespan

Prudence M. Millear

Introduction

The debate about the effects of work, family, and working hours on women is often seen as a wholly negative influence, as a 'tragedy' (Relationships Forum Australia, 2007) and a 'collision' between work and family (Pocock, 2003), with mothers also taking on the double shift beyond what their spouses and partners contribute (Hochschild, 1997). Media portrayal of children as negative economic costs experienced by their parents (e.g., Shin, 2014), either as lost maternal income or costs of upbringing, ignore or downplay the importance of family relationships to psychological well-being. Women are not just passive recipients of the life course and actively make choices about the focus of their lives. Hakim (2000) showed that women can range from being totally focused on their work to being totally focused on family life, with a sizable proportion in the middle interested in both family and work roles. Work and family roles can then be seen as a balance of positive and negative impacts for the individual, where employees can be 'conscripts or volunteers' for long hours (Drago, Wooden, & Black, 2007) and acknowledging that life is a juggle between all roles (Miller, 1997). As such, the choice for part-time work may not be less attachment to employment but a reflection of the person's particular life stage. At the other end of the spectrum, work can be viewed as a wildly exciting, 'extreme job' (i.e., highly paid, challenging, and complex work, Hewlett & Luce, 2006) or as a haven from home life (Damaske, Smtyh, & Zawadzki, 2014). Rather than propose that one role (whether work or motherhood) will lead to fulfilment and the other role should be downplayed, the current study is interested in the experiences across the lifespan and the accumulated resources that both roles bring to women. Mothers of

P.M. Millear (✉)
School of Social Sciences, University of the Sunshine Coast,
Locked Bag 4, Maroochydore DC, QLD 4558, Australia
e-mail: pmillear@usc.edu.au

R.L. Gervais, P.M. Millear (eds.), *Exploring Resources, Life-Balance and Well-Being of Women Who Work in a Global Context*,
DOI 10.1007/978-3-319-31736-6_11

young children are undoubtedly at the busiest time of their lives, but children do become more independent as they grow older, allowing their mothers to focus again on their work roles. By comparing women who represent different stages of the lifespan, it may be possible to explore the long term consequences of having children and the outcomes by the time their children reach adulthood.

Role theory (Goode, 1960; Kahn, Wolfe, Quinn, Snoek, & Rosenthal, 1964) has formed the basis for much research on the work-life interface with the expectations and activities associated with occupational roles long being considered important to an individual's well-being and mental health. In particular, Greenhaus and Beutell's (1985) definition of work-life conflict specified inter-role conflict as being time-based, strain-based and behaviour-based, with sources of conflict coming from both work and family roles and defined by working conditions and/or family structure. Considerable research has since defined the long hours, roles stressors, and work conditions that increase work-life conflict and decrease well-being for employees (for example, Bruck, Allen, & Spector, 2002; Byron, 2005; Casper, Martin, Buffardi, & Erdwins, 2002; Eby, Casper, Lockwood, Bordeaux, & Brinley, 2005; Michel, Kotrba, Mitchelson, Clark, & Baltes, 2011). Women who work in male-dominated occupations face the challenge of accessing flexible work practices which allow them to pursue a career and have family responsibilities, as corporate structures may be inimical to primary care responsibilities. For example, in the large, corporate legal and accountancy firms, time spent maintaining client relationships (usually after hours, or at sporting events) and long working hours are considered crucial to career advancement (Thornton & Bagust, 2007). Among lawyers, the hours billed by mothers increased as her children became older, becoming equivalent with the billing achieved by women without children, when their children were adolescents. Less time spent on housework and parenting activities increased the productivity of the women lawyers (Wallace & Young, 2008). In any workplace, support from immediate supervisors and managers is necessary for family-friendly policies to be enacted (Thompson, Beauvais, & Lyness, 1999), which increases affective commitment for all employees, not only those with children (Anderson, Coffey, & Byerly, 2002). See also the discussion in Siller, Bader, and Hochleitner (2016) on the support offered to female physicians in advancing their profession.

Focusing only on conflict can obscure the beneficial aspects of combining occupational and personal roles. Expanding role involvement and commitment to enjoyable and meaningful activities, and through social relationships, can increase an individual's time and energy (Marks, 1977). The salience of multiple roles is linked to the expectations about the nature and content of each role. In turn, expectations are guided by the personal relevance of the role, the expected standards required to perform the role and the resources that an individual will bring to bear upon the role (Amatea, Cross, Clark, & Bobby, 1986). Role balance occurs then when role quality and enjoyment meet and individuals experience more ease and less strain in performing their roles (Marks & MacDermid, 1996). The benefits of multiple roles are shown as facilitation and enrichment that occurs when positive experiences are transferred between roles (Frone, 2003; Greenhaus & Powell, 2006; Grzywacz & Butler, 2005). By facilitating activities and energy in the other domain, performing multiple roles can have positive effects on psychological functioning for both men and women (Barnett & Hyde, 2001; Galinsky et al., 2003; Geurts & Demerouti, 2003). Multiple roles can contribute to well-being through experiencing success that develops self-efficacy (Greenhaus & Powell, 2006), buffers difficulties in other roles (Greenberger, O'Neil, & Nagel, 1994; Voydanoff & Donnelly, 1999) and decreases financial strains as the additional income adds to the family's economic prosperity (Moen, 1992).

The resources that roles generate are defined as skills and perspectives (e.g., for specific tasks, coping and multitasking), psychological and physical resources (e.g., self-efficacy, positive affect), social capital (e.g., interpersonal relationships), flexibility (e.g., discretion of time and work), and finally, material resources (Greenhaus & Powell, 2006). Resources are broadly defined as such things that are valued for themselves or are valued as a way to obtain other valued resources. Stress and burnout occur when resources are lost, threatened with loss or not gained as expected after investment of time and effort, although individuals can also invest in themselves, their relationships and circumstances to build up their resources and buffer themselves from possible future losses (Hobfoll, 1989, 2002). When individuals have greater resources (of any type), they are more capable of producing successful outcomes to difficult situations. In turn, this 'success' will build their total pool of resources, leading to a gain spiral in resources. Loss spirals occur where limited resources cannot counteract stressors, are then depleted, leading to a further spiral of losses (Hobfoll, 2002). By maximising gains and minimising losses, individuals are able to proactively address possible future problems (Aspinwall & Taylor, 1997; Hobfoll, 2002). It is likely that multiple roles also can be beneficial toward buffering the individual's motivational-affective response to workplace demands, to prevent burnout from developing and the loss of work engagement (Bakker, Demerouti, & Verbeke, 2004; Bakker & Geurts, 2004). Burnout is differentiated from stress by the emphasis on interpersonal relations in the workplace as the basis for the development of burnout (Maslach, Schaufeli, & Leiter, 2001), whereas stress is more often framed as the response to role stressors (Beehr & Glazer, 2005) or challenges to resources (Hobfoll, 1989). Burnout also reflects the negative response an individual has to her or his job and the disengagement from that job as opposed to the distress that the individual experiences (Maslach et al., 2001), whilst work engagement is characterised by absorption, dedication and vigorous involvement with one's job (Schaufeli, Salanova, Gonzalez-Roma, & Bakker, 2002).

Fairly or unfairly, parenthood in women can be taken as disinterest in career development, leaving women in these high status and very high income positions with the choice to postpone motherhood or forgo it completely. When women are childless by choice, they have better outcomes at older ages, reporting less loneliness and depression in later life, when compared to women who would rather have had children but did not for whatever reason (Koropeckyj-Cox, 2002). Whilst the focus on reproduction and parenting in the life cycle does not account for those individuals who chose not to have children, it can be used to account for family demands on the individual, with childless individuals having limited family stressors compared to the parents of pre-school aged children (Frone, Russell, & Cooper, 1992).

In this way, the incremental demands of caring for families is shown, varying from the least, associated with the absence of children, to limited care required by independent adult children, increasing with adolescents, to the greatest demands of caring for preschool children. The 'scarcity' of resources associated with the parental role would therefore be examined. This conception of family or parental demands acknowledges the additional commitments of parents but does not account for the different life experiences of a parent of an adult child compared to an adult without children, and the resources that either life course has developed over time. It may be that the experiences of raising a family to maturity provide a separate source of growth and development that gives the individual greater resources of mastery, skills, purpose (Ryff, Singer, & Seltzer, 2002) and generativity (An & Cooney, 2006) compared to similar aged adults without children. The 'expansion' of resources associated with the parental role would therefore also be examined. The current study will explore these differences by including both life stage and family and parental demands in the comparisons of the women's resources. Actions to accumulate resources would lead the active individual to interact with their environment in ways that promote their competent development in the longer term.

Regardless of the status of a woman's job, family responsibilities do change involvement in the workplace, influencing decisions about jobs, based on the needs of the family schedules (both partners and children as well) with gendered expectations entering the balance. Gender roles still guide life choices with men seeing themselves as breadwinners and women being more involved with their children (Loscoco, 1997). Although the presence of preschool children increases negative family-work spillover (Grzywacz, Almeida, & McDonald, 2002; Stevens, Minnotte, Mannon, & Kiger, 2007) and reduced work-life balance (Kirchmeyer, 2006), parenthood increased the intrinsic value both men and women received from their work (Johnson, 2005) and provided opportunities for psychological growth through involvement in parental roles throughout the child's growth and development (An & Cooney, 2006; Palkovitz, 1996).

Finding a compromise between family and work roles and therefore increasing the income of the household can be difficult because there is no easy, neat solution that allows both roles to be fully expressed (Hand & Hughes, 2004). As children grow older and become more independent, their mothers have ongoing experience of 'managing' more than one role and in consequence, they could be expected to develop a sense of mastery over their lives. Given the focus on over-work as a stressor, there is the possibility that feeling busy has been transformed into being pressured or distressed. By interpreting emotional distress as a possible loss of efficacy, the individual could be underestimating how well they actually manage their role demands (Llorens, Schaufeli, Bakker, & Salanova, 2007), unrealistically comparing themselves to an ideal worker/parent ideal, or not questioning the media representations of 'having it all'. Despite the widespread media preoccupation with negative outcomes, the stability of well-being is important as it denotes a substantial level of happiness that buffers individuals without their being particularly aware of that happiness. Longitudinal studies show that mature coping mechanisms, good relationships, particularly marriage, having sufficient income to meet one's needs and having meaningful work all contribute to well-being across the lifespan (Howard, 1992; Vaillant, 2000, 2002).

In summary, research shows that mothers of small children are busy women, but these findings imply that they will be busy 'forever'. Barring developmental delay or disability, children will grow up, enter school, adolescence, and then the adult world, and mothers of young children will become mothers of adult children. The current study will compare the two views of combining work and family, that 'scarcity' or 'expansion' follow from engaging in multiple roles. For the scarcity view to hold, it is hypothesised that those with the greatest parental and family demands (i.e., mothers of the youngest children) have more demands on their time, are busier, and experience more negative spillover between their work and family roles, compared to women with no children or adult children. In contrast, for the expansion view to hold, it is hypothesised that mothers of adult children will have developed more resources through their life's experiences and a cumulative advantage from their early busy years of parenting and would therefore show less burnout, more work engagement, more job satisfaction and greater work-life balance compared to similar aged women without children.

Method

Participants

Volunteers were recruited ($N=371$) from Australian women (working at least one day per week) from two convenience samples, first from university graduates ($n=152$, 2 % response rate) and second, from administrative employees of a large metropolitan public hospital ($n=219$, 49 % response rate). For the university alumni, monthly e-newsletters contained information of the study and the link to an online survey. Hospital staff received a similar e-mail request through their managers, again containing the information and link to the online survey.

Measures

Demographics Participants reported their age (in years) and how many children they had, from 0 to 6 or more, with children defined as the participant's 'natural, adopted, step, or foster son/s or daughter/s' (Australian Bureau of Statistics, 2006). Educational background was categorised as (1) finished part or all of high school; (2) trade or TAFE qualifications; (3) undergraduate tertiary qualifications (degree or diploma); or (4) postgraduate tertiary qualifications (e.g. masters or PhD).

Life Stage and Family Demands Life stage was defined as (1) younger non-parents, aged under 40 years; (2) older non-parents, aged 40 years and older; (3) parents with youngest child under 6 years; (4) parents with children between 6 and 12 years; (5) parents with children between 13 and 18 years; (6) parents with adult children who live at home; (7) parents with no children living at home (Moen, Harris-Abbott, Lee, & Roehling, 1999). Family and parenting demands were then calculated as (1) no children (Life stages 1 and 2); (2) adult children (Life stages 6 and 7); (3) adolescent children at home (Life stage 5); (4) primary school children at home (Life stage 4); and (5) young children at home (Life stage 3; Frone et al., 1992). Working hours were assessed by the item, 'On average, how many hours do you actually work, including any paid or extra hours that you put in beyond your official work week?' The number of hours worked per week that the participant would prefer to work was assessed by the item, 'How many hours would you ideally like to work each week, compared to hours you CURRENTLY work?' rated as 1 (a lot less hours), 2 (a few less hours), 3 (about the same hours), 4 (a few more hours), or 5 (many more hours) (Moen & Yu, 2000). Participants indicated whether their job was 1, permanent, 2, contract or temporary, or 3, own business, and whether their work was 1, full-time, or 2, part-time.

Salience of Work Role Role salience was measured by the Life Role Salience Scales (LRSS, Amatea et al., 1986), using the reward value and commitment toward occupational role subscales. Each subscale was rated on a Likert scale, from 1 = strongly disagree to 5 = strongly agree. The occupational role reward value scale consisted of 5 items, with e.g., a sample item: 'Having work/a career that is interesting and exciting to me is my most important life goal'. This sub-scale obtained a Cronbach's alpha = .71. One of the sample items of the occupational role commitment scale is: 'I expect to make as many sacrifices as are necessary in order to advance in my work/career'. This sub-scale attained a Cronbach's alpha = .78.

Self-Efficacy Self-efficacy was measured by the Coping Self-Efficacy scale (Chesney, Chambers, Taylor, Johnson, & Folkman, 2003), which included 26 items about confidence in managing various situations, with e.g., a sample item: 'keep from getting down in the dumps'. The scale was rated on a Likert scale ranging from 1 = I cannot do this at all, 4 = I am moderately certain I can do this to 7 = I am certain I can do this. The Cronbach's alpha = .96.

Control of Own Time Perceived control of time was assessed with a single item from the Perceived Control of Time Subscale of the Time Management Scale (Macan, 1994), and was rated on a 5-point Likert scale ranging from 1 = strongly disagree to 5 = strongly agree.

Egalitarian Gender Role Attitude Attitudes to gender roles were assessed with the 4-item Egalitarian Gender Role Attitude scale (Moen, 2003), from which a sample item was: 'a working mother can have just as good relationship with her children as mother who does not work'. It achieved Cronbach's alpha = .71.

Job Autonomy Participants rated the level of control that was experienced in the workplace (Voydanoff, 2004). The scale consisted of 4 items, including 'how often do you have a choice in deciding how you do your tasks at work'. The items were rated on a 5-point Likert scale, ranging from 1 = never, 3 = sometimes to 5 = all the time, with Cronbach's alpha = .85.

Job Social Support The level of support on which the participant can rely on their supervisor and co-workers was measured by the 4-item Job Social Support scale (van Ypern & Hagedoorn, 2003). It includes 2 items about supervisor support and 2 items on co-worker support, comprising e.g., 'can you rely upon your immediate supervisor (co-workers) when things get tough at work'. It is rated on a 5-point Likert scale from 1 = never, 3 = sometimes to 5 = all the time and achieved Cronbach's alpha = .85.

Managerial Support for Work-Life Issues Workplace support for work-life balance issues was measured by the 11-item Managerial Support subscale of the Work-Family Culture scale (Thompson et al., 1999). One of the sample items is 'in the event of a conflict, managers understand when employees have to put their families first'. It was rated on a 5-point Likert scale, ranging from 1 = strongly disagree to 5 = strongly agree and achieved Cronbach's alpha = .90.

Affective Commitment The emotional attachment to the workplace was measured by the 6-item Affective Commitment scale (Allen & Meyer, 1990). One of the sample items is 'I would be very happy to spend the rest of my career with this organisation'. It was rated on a 5-point Likert scale with 1 = strongly disagree to 5 = strongly agree and obtained Cronbach's alpha = .74.

Spillover between work and family life was measured by the Work-Family Spillover scale (Grzywacz & Marks, 2000) with four subscales to reflect the two factor solution of spillover; the direction of influence (work to home and home to work) and quality of interaction (negative or positive). Each Likert-rated subscale had items on how often these items had been experienced in the previous year, ranging from 1 = never, 3 = sometimes to 5 = all the time. The negative work-to-family spillover subscale consisted of 4 items e.g., 'your job reduces the effort you can give to activities at home', and achieved Cronbach's alpha = .86. The positive work-to-family spillover had 3 items, including 'the things you do at work help you deal with personal and practical issues at home', achieving Cronbach's alpha = .76. The 4-item negative family-to-work spillover subscale, e.g., 'personal or family worries and problems distract you when you are at work', achieved Cronbach's alpha = .77. The 3-item positive family-to-work spillover subscale has as a sample item, 'the love and respect you get at home makes you confident about yourself at work', and achieved Cronbach's alpha = .79. Higher scores for negative spillover in either direction indicate more problems and tiredness from one domain to the other. Higher scores for positive spillover in either direction indicate that one domain supports better performance in the other domain.

Satisfaction With Life Domains Satisfaction with family, job, and work-life balance were measured with three single items. Work-life balance: 'all in all, I am satisfied with the balance between my work and family/personal life' (Clarke, Koch, & Hill, 2004); job satisfaction: 'I am satisfied with my work life'; and family satisfaction: 'I am satisfied with my family or personal life'. All items were rated from 1 = strongly agree to 5 = strongly agree.

Stress Stress was measured with the 7-item Stress subscale of the Depression, Anxiety and Stress scale (DASS-21, Lovibond & Lovibond, 1995). One of the items is 'I found it hard to wind down'. Items were rated on a 6-point scale ranging from 0 = did not apply to me, 2 = applied to some degree, 4 = applied to a good degree, or 6 = applied to me very much and achieved Cronbach's alpha = .86.

Burnout The dimensions of burnout were measured with the Maslach Burnout Inventory – General (Maslach, Jackson, & Leiter, 1996). The three subscales comprised emotional exhaustion with 5 items including 'I feel emotionally drained from my work' (Cronbach's alpha = .89); cynicism with 5 items including 'I doubt the significance of my work' (Cronbach's alpha = .84); and professional efficacy with 6 items including 'I feel exhilarated when I accomplish something at work' (Cronbach's alpha = .74). The subscales were rated on a 5-point Likert scale ranging from 1 = strongly disagree to 5 = strongly agree.

Work Engagement Engagement in work was measured with the Utrecht Work Engagement Scale (Schaufeli et al., 2002). Three subscales were used: the 6-item work vigour subscale, i.e., the energy the individual feels when at work including 'when I get up in the morning, I feel like going to work' (Cronbach's alpha = .82); work dedication, i.e., the zest and intrinsic rewards available from work with, 5 item including 'I am enthusiastic about my job' (Cronbach's alpha = .91); and work absorption, i.e., the depth of involvement in work including 'when I am working, I forget everything else around me' (Cronbach's alpha = .79). The scales were rated on a 5-point Likert scale of 1 = strongly disagree to 5 = strongly agree.

Data Analysis

The women were allocated to groups based on their family and parental demands (Frone et al., 1992). In a modification of Frone et al.'s categories, the women without children were kept in two separate groups (under 40 years and 40 years and over, as per Moen et al.'s (1999) life stages) to capture the effects of possible differences of career stages within these diverse age ranges. Analyses of Variance (ANOVAs) compared the groups of women and Bonferroni adjustments were used for all pairwise comparisons to follow-up significant results. Despite the uneven group sizes, Levene's tests for homogeneity were not breached in the ANOVAs and groups' sizes ensured that there was generally sufficient power for the analyses to find significant results. Effects sizes of the partial eta squared (η^2) are given in the results tables, with η^2 rated as small (.01), medium (.06), and large (.14; Fritz, Morris, & Richler, 2012).

Results

The women ($N=371$) were grouped by life stage and parental demands, with women without children under 40 years ($n=152$) the largest grouping; followed by mothers of adult children ($n=70$); and the other groups being reasonably similar in size (women without children over 40 years, $n=36$; mothers of adolescents, $n=26$; mothers of children 6–12 years, $n=46$; mothers of children under 6 years, $n=41$). The groups were sufficiently large to ensure that the ANOVAs had enough power. Most of the mothers ($n=187$) had one ($n=33$), two ($n=102$) or three ($n=34$) children. Education was quite varied across the participants, with about half with university degrees ($n=178$), then those who had finished high school ($n=87$), and achieved postgraduate ($n=68$) or trade qualifications ($n=38$).

The women worked between 8 and 80 h each week ($M=40.0$ h, $SD=11.2$ h) with most in full-time positions ($n=324$), rather than part-time positions ($n=47$). Cross-tabulations showed that the distribution of full-time/part-time work varied with parental demands ($\chi^2(5)=19.51, p=.002$) as women without children under 40 were mostly working full-time (i.e., $n=144$ full-time, 8 part-time), whereas more mothers of children under six were working part-time (i.e., $n=29$ full-time, $n=12$ part-time).

The means, standard deviations, and results of the ANOVAs that compared personal characteristics and workplace conditions are shown in Table 11.1. Where significant differences between the groups were compared, the pairwise comparisons used Bonferroni adjustments and the p values given in the text reflect these adjustments.

As could be expected, age varied substantially from the youngest to the oldest women in the sample (roughly 7 years difference between each group, all $ps<.001$), except for women with adolescent children and childless women 40 years, who were similar in age ($t(60)=1.93$, $p=.807$). Mothers of children under 6 worked fewer hours on average than all other women, although the greatest differences were with the childless women under 40 years ($t(190)=5.14$, $p<.001$) and to mothers with adolescents ($t(65)=4.95$, $p<.001$), and then with mothers of children 6–12 years ($t(85)=3.26$, $p=.018$) and childless women over 40 years, ($t(75)=3.09$, $p=.032$). Despite the differences in working hours, all the women were alike in preferring to work a few less hours than they were currently working.

The women rated how much control they felt they had over their time and their confidence in managing challenging situations. Unsurprisingly, mothers of younger children reported less time control than mothers of older children and women without children, although the significant differences were shown only between mothers of the youngest children and those with adult children ($t(109)=3.38$, $p=.012$).

Table 11.1 Means, SDs and results of the ANOVAs that compared work and family characteristics across women's parental and family demands

	No children		Adult children	Adolescent children	Children 6–12 years	Children <6 years		
	<40 years	≤40 years						
Personal and work characteristics	*M (SD)*	*M (SD)*	*M (SD)*	*M (SD)*	*M (SD)*	*M (SD)*	$F(5,365)$	η^2
Age	28.2 (4.8)	48.4(6.2)	52. 7(5.5)	45.7 (4.7)	41.1 (5.8)	34.8 (5.4)	257.72***	.779
Hours per week	42.1 (9.2)	40.0 (10.0)	37.9 (9.9)	45.7 (16.0)	39.9 (12.8)	32.4 (11.2)	7.31***	.091
Preferred hours	2.4 (0.8)	2.3 (0.8)	2.3 (0.7)	2.2 (0.8)	2.3 (0.9)	2.4 (0.8)	0.32	.004
Control of own time	3.2 (1.1)	3.0 (1.3)	3.6 (1.2)	3.5 (1.2)	2.8 (1.2)	2.8 (1.3)	3.78**	.049
Self-efficacy	117.3 (28.9)	118.1 (33.4)	128.9 (33.1)	118.8 (30.0)	111.9 (27.8)	120.0 (28.0)	2.14†	.033
Egalitarian gender role attitudes	16.2 (3.4)	16.1 (3.8)	16.2 (3.6)	16.0 (3.3)	16.5 (3.5)	16.6 (3.1)	0.24	.003
Occupational role reward	18.2 (3.5)	16.3 (4.2)	16.7 (4.0)	16.3 (4.4)	16.7 (4.0)	15.3 (3.0)	5.50***	.070
Occupational role commitment	15.3 (4.2)	13.4 (4.2)	14.3 (4.9)	14.4 (4.9)	13.9 (4.4)	13.0 (4.1)	2.70*	.036
Job autonomy	13.4 (3.6)	13.7 (4.2)	14.6 (3.2)	14.2 (3.4)	14.5 (3.6)	14.5 (2.9)	1.68	.022
Managerial support for WL issues	38.7 (8.5)	36.8 (9.1)	38.4 (8.9)	40.7 (8.2)	36.2 (10.5)	40.0 (8.1)	1.44	.019
Affective commitment	17.7 (4.5)	18.9 (4.6)	18.6 (5.1)	19.0 (4.5)	18.9 (4.9)	18.7 (3.5)	0.95	.013
Job social support	14.8 (3.6)	14.8 (3.8)	15.0 (3.7)	15.4 (3.4)	14.4 (3.9)	15.1 (3.4)	0.80	.011

Note: 'Preferred hours': Compared to current hours, 1 (a lot less), 2 (a few less), 3 (about the same), 4 (a few more) or 5 (a lot more)
$^{\dagger}p<.10$, $^{*}p<.05$, $^{**}p<.01$, $^{***}p<.001$

Interestingly, when the women rated their self-efficacy, mothers of adult children reported the highest levels, with this being slightly greater than mothers of children 6–12 years ($t(114)=2.98$, $p=.047$), indicating that feeling in control of time may be linked to confidence in one's abilities to manage life's events.

Women's views on employment were compared through their beliefs about egalitarian gender roles and the rewards and commitment to their occupational roles. Despite the differences in ages and the presence or absence of children, the women were very similar in their egalitarian beliefs about women's employment. The differences occurred when considering the rewards of their own employment, with young childless women seeing more occupational rewards than other women, particularly mothers of young children ($t(190)=4.42$, $p<.001$) and to a lesser extent, older childless women ($t(186)=2.79$, $p=.081$) and mothers with adult children ($t(220)=2.86$, $p=.067$). Young childless women were also more committed to their jobs, particularly compared to the mothers of young children ($t(190)=3.04$, $p=.041$).

When the women reported on the characteristics of their jobs, there were surprisingly few differences. All reported similar levels of autonomy in their jobs, felt that their managers were supportive of work-life issues, that they could rely on their supervisors and colleagues for social support, and that they had similar levels of affective commitment to their work. The small effect sizes of these comparisons (i.e., $\eta^2 \approx .01$) highlight that these job resource are available to women generally and do not explain how women's lives differ.

The means, standard deviations and results of the ANOVAs that compared spillover between roles, work-life balance, and workplace outcomes are shown in Table 11.2. As could be expected, mothers with adult children had significantly less negative work-to-family conflict than the other women, and this was significantly less than that of mothers with children 6–12 years ($t(114)=3.63$, $p=.005$) and childless women under 40 years ($t(220)=3.30$, $p=.016$), but interestingly, not for mothers of young children ($t(109)<1.0$, *ns*). Rather, mothers of young children reported the highest levels of negative family-to-work spillover, despite working the least hours per week, compared to mothers of adult children ($t(109)=5.52$, $p<.001$) and the women without children (under 40 years, $t(190)=3.81$, $p<.001$; over 40 years, $t(75)=3.18$, $p=.024$). Along with negative spillover from work, mothers with children 6–12 also reported significantly higher negative family-to-work spillover than the mothers of adult children ($t(114)=4.35$, $p<.001$). In keeping with the limited differences experienced in workplace resources, all of the women reported similar levels of positive work-to-family spillover. However, positive family-to-work spillover was lower for mothers with children between 6 and 18 years, although variability in the scores meant that only mothers of children 6–12 years reported significantly less positive family spillover than childless women under 40 years ($t(196)=3.33$, $p=.015$).

Following on from the negative spillover results, mothers of the younger children (i.e., up to 12 years) reported the highest rating for the 'busy' question of all the women, particularly when compared to mothers of adult children ($ps<.001$) and the childless women ($ps \leq .06$). Mothers of adolescents also felt busier than the mothers

Table 11.2 Means, standard deviations and results of the ANOVA that compared diverse outcomes across women's parental and family demands

	No children		Adult children	Adolescent children	Children 6–12 years	Children <6 years		
	<40 years	≤40 years						
Outcomes	M (SD)	M (SD)	M (SD)	M (SD)	M (SD)	M (SD)	F(5,365)	η^2
Negative work-to-family spillover	11.2 (3.5)	11.0 (2.6)	9.6 (3.0)	10.2 (2.9)	11.9 (3.6)	10.1 (3.1)	3.75**	.049
Positive work-to-family spillover	7.1 (2.4)	7.3 (2.6)	7.6 (2.7)	7.7 (1.9)	7.2 (2.4)	7.6 (2.6)	0.67	.009
Negative family-to-work spillover	8.3 (2.9)	8.2 (2.5)	7.1 (2.4)	8.8 (2.9)	9.5 (3.0)	10.2 (3.4)	7.61***	.094
Positive family-to-work spillover	10.3 (2.7)	9.3 (3.2)	9.9 (3.5)	8.7 (3.3)	8.7 (2.8)	9.5 (3.0)	3.30**	.043
Feeling busy	6.4 (1.4)	6.2 (1.5)	5.9 (1.7)	6.9 (1.6)	7.1 (1.3)	7.2 (1.3)	6.78***	.085
Satisfaction with work-life balance	3.2 (1.3)	3.2 (1.3)	3.2 (1.3)	3.1 (1.3)	2.9 (1.3)	3.0 (1.2)	0.61	.008
Satisfaction with family life	3.8 (1.2)	3.6 (1.3)	4.0 (1.0)	3.7 (1.3)	3.6 (1.3)	3.8 (1.2)	1.03	.014
Stress	12.1 (8.6)	10.1 (6.9)	8.5 (6.9)	9.7 (6.8)	12.0 (8.0)	11.6 (8.1)	2.43*	.032
Job satisfaction	3.4 (1.2)	3.4 (1.3)	3.6 (1.2)	3.9 (1.1)	3.5 (1.3)	3.9 (0.9)	1.42	.019
Emotional exhaustion	15.1 (5.6)	16.2 (4.4)	12.9 (5.5)	14.2 (5.0)	15.5 (5.4)	14.0 (4.9)	2.74 *	.036
Cynicism	13.4 (5.1)	12.6 (5.3)	11.2 (5.2)	11.9 (5.0)	12.0 (4.5)	11.7 (4.4)	2.39*	.032
Professional efficacy	24.4 (3.2)	25.4 (3.4)	25.6 (4.0)	24.4 (3.3)	26.1 (2.9)	25.6 (3.0)	2.94*	.039
Work vigour	20.1 (4.6)	21.2 (4.3)	23.6 (3.7)	21.8 (4.9)	21.1 (4.0)	21.7 (3.7)	6.67***	.084
Work dedication	17.3 (5.1)	18.2 (4.4)	19.2 (4.1)	17.8 (5.4)	18.6 (4.7)	18.4 (4.1)	1.69	.023
Work absorption	15.5 (4.3)	16.4 (4.5)	17.6 (3.8)	15.4 (4.5)	16.5 (4.3)	16.1 (4.0)	2.65*	.035

Note: 'Feeling busy': rated from 1 (life has lots of free time) to 9 (life is hectic all the time)

†$p<.10$, * $p<.05$, ** $p<.01$, *** $p<.001$

of adult children ($t(94)=2.84, p=.072$). In contrast to feeling busy, though, all of the women reported similar levels of satisfaction with their own work-life balance, perhaps indicating that work-life balance is an assessment that takes into account what could be expected for that person's own situation.

Finally, the women's results for stress, job satisfaction, family satisfaction, burnout, and work engagement were compared. Whilst the women reported similar levels of satisfaction with their family and personal lives, satisfaction and dedication to their work, mothers of adult children had more positive outcomes than the other women. They were the least stressed, had less emotional exhaustion and cynicism, and were more absorbed and invigorated by their work. These differences were most marked compared to the women without children, particularly those under 40 (stress, $t(220)=3.16, p=.026$, emotional exhaustion, $t(220)=2.87, p=.066$; cynicism, $t(220)=3.10, p=.031$; work vigour, $t(220)=5.68, p<.001$; work absorption, $t(220)=3.48, p=.009$) and to a lesser extent, those over 40 years (emotional exhaustion, $t(104)=3.01, p=.042$; work vigour, $t(104)=2.73, p=.099$). Whilst mothers of children aged 6–12 years reported work less vigour than the mothers of adult children ($t(114)=3.08, p=.033$), these mothers reported feeling the most confidence in their professional abilities, in particular compared to the women without children under 40 years ($t(196)=3.04, p=.037$).

Discussion

The current study examined the relative merits of scarcity and expansion views of multiple roles, by comparing women of different ages and life stages. The participants included women from the so-defined Baby Boomer generation (born mid 1950s) through to Generation Y (born around 1990), and represent a cross-section of women who have had the opportunity to be continuously employed, have access to effective contraception, and for whom parental status was not a bar for employment. As such, it is possible to compare the different age cohorts at the start of the life course against the later stages of older women with and without children on the consequences of multiple roles.

Firstly, the women were similar in many areas of their lives, in their egalitarian beliefs about gender roles, in the resources available in their jobs and the satisfaction they gained from their work, their personal and family lives, and in their own work-life balance. The resources include control of work tasks and the valuable support of managers for work-life issues and social support more generally from colleagues, and in line with previous research (Anderson et al., 2002; Thompson et al., 1999), these resources support job satisfaction (Wallace & Young, 2008).

The two groups of the youngest participants are at the start of the life course, but were quite different in the salience of the work role. Young women without children reported the greatest rewards and commitment of the occupational role of all the women, whereas the mothers of young children had the least, confirming that in this sample, parenthood changes a women's focus considerably. Mothers of the youngest children demonstrated that scarcity of time and energy are a reality for this life stage, as shown in previous research (Frone et al., 1992; Grzywacz et al., 2002; Stevens et al., 2007). Although on average they were working significantly less than the other women, more of these mothers were working full-time than part-time and felt less control of their time, with more negative family-to-work spillover. Whilst these mothers felt they were very busy, they also were as satisfied with their work-life balance as the other women and did not report more negative work-to-family spillover. These findings contrast with previous research, where parents of young children were likely to report less work-life balance (Kirchmeyer, 2006). It is likely that in this sample, a global assessment of all of the factors in their lives, such as increasingly independent children, a supportive workplace, and satisfaction with their personal and family life leads to a subjective assessment that all these factors together are as balanced as other women find the balance of work and family in their own lives.

Perhaps the most surprising results are for the younger women without children. As a group, they are the most committed to their jobs and feel the work role is most rewarding, but they are more stressed, emotionally exhausted, more cynical, lack professional efficacy, vigour, and are less absorbed by their work than the other women, particularly the older mothers with adult children. Rather than role stress increasing feelings of stress, women with objectively less stress (as the absence of parental demands) reported similar levels of distress as those with the most parental demands, which is contrary to previous research (Beehr & Glazer, 2005). It is likely that stress is generated by a wider range of demands, rather than young children alone. It would seem that greater salience of the occupational role has not buffered the women from negative outcomes and burnout is still problematic for the older women without children. The results for the women without children show that the absence of parental demands does not confer additional benefits apart from feeling less busy and more in control of one's time. The women without children may have more time available to them, but the higher levels of burnout and less work engagement point to some costs associated with a sole focus on work, without the counter-balance of another role in which to achieve a positive identity. In contrast, time may be scarce for mothers of young children in this sample, but there appears to be few other downsides of this life stage. In this case, multiple roles appear to provide more resources to prevent the development of burnout and loss of work engagement (Maslach et al., 2001; Schaufeli et al., 2002), although parenthood did not limit intrinsic value of work as found previously (Johnson, 2005).

The most positive outcomes of all the women were shown by the mothers of adult children, with these women reporting more self-efficacy, more vigour and absorption in their work, less negative spillover between roles, less stress and more control of their time. For these older mothers, it is likely that raising children to adulthood has generated feelings of accomplishment that are not tied to their work and which offers another source of validation for their life's endeavours (Ryff et al., 2002) and that parenting had provided opportunities for generativity in their daily lives (An & Cooney, 2006). These findings would indicate that multiple roles do provide an expansion of resources (Greenhaus & Powell, 2006; Marks, 1977) in the longer term, with the skills, psychological resources, and social capital available from both working and raising children being more apparent amongst the women who have been filling both roles for the longest period of time. Although this is a cross-sectional study of women at different ages, the comparison is based on the women being part of a larger age cohort that had similar opportunities to develop their careers.

Between the mothers of the oldest and youngest children and the young women without children are the mothers of children in the 'middle' years and the older childless women. Mothers with adolescents and older women without children shared many of the same results, and although the mothers worked somewhat longer hours, they had less emotional exhaustion. As with women lawyers (Wallace & Young, 2008), more independent children allow for greater involvement in work and less constraints from family life. Whilst mothers of children aged between 6 and 12 shared some similarities with mothers of children younger and older than their own, this group did show that scarcity of resources does continue before children reach the greater independence of adolescence. These mothers were busy, as were the mothers of younger children, but they reported more negative spillover between work and family and less benefits from family spilling into their work. It is likely that the challenges of longer working hours with children who are not yet independent have impacted on the mothers, although interestingly, they do report higher levels of professional efficacy. This may indicate that the greater involvement with the work role, and the resources of that role (Greenhaus & Powell, 2006), provided both a sense of confidence in their work abilities, but with the counterbalance of continuing family demands.

The results suggest the consequences of two possible trajectories in life for the younger women without children, either to remain without children or to change into the parental life path. If forgoing parenthood is a women's own choice, then she is more likely to have better mental health in later years (Koropeckyj-Cox, 2002), although the women in the current sample were not asked for their reasons for not being parents. The presence of children profoundly changes the career options available to women. Without children, a woman can devote considerably more time to developing her career without dividing her attention. However, the results for the older women without children suggest that this path may also costs, such as more emotional exhaustion, for these women. The second trajectory that the results suggest is when the women without children do become parents, there will be busy years parenting younger children, which later becomes a more relaxed work and family life once the children grow to be adults. The experience of juggling work and family responsibilities appears to have expanded the women's resource base, supporting the benefits of multiple roles (Marks, 1977; Marks & MacDermid, 1996) and resource accumulation over time (Hobfoll, 1989, 2002). As noted by Miller (1997), there is great satisfaction to be gained from managing a busy household and work schedule that builds confidence in oneself and the future.

The limitations of the study must be acknowledged. This is a cross-sectional study and each age cohort is assumed to have had similar work, economic, and family opportunities at similar ages, although this may not have been the case, meaning that the implications of the benefits of parenting would not be sustained in a longitudinal study. The younger women without children are likely to contain women who vary greatly on their views of future parenting and it is not apparent which of the older women without children are childless by choice or for some other reason, which would have unknown impacts on their mental health (Koropeckyj-Cox, 2002) in the current study.

In conclusion, women have many choices in how they construct their lives and being a parent is one of the many roles available to them. Scarcity of time when children are young appears to be replaced with expansion and accumulation of resources when those children reach adulthood. Mothers of adult children appear more relaxed and engaged in their work lives, despite full-time employment. Perhaps another way to view these results is that work and family roles have very different timing of costs and rewards. Work provides many rewards from the beginning, with status, pay, challenging, interesting activities, and a sense of achievement for each task that is completed, but the costs of focusing on the work role may not be apparent for some years, with less time available to establish and maintain relationships, perhaps leading to reduced social capital in retirement. Parenting, on the other hand, gives all the costs in the early days, with the time needed to care for young children coinciding with the main time for establishing one's career. Children however grow and develop and provide many rewards for the long years of older adulthood, including satisfaction for the children's achievements and grandchildren to enjoy. Women without children are not limited by life but may need to seek opportunities to be involved with more than just their work role to continue to expand their resources as the work role progresses toward retirement. Work provides a necessary structure and income for adults, but family life may provide opportunities for contentment in old age.

References

Allen, N. J., & Meyer, J. P. (1990). The measurement and antecedents of affective, continuance, and normative commitment to the organization. *Journal of Occupational Psychology, 63*(1), 1–18.

Amatea, E. S., Cross, E. G., Clark, J. E., & Bobby, C. L. (1986). Assessing the work and family role expectations of career-oriented men and women: The life role salience scales. *Journal of Marriage and Family, 48*(4), 831–838. doi:10.2307/352576.

An, J. S., & Cooney, T. M. (2006). Psychological well-being in mid to later life: The role of generativity development and parent-child relationships across the lifespan. *International Journal of Behavioral Development, 30*(5), 410–421. doi:10.1177/0165025406071489.

Anderson, S. E., Coffey, B. S., & Byerly, R. T. (2002). Formal organizational initiatives and informal workplace practices: Links to work-family conflict and job-related outcomes. *Journal of Management, 28*(6), 787–810. doi:10.1177/014920630202800605.

Aspinwall, L. G., & Taylor, S. E. (1997). A stitch in time: Self-regulation and proactive coping. *Psychological Bulletin, 121*(3), 417–436. doi:10.1037/0033-2909.121.3.417.

Australian Bureau of Statistics. (2006). *Australian social trends*. Canberra, Australia: Commonwealth of Australia.

Bakker, A. B., Demerouti, E., & Verbeke, W. (2004). Using the job demands-resources model to predict burnout and performance. *Human Resource Management, 43*(1), 83–104. doi:10.1002/hmr.20004.

Bakker, A. B., & Geurts, S. (2004). Toward a dual-process model of work-home interference. *Work and Occupations, 31*(3), 345–366. doi:10.1177/0730888404266349.

Barnett, R. C., & Hyde, J. S. (2001). Women, men, work, and family. *American Psychologist, 56*(10), 781–796. doi:10.1037/0003-066X.56.10.781.

Beehr, T. A., & Glazer, S. (2005). Organizational role stress. In J. Barling, E. K. Kelloway, & M. R. Frone (Eds.), *Handbook of work stress* (pp. 7–33). Thousand Oaks, CA: Sage.

Bruck, C. S., Allen, T. D., & Spector, P. E. (2002). The relation between work-family conflict and job satisfaction: A finer-grained analysis. *Journal of Vocational Behavior, 60*(3), 336–353. doi:10.1006/jvbe.2001.1836.

Byron, K. (2005). A meta-analytic review of work-family conflict and its antecedents. *Journal of Vocational Behavior, 67*(2), 169–198. doi:10.1016/j.jvb.2004.08.009.

Casper, W. J., Martin, J. A., Buffardi, L. C., & Erdwins, C. J. (2002). Work-family conflict, perceived organizational support, and organizational commitment among employed mothers. *Journal of Occupational Health Psychology, 7*(2), 99–108.

Chesney, M. A., Chambers, D. B., Taylor, J. M., Johnson, L. M., & Folkman, S. (2003). Coping effectiveness training for men living with HIV: Results from a randomized clinical trial testing a group-based intervention. *Psychosomatic Medicine, 65*(6), 1038–1046. doi:10.1097/01.PSY.0000097344.78697.ED.

Clarke, M. C., Koch, L. C., & Hill, E. J. (2004). The work-family interface: Differentiating balance and fit. *Family and Consumer Sciences Research Journal, 33*(2), 121–140.

Damaske, S., Smtyh, J. M., & Zawadzki, M. J. (2014). Has work replaced home as a haven? Re-examining Arlie Hochschild's Time Bind proposition with objective stress data. *Social Science & Medicine, 115*, 130–138. doi:10.1016/j.socscimed.2014.04.047.

Drago, R., Wooden, M., & Black, D. (2007). *Long work hours: Volunteers and conscripts*. Paper presented at the HILDA Survey Research Conference 2007, Melbourne, Australia.

Eby, L. T., Casper, W. J., Lockwood, A., Bordeaux, C., & Brinley, A. (2005). Work and family research in IO/OB: Content analysis and review of the literature (1980–2002). *Journal of Vocational Behavior, 66*, 124–197. doi:10.1016/j.jvb.2003.11.003.

Fritz, C. O., Morris, P. E., & Richler, J. J. (2012). Effect size estimates: Current use, calculations, and interpretation. *Journal of Experimental Psychology: General, 141*(1), 2–18. doi:10.1037/a0024338.

Frone, M. R. (2003). Work-family balance. In J. C. Quick & L. E. Tetrick (Eds.), *Handbook of occupational health psychology* (pp. 143–162). Washington, D.C.: American Psychological Association.

Frone, M. R., Russell, M., & Cooper, M. L. (1992). Antecedents and outcomes of work-family conflict: Testing a model of the work-family interface. *Journal of Applied Psychology, 77*(1), 65–78. doi:10.1037/0021-9010.77.1.65.

Galinsky, E., Salmond, K., Bond, J. T., Kropft, M. B., Moore, M., & Harrington, B. (2003). *Leaders in a global economy, a study of executive men and women*. New York: Families and Work Institute.

Geurts, S., & Demerouti, E. (2003). Work/non-work interface: A review of theories and findings. In M. J. Schabracq, J. A. M. Winnubst, & C. L. Cooper (Eds.), *Handbook of work and health psychology* (2nd ed., pp. 279–312). Chichester, U.K.: Wiley.

Goode, W. J. (1960). A theory of role strain. *American Sociological Review, 25*, 483–496.

Greenberger, E., O'Neil, R., & Nagel, S. K. (1994). Linking workplace and homeplace: Relations between the nature of adults' work and their parenting behaviors. *Developmental Psychology, 30*(6), 990–1002. doi:10.1037/0012-1649.30.6.990.

Greenhaus, J. H., & Beutell, N. J. (1985). Sources of conflict between work and family roles. *Academy of Management Review, 10*(1), 76–88. doi:10.5465/AMR.1985.4277352.

Greenhaus, J. H., & Powell, G. N. (2006). When work and family are allies: A theory of work-family enrichment. *Academy of Management Review, 31*(1), 72–92. doi:10.5465/AMR.2006.19379625.

Grzywacz, J. G., Almeida, D. M., & McDonald, D. A. (2002). Work-family spillover and daily reports of work and family stress in the adult work force. *Family Relations, 51*(1), 28–36. Retrieved from http://search.proquest.com/docview/213934380?accountid=28745

Grzywacz, J. G., & Butler, A. B. (2005). The impact of job characteristics on work-to-family facilitation: Testing a theory and distinguishing a construct. *Journal of Occupational Health Psychology, 10*(2), 97–109. doi:10.1037/1076-8998.10.2.97.

Grzywacz, J. G., & Marks, N. F. (2000). Reconceptualizing the work-family interface: An ecological perspective on the correlates of positive and negative spillover between work and family. *Journal of Occupational Health Psychology, 5*(1), 111–126. doi:10.1037/1076-8998.5.1.111.

Hakim, C. (2000). *Work-lifestyle choices in the 21st century: Preference theory*. Oxford, UK: Oxford University Press.

Hand, K., & Hughes, J. (2004). Mothers' reflections about work and family life. *Family Matters, 69*, 44–49.

Hewlett, S. A., & Luce, C. B. (2006). Extreme jobs: The dangerous allure of the 70-hour work week. *Harvard Business Review, 84*(12), 49–59.

Hobfoll, S. E. (1989). Conservation of resources: A new attempt at conceptualizing stress. *American Psychologist, 44*(3), 513–524. doi:10.1037/0003-066X.44.3.513.

Hobfoll, S. E. (2002). Social and psychological resources and adaptation. *Review of General Psychology, 6*(4), 307–324. doi:10.1037/1089-2680.6.4.307.

Hochschild, A. R. (1997). *The time bind*. New York: Metropolitan Books.

Howard, A. (1992). Work and family crossroads spanning the career. In S. Zedeck (Ed.), *Work, family, and organizations*. San Francisco: Jossey-Bass Publishers.

Johnson, M. K. (2005). Family roles and work values: Processes of selection and change. *Journal of Marriage & the Family, 67*, 352–369.

Kahn, R. L., Wolfe, D. M., Quinn, R. P., Snoek, J. D., & Rosenthal, R. A. (1964). *Organizational stress: Studies in role conflict and ambiguity*. New York: Wiley.

Kirchmeyer, C. (2006). The different effects of family on objective career success across gender: A test of alternative explanations. *Journal of Vocational Behavior, 68*(2), 323–346. doi:10.1016/j.jvb.2005.05.002.

Koropeckyj-Cox, T. (2002). Beyond parental status: Psychological well-being in middle and older age. *Journal of Marriage & the Family, 64*, 957–971.

Llorens, S., Schaufeli, W. B., Bakker, A. B., & Salanova, M. (2007). Does a positive gain spiral of resources, efficacy beliefs and engagement exist? *Computers in Human Behavior, 23*(1), 825–841. doi:10.1016/j.chb.2004.11.012.

Loscoco, K. A. (1997). Work-family linkages among self-employed women and men. *Journal of Vocational Behavior, 50*(2), 204–226. doi:10.1006/jvbe.1996.1576.

Lovibond, S. H., & Lovibond, P. F. (1995). *Manual for the depression anxiety stress scales*. Sydney, Australia: Psychology Foundation of Australia.

Macan, T. H. (1994). Time management: Test of a process model. *Journal of Applied Psychology, 79*(3), 381–391. doi:10.1037/0021-9010.79.3.381.

Marks, S. R. (1977). Multiple roles and role strain: Some notes on human energy, time and commitment. *American Sociological Review, 42*, 921–936.

Marks, S. R., & MacDermid, S. M. (1996). Multiple roles and the self: A theory of role balance. *Journal of Marriage & the Family, 58*(2), 417–432.

Maslach, C., Jackson, L. M., & Leiter, M. P. (1996). *Maslach burnout inventory manual*. Palo Alto, CA: CPP Inc.

Maslach, C., Schaufeli, W. B., & Leiter, M. P. (2001). Job burnout. *Annual Review of Psychology, 52*, 397–422. doi:10.1146/annurev.psych.52.1.397.

Michel, J. S., Kotrba, L. M., Mitchelson, J. K., Clark, M. A., & Baltes, B. B. (2011). Antecedents of work–family conflict: A meta-analytic review. *Journal of Organizational Behavior, 32*(5), 689–725. doi:10.1002/job.695.

Miller, S. (1997). The role of juggler. In S. Parasuraman & J. H. Greenhaus (Eds.), *Integrating work and family: Challenges and choices for a changing world* (pp. 48–56). Westport, CT: Quorum Books.

Moen, P. (1992). *Women's two roles: A contemporary dilemma*. New York: Auburn House.
Moen, P. (2003). *It's about time: Couples and careers*. Ithaca, N.Y.: ILR Press/Cornell University Press.
Moen, P., Harris-Abbott, D., Lee, S., & Roehling, P. V. (1999). *The Cornell couples and careers study*. Ithaca, NY: Cornell Employment and Family Careers Institute, Cornell University.
Moen, P., & Yu, Y. (2000). Effective work/life strategies: Working couples, work conditions, gender, and life quality. *Social Problems, 47*(3), 291–326.
Palkovitz, R. (1996). Parenting as a generator of adult development: Conceptual issues and implications. *Journal of Social and Personal Relationships, 13*(4), 571–592. doi:10.1177/0265407596134006.
Pocock, B. (2003). *The work-life collision*. Sydney: The Federation Press.
Relationships Forum Australia. (2007). *An unexpected tragedy: Evidence of the connection between working patterns and family breakdown in Australia*. Sydney, Australia: Relationships Forum Australia.
Ryff, C. D., Singer, B. H., & Seltzer, M. M. (2002). Pathways through challenge: Implications for well-being and health. In L. Pulkkinen & A. Caspi (Eds.), *Paths to successful development: Personality in the life course* (pp. 302–328). Cambridge, UK: Cambridge University Press.
Schaufeli, W. B., Salanova, M., Gonzalez-Roma, V., & Bakker, A. B. (2002). The measurement of engagement and burnout: A two sample confirmatory factor analytic approach. *Journal of Happiness Studies, 3*, 71–92. doi:10.1023/A:1015630930326.
Shin, L. (2014, July 7). *How much does it actually cost to have a child?* Retrieved from http://www.dailylife.com.au/life-and-love/parenting-and-families/how-much-does-it-actually-cost-to-have-a-child-20140706-3bgv3.html
Siller, H., Bader, A., & Hochleitner, M. (2016). Support for female physicians at a University Hospital: What do differences between female and male physicians tell us? In R. L. Gervais & P. M. Millear (Eds.), *Exploring resources, life-balance and well-being of women who work in a global context* (Chapter 7, pp. 109–123). Cham, Switzerland: Springer International Publishing Switzerland.
Stevens, D. P., Minnotte, K. L., Mannon, S. E., & Kiger, G. (2007). Examining the 'neglected side of work-family interface': Antecedents of positive and negative family-to-work spillover. *Journal of Family Issues, 28*(2), 242–262. doi:10.1177/0192513X06294548.
Thompson, C. A., Beauvais, L. L., & Lyness, K. S. (1999). When work benefits are not enough: The influence of work-family culture on benefit utilization, organizational attachment, and work-family conflict. *Journal of Vocational Behavior, 54*, 392–415. doi:10.1006/jvbe.1998.1681.
Thornton, M., & Bagust, J. (2007). The gender trap: Flexible work practices in corporate legal practice. *Osgoode Hall Law Journal, 45*(4), 773–811.
Vaillant, G. (2000). Adaptive mental mechanisms. *American Psychologist, 55*(1), 89–98. doi:10.1037//0003-066X.55.1.89.
Vaillant, G. (2002). *Ageing well*. Melbourne, Australia: Scribe Publications.
van Ypern, N. W., & Hagedoorn, M. (2003). Do high job demands increase intrinsic motivation or fatigue or both? The role of job control and job social support. *Academy of Management Journal, 46*(3), 339–348. doi:10.2307/30040627.
Voydanoff, P. (2004). Implications of work and community demands and resources for work-to-family conflict and facilitation. *Journal of Occupational Health Psychology, 9*(4), 275–285. doi:10.1037/1076-8998.9.4.275.
Voydanoff, P., & Donnelly, B. W. (1999). Multiple roles and psychological distress: The intersection of worker, spouse, and parent roles with the role of the adult child. *Journal of Marriage & the Family, 61*(3), 725–738.
Wallace, J. E., & Young, M. C. (2008). Parenthood and productivity: A study of demands, resources and family-friendly firms. *Journal of Vocational Behavior, 72*(1), 110–122. doi:10.1016/j.jvb.2007.11.002.

Part V
Women's Life Changes and Well-Being at Work

Chapter 12
Menstruation as a Work Stressor: Evidence and Interventions

Roxane L. Gervais

Introduction

Over the course of their working lives, women's experiences in the work environment will vary and some of these experiences might be linked to the physiological changes that could occur through menstruation, pregnancy and menopause. Some women may experience all three while in the workplace, while others might not, depending on the time they invest in their careers or jobs. The majority of the research thus far in these areas has focused on the physical health effects of these changes, rather than on women's occupational safety and health (OSH) when undergoing such changes. The research in respect of the OSH aspects of these changes has been increasing over the past few decades, but much more research is required if the well-being of women over their work life course is to be maintained.

The increase in research in these areas could be linked to the expanding use of samples consisting only of women over the past few decades. For the most part, women tended not to be the main group usually selected on which to conduct research, especially within the work environment. One of the reasons cited for this lack of non-extensive use of women in research was the perception that their normal hormonal fluctuations were thought to contaminate research results (Rodin & Ickovic, 1990). Another focus for the lack of women in research outlines the specific ways in which women are considered when conducting research; these could include highlighting their high achievements or their "deficiencies" (e.g., fear of success; Crawford & Maracek, 1989), which do not cover women in general. Such

This chapter is based on data collected independently by the author and represents solely her opinions and/or conclusions.

R.L. Gervais (✉)
Independent Practitioner, Goole DN14 6XN, UK
e-mail: roxane_gervais@alumni.fdu.edu

R.L. Gervais, P.M. Millear (eds.), *Exploring Resources, Life-Balance and Well-Being of Women Who Work in a Global Context*,
DOI 10.1007/978-3-319-31736-6_12

research, with a stronger focus on a male sample, has restricted the applicability of research findings to women, and undermined further women's contributions at work. It also, could have inadvertently led to a lower focus on research on women specific issues within the workplace, such as menstruation and the menstrual cycle, and thereby gain a better understanding of these. The increase in women as *usable* research participants is an acceptance of their viability as active members of the work environment, regardless of any physiological changes that they may experience, during their time at work.

This chapter reviews the literature on menstruation, with a main focus on its influence in the work environment; but acknowledges that research with samples of women who work are not as likely to have been used. It then presents results from a diary study and provides information on various interventions to manage any adverse effects of menstruation.

Perceptions of Menstruation and Associated Symptoms

Within any workplace, workers will have to address the various challenges and stressors of a job; but for women they may have as well the complications that premenstrual symptoms/tension (PMS/PMT) may bring on a monthly basis. It is accepted that for some women, PMS may be an uncomfortable time and for others it is a severe condition that would disrupt their lives and require them to seek some form of treatment (Steiner, Haskett, & Carroll, 1980). While there is no disputing that some women are greatly affected by PMS/PMT, the figures on these differ, ranging from 3 % for severe symptoms (Johnson, McChesney, & Bean, 1988) to an estimated up to 40 % of women experiencing moderate to severe premenstrual symptoms (Ussher, 2003). PMS may function therefore as another source of stress for women. However, menstruation, the menstrual cycle and its consequences such as PMS have not been easy concepts to introduce into the working environment. This is probably due to the fact that they are seen as counter productive to women's health (Golub, 1992; Walker, 1997), cause women to act 'out of character', i.e., less 'feminine' (Nicolson, 1995) and also due to their negative social and religious beliefs, wherein they have been viewed as negative conditions used to restrict women's activities (Golub, 1992; Walker, 1997). Another hypothesis on the topic has argued that women cannot cope with the physical and emotional demands of jobs, so are unable to function effectively; this in turn has reduced systematic searches on the organic causes of menstrual dysfunction (Harlow, 1986). There is no denying that due to the physical discomfort of PMS and at times, the process of menstruation, there would be negative repercussions; for example, those women who see themselves as suffering from PMS tend to see themselves as having negative relationships on the job (Gallant, Popiel, Hoffman, Chakraborty, & Hamilton, 1992). Additionally, women who have been asked about their mood at the pre-menstrual stage tended to report negative behaviours (Golub, 1992). It can be understood therefore why it has been stated that most of the earlier research in this field had focused on assessing the negative aspects of PMS (Walker, 1997). Despite these initial perceptions, these are concepts that should be addressed within the sphere of the working environment, as they are symptoms and behaviours that are real for many women.

Effects of Premenstrual Syndrome

The mood changes and physical discomfort associated with menstruating is commonly known as pre-menstrual syndrome. While the term itself is well understood, it is difficult to get a unified sense of exactly what it entails (Derry, Gallant, & Woods, 1997; Graham & Bancroft, 1993; Lamont, 1995; Ussher & Wilding, 1992) or whether or not it has any clinical value (Bancroft, 1995). Women also have difficulty in voicing how to interpret the term (Marván & Cortés-Iniestra, 2001). Despite a lack of clarity as to what it entails, pre-menstrual syndrome is genuine to many women; although not all women experience mood changes (Golub, 1992). The syndrome's symptoms are far reaching and can range from fatigue (Choi & Salmon, 1995; Golub, 1992), irritability (Choi & Salmon, 1995; Steiner et al., 1980), pain, and water retention (Slade, 1984), low energy, colds, and sore throats (Banks & Beresford, 1979), backache (Banks & Beresford, 1979; Golub, 1992; Shaver & Woods, 1985), abdominal cramps, and headaches (Golub, 1992; Shaver & Woods, 1985), anxiety (Davydova, Shapiro, & Goldstein, 2004; Golub, 1992), depression (Golub, 1992), tiredness (Davydova et al., 2004; Davydova, Shapiro, Goldstein, & Chicz-DeMet, 2005), sleep loss (Baker & Driver, 2004) and feeling stressed (Davydova et al., 2005). Further, while the evidence for a consistent pattern of symptoms across cycles is not readily apparent (Banks & Beresford, 1979; Shaver & Woods, 1985; Walker, 1994), there are women who experience more symptoms than others (Walker, 1994). These women tend to be more neurotic (Bancroft, 1995; Graham & Bancroft, 1993; Ussher & Wilding, 1992), than those who are not prone to such symptoms.

It is important to recognise the negative conditions that can result from the menstrual cycle; but as well the positive situations that can emerge should be acknowledged (Asso, 1992; Graham & Bancroft, 1993; Stewart, 1995). For example, women show greatest feelings of well-being and self-esteem at midcycle (Golub, 1992). These positive aspects of pre-menstrual syndrome should be explored to a greater extent, especially as the positive mood tends to last until the start of the next premenstrual phase (Asso, 1992). The positive aspects of the menstrual cycle are less likely to be researched and if they are, such as happiness experienced over the cycle, they are more likely to be reported in terms of unhappiness over the cycle (e.g. Davydova et al., 2004, 2005).

The Menstrual Cycle and Work Stress

There is a large volume of research that has explored the linkages with the menstrual cycle and both work and non-work stress. The studies have focused on different aspects of the menstrual cycle, and different interpretations of the stress concept, which has made it difficult to arrive at a definitive conclusion of the outcomes. For example, research using a large sample of nurses ($N=746$) reflected that they were more likely to report high levels of job stress if they experienced irregular menstrual cycles and longer menstrual bleeding periods (Lin, Lin, & Shiao, 2007). Other research has shown that low job control, low co-worker social support and low job security were associated with a higher risk for menstrual pain (László, GyŐrffy, Ádám, Csoboth, & Kopp, 2008); while work stress was found to be associated with dysmenorrhoea (painful menstruation; László et al., 2008; László & Kopp, 2009). Another consequence of stress was that women who worked in jobs they considered as stressful were more than twice as likely to be at risk for having a short cycle length (<24 days), when compared with women not working in stressful jobs (Fenster et al., 1999). However, one study has shown that job strain was not significantly associated with any menstrual outcomes (Gordley, Lemasters, Simpson, & Yin, 2000).

While many of the studies found that stress is linked to menstrual irregularity, such as longer or shorter menstrual cycles, the evidence into how menstrual dysfunction is defined still needs to be developed and strengthened (Harlow, 1995; Harlow & Ephross, 1995). In addition, it has been proposed that the relationship between PMS and stress is unsubstantiated as a causal relationship has not been established between the two concepts (Derry et al., 1997), leading to the suggestion that stress and its relationship to PMS and menstruation require more in-depth research (Collins, 1991). Overall, menstruation and PMS are very individual conditions, with some women more prone to these symptoms that may ultimately affect their psychological well-being.

Effects on Work Performance

The discussion thus far in this chapter has illustrated that while women experience negative physical and psychological symptoms due to PMS, with most anxiety, hostility, and depression occurring premenstrually (Golub, 1992); PMS does not seem to have an adverse effect on job performance (Stewart, 1995; Ussher & Wilding, 1992). These results extend also to menstruation, as studies have shown that it does not affect women's performance (Golub, 1992). Other research has highlighted that women's mental work capacity is not affected adversely during the menstrual cycle (Gamberale, Strindberg, & Wahlberg, 1975), with similar results in respect of task performance (Konishi, Kumashiro, Izumi, & Higuchi, 2008). Sommer (1983, 1992) has reviewed extensive amounts of material in respect of women's cognitive abilities and did not find any evidence to support the premise that they are more likely to underperform during their monthly cycle. It can be hypothesised therefore that menstruation does not reduce productivity in the workplace; as there does not seem to be any confirmation to date that it does.

Focus on the Workplace

As women are an active part of the workforce and can menstruate for the majority of their working lives, it is necessary to continue to assess if PMS could contribute to psychological ill health. More research needs to be done on menstruation, with data collected from active workers; especially as a large percentage of the research conducted on the menstrual cycle thus far has been from within a stereotypic concept of womanhood (Walker, 1996). The assessment of menstruation should be undertaken from different perspectives in particular when considered as part of a wider research interest, and not focused solely on PMS and its consequences. One of the reasons that this focus is required is to reduce some of the misperceptions about the meaning of PMS, which women may have, and which in turn causes them unconsciously to intensify their premenstrual changes when remembering these and conform to women's cultural stereotypes on the issue; rather than outline those symptoms that they may have actually experienced (Marván & Cortés-Iniestra, 2001). Other research exploring premenstrual syndrome/late luteal phase dysphoric disorder (LLPDD) has revealed that knowledge of why the data are being collected can cause women to skew slightly what they report (Gallant et al., 1992). Further, women have the tendency to report negative behaviours when asked about their mood at the pre-menstrual stage (Golub, 1992). These are factors to think of when designing studies on menstruation, as they would seem to support the use of a diary method.

There are several research studies that have used a diary method when assessing menstruation and different aspects of its concept (e.g., Banks & Beresford, 1979; Fenster et al., 1999; Freeman, DeRubeis, & Rickels, 1996; Goldberg et al., 2007; Harlow & Zeger, 1991). It is a useful way to collect data on this topic as menstrual data that are collected as part of overall diary measures would provide a better check of mood with respect to PMS, as the participants would not tend to focus solely on negative states. The inclusion of menstrual data as part of wider measures on the work environment and work characteristics should generate data that are less subjective with respect to mood states before the onset of menstruation. Another matter to consider when selecting a method is that the experience of women in respect of menstruation, like the experience of stress, is very individualistic and PMS needs to be explored at the idiographic level (Asso, 1992), as it is relative to the individual level, rather than at the nomothetic level at which it is usually studied.

As mentioned earlier in this chapter, menstruation is a difficult concept to introduce into organisational research. However, as it is a physiological change for women, it should be considered at least as a third variable factor. Frese and colleagues (Frese, 1985; Zapf, Dormann, & Frese, 1996) have promoted the inclusion of more factors as third variables in research studies, and it should be factored into organisational research on women. PMS could impact also how women deal with work demands and while it may not adversely affect performance; the physical and psychological discomfort that can result in some women, may have an effect on how effectively they deal with work demands. Some women, who are sufferers of PMS, may be less effective at addressing demands during their daily routines, despite the amount of resources that are available to them.

Method

The Participants

A large health care trust in the United Kingdom was approached to obtain participants in the nursing profession for the study. As the study was longitudinal in nature and would require the participants to commit fully for a period of one month at two time points, it was decided to provide the nurses with the information about what was involved and allow them to volunteer, rather than asking them to take part in the study. Seventy-one nurses volunteered to participate, 60 of who were women. The 60 women at Time 1 were between the ages of 21 to 60 ($M=40.21$, $SD=8.63$; $n=58$). They worked for an average of 8.24 h per day ($SD=1.12$, $n=60$), had over half-hour of free time ($M=00{:}63$, $SD=00{:}29$), and slept close to seven hours each night ($M=6.82$, $SD=0.89$; $n=60$). At Time 2, 38 women completed the diaries. These were between the ages of 23 to 62 ($M=41.97$, $SD=9.10$; $n=38$). They worked for an average of 8.24 h per day ($SD=0.93$) with just over half-hour of free time ($M=00{:}61$, $SD=00{:}26$), and slept a similar time as in Time 1 ($M=6.81$, $SD=0.83$; $n=38$).

The study was a two-wave panel design, allowing data to be collected from the same participants on two separate occasions. The time lag between the two data points was nine months to enable the capture of any changes in behaviours, moods and work characteristics and has been recommended as one that facilitates the best results from the sample (Zapf et al., 1996) and at demonstrating a moderating effect (Dormann & Zapf, 1999).

The nurses were supplied with one month's supply of diaries, four in total, at each time of the study. They were given freepost envelopes to return them to the researcher once these were completed. The diaries were numerically coded so that the repeated measures would be assigned to the appropriate person.

The participants completed the diaries either at their workplace or at their homes, immediately after completing their shifts, or if they were not at work, in the evening about their mealtime. This enabled more accurate measures to be obtained.

The Measures

The diary was designed to collect structured data on the measures that follow. All of the measures, with the exception of the subjective strain measure, were developed for the study (Gervais, 2002). The work characteristics in terms of the work *demands*, *control* and *support* that the participants experienced were measured on a nine-point Likert scale ranging from 1 = low to 9 = high, with higher scores indicating higher levels of work *demands*, *control* and *social support*.

The nurses' *performance* level in terms of their effectiveness in dealing with the demands made on them was assessed with three items. They were asked, for example, to indicate how good they were at "Taking care of your own needs." These were on a nine-point Likert scale ranging from 1 = not very, to 9 = very. A higher score indicated that a higher level of performance was achieved.

Hassles and *uplifts* were considered from the work and non-work perspectives. These consisted of 24 items with each set of hassles and uplifts consisting of six items. The relationship between work stress and non-work stress is not autonomous and when assessing the effects of work related stress, it is advantageous to assess the effects of non-work related stress, and thereby include elements from both domains in organisational stress assessments (Bolger, DeLongis, Kessler, & Wethington, 1989; Jackson, 1989; Payne, Jick, & Burke, 1982). This study included items from both the work and non-work domains. The items for work included hassles and uplifts by "medical colleagues, interruptions, and having lots to do." Those outside the working environment included "health/appearance, travel/transport, and other people." These were all on a three-point scale ranging from 0 = not at all; 1 = a little; 2 = a lot. The hassles and uplifts were averaged to give a total score. Overall both hassles scores and both uplifts scores (at work, not at work) would total 12. A higher score indicated that the participants experienced more hassles and more uplifts.

Subjective strain was assessed with 16 items detailing various moods and feelings which were scored on a nine-point Likert scale ranging from 1 = did not feel that way at all to 9 = felt that way very much (See Hockey, Payne, & Rick, 1996). Example of the items, some of which were reversed scored (R), were annoyed, at ease (R), calm (R), irritated, contented (R), depressed, enthusiastic (R), energetic (R), lively (R), tired, and weary. A higher score indicated greater level of subjective strain.

Psychosomatic symptoms were assessed with 15 items, including backache, drowsiness, eyestrain, feeling weak, poor appetite, problems of attention or concentration, difficulties with decision making or planning and forgetfulness and slips of mind, They were measured on a three-point scale ranging from 0 = not at all; 1 = a little; 2 = a lot, with higher scores indicating experiences of psychosomatic symptoms.

Menstrual symptoms included two symptoms, menstrual bleeding and menstrual pain and were measured on a three-point scale ranging from 0 = not at all; 1 = a little; 2 = a lot, with higher scores indicating greater experiences of menstrual symptoms.

Analysis

A hierarchical regression analysis, using listwise deletion of missing data, was used to assess the influence that menstrual symptoms have on job strain and job performance. This was based on pooled-time series analysis to control the between and within participant variance, especially as 'day' was the unit of analysis. The data were disaggregated data (individual person days), to allow for the temporal relationships between the daily values to be kept in the analyses, which might otherwise be lost when the data are aggregated to the person level (Eckenrode, 1984). The variables were standardised prior to the analyses to control for within and between participants' variance (Dunlap & Kemery, 1987; Jaccard, Turrisi, & Wan, 1990; Zohar, 1999), for multicollinearity and for differences between the scales (Plewis, 1985). The analyses were conducted separately for each wave of the study.

On the first step, *N*-1 dummy coded variables (representing *N* participants) and thereby accounting for the variance in the dependent variable that was attributable to individual differences (West & Hepworth, 1991; Zohar, 1999), were entered, this was followed by the psychosomatic symptoms on the second step. The demands and resources were entered on the third step, with the fourth step consisting of the daily hassles and daily uplifts. The fifth and final step included the menstrual symptoms. The analyses focused on only those days when the participants were at work. The independent variables described in the five steps were regressed on job strain and job performance.

Results

Descriptive Analyses

The first set of analyses focused on the mean values, standard deviations and reliability values (Cronbach's alpha) for the variables used in the present research. These are detailed in Table 12.1. All of the variables used in the present study had fairly acceptable levels of reliability (Cronbach, 1951), ranging from $\alpha=.52$ for resources to $\alpha=.91$ for job strain (Wave 1). While some of these values are not above the proposed lower limit of .70 that is required to accept the reliability properties of the scales (Nunnally, 1978); it is accepted that alpha values are influenced by the number of items in a scale (Cortina, 1993), and should serve the purpose of this present study.

There was a strong relationship between psychosomatic and menstrual symptoms at both waves (wave 1: $r=.42, p<.001$; wave 2: $r=.39, p<.001$), and similarly between work demands and hassles (wave 1: $r=.46, p<.001$; wave 2: $r=.23, p<.05$). As should be expected, individuals with more resources reported lower job strain (wave 1: $r=-.32, p<.001$; wave 2: $r=-.17, p=.11$), and higher job performance (wave 1: $r=.52, p<.001$; wave 2: $r=.36, p<.001$).

Table 12.1 Alpha values, descriptive statistics and correlations among variables – Time 1 & Time 2

		Wave 1												Wave 2			
		α	Mean	*SD*	*N*									α	Mean	*SD*	*N*
1	Menstrual symptoms	.83	0.98	0.54	139	**1**	.39	.09	.19	.06	.05	.19	.01	.84	0.98	0.55	90
2	Psychosomatic symptoms	.84	0.32	0.29	139	.42	**2**	.23	.10	.36	.11	.30	−.12	.79	0.23	0.26	90
3	Demands	.67	6.03	1.57	138	.03	−.05	**3**	.21	.23	.17	−.03	.33	.59	6.44	1.20	90
4	Resources	.52	5.69	1.50	138	.01	−.22	.16	**4**	.08	.13	−17	.36	.57	5.72	1.56	90
5	Daily hassles	.78	0.65	0.50	138	.05	.22	.46	−.03	**5**	.28	.42	−.11	.78	0.61	0.38	90
6	Daily uplifts	.77	0.56	0.44	130	−.03	−.03	.03	.22	−.04	**6**	−.27	.23	.80	0.57	0.42	90
7	Job strain	.91	4.03	1.36	139	.05	.36	.09	−.32	.41	−.12	**7**	−.59	.91	4.09	1.42	90
8	Job performance	.68	6.39	1.31	137	−.04	−.21	.13	.52	−.10	.26	−.53	**8**	.69	6.43	1.36	90

Note: Wave 1 – values below diagonal: $r \geq \pm .21, p < .05$, $r \geq \pm .22, p < .01$, $r \geq \pm .32, p < .001$, N=Number of Person Days and ranged from 128 to 139; **Wave 2** – values above diagonal: $r \geq \pm .21, p < .05$, $r \geq \pm .27, p < .01$, $r \geq \pm .36, p < .001$; N=Number of Person Days=90

Table 12.2 Hierarchical regression analyses predicting job strain and job performance – Wave 1

Step	Predictors	Job Strain				Job Performance			
		R^2	Adj R^2	ΔR^2	β	R^2	Adj R^2	ΔR^2	β
1	Participants (*N*−1)	.50	.28	.50§		.51	.29	.51§	
2	Psychosomatic symptoms	.56	.35	.05†	.39†	.51	.29	.00	−.08
3	Demands	.61	.42	.06†	.24*	.61	.42	.10§	−.28*
	Resources				−.27†				38§
4	Daily hassles	.66	.48	.05†	.33§	.63	.44	.02	.05
	Daily uplifts				−.12				.25*
5	Menstrual symptoms	.68	.51	.02*	−.21*	.63	.43	.00	.03
	n =	128				126			

Note: * $p<.05$, † $p<.01$, § $p<.001$; Participants (*N*−1): Dummy coded. The table shows standardised β weights for the first entry of each predictor in the analysis. *F* values at the last step of the models were – Job Strain: F (45, 82)=3.92, $p<.001$, Job Performance: F (44, 81)=3.17, $p<.001$

Table 12.3 Hierarchical regression analyses predicting job strain and job performance – Wave 2

Step	Predictors	Job Strain				Job Performance			
		R^2	Adj R^2	ΔR^2	β	R^2	Adj R^2	ΔR^2	β
1	Participants (*N*−1)	.75	.63	.75§		.80	.70	.80§	
2	Psychosomatic symptoms	.80	.70	.05§	.41§	.82	.74	.03†	−.30†
3	Demands	.81	.71	.01	.06	.84	.76	.02*	−.01
	Resources				−.19				.25*
4	Daily hassles	.84	.75	.03†	.29§	.85	.76	.01	−.12
	Daily uplifts				−.04				.14
5	Menstrual symptoms	.85	.75	.01	.13	.85	.76	.00	.03
	n =	90				90			

Note: * $p<.05$, † $p<.01$, § $p<.001$. Participants (*N*−1): Dummy coded. The table shows standardised β weights for the first entry of each predictor in the analysis. *F* values at the last step of the models were – Job Strain: F (34, 55)=9.00, $p<.001$, Job Performance: F (34, 55)=9.23, $p<.001$

Hierarchical Regression Analyses

The results for the multiple regression analyses are presented in Tables 12.2 and 12.3, which display the R^2, Adj. R^2, the change in R^2 (ΔR^2), and the standardised regression coefficients (beta – β). For these analyses, the predictor effect is seen when there is a significant change on the last step of the change in R^2 (ΔR^2; Zapf et al., 1996).

At wave 1 in respect of job strain, all five steps in the model were significant [final step: F (45, 82)=3.92, $p<.001$], with the model realising 51 % of the variance. A review of the beta coefficients showed that psychosomatic symptoms [(β)=.39 (t[126]=3.26, $p<.01$)], demands [(β)=.24 (t[126]=2.19, $p<.05$)], resources [(β)=−.27 (t[126]=−2.73, $p<.01$)], daily hassles [(β)=.33 (t[126]=3.08, $p<.01$)], and menstrual symptoms [(β)=−.21 (t[126]=−2.43, $p<.05$)] were all predictors of job stain. Daily uplifts were not a predictor. Further, psychosomatic symptoms, resources and daily hassles realised significant values throughout all of the steps in the model and highlights their influence on job strain.

The results in respect of job performance showed that while menstrual symptoms were not a predictor [(β)=.03 (t[124]=.38, $p=.70$)], demands [(β)=−.28(t[124]=−2.47, $p<.05$)], resources [(β)=.38 (t[124]=3.86, $p<.001$)] and uplifts were [(β)=.25 (t[124]=2.00, $p<.05$)]. Work demands, resources and uplifts remained significant throughout the model. The overall model was significant, and accounted for 43 % of the variance (F[44, 81]=3.17, $p<.001$).

When the analyses were conducted for wave 2, they showed that menstrual symptoms did not influence job strain [(β)=.13 (t[88]=1.55, $p=.13$)]. The independent variables that predicted job strain when first entered were psychosomatic symptoms [(β)=.41 (t[88]=3.81, $p<.001$)] and daily hassles [(β)=.29 (t[88]=3.35, $p<.001$)]. Neither demands [(β)=.06 (t[88]=.68, $p=.50$)], resources [(β)=−.19 (t[88]=−1.85, $p=.07$)], nor daily uplifts [(β)=−.04 (t[88]=−.38, $p=.71$)], were able to influence directly job strain. Hassles and resources were able to influence job strain on the last step of the model. The overall model was significant (F[34, 55]=9.00, $p<.001$), accounting for 75 % of the variance.

The results for wave 2 for job performance, showed that the predictors of the dependent variable involved psychosomatic symptoms [(β)=−.30 (t[88]=−2.98, $p<.01$)] and resources [(β)=.25 (t[88]=2.59, $p<.05$)]. Neither demands [(β)=−.01 (t[88]=−.12, $p=.91$)], daily hassles [(β)=−.12 (t[88]=−1.41, $p=.16$)], nor daily uplifts [(β)=.14 (t[88]=.13, $p=.20$)] were predictors of job performance. As in wave 1, menstrual symptoms were not a predictor of performance [(β)=.03 (t[88]=.41, $p=.68$)]. Psychosomatic symptoms and resources realised significant values throughout the model and highlights their importance in achieving good job performance. The overall model was significant (F[34, 55]=9.23, $p<.001$), accounting for 76 % of the variance.

Discussion

The present study showed that fewer menstrual symptoms increased job strain during the first wave of the study. It was in the expected direction for wave 2 and for both waves when testing job performance, was not significant. This counterintuitive result suggests that menstrual symptoms might not function as a stressor for this sample of nurses, and is a result that should be explored further. For this study, data were collected for one-month only, and a longer time limit may be more appropriate for researching menstrual symptoms. Some menstrual cycles may extend beyond the 28-day limit of each wave of the present study (Harlow, 1995). Further, menstrual symptoms as a stressor did not reduce job performance at both waves of the study; this might imply that menstrual symptoms are related more strongly to physical symptoms rather than ability to function. As discussed, this present study supports previous research which found also that women's performance levels at work were not adversely affected by their menstrual cycle (e.g., Gamberale et al., 1975; Johnson et al., 1988). Although menstrual symptoms did not have a significant effect on work performance, and may not adversely affect performance, the physical and psychological discomfort that can result from menstrual symptoms in some women may have an effect on how effectively they deal with work demands. Women who are sufferers of these symptoms may be less capable of dealing more effectively with work demands despite the amount of resources that are available to them.

The large percentages of variance that were accounted for by the four models reflect that the variables were strong predictors of job strain and job performance. The strongest predictors though were resources and psychosomatic symptoms. Resources acted as a predictor on job strain (wave 1) and job performance (waves 1 and 2), acknowledging the importance of resources to women who work. Resources have been shown to improve on well-being and performance (see Bakker & Demerouti, 2007). Overall, the importance of resources has been raised in the literature continuously (see de Jonge, Bosma, Peter, & Siegrist, 2000; Gervais & Millear, 2014; Schaufeli, Bakker, & Van Rhenen, 2009). The relevance of psychosomatic symptoms as a predictor in organisational research was shown as it led to higher job strain (waves 1 and 2) and lower work performance (wave 2). Psychosomatic complaints are key components of the stress process, as experiencing symptoms such as headaches, backaches and forgetfulness are usually a preliminary indication that more intense symptoms such as anxiety and depression could result. Higher measures of psychosomatic symptoms have been linked to higher job strain (see de Jonge et al., 2000).

Demands and hassles were more likely to lead to higher job strain (wave 1), while more demands at wave 1 led to lower job performance. Uplifts were only able to improve on job performance in wave 1. The mean values of the variables showed that the nurses reported more demands than resources, but with lower strain and higher performance levels. The positive relationships found in the regression analyses for resources with both job strain and job performance could perhaps indicate that this set of respondents were able to manage their workload effectively.

The importance of gaining data on the work-related needs of women has been raised, in order for these to be met (Quinlan, 1996). A more comprehensive understanding of women's abilities to cope with and function during physiological changes is one of those needs that cannot and should not be ignored. Sommer in 1983 highlighted the belief that menstrual debilitation existed still in the public consciousness; the more evidence that is collected would assist in eradicating this blanket assumption.

Limitations

One of the limitations of the study is the relatively small sample (in terms of person days). However, the use of a diary method and as data were collected on two occasions, do contribute to the usefulness of the data in providing more evidence that menstruation might not function as a debilitating condition for women in general.

Another limitation is the use of self-report data, which could be subject to common method variance. While there is debate in the literature on a definite stance on this topic (see Spector, 1987, 2006; Williams, Cote, & Buckley, 1989), the author helped to control for this issue by standardising the variables before the analyses, in order to control for within and between participants' variance as suggested in methodological discussions (see Dunlap & Kemery, 1987; Jaccard et al., 1990; Zohar, 1999), and also to address the multicollinearity and differences between the scales (Plewis, 1985).

The study consisted of only one profession, nurses, and may not be representative of all women workers. Nurses do have high demands, and the nurses in this sample were able to cope with the demands they encountered at work; their demands did not lead directly to an increase in job strain, or to a reduction in work performance. Despite this, it would be useful to explore this issue in a heterogeneous job sample of women workers.

Managing PMS

Women have been using various methods to improve on the PMS/PMT that they live through on a monthly basis. These can include *diet change* (24.6 %), *exercise* (41.8 %) and *vitamins* (18.9 %) as reported by a sample of 730 nursing school graduates over the period 1963–1984 (Johnson et al., 1988). As women are different and will benefit from using a method with which they are most comfortable; there is no 'one' method that is recommended. The Royal College of Obstetricians and Gynaecologists (RCOG, 2007) acknowledges that various ways should be used to manage premenstrual syndrome and has published a guide to that effect. One of the methods that the RCOG has recommended is *cognitive behavioural therapy* (CBT) as it has proven to be successful when done as a set course, e.g. ten week sessions (RCOG, 2007).

There is substantial evidence that *exercise* will improve physical health (see Penedo & Dahn, 2005; Scully, Kremer, Meade, Graham, & Dudgeon, 1998), as well as mental health (Fox, 1999), allowing individuals to attain overall well-being. The benefit of exercise extends to moderating the effects of PMS. Research in this area has confirmed the use of exercise, with more intensive exercise regimes being more effective than those that were not as intense or for those individuals who did not engage in exercise (Choi, 1992; Choi & Salmon, 1995; Scully et al., 1998; Timmonen & Procopé, 1971).

More evidence of non-traditional ways of managing PMS has been obtained within the past few years and while more research on these methods and medications is required, the preliminary findings have proved useful, especially for those women who may wish to pursue options that might have fewer complications. For example, there is some evidence that *acupuncture* would assist with PMS (Kim, Park, Lee, & Lee, 2011), as would *Chinese herbal medicine* (Jing, Yang, Ismail, Chen, & Wu, 2009). There is some support that *massage* could be used as an additional resource in reducing severe premenstrual symptoms. A randomised controlled trial over a five-week period realised a reduction in anxiety, depressed mood and pain for those in the massage group immediately after the first and last massage sessions (Hernandez-Reif et al., 2000). *Mindfulness* is another, fairly new method that is being explored at present, but there are very few studies, especially randomised controlled trials (RCTs), to present evidence that it could assist with reducing the symptoms of PMS/PMT. As more connection is made to the mind/body connection especially in terms of ill health and well-being (Scheper-Hughes & Lock, 1987), more research should become available, but overall more research is being conducted on the benefits that mindfulness could have on psychological health (e.g., Brown & Ryan, 2003).

Overall, it is important to acknowledge that the old perceptions of the affects of menstruation on women have to be eradicated (Houppert, 2007; Nicolson, 1995), and continuous research in the area would help to achieve this.

References

Asso, D. (1992). A reappraisal of the normal menstrual cycle. *Journal of Reproductive and Infant Psychology, 10*(2), 103–109. doi:10.1080/02646839208403942.

Baker, F. C., & Driver, H. S. (2004). Self-reported sleep across the menstrual cycle in young, healthy women. *Journal of Psychosomatic Research, 56*(2), 239–243. doi:10.1016/S0022-3999(03)00067-9.

Bakker, A., & Demerouti, E. (2007). The job demands-resources model: State of the art. *Journal of Managerial Psychology, 22*(3), 309–328. doi:10.1108/02683940710733115.

Bancroft, J. (1995). The menstrual cycle and the well-being of women. *Social Science & Medicine, 41*(6), 785–791. doi:10.1016/0277-9536(95)00045-9.

Banks, M. H., & Beresford, S. A. A. (1979). The influence of menstrual cycle phase upon symptom recording using data from health diaries. *Journal of Psychosomatic Research, 23*(5), 307–311. doi:10.1016/0022-3999(79)90036-9.

Bolger, N., DeLongis, A., Kessler, R. C., & Wethington, E. (1989). The contagion of stress across multiple roles. *Journal of Marriage and the Family, 51*(1), 175–183. doi:10.2307/352378.

Brown, K. W., & Ryan, R. M. (2003). The benefits of being present: Mindfulness and its role in psychological well-being. *Journal of Personality and Social Psychology, 84*(4), 822–848. doi:10.1037/0022-3514.84.4.822.

Choi, P. Y. L. (1992). The psychological benefits of physical exercise: Implications for women and the menstrual cycle. *Journal of Reproductive and Infant Psychology, 10*(2), 111–115. doi:10.1080/02646839208403943.

Choi, P. Y. L., & Salmon, P. (1995). Symptom changes across the menstrual cycle in competitive sportswomen, exercisers and sedentary women. *British Journal of Clinical Psychology, 34*(3), 447–460. doi:10.1111/j.2044-8260.1995.tb01479.x.

Collins, A. (1991). Premenstrual distress: Implications for women's working capacity & quality of life. In M. Frankenhaeuser, U. Lundberg, & M. A. Chesney (Eds.), *Women, work, and health: Stress and opportunities* (pp. 239–254). New York: Plenum Press.

Cortina, J. M. (1993). What is coefficient alpha? An examination of theory and applications. *Journal of Applied Psychology, 78*(1), 98–104. doi:10.1037/0021-9010.78.1.98.

Crawford, M., & Maracek, J. (1989). Psychology reconstructs the female: 1968–1988. *Psychology of Women Quarterly, 13*(2), 147–165. doi:10.1111/j.1471-6402.1989.tb00993.x.

Cronbach, L. J. (1951). Coefficient alpha and the internal structure of tests. *Psychometrika, 16*(3), 297–334. doi:10.1007/BF02310555.

Davydova, D. M., Shapiro, D., & Goldstein, I. B. (2004). Moods in everyday situations. Effects of menstrual cycle, work, and personality. *Journal of Psychosomatic Research, 56*(1), 27–33. doi:10.1016/S0022-3999(03)00602-0.

Davydova, D. M., Shapiro, D., Goldstein, I. B., & Chicz-DeMet, A. (2005). Moods in everyday situations: Effects of menstrual cycle, work, and stress hormones. *Journal of Psychosomatic Research, 58*(4), 343–349. doi:10.1016/j.jpsychores.2004.11.003.

de Jonge, J., Bosma, H., Peter, R., & Siegrist, J. (2000). Job strain, effort-reward imbalance and employee well-being: A large-scale cross-sectional study. *Social Science & Medicine, 50*(9), 1317–1327. doi:10.1016/S0277-9536(99)00388-3.

Derry, P. S., Gallant, S. J., & Woods, N. F. (1997). Premenstrual syndrome and menopause. In S. J. Gallant, G. P. Keita, & R. Royak-Schaler (Eds.), *Health care for women. Psychological, social, and behavioral influences* (pp. 203–220). Washington, DC: American Psychological Association.

Dormann, C., & Zapf, D. (1999). Social support, social stressors at work, and depressive symptoms: Testing for main and moderating effects with structural equations in a three-wave longitudinal study. *Journal of Applied Psychology, 84*(6), 874–884. doi:10.1037/0021-9010.84.6.874.

Dunlap, W. P., & Kemery, E. R. (1987). Failure to detect moderating effects: Is multicollinearity the problem? *Psychological Bulletin, 102*(3), 418–420. doi:10.1037/0033-2909.102.3.418.

Eckenrode, J. (1984). Impact of chronic and acute stressors on daily reports of mood. *Journal of Personality and Social Psychology, 46*(4), 907–918. doi:10.1037/0022-3514.46.4.907.

Fenster, L., Waller, K., Chen, J., Hubbard, A. E., Windham, G. C., Elkin, E., et al. (1999). Psychological stress in the workplace and menstrual function. *American Journal of Epidemiology, 149*(2), 127–134.

Fox, K. R. (1999). The influence of physical activity on mental well-being. *Public Health Nutrition, 2*(3a), 411–418. doi:10.1017/S1368980099000567.

Freeman, E. W., DeRubeis, R. J., & Rickels, K. (1996). Reliability and validity of a daily diary for premenstrual syndrome. *Psychiatry Research, 65*(2), 97–106. doi:10.1016/S0165-1781(96)02929-0.

Frese, M. (1985). Stress at work and psychosomatic complaints: A causal interpretation. *Journal of Applied Psychology, 70*(2), 314–328. doi:10.1037/0021-9010.70.2.314.

Gallant, S. J., Popiel, D. A., Hoffman, D. M., Chakraborty, P. K., & Hamilton, J. A. (1992). Using daily ratings to confirm premenstrual syndrome/late luteal phase dysphoric disorder. Part I. Effects of demand characteristics and expectations. *Psychosomatic Medicine, 54*(2), 149–166.

Gamberale, F., Strindberg, L., & Wahlberg, I. (1975). Female work capacity during the menstrual cycle. Physiological and psychological reactions. *Scandinavian Journal of Work, Environment & Health, 1*(2), 120–127. doi:10.5271/sjweh.2855.

Gervais, R. (2002), *Patterns of work strain and well-being in nurses*. Dissertation: Thesis (Ph.D.), University of Hull, Hull, OCLC Number: 498567003.

Gervais, R. L., & Millear, P. (2014). The well-being of women at work: The importance of resources across the life course. *Journal of Organizational Change Management, 27*(4), 598–612. doi:10.1108/JOCM-05-2014-0103.

Goldberg, J., Wolf, A., Silberstein, S., Gebeline-Myersm, C., Hopkins, M., Einhorn, K., et al. (2007). Evaluation of an electronic diary as a diagnostic tool to study headache and premenstrual symptoms in migraineurs. *Headache, 47*(3), 384–396. doi:10.1111/j.1526-4610.2006.00441.x.

Golub, S. (1992). *Periods. From menarche to menopause*. Newbury Park, CL: Sage.
Gordley, L. B., Lemasters, G., Simpson, S. R., & Yin, J. H. (2000). Menstrual disorders and occupational, stress, and racial factors among military personnel. *Journal of Occupational & Environmental Medicine, 42*(9), 871–881. doi:10.1097/00043764-200009000-00005.
Graham, C., & Bancroft, J. (1993). Women, mood and the menstrual cycle. In C. A. Niven & D. Carroll (Eds.), *The health psychology of women* (pp. 13–25). Chur, Switzerland: Harwood Academic Publishers.
Harlow, S. D. (1986). Function and dysfunction: A historical critique of the literature on menstruation and work. *Health Care for Women International, 7*(1-2), 39–50. doi:10.1080/07399338609515722.
Harlow, S. D. (1995). *What we know and do not know about the menstrual cycle; or, questions scientists could be asking*. The Robert H. Ebert program on critical issues in reproductive health and population. New York: The Population Council. http://www.popcouncil.org/uploads/pdfs/ebert/MenstrualPaper.pdf. Accessed 29 July 2014.
Harlow, S. D., & Ephross, S. A. (1995). Epidemiology of menstruation and its relevance to women's health. *Epidemiologic Reviews, 17*(2), 265–286.
Harlow, S. D., & Zeger, S. L. (1991). An application of longitudinal methods to the analysis of menstrual diary data. *Journal of Clinical Epidemiology, 44*(10), 1015–1025. doi:10.1016/0895-4356(91)90003-R.
Hernandez-Reif, M., Martinez, A., Field, T., Quintero, O., Hart, S., & Burman, I. (2000). Premenstrual symptoms are relieved by massage therapy. *Journal of Psychosomatic Obstetrics & Gynecology, 21*(1), 9–15. doi:10.3109/01674820009075603.
Hockey, G. R. J., Payne, R. L., & Rick, J. T. (1996). Intra-individual patterns of hormonal and affective adaptation to work demands: An n = 2 study of junior doctors. *Biological Psychology, 42*(2), 393–411. doi:10.1016/0301-0511(95)05169-4.
Houppert, K. (2007, July 17). *Final period*. The New York Times. http://www.nytimes.com/2007/07/17/opinion/17houppert.html?_r=0&adxnnl=1&adxnnlx=1414249607-ogCjtLzoDjsFsKcM0KqHNA. Accessed 04 Aug 2014.
Jaccard, J., Turrisi, R., & Wan, C. K. (1990). *Interaction effects in multiple regression*. Newbury Park, CL: Sage.
Jackson, S. E. (1989). Does job control control job stress? In S. L. Sauter, J. J. Hurrell Jr., & C. L. Cooper (Eds.), *Job control and worker health* (pp. 25–53). Chichester, UK: Wiley.
Jing, Z., Yang, X., Ismail, K. M., Chen, X. Y., & Wu, T. (2009). Chinese herbal medicine for premenstrual syndrome. *Cochrane Database Systematic Review, 21*(1), CD006414. doi:10.1002/14651858.CD006414.pub2.
Johnson, S. R., McChesney, C., & Bean, J. A. (1988). Epidemiology of premenstrual symptoms in non-clinical sample. I. Prevalence, natural history and help-seeking behaviour. *The Journal of Reproductive Medicine, 33*(4), 340–346.
Kim, S.-Y., Park, H.-J., Lee, H., & Lee, H. (2011). Acupuncture for premenstrual syndrome: A systematic review and meta-analysis of randomised controlled trials. *BJOG: An International Journal of Obstetrics & Gynaecology, 118*(8), 899–915. doi:10.1111/j.1471-0528.2011.02994.x.
Konishi, K., Kumashiro, M., Izumi, H., & Higuchi, Y. (2008). Effects of the menstrual cycle on working memory: Comparison of postmenstrual and premenstrual phases. *Industrial Health, 46*(3), 253–260. http://dx.doi.org/10.2486/indhealth.46.253.
Lamont, J. A. (1995). PMS: Methodologic issues. In J. Bitzer & M. Stauber (Eds.), *Psychosomatic obstetrics and gynaecology*, 11th international congress of psychosomatic obstetrics and gynecology 21–24 May, 1995 (pp. 353–358). Basel, Switzerland: Monduzzi Editore S.p.A.
László, K. D., GyŐrffy, Z., Ádám, S., Csoboth, C., & Kopp, M. S. (2008). Work-related stress factors and menstrual pain: A nation-wide representative survey. *Journal of Psychosomatic Obstetrics & Gynecology, 29*(2), 133–138. doi:10.1080/01674820701804423.
László, K., & Kopp, M. S. (2009). Effort-reward imbalance and overcommitment at work are associated with painful menstruation: Results from the Hungarostudy, Epidemiological Panel 2006. *Journal of Occupational & Environmental Medicine, 51*(2), 157–163. doi:10.1097/JOM.0b013e318197ca89.

Lin, H.-T., Lin, L.-C., & Shiao, J. S. C. (2007). The impact of self-perceived job stress on menstrual patterns among Taiwanese nurses. *Industrial Health, 45*(5), 709–714. http://dx.doi.org/10.2486/indhealth.45.709.

Marván, M. L., & Cortés-Iniestra, S. (2001). Women's beliefs about the prevalence of premenstrual syndrome and biases in recall of premenstrual changes. *Health Psychology, 20*(4), 276–280. doi:10.1037/0278-6133.20.4.276.

Nicolson, P. (1995). The menstrual cycle, science and femininity: Assumptions underlying menstrual cycle research. *Social Science & Medicine, 41*(6), 779–784. doi:10.1016/0277-9536(95)00044-8.

Nunnally, J. (1978). *Psychometric theory*. New York: McGraw-Hill.

Payne, R., Jick, T. D., & Burke, R. J. (1982). Whither stress research?: An agenda for the 1980s. *Journal of Occupational Behaviour, 3*(1), 131–145. doi:10.1002/job.4030030110.

Penedo, F. J., & Dahn, J. R. (2005). Exercise and well-being: A review of mental and physical health benefits associated with physical activity. *Current Opinion in Psychiatry, 18*(2), 189–193.

Plewis, I. (1985). *Analysing change. Measurement and explanation using longitudinal data*. Chichester, UK: Wiley.

Quinlan, M. G. (1996). Women and occupational health and safety: The challenges still waiting to be met. *Journal of Occupational Health and Safety, Australia and New Zealand, 12*(4), 409–422.

Rodin, J., & Ickovic, J. R. (1990). Women's health: Review and research agenda as we approach the 21st century. *American Psychologist, 45*(9), 1018–1034. doi:10.1037/0003-066X.45.9.1018.

Royal College of Obstetricians and Gynaecologists. (2007, December). *Management of premenstrual syndrome* (Green-top guideline no. 48). http://www.rcog.org.uk/(last). http://www.rcog.org.uk/files/rcog-corp/uploaded-files/GT48ManagementPremensturalSyndrome.pdf. Accessed 29 July 2014.

Schaufeli, W. B., Bakker, A. B., & Van Rhenen, W. (2009). How changes in job demands and resources predict burnout, work engagement, and sickness absenteeism. *Journal of Organizational Behavior, 30*(7), 893–917. doi:10.1002/job.595.

Scheper-Hughes, N., & Lock, M. M. (1987). The mindful body: A prolegomenon to future work in medical anthropology. *Medical Anthropology Quarterly*, New Series, *1*(1), 6–41. doi: 10.1525/maq.1987.1.1.02a00020

Scully, D., Kremer, J., Meade, M. M., Graham, R., & Dudgeon, K. (1998). Physical exercise and psychological well being: A critical review. *British Journal of Sports Medicine, 32*(2), 111–120. doi:10.1136/bjsm.32.2.111.

Shaver, J. F., & Woods, N. F. (1985). Concordance of perimenstrual symptoms across two cycles. *Research in Nursing and Health, 8*(4), 313–319. doi:10.1002/nur.4770080403.

Slade, P. (1984). Premenstrual emotional changes in normal women: Fact of fiction? *Journal of Psychosomatic Research, 28*(1), 1–7. doi:10.1016/0022-3999(84)90034-5.

Sommer, B. (1983). How does menstruation affect cognitive competence and psychophysiological response? *Women & Health, 8*(2-3), 53–90. doi:10.1300/J013v08n02_04.

Sommer, B. (1992). Cognitive performance and the menstrual cycle. In J. T. E. Richardson (Ed.), *Cognition and the menstrual cycle* (pp. 39–66). New York: Springer. doi:10.1007/978-1-4613-9148-7_2.

Spector, P. E. (1987). Method variance as an artifact in self-reported affect and perceptions at work: Myth or significant problem? *Journal of Applied Psychology, 72*(3), 438–443. doi:10.1037//0021-9010.72.3.438.

Spector, P. E. (2006). Method variance in organizational research truth or urban legend? *Organizational Research Methods, 9*(2), 221–232. doi:10.1177/1094428105284955.

Steiner, M., Haskett, R. F., & Carroll, B. J. (1980). Premenstrual tension syndrome: The development of research diagnostic criteria and new rating scales. *Acta Psychiatrica Scandinavica, 62*(2), 177–190. doi:10.1111/j.1600-0447.1980.tb00605.x.

Stewart, D. E. (1995). Premenstrual dysphoric disorder and women's issues. In J. Bitzer & M. Stauber (Eds.), *Psychosomatic obstetrics and gynaecology*, 11th international congress of psychosomatic obstetrics and gynecology 21–24 May, 1995 (pp. 329–334). Basel, Switzerland: Monduzzi Editore S.p.A.

Timmonen, S., & Procopé, B.-J. (1971). Premenstrual syndrome and physical exercise. *Acta Obstetricia et Gynecologica Scandinavica, 50*(4), 331–337. doi:10.3109/00016347109157334.

Ussher, J. M. (2003). The ongoing silencing of women in families: An analysis and rethinking of premenstrual syndrome and therapy. *Journal of Family Therapy, 25*(4), 388–405. doi:10.1111/1467-6427.00257.

Ussher, J. M., & Wilding, J. M. (1992). Interactions between stress and performance during the menstrual cycle in relation to the premenstrual syndrome. *Journal of Reproductive and Infant Psychology, 10*(2), 83–101. doi:10.1080/02646839208403941.

Walker, A. (1994). Mood and well-being in consecutive menstrual cycles. *Psychology of Women Quarterly, 18*(2), 271–290. doi:10.1111/j.1471-6402.1994.tb00455.x.

Walker, A. (1996). Menstruation and the premenstrual syndrome. In C. Niven & A. Walker (Eds.), *Reproductive potential and fertility control* (pp. 39–58). Oxford, UK: Butterworth-Heinemann.

Walker, A. (1997). *The menstrual cycle*. London: Routledge.

West, S. G., & Hepworth, J. T. (1991). Statistical issues in the study of temporal data: Daily experiences. *Journal of Personality, 59*(3), 609–662. doi:10.1111/j.1467-6494.1991.tb00261.x.

Williams, L. J., Cote, J. A., & Buckley, M. R. (1989). Lack of method variance in self-reported affect and perceptions at work: Reality or artifact? *Journal of Applied Psychology, 74*(3), 462–468. doi:10.1037/0021-9010.74.3.462.

Zapf, D., Dormann, C., & Frese, M. (1996). Longitudinal studies in organizational stress research: A review of the literature with reference to methodological issues. *Journal of Occupational Health Psychology, 1*(2), 145–169. doi:10.1037/1076-8998.1.2.145.

Zohar, D. (1999). When things go wrong: The effect of daily work hassles on effort, exertion and negative mood. *Journal of Occupational and Organizational Psychology, 72*(3), 265–283. doi:10.1348/096317999166671.

Chapter 13
The Relevance of Menopause to the Occupational Safety and Health of Employed Women

Prudence M. Millear and Roxane L. Gervais

Introduction

The opportunities for women in the workplace have grown in recent decades, with the ongoing focus on potential benefits to countries through economic growth; although the economic uncertainty that followed the Global Financial Crisis has made employment less secure for all employees (United Nations Department of Economic and Social Affairs, 2010). Within the workplace, gender-specific health issues, such as menopause, are less frequently or adequately addressed, when compared to for example, pregnancy (Griffiths, MacLennan, & Hassard, 2013). The onset of the menopause typically occurs between the ages of 50 and 51 at the cessation of menstruation and this can be an easy transition from pre to post-menopausal, or last from four to eight years (Hunter & Rendall, 2007). Climacteric symptoms for the peri-menopausal woman include physiological and emotional experiences, such as hot flushes, depression, loss of libido, vaginal dryness, anxiety, poor memory, irritability, mood swings, loss of concentration, insomnia, aching limbs, dry skin, and loss of energy (Hunter & Rendall, 2007). In past generations, where fewer women were in the workforce during this life stage, work conditions or consequences may have been less influential for women and not widely considered by employers. However, the increasing numbers of women in the workforce and likely

This chapter is based on data collected independently by the authors and represents solely their opinions and/or conclusions.

P.M. Millear (✉)
School of Social Sciences, University of the Sunshine Coast,
Locked Bag 4, Maroochydore DC, QLD 4558, Australia
e-mail: pmillear@usc.edu.au

R.L. Gervais
Independent Practitioner, Goole DN14 6XN, UK
e-mail: roxane_gervais@alumni.fdu.edu

R.L. Gervais, P.M. Millear (eds.), *Exploring Resources, Life-Balance and Well-Being of Women Who Work in a Global Context*,
DOI 10.1007/978-3-319-31736-6_13

to be experiencing the menopausal transition during this time, mean that employers and the women's colleagues should take menopause into account in the design and environment of the workplace. Webster (2016) highlights the experience of women in the workplace when they have menopausal symptoms and the challenges of these symptoms on their ability to perform their work.

The Job Demands-Resources (JD-R) model (see e.g., Bakker & Demerouti, 2007) is often used to understand the way in which workplace conditions affect individuals. Greater demands in the workplace, such as physical, social, psychological and organisational aspects of a job that require effort to be sustained, can lead to depletion of energy and eventually, burnout. In contrast, greater job resources, such as the physical, social, psychological and organisational characteristics that can be used to achieve work goals, minimise job demands and related physiological and psychological costs, or promote increases in skill development, growth and learning (Bakker & Demerouti, 2007), increasing reources over time (Schaufeli, Bakker, & Van Rhenen, 2009). For women, having more resources allows them to remain engaged in their work and provides a buffer for poor mental health as well. For example, amongst German nurses, life satisfaction was predicted by more resources, such as support from their supervisors, and the absence of workplace demands, such as poor environmental conditions (Demerouti, Bakker, Nachreiner, & Schaufeli, 2000). For Dutch women working in healthcare, their job satisfaction was increased by greater decision-making, skill discretion, and a positive work climate (Akerboom & Maes, 2006). Intrinsic motivation for work is greater where nurses were able to take greater control of their work, had more support from their colleagues, and had a reasonable workload, whilst fatigue was reduced by greater control in the face of increased workload (Van Yperen & Hagedoorn, 2003). Recent research has included personal resources in the JD-R, showing that these additional resources can assist the individual to overcome challenging situations and thrive in the workplace. For example, amongst Dutch employees of an engineering and electronics firm, both personal and job resources increased work engagement, whilst personal resources buffered the effects of job demands on the exhaustion reported by employees (Xanthopoulou, Bakker, Demerouti, & Schaufeli, 2007). Similarly, for Dutch veterinary professionals (mostly women), personal resources acted directly on work engagement and increased work role performance and buffered them from emotional exhaustion (Mastenbroek, Jaarsman, Scherpbier, van Beukelen, & Demerouti, 2014).

This research on the JD-R adds to the understanding that resources exist beyond the workplace and are generally considered to be things which are valued in their own right, such as optimism, good relationships, social support, or income, or are valued as a method for gaining resources, such as a good job. In addition, individuals will seek to increase their resources where possible, as a buffer for stressors that may occur. Individuals with more resources are less vulnerable to these stressors, although losses can be more salient where resources become exhausted (Hobfoll, 1989, 2001). It could be expected that women with fewer resources, within themselves or in their work, or where they have prolonged or severe menopausal experiences would be more likely to have poorer outcomes, such as poor mental health (e.g., greater depression or anxiety) and less engagement and enjoyment in their work and in life.

Personal resources, such as optimism can assist with transitions across the lifespan and with dealing with other life situations, such as illness. More optimistic university students report less depression and stress and greater social networks at the end of their first semester in college (Brissette, Scheier, & Carver, 2002), whilst optimism is linked to faster recovery from surgery and breast cancer (Scheier, Carver, & Bridges, 1994). Dispositional personality traits such as optimism also play a role in the management of the menopausal experience and healthy adaptations (Caltabioano & Holzheimer, 1999; Elavsky & McAuley, 2009). In a longitudinal study of sedentary women, baseline vasomotor symptoms, along with the women's level of optimism and fitness predicted vasomotor symptoms 12 months later (Elavsky & McAuley, 2009). Women who are optimistic perceive their experience of climacteric symptoms as less severe, as they can focus their attention away from internal and external sensory information, resulting in a more manageable experience of the menopause. Optimists tend to become problem-focussed in their coping processes of difficult symptoms, and believed that post-menopausal life will be filled with personal growth (Caltabioano & Holzheimer, 1999). Problem-solving strategies that are applied to life in general (Armor & Taylor, 1998; Aspinwall, Richter, & Hoffman, 2002) and for dealing with difficult problems (Aspinwall & Richter, 1999) can provide the basis for managing the challenges associated with menopause.

Another personal resource that assists with managing stressors is self-efficacy, as this could increase individuals' confidence in their abilities to deal with their life, to change their behaviours, or to handle unusual or difficult situations (Scholz, Gutierrez, Sud, & Schwarzer, 2002). These situations can include coping with acquired immunodeficiency syndrome (AIDS; Chesney, Chambers, Taylor, Johnson, & Folkman, 2003) or maintaining job satisfaction whilst working long hours and with a high workload (Judge, Locke, Durham, & Kluger, 1998). In addition, self-efficacy is important for successful transitions out of the military (Gowan, Craft, & Zimmerman, 2000) and among teachers (Tang, Au, Schwarzer, & Schmidt, 2001), and for the absence of depression among married professional women, when combined with optimism (Marshall & Lang, 1990). Women who score higher on measures of self-esteem were more likely to experience fewer climacteric symptoms (Bloch, 2002). Self-efficacy, as a sense of personal mastery, also gives individuals the belief that they have more control of their lives (Lachman & Firth, 2004). Along with dispositional optimism, self-efficacy is proposed to give women during menopause a greater ability to manage the challenges of this stage of their lives.

Good health is important for individuals at any time of their lives, and particularly for women during menopause (Stojanovska, Apostolopoulos, Polman, & Borkoles, 2014). Women who reported worse health than their contemporaries, were more likely to have more severe menopausal symptoms (Dennerstein, 1996), but those who engaged in vigorous exercise substantially reduced all forms of symptoms compared to being sedentary, as found in a community sample (Canario et al., 2012), and in a randomised controlled physical activity trial (McAndrew, Napolitano, Albrecht, & Farrell, 2009). Menopause is often associated with many physical and psychological complaints, such as vasomotor symptoms of hot flushes, urinary disorders, and low mood and distress (Stojanovska et al., 2014) and these climacteric symptoms can often influence the capacity a woman has to function at work (Griffiths, Cox, Griffiths, & Wong, 2006; Griffiths et al., 2013). Women report that typical climacteric symptoms associated with the menopause such as having poor concentration (50.9 %), tiredness (50.7 %), poor memory (50.5 %), feeling low/depressed (41.9 %), lowered confidence (38.9 %), and insomnia (37.3 %) decreased their work performance (Griffiths et al., 2013). Uncertainty about work performance could result in stress for both the peri-menopausal woman and colleagues (Griffiths et al., 2013).

The dilemma for women in the workplace however, can be whether disclosing that they are experiencing difficult menopausal symptoms will change how they are perceived by their supervisors and colleagues (Griffiths et al., 2013; see also Webster, 2016). Revealing climacteric symptoms to a manager or colleague represents the women seeking social support from those individuals. When support is provided, the outcome is beneficial for the woman, such that positive initiatives are undertaken to alleviate stress from the individual and there is a reduced likelihood that women will experience burnout in the workplace (Smeur, 2011). In contrast, disclosing can be a source of stress if social support is not provided after private discussions to a manager or colleague. Griffiths et al. (2006) explored women's disclosure patterns in the United Kingdom (UK) and found speaking about menopausal distress was most difficult when it was to a male manager (53 %), or to a younger manager (40.8 %) and caused feelings of embarrassment (45.2 %). About half of the women told their colleagues about their symptoms, compared to only one-third would did this with a line manager. These women were not confident in their managers and colleagues to offer social support to them about a private issue; a situation which could increase a woman's job demands (Griffiths et al., 2006). Interestingly, younger women and men may attribute the signs of a hot flush to some cause other than menopause (Smith, Mann, Mirza, & Hunter, 2011), which might allow menopausal women who are more accepting of their symptoms to better manage any perceived distress associated with these.

In addition to disclosure, there is limited research on the effect the physical conditions of the workplace has on a woman's experience of the menopause, in particular with the most common symptom of hot flushes. Most women in two UK studies identified poor ventilation in hot offices as well as those that were unventilated, as conditions that made coping with hot flushes more difficult (Griffiths et al., 2013), and could worsen the effects of hot flushes (Griffiths et al., 2006). In contrast, Hunter, Gupta, Papitsch-Clark, and Sturdee (2009) found that women in India did not report the same association between problems around employment and experience of hot flushes, when compared to women in the UK. Cross-cultural differences and changes in climate may influence these findings, as women living in the UK may be more likely to notice differences in temperature given the cooler climate than those living in India, whose warm country could make them less aware of hot flushes (Hunter et al., 2009). Other work situations such as formal meetings (62.8 %), high visibility work, such as presentations (45.2 %), and learning new procedures (42.8 %) might prove more challenging for some women when experiencing hot flushes (Griffiths et al., 2013). While employment provides benefits through financial security and access to healthcare and social support, compared to women who are not employed (Williams, Levine, Kalilani, Lewis, & Clark, 2009), some of these benefits might be less evident if menopausal symptoms are more severe. For example, experiencing significantly unpleasant symptoms can leave women feeling less confident about themselves and their work performance, ultimately affecting the professional appearance that they want to portray, and leading to feelings of being ineffective and perhaps contributing to mental health issues.

Mental health conditions sometimes manifest themselves during menopause, although these are likely to be exacerbated by menopause rather than solely due to it (Avis, Crawford, Stellato, & Longcope, 2001; Dennerstein, 1996). The most prominent indicator of post-menopausal depression is previous depression (Amore et al., 2004), as post-menopausal women who report symptoms of depression or anxiety to their doctors also have an extensive medical history of experiencing these symptoms (Deeks, 2003). Longitudinal studies show that women with depression in their early 40s were more likely to have depression during the menopause transition (Strauss, 2011). Regardless of previous levels of depression, for women suffering more persistent and severe menopausal symptoms, depression is proposed to follow from vasomotor symptoms that lead to chronic poor sleep quality, increased irritability and changes in mood (Avis et al., 2001). Further, climacteric symptoms can be very similar to those of an anxious individual, such as rapid breathing, racing heart, sweaty palms, and hot flushes. Studies that link menopause to the development of anxiety should be considered with caution (Deeks, 2003; Sagsoz, Oguuzturk, Bayram, & Kamaci, 2001) and in the current study, the cross-sectional design does not allow for testing causal relationships for existing mental health conditions to be established.

The aim of the current study was to understand women's experiences of menopause in the workplace and the factors that would assist women to manage this stage of their lives. In the current study, the women's resources were measured as Personal Resources (as general health, dispositional optimism, and self-efficacy) and Workplace Conditions (as work climate, job autonomy and skill discretion, work social support and support specific to menopausal symptoms, and an ability to change work conditions if necessary). The women's Poor Experience of Menopause was measured as menopausal symptoms and work performance difficulties associated with menopause. The outcomes for the current study were the women's Well-Being (as job satisfaction and life satisfaction), Mental Health (as depression, anxiety, and stress), and their Performance at Work (as effectiveness in work tasks, interpersonal relationships, and managing their own emotions). The expected relationships between the variables are shown in Fig. 13.1. First, it is hypothesised that more personal and workplace resource would reduce the women's poor experience of menopause. Second, it is hypothesised that the experience of menopause would mediate the effects of the personal and workplace resources on mental health, well-being, and work performance. As such, more severe experience of menopause will be associated with poor mental health, lower levels of well-being and reduced performance at work.

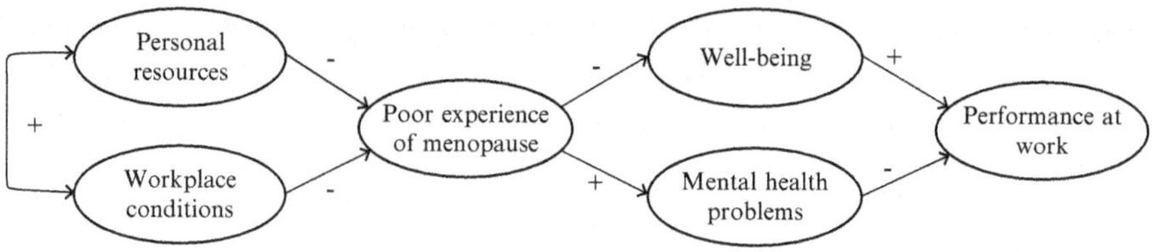

Fig. 13.1 Model of proposed relationships between the women's personal resources, workplace conditions, experience of menopause and the outcomes of well-being, mental health and performance

Methods

Participants

Women were recruited using a snowball sample technique beginning with the family, friends, and work colleagues of the authors to complete an online survey. The present study focuses on those who were employed at least one day per week and aged at least 35 years. Participants (N=424) mostly lived in the UK (n=217) and Australia (n=192), with small numbers in Europe (n=10) and the Americas (n=5).

Measures

Demographics Participants reported their age (in years), marital status (married or de facto relationship, separated or divorced, widowed, or single), and number of children and grandchildren. Women indicated if they were pre-menopausal (regular menstrual periods in last 12 months), peri-menopausal (irregular menstrual periods in the last 2 years), or post-menopausal (no periods in the last 2 years or confirmed by a blood test; Amore et al., 2004). They indicated their general health by responding to the question 'Compared to other women your age, how would you rate your usual state of health?' The range against which they were asked to select were 1 (poor), 2 (fair), 3 (good), 4 (very good), or 5 (excellent; Idler & Benyamini, 1997). Participants were asked how many hours they worked each week (including overtime), whether they worked full-time or part-time, and whether their positions were permanent, causal, temporary, contract, or in their own businesses.

Menopausal Symptoms The women indicated the degree to which they had experienced any symptoms of menopause, using the 11-item Menopause Rating Scale (MRS; Heinemann et al., 2004), including symptoms of, 'hot flushes, sweating (episodes of sweating)' and 'anxiety (inner restlessness, feeling panicky)'. Items were rated on a five-point Likert scale ranging from 1 (none), 2 (mild), 3 (moderate), 4 (severe), or 5 (very severe), with Cronbach's alpha=.89.

Optimism Dispositional optimism was measured with the 6-item Life Orientation Test-Revised (LOT-R; Scheier et al., 1994), including the item 'In uncertain times, I usually expect the best'. Items were rated on a five-point Likert scale ranging from 1 (strongly disagree) to 5 (strongly agree), with Cronbach's alpha = .88.

Self-Efficacy The 10-item General Self-Efficacy scale (Schwarzer & Jerusalem, 1995) provided a measure of self-efficacy, including the item 'I can usually handle whatever comes my way'. Items were rated on a five-point Likert scale ranged from 1 (not like me) to 5 (exactly like me), with Cronbach's alpha = .92.

Work Climate The perceived support for job autonomy provided by managers was measured with the 15-item Work Climate Questionnaire (WCQ; Baard, Deci, & Ryan, 2004), including the item, 'My manager answers my questions fully and carefully'. Items were rated on a seven-point Likert scale from 1 (strongly disagree) to 7 (strongly agree), with Cronbach's alpha = .97.

Job Autonomy Flexibility in decision making was measured by the 4-item Job Autonomy scale (Voydanoff, 2004), including 'How often do you have choice in deciding how you do your tasks at work'. Items were rated on a five-point Likert scale ranged from 1 (not at all), to 5 (all the time), with Cronbach's alpha = .86.

Skill Discretion The ability to use skill and creativity at work was measured with the 6-item Skill Discretion scale (Schwartz, Pieper, & Karasek, 1988), comprising e.g., 'In my job, I keep learning new things'. Items were rated on a five-point Likert scale, 1 (not at all) to 5 (all the time), with Cronbach's alpha = .83.

Social Support The level of social support offered by managers and colleagues was measured with the 4-item Job Social Support scale (Van Yperen & Hagedoorn, 2003), including 'If necessary, I can ask my immediate supervisor (co-workers) for help'. Items were rated on a five-point Likert scale, ranging from 1 (not at all) to 5 (all the time). Two of items applied to the supervisors and two to their colleagues, and these were summed for a total score of support, with Cronbach's alpha = .84.

Menopausal Symptoms and Work The extent to which the women felt they could change their working conditions, seek assistance from colleagues, and the effect on their work was measured by 12 items devised by the authors. Exploratory factor analysis (EFA) found three clear factors that explained 70.9% of the variance ($\chi^2(66) = 2813.0$, $p < .001$, KMO = .81). The factors were: Consideration of others (4 items e.g., 'My colleagues are considerate if I have a hot flush', Cronbach's alpha = .94); Ability to Change (3 items e.g., 'I can change my work schedule if I am feeling unwell or off colour', Cronbach's alpha = .71); and Reductions on performance (5 items e.g., 'If I can't change my work environment, it reduces how I perform my work', Cronbach's alpha = .82). All of the items were along a five-point Likert rating system from 1 (strongly disagree) to 5 (strongly agree).

Job Satisfaction Satisfaction with intrinsic and extrinsic job characteristics was measured with the 15-item Job Satisfaction scale (Warr, Cook, & Wall, 1979) e.g., 'The amount of responsibility you are given'. Items were rated on a seven-point Likert scale from 1 (extremely dissatisfied) to 7 (extremely satisfied), with Cronbach's alpha = .92.

Life Satisfaction Life satisfaction was measured with the 5-item Satisfaction with Life Scale (SWLS; Diener, Emmons, Larsen, & Griffin, 1985) e.g., 'In most ways, my life is close to ideal'. Items were rated on a five-point Likert scale from 1 (strongly disagree) to 5 (strongly agree), with Cronbach's alpha = .89.

Mental Health Depression, anxiety and stress were measured using the short version of the Depression Anxiety and Stress Scale (DASS-21; Lovibond & Lovibond, 1995). Each of the seven-item subscales used a six-point Likert scale rating to assess how much this respective symptom could have applied to them in the past month, from 0 (not at all), 2 (to some degree), 4 (a good part of the time), or 6 (most of the time), with Cronbach's alpha = .91 (depression), .78 (anxiety), and .87 (stress).

Performance at Work Participants rated how effective they felt at work in the past week using three items (Gervais, 2002) to assess 'Getting things done', 'Getting on well with others' and 'Taking care of yourself'. These items were rated, depending on the item from 1 (not very effective/not at all) to 9 (very effective/very much so).

Data Analysis

The fit and parsimony of the proposed model, as shown in Fig. 13.1, was assessed with the Normed Chi-Squared (χ^2/df), the Comparative Fit Index (CFI), and the Root Mean Square Error or Approximation (RMSEA). Good fit is achieved where a model has Normed Chi-Squared between 1 and 3 and where the CFI $\geq .95$. For the point estimate of the RMSEA: 0 indicates perfect fit; $\leq .05$ indicates close or good fit; between .05 and .08 indicates reasonable fit; between .08 and .10 indicates mediocre fit; and estimates over .10 indicate poor and unsatisfactory fit (Browne & Cudeck, 1993; Byrne, 2001; Holmes-Smith, Cunningham, & Coote, 2006). The 90 % confidence intervals for RMSEA are given also, where a lower bound estimate of $< .05$ supports close fit of the model (Browne & Cudeck, 1993) and reasonable fit is supported if the upper bound estimate is $\leq .08$, but poor fit is indicated if this is $> .10$ (MacCallum, Browne, & Sugawara, 1996). Further, a narrow range in the confidence intervals indicates less error in the calculation of the RMSEA (Byrne, 2001). The effect size of the paths in the models is taken as strong ($\beta > .50$), moderately strong ($\beta = .30$ to .50), mild ($\beta = .20$ to .30) and weak ($\beta < .20$) (Holmes-Smith et al., 2006), whilst the squared multiple correlations, as the proportion of variance explained in the latent factors, was considered small ($R^2 = .02$), medium ($R^2 = .15$) or large ($R^2 = .35$) (Cohen, 1992).

Results

Demographics and Country of Origin

The participants ($N=424$) ranged in age from 35 years to 69 years ($M=51.2$ years, $SD=5.6$ years) and were mostly married (71 %), rather than separated or divorced (14 %), widowed (1 %) or single (11 %). Of the women who were mothers ($n=332$), most had one ($n=57$), two ($n=151$), or three ($n=83$) children; whilst most women did not have grandchildren ($n=314$). The women worked between 8 and 80 h per week ($M=36.6$ h, SD = 10.4 h) in small ($n=33$), medium ($n=45$), large ($n=69$), and very large ($n=277$) organisations. Most women were in permanent positions (full-time, $n=249$; part-time, $n=80$), rather than contract positions (full-time, $n=33$; part-time, $n=12$) or part-time causal positions ($n=17$).

The participants were initially compared by country of origin, particularly between Australia and the UK. There were no differences in their ages, hours per week, skill discretion, job social support, the three scales of menopause symptoms affecting work, or how effective they felt at work. Australian women reported greater optimism, self-efficacy, better work climates and job autonomy, and greater life and job satisfaction, whilst women in the UK reported poorer mental health and more severe menopausal symptoms. These differences may be explained by some theories that propose that Australians are more relaxed in their approach to work, and 'work to live', rather than 'live to work' (Winefield et al., 2000).

Menopausal Symptoms

Participants were divided as pre-menopausal ($n=93$, $M=45.67$ years, $SD=3.76$ years), peri-menopausal ($n=142$, $M=50.12$ years, $SD=3.49$ years) or post-menopausal ($n=164$, $M=54.99$ years, $SD=4.82$ years) and gave ratings of symptoms ranged from none or limited impact through to very severe. As expected, occurrence of menopausal symptoms significantly increased as women moved from pre-menopausal to peri- and post-menopausal ($ps<.001$) and remained similar for pre- and post-menopausal women. There were few differences between the women in the menopausal status groups, including the number of hours they worked each week ($F(2,421)=0.359$, $p=.698$, $\eta^2=.002$). The only difference was found for levels of anxiety ($F(2,421)=3.544$, $p=.030$, $\eta^2=.017$). With Bonferroni adjustments, peri-menopausal women reported slightly greater symptoms of anxiety than both the pre-menopausal women ($t(250)=2.21$, $p=.082$), and the post-menopausal women ($t(328)=2.31$, $p=.064$), although pre- and post-menopausal women did not differ from each other.

The means, standard deviations and correlations between variables are shown in Table 13.1. Of note is that hours of work each week had limited predictive associations, being only significantly associated with general self-efficacy, job autonomy and skill discretion, and slightly with levels of anxiety and feelings of effective at

Table 13.1 Means (M), standard deviations (SD) and correlations between the variables in the model

	M	*SD*	2	3	4	5	6	7	8	9	10
1 Age	51.21	5.65	.307***	.119*	.037	.007	−.059	.033	.005	.055	.035
2 Menopausal symptoms	25.40	8.50	(.89)	−.331***	−.359***	−.258***	−.042	−.228***	−.260***	−.081†	−.173***
3 General health	3.22	1.00		–	.351***	.282***	.110*	.162**	.162**	.122*	.161**
4 Dispositional optimism	21.01	4.36			(.88)	.506***	.086†	.218***	.297***	.233***	.238***
5 General self-efficacy	35.21	7.39				(.93)	.189***	.153**	.258***	.294***	.224***
6 Hours per week	36.32	10.43					–	−.034	.136**	.231***	−.040
7 Work climate	72.87	21.67						(.97)	.479***	.304***	.527***
8 Job Autonomy	13.46	3.99							(.87)	.456***	.310***
9 Skill Discretion	21.25	5.07								(.83)	.341***
10 Job Social Support	13.96	4.19									(.85)
11 Considerate others	11.11	4.68									
12 Reduced performance	9.61	4.11									
13 Change work	6.84	3.20									
14 Job Satisfaction	70.75	15.75									
15 Life Satisfaction	16.63	4.44									
16 Depression	8.04	8.77									
17 Anxiety	4.76	5.85									
18 Stress	10.48	8.05									
19 Performance: work tasks	6.93	1.65									
20 Performance: social relationships	7.34	1.50									
21 Performance: own needs	6.13	2.02									

	11	12	13	14	15	16	17	18	19	20	21
1 Age	.081	.112*	.089†	.023	.054	−.030	.017	−.017	.033	.018	.048
2 Menopausal symptoms	−.155***	.376***	−.112*	−.272***	−.321***	.536***	.539***	.539***	−.203***	−.184***	−.287***
3 General health	.151**	−137**	.094†	.230***	.347***	−.355***	−342***	−.326***	.181***	.114**	.290***
4 Dispositional optimism	.254***	−126*	.215***	.342***	.492***	−.555***	−410***	−.430***	.217***	.277***	.336***
5 General self-efficacy	.220***	−.029	.220***	.223***	.322***	−.309***	−.257***	−.299***	.292***	.328***	.224***
6 Hours per week	−.017	−.020	.086	.010	.009	−.038	−.084†	−.054	−.015	.062	−.090†
7 Work climate	.269***	−125*	.264***	.664***	.283***	−.281***	−.264***	−.238***	.171***	.156**	.330***
8 Job Autonomy	.287***	−.239***	.423***	.601***	.274***	−.339***	−.311***	−.287***	.156**	.132**	.239***
9 Skill Discretion	.312***	−.049	.368***	.472***	.262***	−.213***	−.138**	−.157**	.057†	.092†	.090
10 Job Social Support	.489***	−.068	.248***	.538***	.282***	−.238***	−.141**	−.175***	.169***	.247***	.313***
11 Considerate others	(.94)	−.005	.540***	.378***	.280***	−.171**	−.102*	−.137**	.151**	.252***	.236***
12 Reduced performance		(.82)	−.108*	−.283***	−.125*	.280***	.262***	.298***	−.137**	−.071	−.227***
13 Change work			(.71)	.335***	.170**	−.186***	−.097†	−.143**	.131**	.130**	.140**
14 Job Satisfaction				(.92)	.406***	−.407***	−.343***	−.334***	.229***	.171***	.371***
15 Life Satisfaction					(.89)	−.565***	−.350***	−.352***	.256***	.266***	.353***
16 Depression						(.92)	.706***	.729***	−.329***	−.280***	−.475***
17 Anxiety							(.79)	.714***	−.232***	−126***	−387***
18 Stress								(.87)	−.280***	−.197***	−.477***
19 Performance: work tasks									–	.528***	.490***
20 Performance: social relationships										–	.460***
21 Performance: own needs											–

Note. Cronbach's alphas given in brackets on the diagonal with single items shown with '–'
† $p<.10$, * $p<.05$, ** $p<.01$, *** $p<.001$

managing emotions at work. In particular, the numbers of hours worked each week did not have any association with the prevalence of menopausal symptoms, nor the level of support given to the women or their satisfaction with life and their jobs and their mental health. As could be expected, more severe menopausal symptoms are strongly positively correlated with higher levels of depression, anxiety, stress, and reduced performance at work, and strongly negatively correlated with greater dispositional optimism, self-efficacy, and life satisfaction, with other correlations being in the expected directions, although moderate in strength.

The relationships between personal and workplace resources, the experience of menopause, mental health, feeing effective and job and life satisfaction were explored with structural equation modelling (SEM). The latent factors of these relationships are shown in Fig. 13.1. Personal Resources were assessed by the indicators of dispositional optimism, general self-efficacy, and general health. Workplace Conditions were assessed by hours per week, work climate, skill discretion, job autonomy, job social support, consideration from others for menopausal symptoms, and the ability to change one's work conditions, if needed. The Poor Experience of Menopause was assessed by the symptoms of menopause and the reductions in performance associated with menopausal symptoms. Mental Health was assessed by depression, anxiety and stress, whilst Well-being was assessed by life satisfaction and job satisfaction. Finally, Performance at Work was assessed by effectiveness in getting tasks completed, interpersonal relationships, and managing own emotions.

The first model to be tested was the model as hypothesised (as shown in Fig. 13.1), but this model, Model 1, was not supported by the data (i.e., non-positive definite). An examination of the output showed that the latent factor of Well-Being was untenable and separating job satisfaction from life satisfaction did provide a workable solution (Model 2), however the data did not fit well in this model (χ^2/df = 5.26 [χ^2(165) = 867.89], CFI = .78, RMSEA = .10 (90 % CI = .094 – .107)). In evaluating the output, it was found that the total effects of the individual and the workplace on the outcomes were not mediated by the women's experience of menopause. Using the Modification Indices, direct paths were added firstly between Workplace Conditions factors to Life Satisfaction, Job Satisfaction, Mental Health, and Performance at Work factors (Model 3), significantly improving the fit of the model ($\Delta\chi^2$(3) = 239.21, $p < .001$), although the fit was quite poor still (χ^2/df = 3.817 [χ^2(161) = 614.59], CFI = .859, RMSEA = .082 (90 % CI = .075 – .089)). After this the direct paths were added from Personal Resources to Life Satisfaction, Job Satisfaction, Mental Health, and Performance at Work factors (Model 4), significantly improving the fit of the model ($\Delta\chi^2$(20) = 92.247, p < .001), but which could be considered as mediocre still (χ^2/df = 3.705 [χ^2(141) = 522.34], CFI = .879, RMSEA = .080 (90 % CI = .073 – .087)).

Next, the Modification Indices were used to improve the fit of the model, with the addition of a direct path from Life Satisfaction to Depression (which gave better fit than the alternative path from Life Satisfaction to the Mental Health factor, $\Delta\chi^2$ = 54.85), and addition of the correlations between Job Social Support and Consideration of Others, and Consideration of Others and Ability to Change working conditions. Finally, non-significant paths were removed from the model, i.e., working hours as a predictor of Workplace Conditions (β .055, $p = .295$), Personal Resources to Job Satisfaction (β = .019, $p = .697$), and Workplace Conditions to Mental Health (β = −.042, $p = .471$). These changes substantially improved the fit of the model ($\Delta\chi^2(1) = 159.78$, $p < .001$).

The final model (Model 5) is shown in Fig. 13.2 and had reasonable fit, $\chi^2/df = 2.59$, [$\chi^2(140) = 361.95$], CFI = .930, RMSEA = .061 (90 % CI = .054 − .069) and explained substantial variance in the outcomes; 41.0 % for the Experience of Menopause, 74.6 % for Mental Health, 41.1 % for Life Satisfaction, and 78.8 % for Job Satisfaction, each of which were considered as large effects for the models (Cohen, 1992). Of note is the limited range of the 90 % CI for the point estimates for the RMSEA, which indicated that there was less error in their calculation (Byrne, 2001). Strong direct effects (i.e., β > .50; Holmes-Smith et al., 2006) were shown from Personal Resources to Life Satisfaction and to the Experience of Menopause, for Workplace Conditions to Job Satisfaction and from the Experience of Menopause to Mental Health. Moderately strong direct effects (β = .30 to .50) were shown for Personal Resources to Performance at Work and mild direct effects (β = .20 to .30) were shown for Personal Resources to poor Mental Health, Life Satisfaction to Depression, and poor Mental Health to Performance at Work, with the balance of paths having weak direct effects (i.e., β < .20). Finally, the indirect effects were calculated. Personal Resources had strong indirect effects specifically on Depression (β = −.571) and Stress (β = −.502) and moderately strong effects on the Mental Health factor (β = −.378), and specifically on Anxiety (β = −.483) and on the severity of menopausal symptoms (β = −.387), whilst all other indirect effects were weak (i.e., β < .20).

Discussion

The current study explored the factors that influence working women's experiences of menopause and the effects on their well-being, mental health, and performance at work. Rather than the experience of menopause mediating between women's personal and work resources, the presence of resources acted directly on their mental health, life satisfaction, job satisfaction and how effectively they felt they performed at work. Women with a greater pool of individual and organisational resource were substantially buffered from a poor experience of menopause; which in turn protected them from poor mental health and reductions in performance at work, whilst positively impacting on satisfaction with their work and with life in general.

At the centre of the model is the very strong relationship between the poor experience of menopause and the woman's mental health. For the women in the current study, the severity of menopausal symptoms and feelings that their work was suffering as a result (implying a sense of helplessness about managing symptoms and work conditions) were strongly associated with poorer mental health, i.e., greater depression, anxiety and stress. Without considering the positive moderating effects of personal and workplace resources, menopause impacted on their mood and

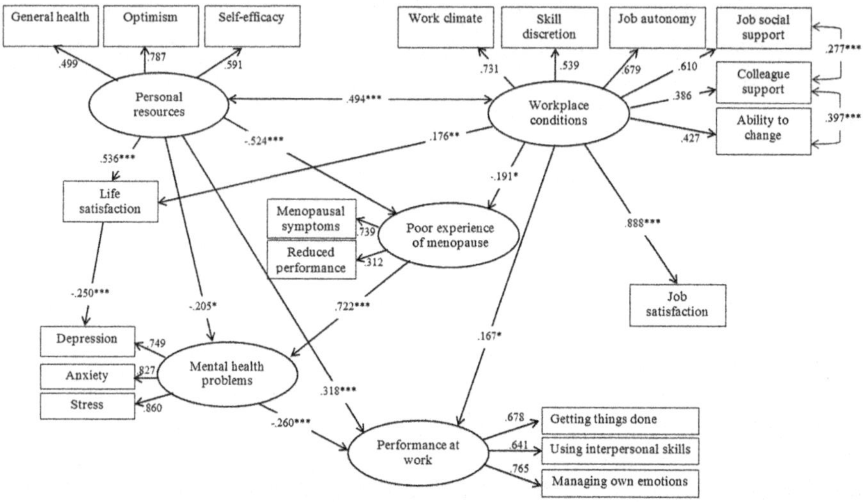

Fig. 13.2 Final model of relationships between the women, their work, experiences with menopause and their well-being, mental health and their performance at work (*Note.* χ 2(140) = 362.565, p < .001, CFI = .930, NFI = .891, TLI = .914, RMSEA = .061, (90% CI = .054 - .069). All factor loadings were significant at p < .001. Squared multiple correlations for the endogenous variables were Poor Experience of Menopause (.410), Mental Health Problems (.746), Life Satisfaction (.411), and Job Satisfaction (.788).† p < .10, * p < .05, **p < .01, *** p < .001)

how effective women feel in their performances at work. As the study is cross-sectional, it is not possible to state whether this is a causal relationship or whether poor mental health was evident prior to the onset of menopause (for example, Sagsoz et al., 2001; Strauss, 2011) but the current study does emphasise that more frequent symptoms are predictive of women experiencing concurrent poor mental health (Avis et al., 2001).

The results do show, however, how a woman's personal and work resources can provide a buffer for the problems that they are experiencing. Interestingly, the benefits provided by a supportive workplace did not rely on the length of the working week. This indicated that in this sample, regardless of the length of time at work, whether this entailed a few hours per week or long working hours; women were equally able to take 'comfort' from their workplace conditions. The removal of the demands of working hours from workplace conditions in the model left the resources that were available to the women. These included a positive work climate, choice and control in work tasks, trustworthy supervisors and colleagues, and specific workplace support for menopausal symptoms. As such, and in line with the JD-R model (Bakker & Demerouti, 2007), a workplace that provides women during menopause with a way to counter their symptoms, by allowing for choice, control, and support, has acted in a similar manner to those workplaces that increased the life satisfaction (Demerouti et al., 2000) and intrinsic motivation (Van Yperen & Hagedoorn, 2003) of nurses and the job satisfaction of women working in health care (Akerboom & Maes, 2006). In addition to the constructs usually measured as job resources, the current study included two measures of the responsiveness of the workplace to the specific needs of the menopausal woman; that of colleagues being considerate of changes in mood and of women being able to alter the immediate environment. These constructs added to the understanding of what constitutes a positive workplace, which can counter the impact of the menopausal experience, as being unable to ameliorate poor ventilation or that work conditions could worsen the impact of vasomotor symptoms (Griffiths et al., 2006, 2013). In addition to the influence on menopausal experience, the workplace resources directly and strongly predicted the job satisfaction of the women in the current study, and enhanced how effective they felt in the performance of their work. Therefore, an important conclusion for OSH is that a workplace that is supportive of women experiencing the menopause, is an extension of the workplace that is well designed and resourced for employees in general to stay engaged and satisfied in their work. The treatment of menopausal women may signal a generally supportive corporate culture, in a similar way to those family-friendly workplaces, which are appreciated by parents and non-parents alike (Grover & Crooker, 1995), leading to greater affective commitment of all employees alike.

The women also showed that their personal resources were important to their experience of menopause, and directly to their life satisfaction, good mental health, and performance at work. These findings confirm the extension of the JD-R to include personal resources to predict work engagement and reductions in exhaustion, as shown in Dutch veterinary employees (Mastenbroek et al., 2014) and engineering employees (Xanthopoulou et al., 2007). Therefore, it can be applied in this present context to predict life satisfaction and mental health. Further, dispositional optimism and self-efficacy have been shown to assist with other transitions in life such as: students starting at college (Brissette et al., 2002), those leaving the military (Gowan et al., 2000), for those coping with serious illness (Chesney et al., 2003), and for those recovering after surgery and breast cancer (Scheier et al., 1994). The results of the current study also confirm previous findings that menopausal women with greater levels of optimism and good health are able to cope better subjectively with menopause, and that they have fewer symptoms (Caltabioano & Holzheimer, 1999; Elavsky & McAuley, 2009). It is likely that women with more optimism and self-efficacy would have better adaptive coping, better self-regulation, and problem solving strategies that proactively manage and reframe the challenges they face, whilst being able to recognise situations that are not amenable to change, such as the severity or frequency of symptoms (Armor & Taylor, 1998; Aspinwall & Richter, 1999; Aspinwall et al., 2002; Scholz et al., 2002). Optimists reframe stressors and are able to moderate their own affect by changing how they view the past. In this way, they change the comparators for outcomes, such that they can reappraise outcomes as more positive and expected, rather than remaining negative or surprising (Sanna & Chang, 2003). Postmenopausal women were found to use direct action, catharsis, and seeking social support as problem-focused coping to manage their symptoms (Simpson & Thompson, 2009), highlighting useful strategies that could be incorporated in future interventions to assist menopausal women, building on the OSH considerations of the benefits of job resources in the workplace. As noted by Webster (2016), having personal and workplace resources available to deal with unexpected menopausal symptoms made this period easier to manage.

One final area that women can act upon is their general health, as this was a strong contributor to their personal resources, and as in previous research, acts as a buffer for increasing symptoms (Deeks, 2003; Dennerstein, 1996). Good health and exercise contribute to good self-esteem in middle-aged women (Elavsky, 2010) and along with optimism, predict reductions in menopausal women's vasomotor symptoms (Elavsky & McAuley, 2009). Exercise has been shown to improve menopausal symptoms across a number of studies with large samples of women (e.g., Canario et al., 2012; McAndrew et al., 2009; Stojanovska et al., 2014), and highlights some easily implemented strategies to improve women's health and menopausal symptomology and thereby builds upon public health and employer campaigns to encourage more physical activity.

In conclusion, increasing numbers of women are remaining in the workforce during their later years, which includes the menopausal transition. There have been limited studies that examine the OSH factors that apply to menopausal women and how employers can assist women to remain in the workforce, manage their symptoms, and maintain work performance. The current study included specific items of consideration from colleagues and modifying the environment that added to the commonly described job resources of social support, job autonomy and a positive work climate, indicating that a 'resourceful' workplace benefits all employees regardless of a specific employee's situation. Personal resources also buffered the women from the poor experience of menopause and the potential for poor mental health, adding to life satisfaction and feeling effective at work. In sum, feeling effective in one's performance at work was the sum of many factors in a woman's life, from her confidence in her abilities, her health and menopausal symptoms, to the conditions of her workplace and the ability to make decisions and be supported by those around her. Organisations can provide conditions which support and acknowledge a woman's symptoms and allow her to change her work situation, which would be seen as part of a 'good' workplace and something that organisations can implement easily. The study has some limitations, such as being a cross-sectional study using self-report measures. However, it is an international sample and provides specific areas that employers could target to assist women in the menopausal transition. Moreover, providing opportunities for physical exercise, developing positive workplace cultures that encourage social support, treating staff with respect, providing jobs that are more autonomous and involved the use of the employees' skills, are all areas that employers could develop to support their employees, not only for menopausal women, but for all staff.

References

Akerboom, S., & Maes, S. (2006). Beyond demand and control: The contributions of organizational risk factors in assessing the psychological well-being of health care employees. *Work and Stress, 20*(1), 21–36. doi:10.1080/02678370600690915.

Amore, M., Di Donato, P., Papalini, A., Berti, A., Palareti, A., Ferrari, G., et al. (2004). Psychological status at the menopausal transition: An Italian epidemiological study. *Maturitas, 48*(2), 115–124. doi:10.1016/j.maturitas.2003.08.010.

Armor, D. A., & Taylor, S. E. (1998). Situated optimism: Specific outcome expectancies and self-regulation. In M. P. Zanna (Ed.), *Advances in experimental social psychology* (Vol. 30, pp. 309–379). San Diego, CL: Academic.

Aspinwall, L. G., & Richter, L. (1999). Optimism and self-mastery predict more rapid disengagement form unsolvable tasks in the presence of alternatives. *Motivation and Emotion, 23*(3), 221–245. doi:10.1023/A:1021367331817.

Aspinwall, L. G., Richter, L., & Hoffman, R. R. (2002). Understanding how optimism works: An examination of optimists' adaptive moderation of belief and behavior. In E. C. Chang (Ed.), *Optimism and pessimism. Implications of theory research* (pp. 217–238). Washington, DC: American Psychological Association.

Avis, N. E., Crawford, S., Stellato, R., & Longcope, C. (2001). Longitudinal study of hormone levels and depression among women transitioning through menopause. *Climacteric, 4*(3), 243–249. doi:10.1080/713605090.

Baard, P. P., Deci, E. L., & Ryan, R. M. (2004). Intrinsic need satisfaction: A motivational basis of performance and well-being in two work settings. *Journal of Applied Social Psychology, 34*(10), 2045–2068. doi:10.1111/j.1559-1816.2004.tb02690.x.

Bakker, A. B., & Demerouti, E. (2007). The job demands-resources model: State of the art. *Journal of Managerial Psychology, 22*(3), 309–328. doi:10.1108/02683940710733115.

Bloch, A. (2002). Self-awareness during the menopause. *Maturitas, 41*(1), 61–68. doi:10.1016/S0378-5122(01)00252-3.

Brissette, I., Scheier, M. F., & Carver, C. S. (2002). The role of optimism in social network development, coping, and psychological adjustment during a life transition. *Journal of Personality and Social Psychology, 82*(1), 102–111. doi:10.1037//0022-3514.82.1.102.

Browne, M. W., & Cudeck, R. (1993). Alternative ways of assessing model fit. In K. A. Bollen & J. S. Long (Eds.), *Testing structural equation models* (pp. 136–162). Newbury Park, CA: Sage.

Byrne, B. M. (2001). *Structural equation modeling with AMOS: Basic concept, applications and programming*. Mahwah, NJ: Lawrence Erlbaum.

Caltabioano, M. L., & Holzheimer, M. (1999). Dispositional factors, coping and adaptation during menopause. *Climacteric, 2*(1), 21–28. doi:10.3109/13697139909025559.

Canario, A. C. G., Cabral, P. U., Spyrides, M. H., Giraldo, P. C., Eleuterio, J., & Goncalves, A. K. (2012). The impact of physical activity on menopausal symptoms in middle-aged women. *International Journal of Gynecology & Obstetrics, 118*(1), 34–36. doi:10.1016/j.ijgo.2012.02.016.

Chesney, M. A., Chambers, D. B., Taylor, J. M., Johnson, L. M., & Folkman, S. (2003). Coping effectiveness training for men living with HIV: Results from a randomized clinical trial testing a group-based intervention. *Psychosomatic Medicine, 65*(6), 1038–1046. doi:10.1097/01.PSY.0000097344.78697.ED.

Cohen, J. (1992). A power primer. *Psychological Bulletin, 112*(1), 155–159. doi:10.1037/0033-2909.112.1.155.

Deeks, A. A. (2003). Psychological aspects of menopause management. *Best Practice & Clinical Endocrinology & Metabolism, 17*(1), 17–31. doi:10.1016/S1521-690X(02)00077-5.

Demerouti, E., Bakker, A. B., Nachreiner, F., & Schaufeli, W. B. (2000). A model of burnout and life satisfaction amongst nurses. *Journal of Advanced Nursing, 32*(2), 454–464. doi:10.1046/j.1365-2648.2000.01496.x.

Dennerstein, L. (1996). Well-being, symptoms and the menopausal transition. *Maturitas, 23*(2), 147–157. doi:10.1016/0378-5122(95)00970-1.

Diener, E., Emmons, R. A., Larsen, R. J., & Griffin, S. (1985). The satisfaction with life scale. *Journal of Personality Assessment, 49*(1), 71–75. doi:10.1207/s15327752jpa4901_13.

Elavsky, S. (2010). Longitudinal examination of the exercise and self-esteem model in middle-aged women. *Journal of Sport & Exercise Psychology, 32*(6), 862–880.

Elavsky, S., & McAuley, E. (2009). Personality, menopausal symptoms, and physical activity outcomes in middle-aged women. *Personality and Individual Differences, 46*(2), 123–128. doi:10.1016/j.paid.2008.09.014.

Gervais, R. (2002). *Patterns of work strain and well-being in nurses.* Dissertation: Thesis (Ph.D.), University of Hull, Hull, OCLC Number: 498567003.

Gowan, M. A., Craft, S. L. S., & Zimmerman, R. A. (2000). Response to work transitions by United States Army personnel: Effects on self-esteem, self-efficacy, and career resilience. *Psychological Reports, 86*(3), 911–921. doi:10.2466/pr0.2000.86.3.911.

Griffiths, A., MacLennan, S. J., & Hassard, J. (2013). Menopause and work: An electronic survey of employees' attitudes in the UK. *Maturitas, 76*(2), 155–159. doi: http://dx.doi.org/10.1016/j.maturitas.2013.07.005.

Griffiths, A., Cox, S., Griffiths, R., & Wong, Y. (2006). *Ageing, work and health.* British Association of Women in Policing. Nottingham: Institute of Work, Health & Organisations, University of Nottingham. http://www.bawp.org/Resources/Documents/Ageing%20Police%20Officers.pdf

Grover, S. L., & Crooker, K. J. (1995). Who appreciates family-responsive human resource policies: The impact of family-friendly policies on the organizational attachment of parents and non-parents. *Personnel Psychology, 48*(2), 271–288. doi:10.1111/j.1744-6570.1995.tb01757.x.

Heinemann, K., Ruebig, A., Potthoff, P., Schneider, H. P. G., Strelow, F., Heinemann, L. A. J., et al. (2004). The Menopause Rating Scale (MRS) scale: A methodological review. *Health and Quality of Life Outcomes, 2*, 45. doi:10.1186/1477-7525-2-45.

Hobfoll, S. E. (1989). Conservation of resources: A new attempt at conceptualizing stress. *American Psychologist, 44*(3), 513–524. doi:10.1037/0003-066X.44.3.513.

Hobfoll, S. E. (2001). The influence of culture, community, and the nested-self in the stress process: Advancing Conservation of Resources theory. *Applied Psychology: An International Review, 50*(3), 337–369. doi:10.1111/1464-0597.00062.

Holmes-Smith, P., Cunningham, E., & Coote, L. (2006). *Structural equation modelling: From the fundamentals to advanced topics.* Melbourne, VIC: School Research, Evaluation, and Measurement Services.

Hunter, M., & Rendall, M. (2007). Bio-psycho-socio-cultural perspectives on menopause. *Best Practice and Research Clinical Obstetrics and Gynaecology, 21*(2), 261–274. doi:10.1016/j.bpobgyn.2006.11.001.

Hunter, M. S., Gupta, P., Papitsch-Clark, A., & Sturdee, D. W. (2009). Mid-aged health in women from the Indian subcontinent (MAHWIS): A further quantitative and qualitative investigation of experience of menopause in UK Asian women, compared to UK Caucasian women and women living in Delhi. *Climacteric, 12*(1), 26–37. doi:10.1080/13697130802556304.

Idler, E. L., & Benyamini, Y. (1997). Self-rated health and mortality: A review of twenty-seven community studies. *Journal of Health and Social Behavior, 38*(1), 21–37. doi:10.2307/2955359.

Judge, T. A., Locke, E., Durham, C. C., & Kluger, A. N. (1998). Dispositional effect on job and life satisfaction: The role of core evaluations. *Journal of Applied Psychology, 83*(1), 17–34. doi:10.1037/0021-9010.83.1.17.

Lachman, M. E., & Firth, K. M. P. (2004). The adaptive value of feeling control during mid-life. In O. G. Brim, C. D. Ryff, & L. L. Bumpass (Eds.), *How healthy are we? A national study of well-being in mid-life* (pp. 320–349). Chicago: The University of Chicago Press.

Lovibond, P. F., & Lovibond, S. H. (1995). The structure of negative emotional states: Comparison of the depression anxiety stress scales (DASS) with the Beck depression and anxiety inventories. *Behaviour Research Therapy, 33*(3), 335–343. doi:10.1016/0005-7967(94)00075-U.

MacCallum, R. C., Browne, M. W., & Sugawara, H. M. (1996). Power analysis and determination of sample size for covariance structure modeling. *Psychological Methods, 1*(2), 130–149. doi:10.1037/1082-989X.1.2.130.

Marshall, M. A., & Lang, E. L. (1990). Optimism, self-mastery, and the symptoms of depression in women professionals. *Journal of Personality and Social Psychology, 59*(1), 132–139. doi:10.1037/0022-3514/90/$00.75.

Mastenbroek, N. J. J. M., Jaarsman, A. D. C., Scherpbier, A. J. J. A., van Beukelen, P., & Demerouti, E. (2014). The role of personal resources in explaining well-being and performance: A study among young veterinary professionals. *European Journal of Work and Organizational Psychology, 23*(2), 190–202. doi:10.1080/1359432X.2012.728040.

McAndrew, L. M., Napolitano, M. A., Albrecht, A., & Farrell, N. C. (2009). When, why, and for whom there is a relationship between physical activity and menopause symptoms. *Maturitas, 64*(2), 119–125. doi:10.1016/j.maturitas.2009.08.009.

Sagsoz, N., Oguuzturk, O., Bayram, M., & Kamaci, M. (2001). Anxiety and depression before and after the menopause. *Archives of Gynecology & Obstetrics, 264*(4), 199–202. doi:10.1007/s004040000108.

Sanna, L. J., & Chang, E. C. (2003). The past is not what it used to be: Optimists' use of retroactive pessimism to diminish the sting of failure. *Journal of Research in Personality, 37*, 388–404. doi:10.1016/S0092-6566(03)00013-8.

Schaufeli, W. B., Bakker, A. B., & Van Rhenen, W. (2009). How changes in job demands and resources predict burnout, work engagement, and sickness absenteeism. *Journal of Organizational Behavior, 30*(7), 893–917. doi:10.1002/job.595

Scheier, M. F., Carver, C. S., & Bridges, M. W. (1994). Distinguishing optimism from neuroticism (and trait anxiety, self-mastery, and self-esteem): A reevaluation of the life orientation test. *Journal of Personality and Social Psychology, 67*(6), 1063–1078. doi:10.1037/0022-3514.67.6.1063

Scholz, U., Gutierrez, B., Sud, S., & Schwarzer, R. (2002). Is general self-efficacy a universal construct?: Psychometric findings from 25 countries. *European Journal of Psychological Assessment, 18*(3), 242–251. doi:10.1027//1015-5759.18.3.242.

Schwartz, J. E., Pieper, C. F., & Karasek, R. A. (1988). A procedure for linking psychosocial job characteristics data to health surveys. *American Journal of Public Health, 78*(8), 904–909. doi:10.2105/AJPH.78.8.904.

Schwarzer, R., & Jerusalem, M. (1995). Generalized self-efficacy scale. In J. Weinman, S. Wright, & M. Johnston (Eds.), *Measures in health psychology: A user's portfolio* (Causal and control beliefs, pp. 35–37). Windsor, UK: NFER-NELSON.

Simpson, E. E. A., & Thompson, W. (2009). Stressful life events, psychological appraisal and coping style in postmenopausal women. *Maturitas, 63*(4), 357–364. doi:10.1016/j.maturitas.2009.05.003.

Smeur, E. (2011). *The effect of menopausal complaints on burnout: Social support and menopausal taboo*. Tilburg, The Netherlands: Tilburg University.

Smith, M. J., Mann, E., Mirza, A., & Hunter, M. S. (2011). Men and women's perceptions of hot flushes within social situations: Are menopausal women's negative beliefs valid? *Maturitas, 69*(1), 57–62. doi:10.1016/i.maturitas.2011.01.015.

Stojanovska, L., Apostolopoulos, V., Polman, R., & Borkoles, E. (2014). To exercise, or not to exercise, during menopause and beyond. *Maturitas, 77*(4), 318–323. doi:10.1016/j.maturitas.2014.01.006.

Strauss, J. R. (2011). The reciprocal relationship between menopausal symptoms and depressive symptoms: A 9-year longitudinal study of American women in midlife. *Maturitas, 70*(3), 302–306. doi:10.1016/j.maturitas.2011.08.002.

Tang, C. S.-K., Au, W.-T., Schwarzer, R., & Schmidt, G. (2001). Mental health outcomes of job stress among Chinese teachers: Role of stress resource factors and burnout. *Journal of Organizational Behavior, 22*(8), 887–901. Stable URL: http://www.jstor.org/stable/3649577.

United Nations Department of Economic and Social Affairs (2010). *The World's women 2010: Trends and statistics*. ST/ESA/STAT/SER.K/19 United Nations publication Sales No. E.10. XVII.11. Retrieved on 14 July, 2014, from http://unstats.un.org/unsd/demographic/products/Worldswomen/WW_full%20report_color.pdf

Van Yperen, N. W., & Hagedoorn, M. (2003). Do high job demands increase intrinsic motivation or fatigue or both? The role of job control and job social support. *Academy of Management Journal, 46*(3), 339–349. doi:10.2307/30040627.

Voydanoff, P. (2004). Implications of work and community demands and resources for work-to-family conflict and facilitation. *Journal of Occupational Health Psychology, 9*(4), 275–285. doi:10.1037/1076-8998.9.4.275.

Warr, P., Cook, J., & Wall, T. (1979). Scales for the measurement of some work attitudes and aspects of psychological well-being. *Journal of Occupational Psychology, 52*(2), 129–148. doi:10.1111/j.2044-8325.1979.tb00448.x.

Webster, J. (2016). Workplace adjustments and accommodations – Practical suggestions for managing the menopause: An overview and case study approach. In R. L. Gervais & P. Millear (Eds.), *Exploring resources, life-balance and well-being of women who work in a global context* (pp. 239–254). Cham, Switzerland: Springer International Publishing Switzerland.

Williams, R. E., Levine, K. B., Kalilani, L., Lewis, J., & Clark, R. V. (2009). Menopause-specific questionnaire assessment in US population-based study shows negative impact on health-related quality of life. *Maturitas, 62*(2), 153–159. doi:10.1016/j.maturitas.2008.12.006.

Winefield, T., Montgomery, B., Gault, U., Muller, J., O'Gorman, J., Reser, J., et al. (2000). *The psychology of work and unemployment in Australia today*. Melbourne, VIC: The Australian Psychological Society Ltd.. Retrieved from: http://www.psychology.org.au/Assets/Files/work_position_paper.pdf.

Xanthopoulou, D., Bakker, A. B., Demerouti, E., & Schaufeli, W. B. (2007). The role of personal resources in the Job demand-resources model. *International Journal of Stress Management, 14*(2), 121–141. doi:10.1037/1072-5245.14.2.121.

Chapter 14
Workplace Adjustments and Accommodations – Practical Suggestions for Managing the Menopause: An Overview and Case Study Approach

Jennifer Webster

Introduction

The menopause, according to the World Health Organization (WHO, 1996, p. 1) '*…is the time of a woman's life when reproductive capacity ceases*'. In epidemiological studies, the peri-menopause is typically defined as the time when women report that they have experienced at least 3–11 months without menstruating (Brambilla, McKinlay, & Johannes, 1994; Prior, 1998). The average age of menopause is 51 years. Often in the lead up to these stages, women may experience or be aware of changes to their menstrual cycle and other physiological and psychological changes, as well as social changes which can have an impact on their quality of life. Some of these changes will be subtle and others less so. During her 40s, a woman may begin to experience menstrual periods of varying lengths. Late in transition in her late 40s, early 50s she may have skipped two or more periods and begun to experience hot flashes, irritability and sleep disturbance. Bone loss also occurs. When periods finally cease; women may experience vaginal atrophy or vaginal dryness, urge incontinence and hot flashes may persist well into their 60s and 70s (National Institute on Aging, 2014).

Although there has been a significant amount of research that explores the clinical presentation of these life stages and their symptoms, relatively little has been written about the impact of the pre-menopause, peri-menopause and menopause on work performance. The purpose of this chapter is to explore potential workplace adjustments and accommodations for women transitioning through these stages

This chapter is based on data collected independently by the author and represents solely her opinions and/or conclusions.

J. Webster (✉)
Independent Practitioner, Stoke-on-Trent ST3 6RR, UK
e-mail: jennifer.webster@hsl.gsi.gov.uk

R.L. Gervais, P.M. Millear (eds.), *Exploring Resources, Life-Balance and Well-Being of Women Who Work in a Global Context*,
DOI 10.1007/978-3-319-31736-6_14

from a brief scoping study that draws on a sample of the available research and primary and secondary case study material. For ease, the transition period will be referred to as 'menopause' throughout the chapter as it is the one term that is most identifiable. As a caveat, the following is not intended to provide a diagnosis, and any woman experiencing symptoms that affect her physical or mental health should seek advice from a qualified medical physician.

Method

Desk-Based Research

A scoping search was undertaken for peer-reviewed journal papers using the Elton B. Stephens Company (EBSCO) databases, the British Psychological Society's PsychSource data-base and Google Scholar. The search terms used included 'menopause and work' and 'menopause and employment' which identified 58 and five peer reviewed journal articles respectively. The same terms were used when searching within Google and Google Scholar, which identified ten items related to women at work during the menopause. Some of the items were grey literature. Grey literature is used to describe non peer-reviewed material and is commissioned through Government agencies, universities, research institutions, trades unions and for example includes such documents as research reports, working papers, guidance, fact sheets and white papers.

Case Studies

In order to identify suitable participants willing to be interviewed a snowball sampling method was used (Goodman, 1961). Given the hidden nature of the menopause at work this method seemed to provide the best chance of gathering participants who would be willing to discuss in person their experience of working through their transition. Three women aged between 52 years and 60 years were approached initially via e-mail and asked to forward an information sheet to anyone else they knew who might be willing to take part. This resulted in five contacts, of whom, three opted out of the study on the grounds that they had gone through the menopause and could not remember making any adjustments to their work. Two contacts agreed to take part. All of those who agreed were asked to complete consent forms. One person agreed to take part in a brief semi-structured interview and the other preferred to provide her own written account as she sent an e-mail message to the researcher to say she was embarrassed to speak in person about her menopause status. In order to identify any recurring themes, permission was sought from the University of Oxford to use its own case study material (healthtalk.org, 2014) from women in the workplace going through the menopause. An interpretative phenomenological analysis (Smith & Osborn, 2008) was carried out to explore how each woman made sense of experiencing menopause whilst being in employment.

Literature Review

The following is a summary of the available literature. Some material written by medical researchers from a clinical perspective have been included, where direct or indirect references to work or employment have been made.

The Case for Workplace Adjustments and Accommodations

By 2047 (United Nations, 2007), the world will have reached a tipping point, with older people outnumbering younger people and already, a number of countries have started to consider how they can support an increasingly older population and still maintain economic growth. Countries in Europe and North East Asia are most affected by an ageing population and one of the ways this effect can be counteracted is to increase participation in the labour market. In Europe, changes to pension policy have been adopted and the extension of working lives in many countries is encouraged, as well as the increased participation of women in the workforce. For instance, Norway adopted family friendly policies, including the right of parents to take leave when their children are ill; making it easier for women of child-bearing age to participate at work and Norway credits its economic growth on having more women in the workplace. However, the contribution that midlife or older women can make to the economy by remaining active in the labour market still tends to be overlooked. In Australia, the Diversity Council Australia (Diversity Council Australia, 2013) and Australian Human rights Commission identified in a joint report, '*Older Women Matter: Harnessing the Talents of Australia's Older Female Workforce*' that participation in the labour market between the ages of 55 years to 64 years is 17 % lower for women that it is for men. In 2010, women over the age of 50 made up 11 % of the world's population and this figure will rise to 18 % by 2050 (Tom & Mishra, 2013). What this suggests is an untapped labour resource and governments will have to look closely at how they can support employers to retain and sustain women in the workplace.

Women also require access to the appropriate advice, guidance and support if needed, during their menopausal transition to retain and/or sustain employment. Any requests for reasonable workplace adjustments and accommodations may be made more difficult because of the variation in menopausal symptoms from woman to woman, both in severity, frequency and duration. However, many women feel uncomfortable discussing their symptoms with their managers or younger colleagues in case their 'condition' harms their employment prospects or because they find it embarrassing. The lack of employment protection afforded to women if they experience menopausal symptoms can also make some women feel that if they openly discuss their work performance with their line manager it could undermine their position at work. Employers are not legally obliged to consider workplace adjustments and accommodations because according to the World Health Organization's (2011) standard definition, the menopause is neither a disability nor a health condition.

Table 14.1 Percentage of women experiencing menopausal symptoms that affect their working lives (Griffiths et al., 2010, p. 41)

Symptoms	%
Poor concentration	51
Tiredness	50
Poor memory	50
Feeling low/depressed	42
Lowered confidence	39
Sleep disturbances	37
Irritability	36
Hot flushes	35
Joint and muscular aches and discomfort	31
Mood swings	29
Anxiety/panic attacks	25
Tearfulness	24
Frequent visits to the toilet	23
Heavy periods/flooding	22
Clumsiness	17
Palpitations/irregular or racing heart	15
Weight gain	11
Night sweats	8
Changes in skin	7

The ambiguity of the menopause status as neither a disability nor a health condition is dealt with more pragmatically in the United States of America (USA). For instance, in the USA, although menopause is not covered by the Americans with Disabilities Act (ADA) and is viewed as very much part of the natural ageing process, the U.S. Department of Labor provides advice and guidance to menopausal women and their employers through their website, the Job Accommodation Network (JAN, no date). In Great Britain, the Trades Union Congress (TUC, 2014) has lobbied for the menopause to be considered as a workplace health issue and many individual Trades Unions in Great Britain now provide information and guidance about the menopause for their representatives and members. Their key source of information has been a study carried out on behalf of the British Occupational Health Foundation (see Griffiths, MacLennan, & Wong, 2010). Their findings are based on interviews with 61 working women and a survey of 912 working women between the ages of 45 and 55 years. Table 14.1 presents the percentage of women who took part in the study who felt their menopausal symptoms had affected their working lives. Around 70 % of the women taking part in the survey said that they had deliberately not talked to their employer.

Other symptoms often cited in epidemiological studies include menstrual flooding during the peri-menopause, headaches, migraines, joint pain, vaginal atrophy which, not only can have an impact on intimate relationships but also increases the risk of urinary tract infections (World Health Organization, 1996). Sleep disturbances can include the need to go to the toilet more often and/or night sweats and poor sleep quality can affect work performance (Shaver & Zenk, 2004, Woods &

Mitchell, 2010). Symptoms also vary across cultures with Japanese and Taiwanese women more likely to report joint pains and headaches than hot flushes and night sweats (Avis, Assman, Kravitz, Ganz, & Ory, 2004).

Quality of Life

The menopause may be a very difficult time for women and a number of studies refer to the impact it has on a woman's quality of life (Avis et al., 2004, Jacobs, Hyland, & Ley, 2000, Moilanen et al., 2012, Wu, Lai, & Hwang, 2011). Avis et al. defines quality of life (QoL) as comprising objective and subjective well-being and refers to both specific and global measures of QoL although they are not clearly defined. Clinical studies tend to refer to health-related quality of life (HRQoL). For example, Thurston, Blumenthal, Babyak, and Sherwood (2006) highlight that whilst the incidence of hot flashes will improve, vaginal atrophy and the associated vaginal and bladder issues do not, which accounts for a decline in HRQoL for midlife women. Women who experience hot flushes have been found to have a lower HRQoL than women with other symptoms (Hess, Thurston, & Matthews, 2012, Jacobs et al., 2000, Nakano, Pinnow, Flaws, Sorkin, & Gallicchio, 2012). The Study of Women's Health Across the Nation (SWAN) looked at the quality of life of 13,874 women in a multi-ethnic, multi-race study of middle aged women (Avis et al., 2004) and found that women experiencing early peri-menopause reported lower quality of life than women who were pre-menopausal and differences were found in educational attainment, marital status, perceived stress and social support and that varied across all racial/ethnic groups. This study found that whilst Chinese and Japanese women had similar views on the importance of education and family, the analysis identified that there were enough differences between the other factors associated with quality of life to suggest that Asian heritage groups should not be considered as a homogenous group for similar studies of this nature.

The age that women typically go through the menopause means that they may be part of the 'Sandwich' generation (Miller, 1981), sandwiched between the demands of caring for their children and caring for parents (Scalea et al., 2012). At this stage in their lives, they may wonder what their purpose is in life. In a study carried out by Deeks and McCabe (2004), women's feelings about their social roles were explored through a 'Purpose in Life' sub-scale comprising of 14 statements which asked women about their goals in life, their sense of directedness and meaningfulness in life. One of its findings suggest that pre-menopausal women rated their feelings about their role(s) in life as more positive than all menopausal women and that quality of life, including well-being, appears to change with the menopause stage. The authors suggest this is around the time when children become more independent. Although there are references to potential workplace adjustments and accommodations the psychosocial aspects of women's lives are rarely taken into account (Pimenta, Leal, Maroco, & Ramos, 2012). Those that fare better during the menopause appear to be either educated women or are those women who remain in the workforce (Jacobs et al., 2000). Although, it is not entirely clear whether it is because the former are more assertive at getting the right information and help, or that the latter affords the menopausal woman greater social contact. Further insights into this area can be gleaned from Millear and Gervais (2016) who suggest that the availability of resources within the workplace to individuals, as advocated by the Job Demands-Resources (JD-R) model (see e.g., Bakker & Demerouti, 2007), may act as a protective buffer for challenging situations.

Fatigue and the Importance of Sleep

Most people would generally accept that they function better after having had a good night's rest, but for some women going through the menopause this is more difficult to achieve. Night sweats can cause a reduction in sleep quality through awakening. At their worst, night sweats may necessitate a change of clothing or bedding. Some women experience an increased urgency to urinate during the day that may lead also to bladder sensitivity. This in turn can result in disturbed sleeping patterns at night. This has implications for a range of occupations and patterns of employment. Shift workers may find that without adequate workplace adjustments they may be unable to achieve sufficient rest to enable sleep recovery and circadian readjustment (Costa, Haus, & Stevens, 2010). Women in demanding professional and technical occupations, around the age of 55, are more likely to report feeling exhausted (Helkavaara, Saastamoinen, & Lahelma, 2011), although it is unclear whether this is because of sleep disturbances affecting their ability to concentrate, or hot flushes, or weight gain affecting how they perceive themselves. This finding also appears to contradict some of the evidence presented from the SWAN research series (Avis et al., 2004) that suggests that educated women are better able to cope with menopausal symptoms. There is also a higher prevalence for exhaustion amongst women who report having low job control, who perceive organisational injustice within their workplace or frequently witness workplace bullying. However, the link with their transition through the menopause is unclear.

Although some of the more typically reported menopausal symptoms, such as hot flashes, are not usually considered to be an issue affecting Japanese women, two studies from Asia exploring insomnia during the menopause have found their results are comparable to those carried out with Western subjects (Shin et al., 2005, Wu et al., 2011). In a study of 1098 menopausal women in Taiwan (Wu et al., 2011), subjective sleep quality was found to affect the physical, psychological and social aspects of one's life. Feeling tired at work makes it harder to maintain any enthusiasm and easier to make mistakes. Sleep deprivation can alter *'numerous endocrine rhythms'* at work (Costa et al., 2010) and make women more prone to anxiety and emotional outbursts.

Although the evidence is inconclusive, some of the fatigue or exhaustion experienced around the menopause may be the result of running out of bio-psychosocial resources in maintaining usual activities when one's actual or perceived functioning is transitioning. Work should not be seen in isolation but rather within the context of the whole life. When individuals do not have sufficient resources in one area of their life, they call on resources from another (Barnett et al., 2012). As a result, a deficit occurs. The previous section touched on the importance of women's social roles and with changes to working patterns and in some countries, women putting off having children until later in life, they may find themselves becoming part of what is colloquially referred to as the 'Sandwich' generation. This involves having caring responsibility not only for their children, but also for their parents or other elderly relatives. Finding ways to maintain one's internal resources would appear to be most important during the transition.

The Importance of Physical Activity

Although it is not inevitable, many women experience changes to their weight and body shape during their menopause that they find difficult to resolve. These changes are not necessarily related to menopause but part of the ageing process. In a longitudinal study of 1165 Finnish women between the ages of 45–64, those who increased their physical activity not only improved their quality of life during the menopause transition but also had fewer episodes of hot flushes, night sweats and vaginal dryness (Moilanen et al., 2012). Leaner women tend to have more hot flushes at the time of menopause and some might use hormone replacement therapy (HRT) more frequently; but overall, women who increase their physical activity and maintain a stable weight, tend to have an improved quality of life (Moilanen et al., 2012). Physical activity can also have more broader health benefits for a healthy ageing including decreased risk of cardio-respiratory and metabolic diseases and some cancers (colon and breast), improved musculoskeletal, functional and mental health (Sternfeld & Dugan, 2011).

What the Grey Literature Says About Workplace Adjustments and Accommodations

There are numerous sources of information on the Internet and from grey literature, about the different types of adjustments and accommodations where the evidence base is unclear or where they are used as a device to promote products. As a result this chapter refers to the advice provided within Griffiths et al. (2010), and the Trades Union Congress (TUC, 2013). These include several evidence-based recommendations around the key themes of positive communications, training for line managers, and appropriate employment policies. They advise to look at possible flexible working arrangements and adapting sickness related procedures to take into account menopause related absences. They also suggest conducting risk assessments to ensure the immediate working environment does not worsen any menopause symptoms. For example, this could consist of paying attention to temperature and ventilation within the work envisioned and the access to welfare facilities/toilets.

Another reputable source of information is The US Department of Labor's website, The Job Accommodation Network (JAN, no date). It focuses mainly on solutions that deal with temperature sensitivity. The solutions they suggest are modifying or reducing worksite temperatures; modifying the dress code, wearing cooling clothing; the use of a fan/air-conditioner at the workstation; flexible working, working from home during hot weather or during breakdowns in air conditioning units; maintaining ventilation systems, as well as providing an office with separate temperature controls.

Findings

This section provides the findings from the present research and shows how the menopause affected these women in the workplace. The information that is presented explored the verbal and written narratives from the six women, all of whom addressed the challenges they encountered while experiencing the menopause whilst maintaining their employment. Their accounts are clustered around four superordinate themes: (1) going through a period of uncertainty; (2) hiding symptoms; (3) stay or leave the job and (4) carrying on as usual. Most of the accounts share all the themes, but for the purposes of this section the narrative which is the best illustration of the theme has been selected. Substantial quotations from the women's narratives are used because they provide richer, evocative insights into how each of them coped with their individual experiences. Only the first names, ages and occupation of the participants are provided.

Going Through a Period of Uncertainty

All the narratives express some degree of uncertainty about what is happening to their bodies when the menopausal symptoms begin to surface and affect their working lives. Carole's account refers to her beginning to notice changes to her mood, then hot flushes and memory. There is some variation in how Carole's symptoms manifest. Sometimes she reports being unable to do more than a couple of tasks at a time and at other times, she can undertake several tasks.

> By the end of the following summer I'd started to notice that I was getting, I wouldn't say depressed but I was getting quite weepy, I was having trouble concentrating on work. And I found I just couldn't cope with things and I started getting a bit tearful. This went on for about another four months towards the end of 2006 and everything got on top of me. I thought I was slightly depressed, then the hot flushes started and they'd been going on for

> about 3 or 4 months, mainly during the day, not any at night at the time, but then I found I couldn't concentrate on things, I had no co-ordination, I couldn't do two things at once. I'd be out in the kitchen thinking I've opened the drawer, yes, what am I getting, other times I could do two or three things at once but this was just getting me down. I think you start to think what the hell's wrong with me, have I got some disease that, the big C,[1] what is making me like this, am I depressed, am I going to have a nervous breakdown. I thought I was going to have a nervous breakdown until I found the website and I read the forum and I thought Jesus there's hundreds of women like me, I'm not going bonkers, I'm not going mad, this is quite normal. It's not abnormal, you're not mad, you're not stupid, you're just going through a stage of your life and you're not the only one.

Carole, 51 years, part-time office administrator

Carole's account captures the extent to which she became disturbed by the changes in her ability to concentrate at work and also the feelings of fear; '*what the hell's wrong with me.*' Her ability to function changes to such an extent that she worries she is heading for a '*breakdown*' or has cancer. The uncertainty about what she is going through is only alleviated when she finds out that this is something that happens to other women and that she is not alone.

Hiding Symptoms

A concern about being perceived as 'stupid' or unable to maintain a good level of job performance was shared by a number of the narratives. Some of the participants wondered whether their colleagues noticed the change in their performance. Susan's account illustrates the confusion that comes from finding herself unable to do jobs as well as she had in the past. Susan began to lose her confidence and started to craft her job, which allowed her to undertake tasks that enabled her to withdraw from a public facing role in which she was now less confident.

> My biggest thing was the loss of confidence, the loss of self-esteem, the loss of putting myself out there. Up until then I would have been a confident, out and about kind of person doing talks, going to meetings, all of that. I completely lost my confidence with the result that I very much retreated in back to the centre here, much happier to work on books, planning systems, working within the centre. I certainly stopped being out there. Going to meetings I felt awkward, lacked confidence and I felt that as a representative of the organisation I was letting it down in some ways. That paranoia, stupid jealousies sometimes, every kind of emotion you can think of was exaggerated. The impact on work then was probably I didn't feel I was doing the job. I felt, "I'm going to be caught out. I'm not doing this job as well." A lack of belief in my own ability, so looking for reassurance all the time and wanting to be reassured that I was doing, that I was okay, that I'm doing the job all right. That kind of, paranoia is the word for it, that not saying that people are talking about you, it's not that sort of thing but that you're going to be found out that you're not doing your job properly or you're going to be found out that you're not the great person you thought they think you are.

[1] The big 'C' is a colloquial term for cancer

Susan, 55 years, manager
Reproduced with the kind permission of the University of Oxford ©

Susan seemed worried that she would be '*found out*' and her account is very much about trying to carry on at work as normal but inwardly becoming more insecure about her abilities. Ultimately, there is an implied sense of vulnerability about '*not doing your job properly*'.

Christina's account illustrates also how she has developed her own coping strategies in order to hide the fact that 'everything kind of disintegrates.' Like Susan, Christina also had concerns that she was not functioning as well at work when compared to before her menopause. She talked about it being '*extremely hard to admit*' that her memory was no longer as '*sharp*'.

> It seems like everything kind of disintegrates but the worse thing is the memory. It is the worst thing. The lack of concentration, the appalling inability to remember people's faces and names, forgetting appointments. I was running a two million pound operation I couldn't afford to forget a thing. So, I developed coping strategies but if you've always had a really sharp memory it's extremely hard to admit…Notes, all the time. Notebook, notebook. All the time notebook. If ever I said to somebody, "Oh, I'll send you one of those" or "let me get in touch with you and talk to you about such and such" or "I'll ring you and we'll make an appointment" I would, the first moment, I would even disappear into the loo [bathroom] to do it. I would go into the loo, get my notebook out and write send such and such to Fred or ring Jean to fix an appointment to meet John. It was the only thing I could do. It was absolutely impossible. And I developed the electronic diary as being an important thing with massive numbers of reminders that come up which say do such and such, buy such and such, go to such and such.

Christina, 57 years, self-employed
Reproduced with the kind permission of the University of Oxford ©

Although Christina is not explicit on whether it was hard to admit to herself or to others about her memory problems, rather she hid in the toilet to take notes and sets up electronic reminders to herself. Although not explicitly stated here, Christina took steps to maintain a certain image that she was capable of '*running a two million pound operation.*'

Stay in or Leave the Job

A number of the narratives alluded to withdrawing from being in the 'spotlight.' Joyce's narrative describes that even though she had been preparing for a presentation for a year she developed a panic attack. Joyce did not explicitly admit to lacking in confidence but she described her anxiety at encountering possible resistance at the meeting and talking to people in a big room. She could not admit in a work setting to having had a panic attack so she explains away her performance as something she ate.

> I remember one day, this was in July of last year, going to a meeting to give a presentation about something, which again I'd been working on for 12 months, this wasn't new territory to me but I'd got an e-mail from another person who's a friend and an associate, who said,

> "You could meet some resistance at this meeting on this particular issue that you're going to describe. Suggest that you really are prepared for the difficult questions." Which, he was giving me a heads up it, there was nothing more to it than that, but I really became very very anxious about this to the point where I actually had a panic attack in the meeting. The meeting was being [held] unfortunately in a very big room and as I started to speak people at the top end of the table said, "We can't hear you, would you stand up?" And so that kind of added to being under a spotlight that not only can I not sit here and say this, I had a presentation and I needed to touch the keys on the laptop to bring it up. Not only could I not do that but now I had to stand up and the words came up, the words were in front of me and I could see the words but I couldn't read them if that made sense. And I just said, "I'm really sorry, I'm feeling really unwell at the moment, you're going to have to excuse me," and I walked out the room. And fortunately a colleague came out and said, "Are you okay?" And I didn't admit to having a panic attack but I just said, "Look, I just thought I was going to faint and pass out, I think I've eaten something, I think I've got a stomach upset."
>
> Fortunately a colleague was with me at that meeting and said, "Actually what [name] wants to tell you is X, Y & Z" and she conveyed the message. So it wasn't a big problem but I just felt so embarrassed, I wanted the ground to open up and swallow me and I just thought I can't go on like this.

Joyce, 48 years, police officer
Reproduced with the kind permission of The University of Oxford ©

Joyce appeared to have reached a point where she was not able to continue as she has been and would probably have had to do something. The next narrative describes Sue's account of how a change in line manager and job role left her on the verge of handing in her notice. Sue described herself as '*just about coping*' and being '*worried all the time.*' In Sue's case she had to disclose her menopause status when her job changed. Like many of the other participants, Sue had a different perception of her abilities than her colleagues. Sue reported that the human resources manager called her one of their '*best workers*' and that she was '*in line for promotion.*'

> When I was putting stock out in the shop it was really easy for me to go to the toilet when I needed to. Then my periods started to get really heavy and could go on for weeks. I felt really uncomfortable when this happened, especially during the first couple of days of my period when just to be on the safe side I would wear a tampon and a sanitary towel. I was just about coping when they brought a new manager in and he decided to move me to work on the tills. It was much more difficult to get away to visit the toilet and I was worried all the time I would have an accident. The more worried I got about it the more hot flushes I got and I knew I was making mistakes. I could not talk to my manager about my personal business because I was too embarrassed. Besides, how do you explain something like this to a man who is young enough to be your son? One day I decided I could not go on like this and when I went to hand my notice into the human resources manager, she was really surprised because she said I was one of their best workers and was in line for a promotion. I just burst out crying and told her my problems. She is the same age as me so she understood and said she would fix things. She went to my manager and told him that he was not to ask any questions but accept that sometimes I have to go to the toilet more often. It is sort of accepted now at work. I still do not feel great about it, leaving the tills when there is a queue of customers so I go the extra mile when I am there and everything is going smoothly. At least I can still work.

Sue, 51 years, shop worker
Source: Author

Sue described feeling 'great' once she had disclosed the information and been supported to find a solution that would not embarrass her in front of her younger male manager.

Carrying on as Usual

All of the participants in their own way were carrying on with their working lives as usual without the help of others. Chris was in a different situation to the others because she had clear responsibilities for employees. She noted that no one had come to her for help or advice about working through the menopause. Her own approach was to make any changes or adjustments that made her feel more comfortable. Chris used humour to brush off her symptoms at work and appeared to be part of a group of women of a similar age who were happy to make jokes about their menopause.

> My main problems at work are feeling tired and at times I have the overwhelming feeling of being too hot which, makes it difficult to concentrate. I know I use the wrong words at home on occasions (my husband tells me!) so I must do it at work too but no one ever says anything. I work in Human Resources for a charity, and have never had a member of staff come to me to say they need any help or adjustments at work. I think most women, including myself just get on with it. I have taken the opportunity to move to a desk near to a window that I could open and have asked for a desk fan, both of which have helped with my hot flushes. I drink a lot more water at work now and less coffee and take a proper lunch break to help re-charge my batteries. I bought a summer weight duvet, which, I use throughout the year. It has helped me sleep a bit better, but not much. There are a group of us at work who are of a similar age and we tend to just make a joke of the fact that we are "women of a certain age". I still have occasional night sweats, hot flushes and red cheeks but these occurrences have reduced significantly over the last 6 months. I feel as though I am coming out of the fog and have managed with minimal adjustment at work.

Chris, 57 years, human resources manager
Source: Author

Chris also described her menopause as a 'fog' from which she was coming out. 'Coming out of the fog' captures how dark and miserable she must have felt when her menopausal symptoms were at their height. It was something she 'managed' to emerge from with minimal interventions but unlike the others, Chris had peer support and one imagines that as a human resource professional she would have access to information about the menopause.

Summary and Conclusions

Although there is a great deal of literature available to women on the Internet about the menopause, the narratives underline how ill-prepared there women were for the menopause. As menopause is often associated in most peoples' minds with hot flushes/flashes, the manifestation of the other symptoms such as poor concentration, tiredness, poor memory and feeling low and depressed (see Table 14.1, Griffiths et al., 2010) for no apparent reason, may be unsettling to those experiencing these for the first time. As the narratives from the two participants from the snowball sample and the four narratives from the University of Oxford's 'healthtalk.org' programme have shown, they share many commonalities with the research carried out by Griffiths et al., which to date provides one of the few examples of research into how some women at work experience their menopause. However, it is important to remember that not all women will experience all or any symptoms related to the menopause. It also has to be remembered that although the definition of the menopause is a year without a menstrual period, many women may experience symptoms over a substantial time period, in some cases years. Symptoms may come and go so it may be difficult to predict when workplace support will be required and for how long. In addition, as the examples in this brief scoping study have illustrated, women are reluctant to admit that they have any impairment, albeit temporary, which may affect their overall job performance although to date little evidence (DiBonaventura, Wagner, Alvir, & Whiteley, 2012) could be found that menopause in itself affects workplace performance. If, as the narratives have shown, that women are more likely find solutions that work for them in the workplace, some may be willing to disclose their menopause status only when their symptoms become incompatible with their work environment. This suggests that there may be further work required to look at whether requests for changes in working patterns from say full time to part time working amongst midlife women is seen as the default position when insufficient consideration is made to other types of workplace adjustment and accommodation. If it is, then it is not a tenable position for many countries that need to keep as many of their citizens economically active for longer, in order to counteract the effects of an ageing population.

To suggest that all women of a certain age should be offered a fan and control of the ambient temperature of their working environment also perpetuates the misconception that the menopause manifests itself solely as inconvenient hot flushes/flashes. Poor sleep quality and other psychological and physiological changes require a more holistic approach rather than adjusting to a set of varying symptoms. One area that deserves to be explored further is the connection between quality of life, quality of working life and conservation of resources during the menopause. Also, some symptoms such as vaginal atrophy may lead to a decline in health related quality of life but because of the sensitive nature of the topic a woman may find it difficult to discuss these with her medical practitioner, let alone her employer. Quality of life, quality of working life, health-related quality of life in respect of working women are still not clearly defined in the literature. If the relationship between them as well as conservation of resources during the menopause were better defined and understood, this may provide further insights into appropriate workplace adjustments and accommodations. As Joyce says in her narrative, '*I can't go on*'. The quality of her working life appears to be poorer than before, but she is drawing on something within herself to keep going. Similarly, the others also find ways of dealing with specific symptoms like making notes, or like Susan, withdrawing from certain tasks by making discreet changes to their jobs.

Overall, one of the best ways of coping is to educate women to make them more aware of the menopause and potential symptoms and this applies equally to employers. The information provided through the Trades Union Congress to unions is very helpful. Unions representing women employees such as the Union of Shop, Distributive and Allied Workers (USDAW, No date) and UNISON (No date) which represents workers in the public sector, provide their safety representatives with training literature about the menopause and workplace adjustments. The menopause is not a disability, but it can be an exceptional period in a woman's life. As such, in recognising it as an occupational health issue may help further with the discussion about the range of adjustments and accommodations that could be made, both inside and outside of the workplace. Also, no-one functions well without sleep at any age and the literature appears to support the importance of adhering to good sleep hygiene (Guidozzi, 2013, Shaver & Zenk, 2004, Woods & Mitchell, 2010). With disturbed sleeping patterns, women may need to re-evaluate whether they need to go to bed earlier to compensate, or discuss flexible working with their employer. Finally, it is time for a wider debate about improving the quality of working life for midlife women as until such time, they will remain quiet about their needs for workplace adjustments and accommodations.

References

Avis, N. E., Assman, S. F., Kravitz, H. M., Ganz, P. A., & Ory, M. (2004). Quality of life in diverse groups of midlife women: Assessing the influence of menopause, health status and psychosocial and demographic factors. *Quality of Life Research, 13*, 933–946.

Bakker, A. B., & Demerouti, E. (2007). The job demands-resources model: State of the art. *Journal of Managerial Psychology, 22*(3), 309–328. doi:10.1108/02683940710733115.

Barnett, R., Brennan, R. T., Gareis, K. C., Ertel, K. A., Berkman, L. F., & Almeida, D. M. (2012). Conservation of resources theory in the context of multiple roles: An analysis of within- and cross-role mediational pathways. *Community, Work and Family, 15*(2), 131–148. doi:10.1080/13668803.2010.539066.

Brambilla, D. J., McKinlay, S. M., & Johannes, C. B. (1994). Defining the perimenopause for application in epidemiologic investigations. *American Journal of Epidemiology, 140*, 1091–1095.

Costa, G., Haus, E., & Stevens, R. (2010). Shift work and cancer – Considerations on rationale, mechanisms, and epidemiology. *Scandinavian Journal of Work, Environment & Health, 36*(2), 163–179. doi:10.5271/sjweb.2899.

Deeks, A. A., & McCabe, M. P. (2004). Well-being and menopause: An investigation of purpose and social role in premenopausal, perimenopausal and post-menopausal women. *Quality of Life Research, 13*, 389–398.

DiBonaventura, M. D., Wagner, J. S., Alvir, J., & Whiteley, J. (2012). Depression, quality of life, work productivity, resource use, and costs among women experiencing menopause and hot flashes: A cross-sectional study. *The Primary Care Companion CNS Disorders, 14*(6), pii: PCC.12m01410. doi:10.4088/PCC.12m01410.

Diversity Council Australia. (2013). *Older women matter – Harnessing the talents of Australia's older female workforce*. Sydney, Australia: DCA Ltd, http://dca.org.au/files/file/DCA%20Older%20Women%20Matter%20Exec%20Summary%20online.pdf. Accessed 28 Aug 2014.

Goodman, L. A. (1961). Snowball sampling. *Annals of Mathematical Statistics, 32*(1), 148–170. doi:10.1214/aoms/1177705148.

Griffiths, A., MacLennan, S., & Wong, Y. Y. V. (2010). *Women's experience of working through the menopause*, University of Nottingham/British Occupational Health Research Foundation 2010. http://www.bohrf.org.uk/downloads/Womens_Experience_of_Working_through_the_Menopause-Dec_2010.pdf. Accessed 3 Apr 2014.

Guidozzi, F. (2013). Sleep and sleep disorders in menopausal women. *Climateric, 16*(2), 214–219. doi:10.3109/13697-137.2012.753873.

Helkavaara, M., Saastamoinen, P., & Lahelma, E. (2011). Psychosocial work environment and emotional exhaustion among middle-aged employees. *BMC Research Notes, 4*(101), 1–8. http://www.biomedcentral.com/1756-0500/4/101. Accessed 3 Apr 2014.

Hess, R., Thurston, R. C., & Matthews, K. A. (2012). The impact of menopause on health-related quality of life: results from the STRIDE longitudinal study. *Quality of Life Research, 21*(3), 535–544.

Jacobs, P. A., Hyland, M. E., & Ley, A. (2000). Self-rated menopausal status and quality of life in women aged 40–63 years. *British Journal of Health Psychology, 5*(4), 395–411. doi:10.1348/135910700169008.

Millear, P. M. & Gervais, R. L. (2016). The relevance of menopause to the occupational safety and health of employed women. In R. L. Gervais & P. Millear (Eds.), *Exploring resources, life-balance and well-being of women who work in a global context* (pp. 219–238). Cham, Switzerland: Springer International Publishing Switzerland.

Miller, D. A. (1981). The 'Sandwich' generation: Adult children of the aging. *Social Work, 26*(5), 419–423.

Moilanen, J. M., Aalton, A. M., Raitanen, J., Hemminki, E., Aro, A. R., & Luoto, R. (2012). Physical activity and change in quality of life during menopause – An 8 year follow up study. *Health and Quality of Life Outcomes, 10*(8), 1–7. doi:10.1186/1477-7525-10-8.

Nakano, K., Pinnow, E., Flaws, J. A., Sorkin, J. D., & Gallicchio, L. (2012). Reproductive history and hot flashes in perimenopausal women. *Journal of Women's Health, 21*(4), 433–439.

National Institute on Aging. (2014). *Menopause: Time for a change – An introduction to menopause*. http://www.nia.nih.gov/health/publication/menopause-time-change/introduction-menopause?utm_source=ad_box&utm_medium=website&utm_content=onset&utm_campaign=menopauseFAQ. Accessed 28 Aug 2014.

Pimenta, F., Leal, I., Maroco, J., & Ramos, C. (2012). Menopausal symptoms: Do life events predict severity of symptoms in peri- and post – menopause? *Maturitas, 72*, 324–331. http://dx.doi.org/10.1016/j.maturitas.2012.04.006. Accessed 6 Feb 2014.

Prior, J. C. (1998). Perimenopause: The complex endocrinology of the menopausal transition. *Endrocrine Reviews, 19*(4), 397–428.

Scalea, d. T. L., Matthews, K. A., Avis, N. E., Thurston, R. C., Brown, C., Harlow, S., et al. (2012). Role stress, role reward, and mental health in a multiethnic sample of midlife women: Results from the Study of Women's Health Across the Nation (SWAN). *Journal of Women's Health, 21*(5), 481–489. doi:10.1089/jwh2011.3180.

Shaver, J. L. F., & Zenk, S. N. (2004). Sleep disturbance in menopause. *Journal of Women's Health and Gender-Based Medicine, 9*(2), 109–118. doi:10.1089/152460900318605.

Shin, C., Lee, S., Lee, T., Shin, K., Yi, H., Kimm, K., et al. (2005). Prevalence of insomnia and its relationship to menopausal status in middle-aged Korean women. *Psychiatry and Clinical Neurosciences, 59*, 395–402.

Smith, J. A., & Osborn, M. (2008). Interpretative phenomenological analysis. In J. A. Smith (Ed.), *Qualitative psychology: A practical guide to research methods* (pp. 51–80). London: Sage.

Sternfeld, B., & Dugan, S. (2011). Physical activity and health during the menopausal transition. *Obstetrics and Gynecology Clinics of North America, 38*(3), 537–566.

Thurston, R. C., Blumenthal, J. A., Babyak, M. A., & Sherwood, A. (2006). Association between hot flashes, sleep complaints, and psychological functioning among healthy menopausal women. *Journal of Behavioral Medicine, 13*(2), 163–172.

Tom, S. E., & Mishra, G. D. (2013). A life course approach to reproductive aging. In V. Dvornyk (Ed.), *Current topics in menopause* (pp. 3–19). Oak Park, IL: Bentham e Books. doi:10.2174/978160805453411301004.

Trades Union Congress. (2013). *Supporting working women through the menopause: A guide for union representatives*. TUC, London. http://www.tuc.org.uk/equality-issues/gender-equality/supporting-women-through-menopause. Accessed 6 Feb 2014.

Trades Union Congress. (2014). *Age immaterial – Women over 50 in the workplace*, A TUC report, London. https://www.tuc.org.uk/sites/default/files/TUC_menopause_0.pdf. Accessed 6 Feb 2014.

UNISON. (No date). *The menopause and work: A guide for UNISON safety reps*. https://www.unison.org.uk/upload/sharepoint/On%20line%20Catalogue/20472.pdf. Accessed 5 Sept 2014.

United Nations. (2007). *World population ageing*, DESA, Population Division, xxvi. http://www.un.org/en/development/desa/population/publications/pdf/ageing/WorldPopulationAgeingReport2007.pdf. Accessed 6 Feb 2014.

United States Department of Labor's Office of Disability Employment Policy. (No date). *Job accommodation network*. http://askjan.org/corner/vol09iss01.htm. Accessed 6 Feb 2014.

University of Oxford. (2014). *Healthtalk.org*. http://www.healthtalk.org/peoples-experiences/later-life/menopause/topics. Accessed 6 Feb 2014.

USDAW. (No date). *Women in USDAW talking about menopause*. http://www.usdaw.org.uk/idoc.ashx?docid=e1564e86-5e10-4b0d-8cd3-84468e10cfde&version=-1. Accessed 5 Sept 2014.

Woods, N. F., & Mitchell, E. S. (2010). Sleep symptoms during the menopausal transition and early post menopause: Observations from the Seattle midlife women's health study. *Sleep, 33*(4), 539–549. http://www.ncbi.nlm.nih.gov/pmc/articles/PMC2849794/. Accessed 3 Sept 2014.

World Health Organization. (1996). *Research on the menopause in the 1990s: Report of a WHO scientific group*. WHO technical report series 866, Geneva. http://apps.who.int/iris/handle/10665/41841. Accessed 25 Feb 2014.

World Health Organization (WHO). (2011). *International Classification of Functioning, Disability and health: ICF*. Geneva: WHO Library Cataloguing-in-Publication Data, 2001. http://www.who.int/classifications/icf/en/. Accessed 25 Feb 2014.

Wu, H. C., Lai, J. N., & Hwang, J. S. (2011). Quality of life and sleep quality amongst climacteric women seeking medical advice in Northern Taiwan. *Sleep Medicine, 13*, 906–912. doi:10.1016/j.sleep.2012.04.008.

Part VI
Exploring the Future for Women at Work

Chapter 15
Women at Work: Challenges for the Future

Roxane L. Gervais

Introduction

The present volume has covered various aspects of women and their work. One of the main tenets that has emerged from the various chapters is that despite the various discourses on gender and its construct that have occurred over the past 50 years or more; the various levels of equality that have been enacted across countries; and the resources provided within the home and organisations, that irrespective of women's role in the workplace, they are seen as the ones mainly responsible still for caring and household responsibilities. This is regardless of having their own business, such as discussed in Chap. 3 by Al-Dajani and colleagues, or working within very professional roles, as outlined in Chap. 7 by Siller and colleagues and Chap. 8 by Kinman. The unequal distribution of work and caring responsibilities whether across age or profession (see Chap. 9 by Boyd and colleagues, Chap. 7 by Siller and colleagues), or across economies, whether formal and informal (see Chap. 3 by Al-Dajani and colleagues) is obvious still. While, this caring role is not a negative one, it does highlight the underlying perceptions of women's overall function, despite the acknowledgement at the macro level that more women are required to enter the workforce.

As shown in Chap. 5 (Lyonette and colleagues) and Chap. 11 (Millear), working part-time remains an 'option' for women in order to fulfil their caring responsibilities; as does working at home (Chap. 8 by Kinman). In addition, choosing the activity in which to engage (Chap. 7 by Siller and colleagues) that could impact negatively on career advancement, is another 'option' that women have to choose to address caring responsibilities. These various facets of how women have to work have to be

This chapter is based on data collected independently by the author and represents solely her opinions and/or conclusions.

R.L. Gervais (✉)
Independent Practitioner, Goole DN14 6XN, UK
e-mail: roxane_gervais@alumni.fdu.edu

R.L. Gervais, P.M. Millear (eds.), *Exploring Resources, Life-Balance and Well-Being of Women Who Work in a Global Context*,
DOI 10.1007/978-3-319-31736-6_15

considered when propounding the entry of more women into work, especially in non-traditional female occupations.

The challenges that women continue to face in moving into less 'traditional' female occupations, such as medicine (see Chap. 7, Siller and colleagues) is evident still. Even when moving into higher positions within an organisation remains very much about perceptions, the availability of resources and the support that is in place as Rink and colleagues presented in Chap. 6. Challenges are abundant also when women choose to start their own business, even within the 'informal' economy (see Chap. 3, Al-Dajani and colleagues). However, trying to do everything with respect to work/non-work could have negative consequences as discussed in Chap. 8 by Kinman and Chap. 4 by Huda; with Katsikitis and colleagues (Chap. 10) proposing one way to address one of the consequences of modern society, i.e., the decrease in communication within families and especially between mothers and daughters due to the many 'pulls' on their time.

Women and their physiology cannot be separated and this was outlined by Gervais, Millear and Webster (Chaps. 12, 13 and 14). Women who work will go through various physiological changes over their life course, i.e., during their working lives. While, some of these are considered within a work environment, e.g., pregnancy; for the most part there are no established resources to assist women when dealing with menstruation and the menopause. The three chapters outline various recommendations that could assist with the changes.

The sections that follow explore the various challenges to women's career advancement and some of the resources that would assist them when in the workforce. These are not exclusive and it is hoped that this volume supports this discussion.

Influences on Women's Work

> Women who work gain less, financially, socially and politically, than the typical working man (ILO, 2010).

The World Bank (2011) has presented key facts that illustrate how women's life situation has improved over the past 20–30 years. These include:

- *Increased education levels.* There has been a reduction in the gender gap in primary education across most countries across the world, with most girls now being educated. With respect to secondary education, a similar result is found, as the gaps are closing quickly, but in some countries, a reversal of who is educated has occurred, especially in Latin America, the Caribbean, and East Asia, in that boys and young men are disadvantaged with respect to attaining a secondary level education.
    - Among the developing countries, more girls than boys are attending secondary schools within 45 countries, with more young women than men gaining a university education in 60 countries.

- *Increased life expectancy.* Women are benefiting from an increased life expectancy since 1980, as they are living longer than men across all parts of the world. This increase is especially advantageous in low-income countries, where women are now living on average 20 years longer than they did in 1960.
- *Increased labour force participation.* Over half a billion women joined the world's labour force over the last 30 years as women's participation in paid work has risen in most of the developing world. An important reason for this has been the unprecedented reduction in fertility in developing countries as diverse as Bangladesh, Colombia, and the Islamic Republic of Iran.

These facts support a better integration of women into the workforce at present and continuing into the future. As the chapters in this volume have shown, women's contribution to the economy is constant; although they may have faced various challenges in making this contribution, which are linked to the organisational, cultural and social constraints around them. In this volume, women have experienced many diverse and different conditions that required them to adapt to their situations and to find solutions, which allow them to prosper in their working lives and for their families to have economic security and positive relationships. Despite these challenges, women will continue to contribute to the economy. The intensity of work has not decreased over the past few decades, nor has women's unpaid work (Gershuny & Fisher, 2014), and it can be hypothesised that these trends will remain consistent over the next few decades. These trends are especially relevant as more women continue to enter the labour market in both developed and developing countries (The Economist, 2014). It is estimated that one billion women across the world could enter the workforce over the coming decade (Aguirre, Hoteit, Rupp, & Sabbagh, 2012). They are moving to a greater extent into male-dominated professions (European Agency for Safety and Health at Work (EU-OSHA), 2013) and are increasingly more likely than men to gain tertiary level education (World Bank, 2011). But while men benefit when they move into female-dominated professions, in terms of career advancement (Williams, 1992) and support (Taylor, 2010), the same cannot be said for women when they move into male-dominated professions (Martin & Barnard, 2013; Taylor, 2010). This is especially when the choice between 'family' and 'career' is made even more difficult in those more demanding work roles (Frome, Alfeld, Eccles, & Barber, 2006; Slaughter, 2012). This ability to select demanding work roles seems to remain a challenge for women over the next few decades, as will be illustrated as this present chapter develops.

However, despite these gains, women's status is driven still, depending on country, by maternal mortality and economic dependence at the micro and macro levels (Shen & Williamson, 1999; World Bank, 2011). These in turn could impact negatively on economic growth (Shen & Williamson, 1999). In addition, maternity benefits remain unavailable or are inadequate to 830 million women globally, of whom 80 % work in Africa and Asia (International Labour Organization (ILO), 2014a) The ILO report goes on to state that less than one-third (28 %) of employed women worldwide are likely to receive cash maternity benefits. If women's work conditions are to continue to improve, and their contributions to the world's economy are to increase and to be sustained, these are issues that have to be considered and addressed rigorously.

Although women are able to be more selective in their choice of occupation, they continue to work mainly in the service sector (EU-OSHA, 2013; Young, Fort, & Danner, 1994), except in the poorest countries (Young et al., 1994), where they work mainly in agriculture (World Bank, 2011). The work in the service sector tends to be an extension of their domestic responsibilities and constitute jobs that are low paid and of low status (EU-OSHA, 2013; Young et al., 1994). While they are entering male-dominated professions, with more opportunities inclusive of higher pay; women with children are more likely to leave their jobs, than men or women without children when they work 50 h or more (Cha, 2013). The care factor determines still the gender segregation of the labour market and has implications for women's sustained employment levels.

Other factors that influence directly women's work patterns and sustainability are work intensification and the growth in non-standard work (Ghosh, 2014); the decline in fertility together with the simultaneous growth in the ageing population; and those changes in the pattern of how families are constructed, for example the growth of single-parent households (ILO, 2011). Although at a global level women (48.7 %) are only slightly more likely than men to be in vulnerable employment (46.9 %; ILO, 2014b), non-formal contracts and the growth of precarious forms of self-employment rather than decent work (ILO, 2014b), remain options that women may choose to address caring responsibilities.

One of the ways that has been promoted to improve on women's overall conditions, inclusive of the workplace, is for them to gain more public power. However, the disparity between men and women in national legislative bodies continues to exist with men's dominance in this arena (World Bank, 2011; Young et al., 1994). Women's power remains limited when they become politicians, as they tend to be assigned social portfolios rather than economic positions (World Bank, 2011). This in turn could diminish their ability to influence effectively '*women's work-related concerns*'.

In acknowledging the various challenges as outlined, it is useful to explore different ways in which these could be addressed. Work remains important for women. It has already been established that individuals' well-being improves when they work (Waddell & Burton, 2006). This finding is even more relevant for women. One Swedish study showed that women's mortality rate increased due to unemployment (Nylén, Voss, & Floderus, 2001). In addition to the health benefits that work brings, what are some of the issues that should be considered to facilitate the movement of more women into the workplace as a healthy and available resource that would assist economic development worldwide? There are various elements to support women's occupational safety, health and well-being; with some of these discussed in this present chapter.

Increasing the Labour Pool

> If all forms of discrimination against female workers and managers were eradicated, then productivity per worker could rise by up to 40 per cent (Cuberes & Teignier-Baqué, 2011).

It is important to get all individuals who wish to work, into work, but this is not consistent across countries with respect to women, as in less developed countries, young women are more likely than young men to be neither in employment nor in education nor training (NEET; Organisation for Economic Co-operation and Development (OECD), 2012). When these women enter the labour market, it is likely to be in vulnerable jobs and in the informal economy (OECD, 2012). It is known that women experience higher unemployment rates globally. In 2014, the unemployment rate for women was estimated at 6.4 %, when compared to a 5.7 % rate for men (ILO, 2014b). This disparity in the unemployment rates between the genders is consistent in most regions in the world, with the exception of higher male unemployment rates in East Asia and Central and South-Eastern Europe and in the Commonwealth of Independent States (CIS; ILO, 2014b).

In 1994, Young et al. proposed that industrial work was the area that had the greatest potential to empower women, as it was most likely to be organised and had the greatest investment of resources. In view of this recommendation, women should be encouraged to focus their efforts in this area, as well as to enter male-dominated fields, such as law, medicine, finance and engineering, as these provide higher salaries than those industries dominated by female workers. However, the lack of support to women in assisting them to advance in their career as well as overall organisational support in male-dominated industries has been noted (for example Cha, 2013; Kessler, 2007, Martin & Barnard, 2013). This aspect of the work environment has to improve to ensure that women's employment can be sustained long-term, regardless of their caring responsibilities when they work in these industries. It would be constructive to address from an early age therefore, the stereotyping of the genders in their educational choices at school: such as adapting teaching strategies and material to increase engagement of boys in reading and of girls in mathematics and science; by supporting more girls in choosing science, engineering and mathematics courses in higher education, and in applying for jobs in these fields (OECD, 2012).

There is great potential to get more women into work. The global employment rate for women in 2014 stood at 50.3 %, which indicated that half of all women of working age were either in employment or looking for work, while the other half were economically inactive, that is, neither in work nor looking for work (ILO, 2014b). This is a very large labour pool that could be accessed. This is especially relevant for rapidly ageing economies, where increased female labour force participation can boost economic growth by mitigating the impact of a shrinking workforce (Elborgh-Woytek et al., 2013). However, there are constraints to how and where women work in terms of social, personal and cultural factors. Taking Japan as one example, the female participation rate in Japan is 63 %, which is much lower than in comparable OECD countries, but the rate is further compounded as 70 % of women on having their first child stop working for a decade or more, with some of them never re-entering the workforce (The Economist, 2014). Research has indicated that Japan's annual growth rate could increase by about one-quarter of a percentage point, if the female labour participation rate was to reach the average for the Group of 7 (G7; Canada, France, Germany, Italy, Japan, the United Kingdom and the United States) countries, and thereby result in a permanent rise in per capita gross domestic product (GDP) of 4 % (International Monetary Fund (IMF), 2012). Steinberg and Nakane (2012) noted also that due to Japanese women's higher education levels, their greater involvement in the labour force would result in a more skilled labour force.

The Health of Women Who Work

> When women's education and health have improved, these improvements have facilitated better outcomes for their children (World Bank, 2011).

Due to the social, economic and cultural changes that have changed forever the employment landscape, women, as are men, are expected to be in the workforce far longer than they might have anticipated. Some countries have started to increase the 'mandatory' retirement age, e.g., in the United Kingdom (Wunsch & Raman, 2010) and in the Netherlands (van der Smitte, 2013), removing the choice of an earlier exit from work for many employees. And while, there are economic reasons for encouraging workers to retire later in life, there are aspects of an older workforce that should be considered, but for which there is a limited evidence base. The research in respect of an ageing workforce is increasing, but there are still various unknowns. What is known is that if workers are required to work longer, then the maintenance of their health is a prime concern; this is especially relevant as healthy workers can influence directly the productivity and overall return on investments of organisations (Chenoweth, 2011).

There are factors in the work environment that augment ill health and only a few of these will be considered in this chapter. One of these is the amount of control or job autonomy that workers have over their tasks. Low work control has been shown to increase workers' sickness absence (Vahtera, Kivimaki, Pentti, & Theorell, 2000), while women with less control over work processes were more likely to report poorer health and psychological distress than men, and thereby increase their sickness absence (Ala-Mursula, Vahtera, Kivimäki, Kevin, & Pentti, 2002). Work control is one of the ways to improve on women's health in the workplace and is an essential feature that all organisations should consider to assist with managing any workforce, and especially an ageing workforce.

Another issue to consider is a long hour work culture that could exist in many western societies. Although, generally women work fewer hours than men (Burchell et al., 2009), when they do work long hours, for example, 56 or more hours a week, they are more likely to display more psychosomatic symptoms, to have a higher levels of satisfaction with friends, and to report higher levels of perfectionism and job stress, as research among female and male managers has shown (Burke & Fiksenbaum, 2009). Burchell, Fagan, O'Brien, and Smith (2007) explored the negative impact of long hours, finding that workers in the European Union were more likely to report health issues if they worked more than 48 h per week. This intensity of work is more likely to affect adversely women's health than that of men (Burchell & Fagan, 2004). This is very relevant as one of the interesting concerns about long work hours is that even when working part-time, women tend to have a longer 'work week' than men (Fagan, Lyonette, Smith, & Saldaña-Tejeda, 2012), due to their unpaid work, which would involve caring responsibilities. In general, work intensification is not sustainable over time (Burchell et al., 2009), neither for men nor women.

As this section has illustrated briefly, there are health concerns specific to women, which are compounded further when considering that men and women differ biological and are affected differently in the health risks they face (World Bank, 2011). This is in respect of exposures that occur within the work environment, with women more exposed to jobs involving lifting or moving people, and to jobs with the potential to experience musculoskeletal disorders (MSDs), than are men (see EU-OSHA, 2013). It is necessary therefore to continue to devise and support work-related interventions that concentrate on improving women's health, and of course that of men's as well. A consistent focus on progressing work practices benefits not only the workers, but the organisations in which they work.

Pay, Leadership and Choices

> The continual gender pay gap has been (and is) influenced by the horizontal and vertical job segregations that exist (European Commission, 2011).

Pay

The sustainability of economies is a prime concern globally. One of the ways to address this concern is to not only increase the number of women in the workforce; but to then value the skills and talent that they bring to the workplace (European Commission, 2014). The underutilisation of women's work-relevant assets is reflected in women continuing still to have disparate salaries from men; with women still paid less than men, even when doing comparable work (Catalyst Inc, 2014a; ILO, 1995; OECD, 2012). The feminisation of poverty is essential in this discussion (United Nations, 2010), especially in the context of women as they age. Further, women continue to do most of the unpaid work that occurs across societies and when this aspect of work is ignored, it undervalues the contribution that women make to economies (Miranda, 2011), and could be seen as playing a part in the feminisation of poverty.

Projections on earnings and the frequencies of changes in earnings in the United States of America's (US) economy have proposed that women are not expected to earn the same as men until 2050 (Lorenz, 2007) and perhaps beyond 2050 (AFL-CIO, n.d.; Institute for Women's Policy Research, 2013). Similar projections exist in respect of pensions, with women not receiving comparable pensions with men until 2050 (Ritchie, 2010). In 2008, in the United Kingdom, women were not as entitled to receive a full state pension as were men, showing a fairly large disparity between the genders (40 % compared with 90 % respectively; Pensions Policy Institute, 2009).

Leadership

> Cultural stereotypes about men, women, and leaders influence the attitudes, judgments, and decisions that others make about women and the choices women make for themselves (Isaac, Kaatz, Lee, & Carnes, 2012, p. 307).

Leadership remains a stereotypical position for women, as women have tended to be viewed less favourably as leaders than have men (Eagly & Karau, 2002). Global social norms prevail in how women are perceived, in that they are less likely to be seen as leaders, as even among other women, they are considered still as responsible for 'home' related concerns and as such they are expected to focus on the home and thereby accept their caring role within this environment (World Bank, 2011). While women do attain leadership positions, the disparity with men is obvious still. There are very few women who hold Chief Executive Officers (CEOs) positions at companies that rank on the 2014 Fortune 1000 lists; in 2014, women held 5.0 % of Fortune 500 CEO positions and 5.3 % of Fortune 1000 CEO positions (Catalyst Inc, 2014b). Women are underrepresented also at the top level of corporations, ranging in 2013, from 34 % in Norway to 18 % in Belgium and to 2 % in Japan (Devillard, Sancier, Werner, Maller, & Kossoff, 2013). Devillard et al. (2013) noted that this should be viewed less as a glass ceiling effect, but constituted more of a leaky pipeline, especially when considering that organisations have been making concerted efforts to improve gender diversity within their workforce. Some of the reasons for the slow increase are due to the time it requires for strategies to be implemented rigorously and to be monitored and adjusted if necessary, combined with the mindset of the corporate culture (Devillard et al., 2013). Other figures of women's visibility in leadership positions reflect that in 2013 women around the world held only 19 % of board roles (Grant Thornton, 2013).

Despite the present state of women's organisational leadership, it does not reflect what women can achieve once they lead companies. Organisations with three or more women in managerial positions tend to perform better in terms of organisational effectiveness (Sperling, Marcati, & Rennie, 2014). One study in tracking results from Fortune 500 companies from 2004 to 2008, established that those companies with more women board directors outperformed those with the least amount by at least 16 % in respect of return on sales and 26 % on their return on invested capital (Carter & Wagner, 2011). Carter and Wagner (2011) were able to determine as well that those companies with a sustained high representation of women board directors, i.e., those companies which employed three or more women board directors for no less than four of five years, were able to outperform greatly those with continued low representation. They did this by showing an 84 % return on sales, a 60 % return on invested capital, and a 46 % return on equity. Other research has shown a direct link of success between those companies with more female executives than those with fewer. The more successful companies tended to employ a median proportion of 7.1 % female executives compared to those less successful companies that employed 3.1 %; 61 % of start-up businesses with five or more females were successful with only 39 % failing; thereby illustrating the value that women as leaders can add to successful business outcomes (Canning, Haque, & Wang, 2012).

So although women do add value at the managerial level, as previously discussed, they could struggle when working long hours. Further, the intensive work patterns that are associated with senior level positions in organisations may work as a deterrent for women to work in these types of roles (Burchell et al., 2009). One of the suggested ways to increase women accepting and staying in leadership positions is to remove the 'stigma' of part-time working and also job sharing. Job sharing is a useful alternative as it can consist of different dimensions to meet the needs of women and is one way to recruit and to keep women at senior level (Daniels, 2011).

Entrepreneurship

> Women could become more economically empowered, achieve gender equality and be able to sustain economic growth and jobs by the removal of various barriers, which they face, for example, discriminatory property and inheritance laws, cultural practices, the lack of access to formal financial institutions, and time constraints due to family and household responsibilities (ILO, 2012).

While women for the most part are not self-employed (Burchell et al., 2007; World Bank, 2011), entrepreneurship is one of the ways that women could improve their work choices and make the most of their abilities. However, women are less likely than men to be entrepreneurs (Pines, Lerner, & Schwartz, 2010). There are several challenges as outlined that have hindered women in the past from taking up entrepreneurial opportunities, and it could be expected that these could continue in the future.

- In respect of starting their own business women are less likely than men to do so, resulting in fewer female entrepreneurs at a global level,
- When women do set up their own enterprises, these are usually smaller and less well represented in capital-intensive sectors; thereby restricting their sales, profits and labour productivity,

- Women entrepreneurs tend to rely substantially less than men on loans, and this includes for starting up their business and for financing their activities,
- Women who are self-employed women usually earn 30–40 % less than self-employed men (OECD, 2012).

These challenges could be minimised, or even reversed, if more resources are made available to women, including changes to financial support and rights to ownership. Women's right to own and inherit property is increasing at a global level, as is their access to credit and other resources, and are all factors that are helping to reduce the gender productivity gap (Elborgh-Woytek et al., 2013). It is important to note however that while microfinance is able to assist low-income individuals and those without access to typical banking services, with much needed financial assistance; it should not be seen as the one tool that will empower poor women and lift them out of poverty (Kabeer, 2005). The high credit ratings in respect of microfinance might limit, rather than allow women entrepreneurs to grow (OECD, 2011a).

This section has shown that supporting women in developing their own businesses, either in developed or developing countries should assist in greater independence and in the reduction of poverty. A greater focus on the entrepreneurial support of women has been recognised (OECD, 2011a) and it is anticipated that this focus would improve on women's work in the future. This could be ensured if those support policies that are put in place for women-owned enterprises are used to target all existing firms, not just start-ups and small enterprises; as both genders have to be assured of the same access in respect of finance (OECD, 2012).

The Care Factor: Balancing Work and Life

> Caring activities are essential challenges for all societies, as they are required at each stage of the lifecycle (Brodolini, 2011).

Achieving a balance between work and life will remain a challenge for women over the next few decades. The amount of time that they will have to invest in household chores is not expected to decrease significantly (Kan, Gershuny, & Sullivan, 2011), and it can be hypothesised that due to social and cultural mores that their caring responsibilities are expected to increase. As the profile of the population changes, with individuals living longer than previous generations, it could be reasoned that health requirements would change. One of these changes would involve individuals having to invest in long-term care due to the increase in conditions like Alzheimer's. Data from the US in respect of this condition show that women bear the brunt of caring and are more likely also to develop the condition (Alzheimer's Association, 2014). So while a woman in her 60s has an estimated lifetime risk of 1 in 11 to develop breast cancer, for Alzheimer's it increases to 1 in 6. The data reflect also that close to two-thirds of Americans with Alzheimer's are women; that 2.5 times more women than men provide intensive "on-duty" care 24 h a day for someone with Alzheimer's; and that overall more than 60 % of Alzheimer's and dementia caregivers are women (Alzheimer's Association, 2014).

As women are the ones who mainly provide care for elderly parents (Aguirre et al., 2012), the care of elderly parents/relatives could affect adversely their job prospects, especially in cultures, where care by one's children, usually one's daughters, is accepted as a norm, rather than relying on social facilities (Hewlett & Rashid, 2010). In Brazil, for example, over two-thirds (69 %) of women care for their ageing relatives, which is much less when compared to under one-half (48 %) of American women (Hewlett & Rashid, 2011).

While women maintain caring responsibilities worldwide, the way in which this is managed depends on the development of the country. In the more developed and richer countries, the state and market tends to support caring responsibilities, while in the less developed and poorer countries, care is provided by unpaid family members and the community (United Nations Research Institute for Social Development (UNRISD), 2010). These distinct approaches to care across countries impact on the numbers of women who enter the workforce. This is displayed in the spend on care services, as OECD countries with the highest public spending as a percentage of GDP on child care and education services for children under the age of five, tend to have higher employment rates among mothers with young children (OECD, 2011a). In this respect, the necessity to have care as a focus for public policy has been stressed (UNRISD, 2010).

So why is the provision of care of such importance? The estimated figures for caring responsibilities, if these were assigned a monetary value would constitute between 10 % and 39 % of GDP (UNRISD, 2010). This 'unpaid job', in particular as it relates to child care, is vital to the future development of national economies, as it assists in creating a new generation of healthy, educated citizens (Aguirre et al., 2012) who in turn would sustain economies and societies. This outcome stresses the importance of promoting to governments when implementing policies for child care requirements, to ensure that this level of care work is not 'pushed' into low-quality jobs that are often filled by women (OECD, 2011a). The Finnish government, for example, has recognised the importance of having trained staff in day care facilities and there is an obligation for all kindergarten teachers and special kindergarten teachers to have received tertiary education (OECD, 2002). More importantly, the state provides affordable child care (Finnish National Board of Education, n.d.; OECD, 2002) as it acknowledges that all children under school-age are entitled to early childhood education and care (ECEC; Finnish National Board of Education, n.d.; OECD, 2002). The provision of good and affordable childcare is a major component in achieving better gender equality in employment; and when combined with parental leave policies that unambiguously include fathers, could lead to a fairer distribution of the housework and caring that women in many countries tend to do for the most part (OECD, 2012).

The Structure of the School Day

Another factor that impacts on women's work patterns is the school day, which for the most part, does not align with the work day. Family responsibilities are a major problem that working women face on a daily basis. One of the reasons why women work part-time is to facilitate child care; and while a return to work after having children might not be based on one factor, it would be easier to do so based on the availability of child care with which they felt comfortable or when the child reached school age (Bashir, Crisp, Gore, Reeve, & Robinson, 2011). A return to work and working in a full-time position would then become much more difficult for women when they have to work around set school times. For example, the school day in Brazil is very short, and could only last up to 4 h in some areas, with most schools offering very few after-school activities; further, children are required only to attend up to the age of 14; there are very few day-care facilities for preschool children and the ones that are available are expensive, and thereby affordable only to those with the financial means; and in addition, around 75 % of children who are between 1 month and 4 years old, do not attend formal day care (Aguirre et al., 2012). The structure of the school day could therefore act as a deterrent to many women who wish to work full-time.

The Virtual Workplace

One of the ways that could assist women with child care is the virtual workplace. The rapid advances in information technology over the past 20–30 years have made it possible for individuals to work in different locations, inclusive of their homes. Due to this, companies are able to increase their potential labour markets, by allowing them to hire and to retain the best workers despite their physical location (Cascio, 1998). The ability to telecommute, one aspect of virtual working, can assist women with their caring responsibilities; as it assists employees in managing their personal and professional lives (Cascio, 1998, 2000; Fathy El Dessouky, 2011). Telecommuting, as one way to work is expected to increase in the future (OECD, 2011b), and thereby allowing workers more flexible working patterns.

The virtual workplace continues to adapt and change; with new technologies expected to emerge as innovations and adaptations are encouraged, especially ones that combine living and non-living systems (Saurin, Ratcliffe, & Puybaraud, 2008). Of course, virtual workplaces would not suit all jobs, but organisations that choose to use it as one work option are able to gain a return on their investment by way of increased profit and productivity (Cascio, 2000).

Part-Time Work Remains Important for Women

As mentioned, one of the ways that women will continue to address care responsibilities is to work part-time; and as this type of work is and will remain an established feature of modern life, it is important that organisations improve on its condition and quality (OECD, 2010; European Foundation for the Improvement of Living and Working Conditions (Eurofound), 2011). Some of the challenges associated with working part-time are that part-time workers are more likely to encounter poorer psychological working conditions, to have fewer available opportunities to support socioeconomic integration and to not have career opportunities (Burchell et al., 2009). In addition to improving part-time work, another way to address care responsibilities is for companies to offer flexible working. Again this differs globally, so while 71 % of companies surveyed in China do not offer flexible working options, in India, half of companies offer it (51 %), while in Denmark, most companies do at 93 % as happens in Finland, reported at 90 %; overall 67 % of global organisations offer flexible working (Grant Thornton, 2013).

Men and women have to be able to find a work-life balance that suits them, regardless of family status or household income. This could be difficult for men in some cultures, due to the underlying perception that household tasks should be delineated into gender specific ones, and which in turn could adversely affect women's career path, if they choose to take time away from work (OECD, 2012).

Moving Forward

Change is the one constant that is expected to prevail in the workplace over the coming decades, and any changes that occur will have implications for workforce planning (Saurin et al., 2008). Some of these changes have been discussed in this chapter in the context of women who work, especially if more women are to enter the workforce. Despite the various changes that have occurred to date, it has been noted that organisations are trying to move forward in the twenty-first century using twentieth century solutions, designed by men and for men (Hay Group, 2013). This approach to organisation development has to change if women are to enter and remain in the workforce. The ILO (2010) recognises that women's 'fit' in the labour force should not be forced into the existing male-focused construct, but that the market has to take account of those unique values that women bring, as well as those constraints of which they have to take account when choosing to work. This is very relevant to an older workforce; with Merkes (2003) suggesting that policies developed for an ageing female workforce should focus on the values of inclusiveness, fairness, self-determination and social justice.

In working to continue to reduce the differences between the genders in respect of work, it must be acknowledged that women require financial, educational, and cultural investments in their future, all of which are interdependent (Aguirre et al.,

2012). Aguirre et al. (2012) go on to state that improvements for women in one area would not guarantee a positive outcome necessarily; so if women are provided with the capital to invest in their business, then this investment would succeed only if they have the education to run a business successfully, and if there is a cultural perception that they are able to compete economically with men. The education of girls is a key factor in getting women to compete on the same level as men. However, there are some simple and easily addressed factors that could restrict girls from being educated. One of these is having access to sanitary protection, one that is a relatively inexpensive 'fix', but one that many young girls across the world struggle with still (see Jewitt & Ryley, 2014; Venema, 2014). Further, in terms of the overall investment in the education of girls, it would be useful to secure financial investments to ensure that jobs are created for those receiving an education; as if there are cultural restrictions that restrict girls from attending school, any subsequent actions that are implemented to let women know that they are moving forward and being empowered will not be accepted, as women will not be educated enough to take their place in rapidly advancing societies, nor will they be able to have an impact as they would not be involved in the economy (Aguirre et al., 2012). It has been established that when greater gender equality in educational attainment has been attained, this has a strong positive effect on economic growth (OECD, 2012).

It is vital that women are empowered, but as mentioned earlier in this chapter, there are various challenges that have to be considered to support women, and girls, in the workplaces of the future.

Despite the advances made to the provision of equal opportunities for women, there are several basic elements that should be considered as outlined. These include:

- Investing in the infrastructure and transportation services as these can reduce the costs related to working outside the home. In rural Bangladesh, the upgrading and expansion of the road network increased labour supply and incomes.
- Improving access to electricity and water sources closer to individuals' homes frees up women's work time and allows them to integrate into the formal economy. In rural South Africa, electrification was found to have increased women's labour market participation by 9 %.
- Ensuring better access to information and communication technologies, as these can facilitate access to markets and market work. Mobile banking, such as M-PESA in Kenya, facilitates financial and banking transactions and lowers transaction costs in market access (Elborgh-Woytek et al., 2013, p. 20).

Of course any policies that are implemented should consider using a "six sector approach", inclusive of incorporating demographic, economic, governance, environmental, societal, and technological factors into policies, as proposed by Saurin et al. (2008). This type of holistic consideration should always be included as social sustainability is more likely to occur when health, lifelong learning and the development of social capital is in place (Merkes, 2003).

Finally, in addition to all that has been done and that societies and organisations will continue to do to encourage and support women in their job and career choices, as has been stated previously and deserves to be stated again, there is a need for detailed, frequently updated, and gender-disaggregated data, to further the understanding of those issues that women face and thereby allow more effective and relevant solutions (Aguirre et al., 2012; EU-OSHA, 2013). This chapter has highlighted some of the ongoing challenges for women who work and, unfortunately, most of which will continue into the future. Changes are happening and will continue to happen, and the ongoing focus on women's work challenges should guarantee that these will improve.

References

AFL-CIO. (n.d.). *Long and winding road to equal pay national summary table*. Retrieved from http://www.pay-equity.org/PDFs/payequitysummarytable.pdf. Accessed 18 Oct 2014.

Aguirre, D., Hoteit, L., Rupp, C., & Sabbagh, K. (2012). *Empowering the third billion women and the World of work in 2012*. Booz & Company Inc. http://www.strategyand.pwc.com/media/file/Strategyand_Empowering-the-Third-Billion_Full-Report.pdf. Accessed 21 Sept 2014.

Ala-Mursula, L., Vahtera, J., Kivimäki, M., Kevin, M. V., & Pentti, J. (2002). Employee control over working times: Associations with subjective health and sickness absences. *Journal of Epidemiological and Community Health, 56*(4), 272–278. doi:10.1136/jech.56.4.272.

Alzheimer's Association. (2014). Alzheimer's disease facts and figures. *Alzheimer's & Dementia, 10*(2). Retrieved from http://www.alz.org/downloads/Facts_Figures_2014.pdf. Accessed 20 Sept 2014.

Bashir, N., Crisp, R., Gore, T., Reeve, K., & Robinson, D. (2011). *Families and work: Revisiting barriers to employment*. Research report No 729. Department for Work and Pensions. Retrieved from http://www.shu.ac.uk/research/cresr/sites/shu.ac.uk/files/families-work-barriers-employment.pdf. Accessed 19 Oct 2014.

Brodolini, F. G. (2011). *Gender equality in caring responsibilities over the lifecycle*. European Commission. http://ec.europa.eu/justice/gender-equality/files/conference_sept_2011/background-paperiii-equality-in-caring_en.pdf. Accessed 01 Nov 2014.

Burchell, B., & Fagan, C. (2004). Gender and the intensification of work: Evidence from the European working conditions surveys. *Eastern Economic Journal, 30*(4), 627–642.

Burchell, B., Fagan, C., O'Brien, C., & Smith, M. (2007). *Working conditions in the European Union: The gender perspective*. European foundation for the improvement of living and working conditions. Luxembourg: Office for Official Publications of the European Communities. Retrieved from http://www.eurofound.europa.eu/pubdocs/2007/108/en/1/ef07108en.pdf. Accessed 13 Sept 2014.

Burchell, B., Cartron, D., Csizmadia, P., Delcampe, S., Gollac, M., Illéssy, M., et al. (2009). *Working conditions in the European Union: Working time and work intensity*. European foundation for the improvement of living and working conditions. Luxembourg: Office for Official Publications of the European Communities. Retrieved from http://www.eurofound.europa.eu/pubdocs/2009/27/en/1/EF0927EN.pdf. Accessed 13 Sept 2014.

Burke, R. J., & Fiksenbaum, L. (2009). Are managerial women in "extreme jobs" disadvantaged? *Gender in Management: An International Journal, 24*(1), 5–13. doi:10.1108/17542410910930716.

Canning, J., Haque, M., & Wang, Y. (2012). *Women at the wheel: Do female executives drive start-up success*? Dow Jones and Company Inc. Retrieved from http://www.dowjones.com/collateral/files/WomenPE_report_final.pdf. Accessed 27 Sept 2014.

Carter, N. M., & Wagner, H. M. (2011). *The bottom line: Corporate performance and women's representation on boards (2004–2008)*. Catalyst Inc. Retrieved from http://www.catalyst.org/system/files/the_bottom_line_corporate_performance_and_women%27s_representation_on_boards_%282004-2008%29.pdf. Accessed 27 Sept 2014.

Cascio, W. F. (1998). The virtual workplace: A reality now. *The Industrial-Organizatonal Psychologist (TIP), 35*(4). Retrieved from http://www.siop.org/tip/backissues/TIPApril98/Cascio.aspx. Accessed 20 Sept 2014.

Cascio, W. F. (2000). Managing a virtual workplace. *Academy of Management Executive, 14*(3), 81–90.

Catalyst Inc. (2014a). *High-potential women in Europe. Underutilized talent.* Catalyst Inc. Retrieved from http://www.catalyst.org/knowledge/high-potential-women-europe. Accessed 27 Sept 2014.

Catalyst Inc. (2014b). *Women CEOs of the Fortune 1000.* Catalyst Inc. Retrieved from http://www.catalyst.org/knowledge/women-ceos-fortune-1000. Accessed 19 Sept 2014.

Cha, Y. (2013). Overwork and the persistence of gender segregation in occupations. *Gender & Society, 27*(2), 158–184. http://dx.doi.org/10.1177/0891243212470510.

Chenoweth, D. (2011). *Promoting employee well-being: Wellness strategies to improve health, performance and the bottom line.* Society for Human Resource Management (SHRM). Alexandria: SHRM Foundation. Retrieved from http://www.shrm.org/about/foundation/products/documents/6-11%20promoting%20well%20being%20epg-%20final.pdf. Accessed 27 May 2013.

Cuberes, D., & Teignier-Baqué, M. (2011). *Gender inequality and economic growth.* World Development Report 2012. Background Paper. Retrieved from http://disde.minedu.gob.pe/xmlui/bitstream/handle/123456789/1418/Gender%20Inequality%20and%20Economic%20Growth.pdf?sequence=1. Accessed 18 Oct 2014.

Daniels, L. (2011). *Job sharing at senior level: Making it work.* Capability Jane. Retrieved from http://candidates.capabilityjane.com/sites/default/files/uploads/Report%20-%20Job%20Share%20Summary%20Report.pdf. Accessed 15 Sept 2014.

Devillard, S., Sancier, S., Werner, C., Maller, I., & Kossoff, C. (2013). *Women matter 2013. Gender diversity in top management: Moving corporate culture, moving boundaries.* McKinsey & Company. Retrieved from http://www.mckinsey.de/sites/mck_files/files/womenmatter_13.pdf. Accessed 13 Sept 2014.

Eagly, A. H., & Karau, S. J. (2002). Role congruity theory of prejudice toward female leaders. *Psychological Review, 109*(3), 573–598. doi:10.1037//0033-295X.109.3.573.

Elborgh-Woytek, K., Newiak, M., Kochhar, K., Fabrizio, S., Kpodar, K., Wingender, P., et al. (2013). *Women, work, and the economy: Macroeconomic gains from gender equity* (SDN/13/10). Washington, DC: International Monetary Fund. Retrieved from http://www.imf.org/external/pubs/ft/sdn/2013/sdn1310.pdf. Accessed 21 Sept 2014.

European Agency for Safety and Health at Work. (2013). *New risks and trends in the safety and health of women at work.* Luxembourg: Publications Office of the European Union. Retrieved from https://osha.europa.eu/en/publications/reports/new-risks-trends-osh-women. Accessed 27 May 2013.

European Commission. (2011). *Tackling the pay gap between women and men.* Retrieved from http://europa.eu/legislation_summaries/employment_and_social_policy/equality_between_men_and_women/c10161_en.htm. Accessed 18 Oct 2014.

European Commission. (2014). *Tackling the gender pay gap in the European Union.* Luxembourg: Publications Office of the European Union. doi:10.2838/42323. Accessed 18 Oct 2014.

European Foundation for the Improvement of Living and Working Conditions. (2011). *European company survey 2009. Part-time work in Europe.* Retrieved from http://www.eurofound.europa.eu/pubdocs/2010/86/en/3/EF1086EN.pdf. Accessed 23 Aug 2014.

Fagan, C., Lyonette, C., Smith, M., & Saldaña-Tejeda, A. (2012). *The influence of working time arrangements on work-life integration or 'balance': A review of the international evidence* (Conditions of work and employment research series No. 32). Geneva, Switzerland: International Labour Office. Retrieved from http://www.ilo.org/wcmsp5/groups/public/---ed_protect/---protrav/---travail/documents/publication/wcms_187306.pdf. Accessed 24 Sept 2014.

Fathy El Dessouky, N. (2011). *The virtual workplace: A new alternative merging technology and policy for more environmental, economic and social sustainability*. Paper presented at the 15th world multi-conference on systemics, cybernetics and informatics: WMSCI 2011, July 19th–July 22nd, 2011, Orlando. Retrieved from http://www.iiis.org/CDs2011/CD2011SCI/SCI_2011/PapersPdf/SA409CC.pdf. Accessed 19 Oct 2014.

Finnish National Board of Education. (n.d.). *Early childhood education*. Retrieved from http://www.oph.fi/english/education_system/early_childhood_education. Accessed 19 Oct 2014.

Frome, P. M., Alfeld, C. J., Eccles, J. S., & Barber, B. L. (2006). Why don't they want a male-dominated job? An investigation of young women who changed their occupational aspirations. *Educational Research and Evaluation, 12*(4), 359–372. doi:10.1080/13803610600765786.

Gershuny, J., & Fisher, K. (2014). *Post-industrious society: Why work time will not disappear for our grandchildren*. Sociology working papers paper number 2014–03, Centre for Time Use Research, Department of Sociology, University of Oxford. Retrieved from http://www.sociology.ox.ac.uk/materials/papers/wp20143.pdf. Accessed 20 Sept 2014.

Ghosh, J. (2014). Financial crises and their gendered employment impact. Emerging trends and past experiences. In R. Antonopoulos (Ed.), *Gender perspectives and the gender impacts of the global economic crisis* (pp. 17–48). London/New York: Routledge.

Grant Thornton. (2013). *Women in senior management. Setting the stage for growth*. Grant Thornton International Business Report 2013. Grant Thornton International Ltd. Retrieved from http://www.gti.org/files/ibr2013_wib_report_final.pdf. Accessed 27 Sept 2014.

Hay Group. (2013). *Stop blaming women: Prescribing a 21st century approach to gender diversity*. Retrieved from http://www.haygroup.com/downloads/uk/stop%20blaming%20women%20-%20gender%20diversity%20viewpoint.pdf. Accessed 27 Sept 2014.

Hewlett, S. A., & Rashid, R. (2010). The battle for female talent in emerging markets. *Harvard Business Review, 88*(5), 101–106. Retrieved from http://asiasociety.org/files/pdf/101206_HBR_BattleForFemaleTalent.pdf. Accessed 27 Sept 2014.

Hewlett, S. A., & Rashid, R. (2011). *Winning the war for talent in emerging markets. Why women are the solution*. Boston: Harvard Business Review Press.

Institute for Women's Policy Research. (2013). *Gender wage gap projected to close in year 2058*. Retrieved from http://www.iwpr.org/publications/pubs/gender-wage-gap-projected-to-close-in-year-2058-most-women-working-today-will-not-see-equal-pay-during-their-working-lives/at_download/file. Accessed 18 Oct 2014.

International Labour Organization. (1995). *Women work more, But are still paid less*. Geneva, Switzerland: International Labour Office. Retrieved from http://www.ilo.org/global/about-the-ilo/newsroom/news/WCMS_008091/lang--en/index.htm. Accessed 19 Sept 2014.

International Labour Organization. (2010). *Women in labour markets: Measuring progress and identifying challenges*. Geneva, Switzerland: International Labour Office. Retrieved from http://www.ilo.org/wcmsp5/groups/public/---ed_emp/---emp_elm/---trends/documents/publication/wcms_123835.pdf. Accessed 16 Aug 2014.

International Labour Organization. (2011). *Work-life balance*. Governing Body GB.312/POL/4, 312th Session, Geneva, November 2011. Geneva: International Labour Office. Retrieved from http://www.ilo.org/wcmsp5/groups/public/---ed_norm/---relconf/documents/meetingdocument/wcms_163642.pdf. Accessed 27 Sept 2014.

International Labour Organization. (2012). *Women's entrepreneurship development. The ILO approach to women's entrepreneurship development – Sustainable enterprises*. Retrieved from http://www.ilo.org/wcmsp5/groups/public/---ed_emp/---emp_ent/---ifp_seed/documents/publication/wcms_175471.pdf. Accessed 01 Nov 2014.

International Labour Organization. (2014a). *Maternity and paternity at work. Law and practice across the world*. Geneva, Switzerland: International Labour Office. Retrieved from http://www.ilo.org/wcmsp5/groups/public/---dgreports/---dcomm/---publ/documents/publication/wcms_242615.pdf. Accessed 17 Aug 2014.

International Labour Organization. (2014b). *World of work report 2014: Developing with jobs*. Geneva, Switzerland: International Labour Office. Retrieved from http://www.ilo.org/wcmsp5/groups/public/---dgreports/---dcomm/documents/publication/wcms_243961.pdf. Accessed 16 Aug 2014.

International Monetary Fund. (2012). *Country report No. 12/208, Japan*. Washington, DC: International Monetary Fund. Retrieved from http://www.imf.org/external/pubs/ft/scr/2012/cr12208.pdf. Accessed 21 Sept 2014.

Isaac, C., Kaatz, A., Lee, B., & Carnes, M. (2012). An educational intervention designed to increase women's leadership self-efficacy. *CBE Life Sciences Education, 11*(3), 307–322. doi:10.1187/cbe.12-02-0022.

Jewitt, S., & Ryley, H. (2014). It's a girl thing: Menstruation, school attendance, spatial mobility and wider gender inequalities in Kenya. *Geoforum, 56*, 137–147. doi:10.1016/j.geoforum.2014.07.006.

Kabeer, N. (2005). Is microfinance a 'Magic Bullet' for women's empowerment? Analysis of findings from South Asia. *Economic and Political Weekly, 40*(44/45), 4709–4718. doi:10.2307/4417357.

Kan, M. Y., Gershuny, J., & Sullivan, O. (2011). Gender convergence in domestic work: Discerning the effects of interactional and institutional barriers from large-scale data. *Sociology, 45*(2), 234–251. doi:10.1177/0038038510394014.

Kessler, L. T. (2007). Keeping discrimination theory front and center in the discourse over work and family conflict. *Pepperdine Law Review, 34*(2), 313–332. Retrieved from http://digitalcommons.pepperdine.edu/plr/vol34/iss2/10. Accessed 05 Oct 2014.

Lorenz, K. (2007). *Equal pay for women? Not till 2050*. CareerBuilder, LLC. Retrieved from http://www.careerbuilder.com/article/cb-709-getting-ahead-equal-pay-for-women-not-til-2050/. Accessed 21 Sept 2014.

Martin, P., & Barnard, A. (2013). The experience of women in male-dominated occupations: A constructivist grounded theory inquiry. *SA Journal of Industrial Psychology/SA Tydskrif vir Bedryfsielkunde, 39*(2), Art. #1099, 12 pages. http://dx.doi.org/10.4102/sajip.v39i2.1099

Merkes, M. (2003). Women's working futures – Views, policies and choices. *Foresight, 5*(6), 53–60. doi:10.1109/14636680310508991.

Miranda, V. (2011). *Cooking, caring and volunteering: Unpaid work around the world*. OECD social, employment and migration working papers, No. 116, OECD Publishing. doi: 10.1787/5kghrjm8s142-en

Nylén, L., Voss, M., & Floderus, B. (2001). Mortality among women and men relative to unemployment, part time work, overtime work, and extra work: A study based on data from the Swedish twin registry. *Occupational and Environmental Medicine, 58*(1), 52–57. doi:10.1136/oem.58.1.52.

Organisation for Economic Co-operation and Development. (2002). *Early childhood education and care policy in Finland*. Retrieved from http://www.oecd.org/finland/2476019.pdf. Accessed 19 Oct 2014.

Organisation for Economic Co-operation and Development. (2010). *OECD employment outlook 2010. Moving beyond the jobs crisis*. doi: 10.1787/19991266. Retrieved from http://www.oecd-ilibrary.org/employment/oecd-employment-outlook-2010_empl_outlook-2010-en. Accessed 23 Aug 2014.

Organisation for Economic Co-operation and Development. (2011a). *Report on the gender initiative: Gender equality in education, employment and entrepreneurship*. Meeting of the OECD Council at Ministerial Level Paris, 25–26 May 2011. Retrieved from http://www.oecd.org/education/48111145.pdf. Accessed 27 Sept 2014.

Organisation for Economic Co-operation and Development. (2011b). *The future of families to 2030. A synthesis report*. Retrieved from http://www.oecd.org/futures/49093502.pdf. Accessed 18 Oct 2014.

Organisation for Economic Co-operation and Development. (2012). *Closing the gender gap. Act now*. doi: 10.1787/9789264179370-en. Retrieved from http://www.oecd-ilibrary.org/social-issues-migration-health/close-the-gender-gap-now_9789264179370-en. Accessed 27 Sept 2014.

Pensions Policy Institute. (2009). Pension facts. In Ritchie, A. (2010). *Equal pay and pensions: The role of trade union reps in addressing women's inequality in retirement. Close the gap.* Retrieved from http://www.closethegap.org.uk/content/resources/Pensions-briefing.pdf. Accessed 18 Oct 2014.

Pines, A. M., Lerner, M., & Schwartz, D. (2010). Gender differences in entrepreneurship: Equality, diversity and inclusion in times of global crisis. *Equality, Diversity and Inclusion: An International Journal, 29*(2), 186–198. doi: http://dx.doi.org/10.1108/02610151011024493.

Ritchie, A. (2010). *Equal pay and pensions: The role of trade union reps in addressing women's inequality in retirement. Close the gap.* Retrieved from http://www.closethegap.org.uk/content/resources/Pensions-briefing.pdf. Accessed 18 Oct 2014.

Saurin, R., Ratcliffe, J., & Puybaraud, M. (2008). Tomorrow's workplace: A futures approach using prospective through scenarios. *Journal of Corporate Real Estate, 10*(4), 243–261. doi:10.1108/14630010810925118.

Shen, C., & Williamson, J. B. (1999). Maternal mortality, women's status, and economic dependency in less developed countries: A cross-national analysis. *Social Science & Medicine, 49*(2), 197–214. doi:10.1016/S0277-9536(99)00112-4.

Slaughter, A-M. (2012, June 13). *Why women still can't have it all.* The Atlantic. Retrieved from http://www.theatlantic.com/magazine/archive/2012/07/why-women-still-cant-have-it-all/309020/. Accessed 10 Oct 2014.

Sperling, J., Marcati, C., & Rennie, M. (2014). *Women matter 2014. GCC Women in leadership – From the first to the norm.* McKinsey & Company. Retrieved from http://www.mckinsey.com/~/media/McKinsey%20Offices/Middle%20East/Latest%20thinking/GCC_Women_In_Leadership_FINAL.ashx. Accessed 13 Sept 2014.

Steinberg, C., & Nakane, M. (2012). *Can women save Japan?* (IMF working paper 12/48). Washington, DC: International Monetary Fund. Retrieved from https://www.imf.org/external/pubs/ft/wp/2012/wp12248.pdf. Accessed 13 Sept 2014.

Taylor, C. J. (2010). Occupational sex composition and the gendered availability of workplace support. *Gender & Society, 24*(2), 189–212. doi:10.1177/0891243209359912.

The Economist. (2014, March 29). *Japanese women and work. Holding back half the Nation.* The Economist Newspaper Limited 2014. Retrieved from http://www.economist.com/news/briefing/21599763-womens-lowly-status-japanese-workplace-has-barely-improved-decades-and-country. Accessed 20 Sept 2014.

United Nations. (2010). *The World's women 2010. Trends and statistics.* New York: United Nations. Retrieved from http://unstats.un.org/unsd/demographic/products/Worldswomen/WW_full%20report_color.pdf. Accessed 25 May 2013.

United Nations Research Institute for Social Development. (2010). *Why care matters for social development* (UNRISD research and policy brief 9). Geneva, Switzerland: United Nations Research Institute for Social Development. Retrieved from www.unrisd.org/publications/rpb9e. Accessed 21 Sept 2014.

Vahtera, J., Kivimaki, M., Pentti, J., & Theorell, T. (2000). Effect of change in the psychosocial work environment on sickness absence: A seven year follow up of initially healthy employees. *Journal of Epidemiology & Community Health, 54*(7), 484–493. doi:10.1136/jech.54.7.484.

van der Smitte, J. (2013). *Short introduction to the pension system in the Netherlands.* ÖSB Consulting, the Institute for Employment Studies (IES) & Applica. Retrieved from http://ec.europa.eu/social/BlobServlet?docId=10403&langId=en. Accessed 12 Oct 2014.

Venema, V. (2014, March 4). *The Indian sanitary pad revolutionary.* BBC World Service. Retrieved from http://www.bbc.co.uk/news/magazine-26260978. Accessed 20 Sept 2014.

Waddell, G., & Burton, A. K. (2006). *Is work good for your health and well-being?* Norwich, UK: Department for Work and Pensions, The Stationery Office. Retrieved from http://www.dwp.gov.uk/docs/hwwb-is-work-good-for-you.pdf. Accessed 26 Mar 2013.

Williams, C. L. (1992). The glass escalator: Hidden advantages for men in the "female" professions. *Social Problems, 39*(3), 253–267. http://dx.doi.org/10.1525/sp.1992.39.3.03x0034h.

World Bank. (2011). *World development report 2012. Gender equality and development.* Washington, DC: The International Bank for Reconstruction and Development/The World Bank. Retrieved from http://siteresources.worldbank.org/INTWDR2012/Resources/7778105-1299699968583/7786210-1315936222006/Complete-Report.pdf. Accessed 26 Mar 2013.

Wunsch, C., & Raman, J. V. (2010). *Mandatory retirement in the United Kingdom, Canada and the United States of America.* London: TAEN – The Age and Employment Network. Retrieved from http://taen.org.uk/uploads/resources/Combined_dissertation_final_formatted.pdf. Accessed 12 Oct 2014.

Young, G., Fort, L., & Danner, M. (1994). Moving from 'the status of women' to 'gender inequality': Conceptualisation, social indicators and an empirical application. *International Sociology, 9*(1), 55–85. doi:10.1177/026858094009001005.

CPSIA information can be obtained at www.ICGtesting.com
Printed in the USA
BVOW06*0217160616

452304BV00008B/19/P

9 783319 317342